Cyprus, a Modern History

To my family

CYPRUS

A MODERN HISTORY

William Mallinson

I.B. TAURIS

LONDON · NEW YORK

Published in 2005 by I.B.Tauris & Co Ltd
6 Salem Road, London W2 4BU
175 Fifth Avenue, New York NY 10010
www.ibtauris.com

In the United States and Canada distributed by Palgrave Macmillan,
a division of St. Martin's Press, 175 Fifth Avenue, New York NY 10010

ISBN 1 85043 580 4
EAN 978 1 85043 580 8

A full CIP record for this book is available from the British Library
A full CIP record for this book is available from the Library of Congress
Library of Congress catalog card: available

Typeset in Stone by Dexter Haven Associates Ltd, London
Printed and bound in Great Britain by MPG Books Ltd, Bodmin

CONTENTS

FOREWORD

This is a book about Cyprus' past, present and future and, as a professional historian I should really provide an introduction that is chronologically sound and works its way from past to present. However, at the risk of being perverse, I think it best to sketch out the present international context of 'the Cyprus problem' before considering how Bill Mallinson's book fits into it. He has a superb command of the historical sources for a modern history of the island. Yet the chief purpose of his book is to help illuminate the present crisis concerning Cyprus' entry into the European Union, to explain how Cyprus has reached this position and perhaps to imply what should be the right policy for the international community to pursue in the future. So here goes.

International relations in the era of the cold war appear in retrospect to have been relatively stable and predictable. Since 1989, on the other hand, everything has been in flux. At first it seemed as if a new, united Germany would be the state to watch, although the 'clean hands' revolution in Italy with its promise of a 'second Italian republic' diverted the attention of political observers in the first half of the 1990s. As things turned out, however, Germany entered a period of relative economic decline and Italy fell into the dubious embrace of Silvio Berlusconi. Both NATO and the EU, meanwhile, expanded to absorb the former satellite states of the Soviet Empire with the grudging acquiescence of a bankrupt Russia, so that it was the USA which emerged supreme – economically, militarily and therefore diplomatically – in a class of its own as the only 'hyper-power', with military victories to its credit in the Gulf, Bosnia, and Kosovo. Its main European ally was the United Kingdom, whose economic renaissance and military capacity made it the foremost European power. In a sense then, despite the fall of Communism (admittedly no small matter) and the implosion of Yugoslavia, the end of the cold war brought relatively little change.

The events of 11 September 2001, on the other hand, altered everything. The USA woke up to discover that it had been the target of an outrageous terrorist attack by Muslim extremists, an attack which forced the administration of George W. Bush to reassess America's world role and its whole defence strategy. The response was to declare world war on terrorism, to proclaim America's readiness to take preventive action, and to go to war first in Afghanistan and then Iraq in order to defeat the terrorists and their possible sponsors. Militant Islam was to be defeated by the world's most militant democracy, although, to be fair, the war in Iraq was primarily occasioned by the need after more than a decade to force Saddam Hussein to comply with agreements made with the UN at the end of the first Gulf war, agreements he continued to flout.

The second Gulf war, however, brought the USA into diplomatic confrontation with France and Russia (both deeply involved in Saddam's oilfields) and with Germany, whose pacifistic instincts had already forced it to refuse to participate in the first Gulf war. In the Arab world, the US victory (aided by the UK) was condemned as an attack on Islam, despite the fact it had led to the emancipation of millions of Muslims (Kurds, Shi'ites and Sunnis) from terror and tyranny and despite the fact, too, that the USA had recently already liberated Muslims from tyranny in Bosnia, Kosovo and Afghanistan. (In Kosovo, for example, the Americans and even the Israelis, who had offered aid and education to many refugees from the Milosevic regime, were much more popular among Kosovar Muslims than Arabs who had previously dealt profitably with the Serb dictatorship and whose late offers of aid were accompanied by efforts to get Kosovar women to wear veils and men to grow long beards.) Nonetheless, President George W. Bush became a hate-figure for the European Left, and was pilloried all the more for apparently protecting his unlovely ally, that other great hate-figure of the European Left, the Israeli prime minister, Ariel Sharon.

In Europe two somewhat discredited political leaders, Chancellor Schroeder and President Chirac, exploited the crisis over Iraq to rehabilitate themselves. Building on anti-American sentiment, they declared that France and Germany (along with Belgium and Luxembourg) would create a new European army independent of NATO within the EU. It would have its own planning staff and command structure and independent military assets. European defence, in short, would no longer be restricted to merely a 'separate identity', dependent on NATO assets and operational control. Parallel to this the former president of France, the ineffable Valéry Giscard d'Estaing, presided over the drafting of a new European constitution, the complexity of which nonetheless did not disguise the fact that the EU was to become a single legal entity – in short a state – whose sovereignty would henceforth derive from this same constitution. The EU *Staatenbund* would become a *Bundestaat* should this document be ratified. Soon, therefore, some Europeans hoped, the USA would face a rival superpower, completely overlooking the fact that the EU was economically stagnant, in relative economic decline, demographically shrinking, lacking money and troops, and, in the realm of defence, technologically obsolete. It was also dependent on the USA for nuclear technology.

This then is the background against which Bill Mallinson's new history of Cyprus is to be read. It is an extremely lively and controversial book and few will endorse every line of it. Yet, along with works such as Vassilis Fouskas's recent *Zones of Conflict: US Foreign Policy in the Balkans and the Greater Middle East*,[1] it not only sets the history of Cyprus in its international context – and Mallinson knows the archives inside out – but also takes the story right up to the present and interprets it in the light of both US policy in the Middle East and the emergence of an expanded and constitutionally united European Union.

Mallinson is absolutely right to draw our attention to both factors. He is also correct to point out that there is a growing tension between the EU and the USA.

For it is the key contribution of his book to show that Cyprus has been and remains the victim of great power politics and rivalries.

The British should have handed Cyprus to Greece after the Second World War as Sir Oliver Harvey proposed and as both Cypriots and Greeks desired. Instead, in order to keep her military bases and information-gathering facilities secure on sovereign British soil during the cold war, Britain refused to take the honourable path of straightforward decolonisation. Rather, a policy of divide and rule was implemented and Turkish Cypriots manipulated, and when even that failed, in an astonishing piece of diplomatic impudence, the United Kingdom ignored the 1923 Treaty of Lausanne (by which Turkey renounced all interest in Greek territories) and in 1960 granted Cyprus independence under treaties guaranteed by Greece and Turkey as well as the UK. Cyprus was also given a completely unworkable constitution that gave separate status to Greeks and Turks; the result was that under this new order the island became something akin to an international protectorate. Needless to say, Britain retained her bases. Thereafter, she exacerbated tensions between Greeks and Turks by encouraging Archbishop Makarios to amend the constitution (riots followed in Cyprus and Turkey), while Greek interference also radicalised the situation, especially once parliamentary government in Athens had been overthrown by the infamous Greek colonels. Eventually their coup d'état against Makarios in 1974 gave the Turks the opportunity to intervene – yet despite the failure of the coup and the return to power of Makarios, the Turks remained in possession of the northern third of the island.

Since 1974 there have been continuous international and intercommunal negotiations to settle 'the Cyprus problem'. Ethnic differences have played their part in this, but the main problems have been international: Britain and the USA (which by the mid-1960s wanted to partition the island) were concerned to maintain their bases and intelligence-gathering facilities; Greece favoured a united independent Cyprus without any Turkish military presence; while the Turks in 1983 eventually approved the establishment of a Republic of Northern Cyprus, given that the Greek Cypriots were not prepared to agree to disproportionate rights for Turkish Cypriots. After Greece's entry into the EEC, however, the complications increased.

They did so particularly once the EU inaugurated a separate security policy. Hitherto NATO had managed to contain both Greece and Turkey (despite all their differences over airspace, territorial waters, islands and oil exploration rights) but Turkey was not a member of the EU, although she wanted to become one. Both Britain and the USA lent her their support since Turkey was needed as an ally in the Middle East. It was in US interests, therefore, to keep Turkey sweet. The EU and the Greeks had no such incentive. They were critical of Israeli policies, hostile to Turkey (which Giscard d'Estaing said was not European and should never enter the EU) and in 2003 opposed US and UK policy on Iraq. Meanwhile, they agreed to accept Cyprus as a full member of the EU in May 2004.

All sorts of efforts were made to reunite the island. The UN produced the Annan Plan to balance Greek and Turkish Cypriot interests (and maintain the

British bases and US intelligence facilities) and to allow a united and independent Cyprus to take its place in the EU. Greek Cypriots, however, rejected the plan with the result that when Cyprus joined the EU, the northern part of it (and therefore part of the EU) remained occupied by Turkey. Fortunately the EU stipulated that the *acquis communautaire* will not apply to Turkish Cyprus. Meanwhile, membership talks have begun with Turkey itself. However, Cyprus still bedevils international relations. For example, in 1993 she entered into a 'Joint Defence Doctrine' with Greece by which any attack on Cyprus would be considered one on Greece as well. Presumably she now possesses a 'Joint Defence Doctrine with the EU'? Turkey, meanwhile, only allows the EU to use NATO military assets so long as Greece promises not to allow other NATO assets to be used for an attack on Turkey. These problems might well prove manageable, but, fundamentally there seems no objective reason why Turkey should surrender her hold on Northern Cyprus without first being guaranteed membership of the EU. The trouble is that she is much poorer than most EU members, has a dubious civil rights record, might in future be subject to Islamic fundamentalist pressure, and in any case threatens to dominate the EU demographically in fifty years' time, should she be allowed to join. Greece, however, appears at present to support Turkish membership.

The international history of, as well as the foreign policy dilemmas confronting that country, are all covered in Bill Mallinson's book. He treats the subject passionately but historically accurately. He is deeply critical of the UK (whose record is indeed a miserable one), the USA and Turkey and his sympathies lie with the EU. His contribution, nonetheless, is based on wide and original archival research; even when lack of historical documentation forces him to be more speculative, his views deserve to be read with respect and to be debated. No one interested in 'the Cyprus problem' will fail to respond to them. The hope is that as a result of informed debate the future of Cyprus will be a happy and peaceful one.

Alan Sked

ACKNOWLEDGEMENTS

I am grateful to the following.

Yigit Alpogan, Turkish Ambassador to Greece, for a thoughtful discussion; Pavlos Apostolidis, former Head of the Greek Intelligence Service, for an intriguing discussion; Panayiotis Beglitis, former Foreign Ministry and George Papandreou's spokesman, for a difficult interview; Kypros Chrysostomidis, Chief Spokesman of the Government of the Republic of Cyprus, for his subtle frankness. Marie Ermine Chrysanthopoulos for lending me the extensive press collection of her deceased husband, Dimitris Pentzopoulos, Greek diplomat and scholar; Themistocles Chrysanthopoulos, former Greek Ambassador and Consul-General in Istanbul, for saying the truth; Elias Clis, former head of the Department of Greek–Turkish relations at the Greek Ministry of Foreign Affairs, for expounding on his government's views; Tam Dalyell, M.P., Father of the House of Commons, for his honesty and guts; Elias Demetracopoulos, courageous Greek journalist and former Washington correspondent of *Kathimerini*, for a long and frank interview; Marios Evriviades, former Press Counsellor at the Cyprus Embassy in Washington, for an interesting interview; Atillâ Günay, former Minister Counsellor at the Turkish Embassy, Athens, for a long and incisive interview; Vassilis Fouscas, leading academic on the Balkans and editor of the *Journal of Southern Europe and the Balkans*, for intellectual stimulation; Kyriakos Kouros, former Counsellor at the Embassy of Cyprus in Athens, for his frankness; Theodoros Kouloumbis, for a searching interview; Giannis Marinos, MEP and former co-editor of *Oikonomikos Tachidromos*, for his views; Constantinos Mitsotakis, former Prime Minister of Greece, for an enlightening interview; Martin Packard, former British naval Intelligence Officer, for his reminiscences and observations on British and American policy towards Cyprus; Tassos Papadopoulos, President of the Republic of Cyprus, for showing the acumen to finally answer some incisive questions; Stylianos Pattakos, former Minister of Home Affairs in the Greek Junta, for his precision and candidness; Dimitris Pavlidis, former resident of Istanbul, for his views; John Spanopoulos, for lending me the press archives of his father Vassilis Spanopoulos, former editor-in-chief of *Kathimerini*; Themos Stoforopoulos, former Greek Ambassador to Cyprus, for his experience and incisive, independent views. Theodoros Tritaris, Head of the Cyprus Department at the Greek Ministry of Foreign Affairs, for expanding on his government's views; and Yiannis Valinakis, former International Secretary of New Democracy, for a precise and stimulating interview.

No thanks possible, unfortunately, to Dimitris Ioannidis, head of the Greek Military Police during the Junta; the Ministry of Justice, after giving me permission over the telephone to interview him, then wrote to say that as he did not wish to be interviewed, they could not after all grant permission.

My special thanks to Robin Cosby for incisive textual advice.

LIST OF ABBREVIATIONS

AKEL   Progressive Working People's Party
CFSP   Common Foreign and Security Policy
CIA   Central Intelligence Agency
EAM   National Liberation Front
EDES   National Republican Greek League
ELAS   Greek People's Liberation Army
EOKA   National Organization of Cypriot Fighters
ERRF   European Rapid Reaction Force
ESDI/P   European Security and Defence Initiative/Identity/Policy/Personality
EYP   Greek Intelligence Service
ICC   International Criminal Court
IRD   Information Research Department
KYP   Greek Intelligence Service (original name)
NATO   North Atlantic Treaty Organization
TNT   Turkish Defence Force

SOME KEY DATES

1191 Richard Coeur de Lion, England's French King, captures Cyprus, then sells it to the Knights Templar.

1192 Guy de Lusignan acquires Cyprus.

1473 Venice becomes protector of Cyprus.

1489 Venice introduces direct rule.

1571 Ottoman Turks capture Cyprus.

1878 Ottomans lease Cyprus to Britain.

1914 Britain annexes Cyprus.

1931 Cypriots burn down Government House.

1950 Election of Makarios III as Archbishop.

1955 EOKA campaign to free Cyprus and unite with Greece begins; British–Greek–Turkish Conference blows up; anti-Greek riots in Turkey.

1960 Cyprus gains nominal sovereignty over most of its territory.

1963 Archbishop Makarios introduces his 'Thirteen Point Plan', with British support, to amend the constitution; 'communal troubles' begin.

1964 War between Greece and Turkey averted by Soviet and American pressure.

1967 War between Greece and Turkey threatens; Greece withdraws General Grivas and 12,000 men.

1973 17 November demonstrations in Athens: Brigadier Ioannides takes over behind the scenes.

1974 General Grivas dies; Turkey invades Cyprus and occupies thirty-eight per cent of the island.

1977 Archbishop Makarios dies.

1983 Turkish Cypriots declare 'Turkish Republic of Northern Cyprus'.

1990 Cyprus applies to join the European Union.

1996 Imia incident: threat of war between Greece and Turkey.

2002 Kofi Annan presents plan to the leaders of the two main Cypriot communities.
      (December) Copenhagen Summit.

2003 (February) Britain offers half its Cyprus territory to Cyprus if 'Annan Plan' is accepted; Tassos Papadopoulos elected President of Cyprus.
      (March) Talks on 'Annan Plan' fail.
      (April) Cyprus signs EU accession treaty. Rauf Denktash eases travel restrictions to the South: Greek and Turkish Cypriots cross the dividing line.
      (May) Massive increase in Turkish violations of Greek airspace.
      (June) David Hannay, Britain's special envoy for Cyprus, steps down.
      (July) Rauf Denktash declares that the 'Annan Plan' is unacceptable.
      (December) Talks on EU constitution collapse.

2004 (January) Turkey urges resumption of Cyprus negotiations. Elections in occupied Cyprus lead to inclusion of pro-negotiation party in coalition. Greek Prime Minister cites Cyprus developments as the main reason for holding Greek general election two months earlier than necessary.
(February) Following intense American pressure and meeting in New York, the Cypriot sides resume negotiations on the Annan Plan, to be put to referenda on 24 April.
(March) President Papadopoulos advises Cypriots to vote against the Annan Plan. They do.
(April) Russia vetoes Security Council resolution intended to strengthen the Annan Plan.
(May) Republic of Cyprus joins the European Union.
(October) European Commission recommends opening of EU accession talks with Turkey.

PREFACE

The essential to good diplomacy is precision. The main enemy of good
diplomacy is imprecision.[1]

War between Greece and Turkey has almost broken out thrice since Cyprus gained
its alleged independence from Britain in 1960, largely as a result of Britain having
divided the two main communities on Cyprus and because of the unworkable
constitution that was thrust on the fledgling republic. Another negative factor has
been the incapacity of the major stakeholders to agree on a permanent solution
– an incapacity fuelled by a web of intrigue, hidden and overt fanaticism, deceit
and geopolitical self-interest that has reduced Cyprus to a chip in a cynical game of
international poker.

Some irresponsible things have been said by some irresponsible people involved
in international relations. One political scientist and politician, Henry Kissinger,
considered by a senior British diplomat in 1972 as seeing himself as a 'modern
Metternich',[2] has displayed a rather intemperate and undiplomatic streak by
saying:

> The Greek people are a difficult if not impossible people to tame, and for this
> reason we must strike deep into their cultural roots: perhaps then we can force
> them to conform. I mean, of course, to strike at their language, their religion,
> their cultural and historical reserves, so that we can neutralise their ability to
> develop, to distinguish themselves, or to prevail, thereby removing them as an
> obstacle to our strategically vital plans in the Balkans, the Mediterranean, and
> the Middle East.[3]

The power-hungry bull in a diplomatic china shop was reported to have spoken
these words in 1994. Some one hundred and seventy years earlier, Metternich
had said of the Greeks, when they revolted against the Turks: 'Over there, beyond
our frontiers, three or four hundred thousand individuals hanged, impaled or with
their throats cut, hardly count.'[4] Of course, it is not only the Greeks who come in
for attack within the context of international relations. Writing about the Turks
within the context of the Versailles negotiations in 1919, the distinguished British
diplomat Harold Nicolson, said:

> For the Turks I had, and have, no sympathy whatsoever. Long residence at
> Constantinople had convinced me that behind his mask of indolence, the Turk
> conceals impulses of the most brutal savagery [...] The Turks have contributed
> nothing whatsoever to the progress of humanity: they are a race of Anatolian
> marauders: I desired only in the Peace Treaty they should be relegated to
> Anatolia.[5]

Nicolson's and Kissinger's views regarding Cyprus are also worth considering. The latter is well known for saying that the Cyprus problem was solved in 1974 (with the Turkish invasion), while the former wrote:

> I am distressed about Cyprus. The British Empire Delegation have decided to retain it on strategical and other grounds. They are wrong entirely: its retention compromises our whole world position in regard to the Italians.[6]

While these two views are separated both by time and by the very different mentalities of the individuals who held them, they have one significant factor in common: the position of Cyprus as a pawn in the dangerous game of 'world positioning' played by great powers. Nicolson was concerned that Britain's hanging on to Cyprus would justify Italy's hanging on to the Dodecanese Islands, thereby challenging British Mediterranean power – the 'me too' factor – while the Metternich-obsessed Kissinger wanted Cyprus to be a 'staging area' for the Middle East.[7] In 1966, Patrick Leigh Fermor wrote:

> Ever since the Greek War of Independence, England has enjoyed a singular pre-eminence in Greek affections [...] solid reasons support this flattering image [...] an image, alas, which recent conflict in Cyprus has battered [...] premature to say whether things will revert in time to their previous happy state. There are hopeful signs. But lilies that fester smell worse than weeds.[8]

As the Cyprus problem festers on, a new player, the EU, has now joined the USA, Britain, Russia, Turkey and Greece around the poker table. As the tension surrounding Cyprus' membership of the EU increases, with all the concomitant issues of EU–US–NATO relations that are coming to the fore, one wonders which of these players, frustrated with the forty-four-year-old control game, will draw a gun. In 1964, it was the Cypriot nationalist Grivas; in 1967, the Greeks and the Cypriots; while in 1974, it was the Greek Junta, with covert US support, aided by Cypriot extremists. If guns are going to be drawn in Cyprus for a fourth time, they may well be those of the Turkish armed forces.

This book proceeds from the contention that international relations problems can only be reasonably comprehended through serious study of historical primary, as well as secondary, sources. Foreign ministry files are the stuff of diplomatic history. Without adequate knowledge of the past, the future cannot seriously be considered, other than emotionally, since foreign policy formulation is essentially an atavistic business, which is itself dependent on historical 'archives', in other words on policy files. The first thing that a Foreign and Commonwealth Office official does when looking at a question is to call for the file, which will point him in the 'right' direction.

Predicting war is a risky and controversial business. While the benefit of hindsight helps us to understand that the most obvious cause of the Second World War was the Great War and its unsatisfactory outcome, there were few who were prepared to stick their necks out during the one-sided negotiation of the Treaty of Versailles, and to warn of another war. One such brave figure was John Maynard Keynes, who withdrew in protest from the negotiations.

Many historians develop an understanding of the present, and often of the future, that lies somewhere between realism and cynicism. A. J. P. Taylor wrote that one learns from history how to repeat one's mistakes. Conversely, the trite assumption that history repeats itself is only another way of saying something more obvious: that human characteristics and behaviour, whether individual or corporate, remain remarkably constant. It is only historians who tend to repeat themselves. History is merely an exposé of the immutable human condition.

Chapter Fourteen is devoted to an analysis and evaluation of answers received from governments involved in the Cyprus question. The comparison is quite revealing. Russia, France and the Netherlands, after wriggling around, refused to answer any of the questions, while the USA delayed and obfuscated. Israel, Britain, Cyprus, Turkey and Greece were reasonably forthcoming. The inconsistency of responses to similar questions posed by the author suggests that whatever 'solution' is found, it could end up as a watered-down compromise, further muddying the already opaque waters of international political expediency and power politics.

The book ends with an analysis and evaluation of the likelihood of further conflict as a result of the Cyprus problem. It also demonstrates that the ability of the island's inhabitants to determine their own future is severely constrained. This contention is supported by the curious length of time (ten months) on the part of the Cyprus government to reply to a series of straightforward and precise questions put by this author to the then president in September 2002. One was: 'Do you support Cyprus' possible membership of NATO?'; another was: 'Do you believe that the British Sovereign territories should remain?'; while yet another was: 'Do you think that Cyprus should be part of a future European Army?' The most curious aspect of the lack of a response was that the Embassy of Cyprus in Athens actually asked this author to pose questions in the first place, and could not itself initially elicit any coherent response from its own government. The relevant official insisted to both the Cypriot Embassy in Athens and this author that the answers were awaiting the president's signature.

Any historical and current analysis of the Cyprus problem is limited by several factors. First, key documents have not been released by the Foreign and Commonwealth Office, despite the Thirty Year Rule. Second, the United States government withheld between 1999 and 2002 distribution of its already printed 'Foreign Relations of the United States, Greece, 1964 to 1968',[9] then releasing a carefully re-edited version. Third, the Greek government refuses to release crucial documentation, even as far back as 1955, on the Cyprus question, thus leading to justified academic concerns about a murky past. This withholding of key documentary evidence suggests that the increasing interest in Cyprus, as the island joins the European Union without a solution to its problems, has worried some of the key information gatekeepers. A fourth constraint is that although the importance of the Soviet stance is dealt with, Soviet primary source material has not been consulted; neither has Ottoman and Turkish primary material, which is in any case not easy to come by. There are also gaps in Greek primary sources. However, since a good deal of the book concentrates on the last thirty years, government primary source material is in any case generally unavailable, and we have to make do with interviews and secondary sources.

Recognising these limitations, I can but claim an attempt at objectivity, as I am shackled by the source material itself: it is important to recognise that the Foreign Office files used are themselves constrained by the professional consciousness of the diplomats who wrote their letters, dispatches, memoranda and comments. These last documents nevertheless constitute the most valuable source of information for the book. Some of the diplomats' analyses are remarkably frank, and occasionally emotional, almost certainly because 'in-house' diplomat-to-diplomat communications are far more revealing than public statements. The backstage reveals far more of the truth than the frontstage.

Britain has borne the greatest responsibility for the condition of Cyprus since 1878, and still does, especially because of the ninety-nine square miles of Cyprus that are, literally, part of the United Kingdom. Britain's 'dividing' tactics can be traced back at least to the Colonial Constitution of 1925, when separate Greek Cypriot and Turkish categories were established.

In geopolitical terms, the USA is now the elephant as regards Cyprus' future, with Britain as the behind-the-scenes PR consultant, occasionally trying to prevent embarrassing excesses, but not always succeeding, as the Turkish invasion of 1974 shows. The advent of the Junior Bush administration has seen a serious shift in American policy on Greece: while, in the Clinton administration, the American ambassador in Athens was telling people (see Chapter Fourteen) that the islet of Imia was marked as Greek, the current administration did not 'recognize all the territorial waters implications which Greece asserts' and had 'not taken a position on sovereignty over Imia/Kardak, in part because of the lack of an agreed maritime boundary'. Since the Turkish government links the Cyprus question to its claims on Greek islands, US policy has major implications for any Cyprus solution, even though the country is not officially involved.

One useful side effect of this book is that it demonstrates British foreign policy formulation. Another is that it juxtaposes Machtpolitik – *à la* Metternich and Kissinger – with the exercise of 'pure' diplomacy,[10] to the extent that one of its conclusions is that if the 'might is right' concept prevails over diplomacy, the question will not be whether a war breaks out, but, rather, how limited – or otherwise – that war will be. One respected expert has recently written: 'The failure of the parties to the Cyprus problem to agree has created the threat of a regional war on many occasions, and continues to do so.'[11]

INTRODUCTION

It is the primary right of man to die and kill for the land they [sic] live in.[1]

'F*** your Parliament and your Constitution, America is an elephant, Cyprus is a flea. Greece is a flea. If those two fleas continue to itch the elephant, they just may get whacked by the elephant's trunk, whacked good.'[2] These intemperate words were addressed by President Johnson to the Greek ambassador in Washington, in 1964. The itching continued for another ten years, and then, in 1974, came the whacking, courtesy of the Turkish armed forces, which remain firmly entrenched in the northern thirty-eight per cent of the island – minus almost all its 200,000 Christian population – avowedly to protect the 100,000 Turkish settlers and those of the original Muslim population (about 45,000) who have not emigrated. Such a massive forced demographic change in Cyprus has not occurred since 1571, when, upon the capture of Cyprus from Venice, the Ottoman Empire settled Turkish-speaking Muslims in the island. These were the janizaries, (from 'yeni çeri', which means 'new soldier' in Turkish) many of whom had been 'acquired' as Greek toddlers, to be raised in the Ottoman military fashion as the elite guard of the sultan.[3]

Ever since Cyprus gained its qualified independence from Britain in 1960 – apart from the ninety-nine square miles that became British sovereign territory – NATO members Greece and Turkey have come close to war three times over the island. Up to today, the world has witnessed forty-five years of continuous diplomatic and political wrangling, intercommunal fighting, United Nations involvement, threats of war, the above-mentioned invasion, more threats of war, and abortive attempts to solve the Cyprus problem to everybody's satisfaction. It appears to be an impossible task. We are currently witnessing yet another round of talks, secret and semi-public, on a problem that Henry Kissinger, the former US secretary of state, and Bulent Eçevit, the executor of the invasion and recent prime minister of Turkey, have stated was solved in 1974, as if invasions and occupation are the solutions to the ills of the world.

Perhaps the most immutable ingredients of the problem are the interests that need to be satisfied. First is America's insistence that Cyprus must be NATO-friendly, and that it continues to house US listening posts; second, but strongly connected to this, is the British government's fear that real independence for Cyprus could undermine Britain's insistence on hanging on to its sovereign territories; third, and clearly connected to the first two, is the fear, felt by the USA and Britain, that Russia, which supports the UN and Greek position, is still a threat to NATO, and could exploit the situation. The S-300 saga, which resulted in Turkish threats in

1998 to bomb the sophisticated Russian anti-aircraft missile systems if they were delivered to Cyprus, has not been forgotten;[4] fourth, opinion both in Greece and Turkey is highly sensitive to the Cyprus issue, and national pride plays a leading role; fifth, and perhaps the least well comprehended, are the treaties involved. The final factor which, for an allegedly sovereign state, should be the most important one, is that of the Cypriots' own aspirations. From the beginning of independence, however, the treaties imposed various constraints, which were clearly forced upon unwilling Cypriots by Britain, Greece and Turkey, and the constitution proved unworkable, as we shall see.

Outside pressure, particularly from Britain, appears to have reached near-farcical proportions, with Archbishop Makarios allegedly being blackmailed about 'unusual homosexual proclivities'.[5] From 1960, certainly, Makarios tried his best to keep Cyprus independent, but increasing radicalisation between the two communities, with unwarranted outside interference from Greece and Turkey, limited his freedom of action. By 1969, the British high commissioner was writing:

> Undoubtedly the most able and dove-like leaders to emerge are Glafcos Clerides on the Greek side and Rauf Denktash on the Turkish side. If the negotiations were left to these two men, it is probable that an early solution, or at any rate a 'modus vivendi', could be reached... In the last resort the authorities in Ankara undoubtedly run the Turkish–Cypriot Administration [...].[6]

As we shall see, Makarios was increasingly regarded as an irritant by the Greek military Junta and the US government, in particular by Kissinger. It is clear that external factors after 1960 severely constrained the ability of the Cypriots themselves, particularly after radicalisation, to determine their destiny with confidence. Indeed, when Makarios openly criticised the Junta, the result was a coup, providing Turkey with the perfect excuse to carry out its threat and to invade.

It is perhaps paradoxical that Britain, which bears the most responsibility for dividing not only the two communities on Cyprus, but also the Greek and Turkish governments, was later content to allow the USA to make the running, while nevertheless seriously considering *enosis* (union). Behind the many options that the British government considered lay the primary aim of keeping its sovereign territory on Cyprus sacrosanct. Fear of the Soviet Union played perhaps a key role. After the USA came to regard Cyprus as a geostrategic necessity, a totally sovereign Cyprus was out of the question, both for the USA and for Britain, whatever the inhabitants thought and whatever the US government had once thought, in its post-war decolonisation enthusiasm.

The cold war, geopolitics and NATO solidarity were far more important than considerations of self-determination for Cyprus. Any tension between Greece and Turkey was bound to affect Cyprus negatively, as has been proved, and the key year of 1955 marked the beginning of the end of correct Graeco–Turkish relations, when Britain managed, in defiance of Article 16 of the Treaty of Lausanne of 1923, to involve Turkey in Cypriot affairs.

It is interesting to compare the fates of Crete and Cyprus, islands of approximately the same size.[7] By 1821, the Muslim population of Crete was far larger (c. fifty per cent) than that of Cyprus (c. twenty-five per cent).[8] Crete and Cyprus sought freedom and union with Greece, and began a long struggle to achieve this. In Cyprus, the Turks hanged the archbishop and beheaded three bishops. Following the Graeco–Turkish war of 1897, the Great Powers (Britain, France, Italy, Russia, Germany and Austro-Hungary) sent a peacekeeping force to Crete, and forbade *enosis*, but, after the withdrawal of the Turkish troops, allowed Crete to proclaim independence. Following the Balkan wars, in which Turkey lost huge swathes of Christian territories, Crete was united with Greece. The Muslim Cretans emigrated or were forcibly sent to Turkey following the First World War and the subsequent Greek 'catastrophe', when the ill-fated Greek campaign in Turkey ended in failure and in the expulsion of over one million Greeks.[9]

Cyprus and Crete were undoubtedly part of the Greek world. Both were captured from Venice by the Ottoman Turks, in 1571 and 1669 respectively. Crete, perhaps because it had never been a British colony, was able to join Greece. The Greek navy, however, could not reach Cyprus easily during the Balkan wars. Nor would Greece have ever considered attacking Cyprus, since it was now occupied by Britain, with Ottoman permission. Britain had returned the Ionian Islands to Greece in 1864, which gave many Cypriots the hope of union with Greece.[10] Winston S. Churchill, when parliamentary secretary to the Colonial Office, had said in 1907:

> It is only rational that the Cypriot people who are of Greek descent should regard their incorporation with what can be called their mother country as an ideal to be earnestly, devoutly and fervently cherished. Such a feeling is an example of the patriotic devotion, which so nobly characterises the Greek nation.[11]

Such statements understandably gave rise to the hope that Cyprus would eventually go the way of Corfu and Crete; Greece was even promised Cyprus if she would join Britain in the First World War. When she eventually did so, Britain claimed after the war that she had joined in too late. By the end of the Second World War, in which Cypriots served in the British armed forces, there was again an expectation that Britain would relinquish Cyprus; but the world was no longer as multilateral as it had been fifty years earlier, and, as we shall see, the cold war began to clash with moralistic decolonisation arguments, particularly in the case of Cyprus. Hard-nosed strategic interests took priority, even when the Dodecanese Islands were handed back to Greece; and Cyprus remained British, despite strong arguments in favour of giving it to Greece to strengthen the Greek government's war against the Communists.

The rights of the people of Cyprus certainly seem to have been subordinated to the strategic interests of strong powers and to the vagaries of international and regional politics. The number of UN Security Council and General Assembly resolutions ignored by Turkey is large, exceeded perhaps only by those ignored by Israel, with whom Turkey has formed increasingly close formal military links over the past forty-five years. In 1998, two Mossad agents were arrested in Cyprus for spying on the installations being prepared for the (eventually abortive) arrival of the Russian S-300s. The agents were briefly imprisoned, before being released in a secret deal.

Since the 1974 invasion of Cyprus, partition of the island is now a reality; the island is, in one author's words, a hostage to history,[12] although 'hostage to hypocrisy' would also be an apt term. The measure of radicalisation, entrenchment and emotion on the part of the British, Americans, Greeks and Turks, not to forget the Cypriots, transcends serious attempts to solve the problem equitably.

One important factor is that Cyprus is a victim of the problems of Graeco–Turkish relations, particularly as regards Turkey's claims to some Greek Aegean islands. As well as a victim, however, it has been the cause of the expulsion of almost the whole Greek-speaking population of Turkey in 1964 and 1965 (see Chapter Three). Many experts have mooted the idea of trading Cyprus for peace in the Aegean: in other words, recognition of the occupied zone, in the hope that Turkey would formally drop its claims to Greek territory. Four retired Greek ambassadors have advocated the recognition of occupied Cyprus to accelerate the remaining Cyprus' membership of the EU.[13]

The stakes have now risen over Cyprus, and matters are coming to a head, as Cyprus' EU membership has engulfed us. As if US, British, Russian, NATO, Turkish and Greek interests were not enough, the EU interest is a new, and possibly, vital factor, contrasting, as it does, US and EU interests.[14] The obvious point arises that as Cyprus becomes an EU member, then Turkey, a non-member, will be occupying European Union territory. Immense behind-the-scenes pressure is being exercised on the Greek government, which has a 'joint defence doctrine' with Cyprus, to recognise the occupied zone as a separate entity, and even to discuss bilaterally Turkey's claims to Greek territory, which would entail the Greek government having to entertain such claims, when the only matter it is prepared to discuss is the delimitation of the continental shelf between the two countries.

Behind all the manoeuvring lies the American and, therefore, British fear, that an already economically and politically unstable Turkey could slide into chaos and then 'anti-western' radicalism, most likely of the Islamic variety, which would help Russia.

Britain's relationship with the USA is another factor: the Blair government is trying to increase its weight within the EU by presenting itself as America's staunch ally in the fight against terrorism; and since Turkey is crucial to the USA, Britain is not prepared to upset that particular apple cart.

Allied to this is Britain's attempt to subtly weaken EU independence, not only by enthusiastically supporting enlargement willy-nilly, including Turkey's application, but also by supporting, with the USA, the Turkish position on the European Rapid Reaction Force. In short, Britain and the USA want Turkey in the force on Turkey's terms, namely that the fledgling EU force will not be allowed to operate in the Eastern Aegean and Cyprus. In December 2001 a secret agreement signed by Britain, the USA and Turkey assured the latter of precisely this. Greece, which obtained a copy of the agreement, understandably rejected it, on the grounds that it would limit EU independence and that it was not signed within an EU framework. When amendments to the agreement were inserted to the effect that no NATO or EU member would threaten or attack each other, Greece withdrew its objections, while Turkey equivocated. In this sense, Cyprus represents an Achilles' heel of European Union defence integration.

Another significant factor in the Cyprus conundrum is the powerful arms lobby; the majority of Greece's and Turkey's arms purchases are from US companies. Competition between US and European arms manufacturers is intense (see Chapter Sixteen) and helps to explain why the USA is promoting NATO enlargement so keenly, while trying to undermine purely EU solutions. Pressure on both the Greek and Turkish governments to 'buy American' is heavy, as Greece's recent purchases of Patriot defence systems suggests. It follows that a united truly independent Cyprus as an EU member, linked to a solution to Graeco–Turkish problems, would not be welcome to the arms lobby, which would have to find new markets or cut its large workforce. A Cyprus–Greece–Turkey solution could also call into question the relevance of the British bases, particularly if Cyprus were to be a member of a future European army or even only of NATO.

Thus, the situation is tense: Turkey even threatened, at the very least, to annex the northern part of the island if Cyprus joined the EU without being reunited. The big question remains whether, despite Cyprus' membership, the problem will be solved, or whether, whatever arrangements are agreed, they will simply be a recipe for further trouble and war. The former British prime minister, James Callaghan, is reported to have told two authors that in 1974 Britain nearly went to war with Turkey.[15] This book, mainly through earlier documentary evidence and Lord Callaghan's own recent denial, elicited by this author, questions that view. (It is however possible that there was a near-incident.) What *is* certain is that Greece nearly went to war with Turkey. According to an opinion poll, seventy-two per cent of Turks believe that there will be a war with Greece.[16]

Part of the 'spin-off' of this book is that the primary sources show how dangerously muddled British foreign policy formulation was, at least on the Cyprus issue. As we shall see, the Foreign Office admitted *a posteriori* that the Cyprus constitution was unworkable and even that the Treaty of Guarantee was questionable, particularly in a United Nations context. To this one can add the foreign policy muddle in the USA at the time of the Turkish invasion, exacerbated not only by the Watergate scandal, but also by those who took advantage of the confusion. Here, Henry Kissinger played a dangerous, irresponsible and egotistical role. Writing about him – officially – in December 1971, the British chargé d'affaires to the embassy in Washington wrote:

> It is impossible to square Kissinger's expressed views with reality [...]. It is rather his manner of conceiving and conducting foreign policy without reference to, or knowledge of, the State Department or anyone else which is most worrying. It leaves one with the fear that any day something could go seriously wrong because the normal sources of advice, restraint and execution are wholly by-passed.[17]

Coming from an insider, this lends great credibility to what authors like Hitchens, Craig and O'Malley have written.[18] Chapters Five and Six have more such comments, which paint a negative picture.

American foreign policy has certainly played, and plays, a vital part in Cyprus' fate. The British chargé d'affaires' premonition was proved correct in 1974. Although Kissinger is now largely discredited outside the USA, unilateralism and some of the rather strident characters involved in the Bush administration discourage moderation and restraint. The moderate Chris Patten, the former EU external affairs commissioner, has said that while Europeans believe in acting together, multilaterally, the USA seems 'ever more bent on acting alone'.[19] Although the USA has no formal responsibility for Cyprus, it's the increasing involvement there, through its 'troubleshooter', Thomas Weston, and increasing American influence in the region, cannot be ignored. This clearly has implications for Cyprus, as it moves into the EU.

The first section of this book is essentially the historical background so necessary to understand the second section, which will scrutinise the views of the different *partis pris* and evaluate the legal and moral aspects, while the third section will look at the 'geopolitical' aspects, the wider but intimately related question of Graeco–Turkish relations, developments after the invasion, the EU factor and the likelihood of some kind of conflict.

We shall now consider why, unlike Crete, Cyprus is a divided aircraft carrier, after decades of futile lip service to the reunification of the island.

PART I

The Poker Table

INTRODUCTION

Part I covers the history of Cyprus, using mainly diplomatic papers, to enable you to get a 'first-hand view' of the story. It goes without saying that one cannot properly comprehend the power of the forces at work around Cyprus without sufficient insight into the backstage diplomacy of the story. It follows that one needs this historical perspective to attempt an analysis and evaluation of the international relations aspects of the conundrum, with which we deal later in the book.

1 British Property and the Russian Factor

A truly independent Greece is an absurdity. Greece can either be English or Russian, and since she must not be Russian, it is necessary that she be English.[1]

INTRODUCTION

The precise ethnic mix of those who lived in Cyprus in 7000 BC is a bit of a moot point, although they were certainly mainly neolithic farmers. The Ottoman Turks were not to put in an appearance there for another 8,570 years. The island was settled by Greeks in the second millennium BC. Since then, whatever political arrangements were in force, the population has remained intrinsically Greek, while controlled successively by Mycenaeans, Phoenicians, Assyrians, Egyptians, Persians, Macedonians, Romans, Byzantines, Franco–English (Richard the Lionheart), Franks, Venetians, Turks, British and, since 1960, also by its own people, albeit with severe constraints on its sovereignty. At independence in 1960, some eighteen per cent of the population was described as Turkish Cypriot, while today this figure is about double, owing to the import of Turkish settlers since the Turkish invasion, a far cry from Ataturk's policy of the 1920s, to encourage Turkish-speaking Cypriots to return home, to encourage national homogeneity. Interestingly, the ratio of Turkish Cypriots and illegal settlers to Greek Cypriots now corresponds more closely to the percentage of territory taken and occupied by the Turkish armed forces, of which there are some 40,000 soldiers.

This chapter will consider the British interest in Cyprus as well as why, unlike India and other British possessions, Cyprus was unable to buck the trend of the post-war decolonisation process sponsored by the USA – and USSR – and achieve independence or *enosis*, despite the anti-colonial uprising of Colonel (later General) Grivas which broke out on 1 April 1955. Whether the date of April Fool's Day was fortuitous or reflected dark humour is a moot point.

THE RUSSIAN OBSESSION AND 1878

It is no exaggeration to say that, during almost the whole of the nineteenth century, one of the British Empire's most obsessive preoccupations was with Russia, and particularly with the latter's usually hostile attitude towards the Ottoman Empire. This reached its fulfilment in the case of Greece when the British and their French junior partners occupied Piraeus during the Crimean War, to force Greece not to cooperate with Russia.[2] The British motive for waging the Crimean War against Russia was essentially to help preserve British hegemony in the Eastern Mediterranean, by combating Russia's desire to weaken Turkey.[3] The conclusion of the war did not, however, stop future Russian territorial pressure on Ottoman possessions: Russia defeated the Ottomans in 1877, and reached the gates of Constantinople. The terms of the Treaty of San Stefano concluded between the Russians and the Ottomans were so advantageous to the former, including, for example, the establishment of a large and independent pro-Russian Bulgaria, that the British intervened diplomatically (and by moving more naval vessels into the Mediterranean), actions which led to the 'Great Eastern Crisis', and the Congress of Berlin in 1878. Although the main aim of the Congress was to establish peace in the Balkans, in the face of Russian power and a crumbling Ottoman Empire, Britain realised that the Ottoman Empire was no longer a 'genuine reliable power',[4] and that she would need not only to combat Russia, but also to watch over Anatolia. Britain therefore leased Cyprus from the Ottomans as a 'place d'armes' in a convention approved by the Congress of Berlin, to guarantee Asiatic Turkey against Russian attack. The main objective was to keep the Russians at bay and to 'prop up some sort of Turkish state, in Asia Minor – much the arrangement, in fact, which still existed in the middle half of the twentieth century',[5] and, at least in (IMF) financial and US-sponsored military terms, today. By 1878, Britain enjoyed naval strategic supremacy in the Mediterranean, controlling Gibraltar, Malta and Cyprus, after the latter pawn had changed hands.

ENOSIS

Although the campaign for union with Greece was not to become a serious problem for its colonial masters until the EOKA campaign of the 1950s, its roots had been put down much earlier, arguably with the outbreak of the Greek War of Independence in 1821, when the archbishop of Cyprus, his archdeacon and three bishops were beheaded, and other atrocities occurred. In 1828, modern Greece's first president, Count Kapodistria, called for the union of Cyprus with Greece, and various minor uprisings took place.[6] When General Wolsely stepped ashore in Cyprus in 1878 formally to establish British control, he was welcomed by the archbishop of Kition with a request that Britain hand Cyprus over to Greece.[7] At all events, the *enosis* movement remained 'patchy and incidental in its extent, but nevertheless retained a high degree of continuity and fixity of purpose, essentially because of the existence of high Greek culture within the milieu of the powerful and respected Greek Christian Orthodox Church'.[8] *Enosis* was always in the background, and expectation in Greece and Cyprus rose and came into the open during the Graeco–Turkish War of 1897 and with Crete's subsequent de facto independence and final incorporation into Greece in 1912. When Turkey joined Germany in the First World War, Britain formally annexed the island, although it had discussed ceding it to Greece at the end of 1912, in return for a base in the Ionian Islands.[9] In 1915, Britain actually offered to cede Cyprus, if Greece were to join her in the war,[10] but as Greece did not join until 1917, Britain did not grant Greece's request, made at the Versailles negotiations in 1919, to give up the island. Expectations for *enosis* had nevertheless been raised. Under the terms of the Treaty of Lausanne in 1923, Turkey formally ceded Cyprus to Britain, which declared it a Crown Colony in 1925. In the Treaty (Article 16), Turkey agreed to renounce all claims of any kind to territories under its former jurisdiction. Britain was to change that, effectively bringing to an end all the good achieved in the Friendship Treaties of 1930 between Greece and Turkey.[11]

The *enosis* campaign grew in strength. When, in 1931, the Colonial Admin-istration proposed a temporary levy of five per cent on official salaries of over £100 a year, the Legislative Council voted thirteen to twelve to reject it. The twelve Greek Cypriots who voted against the measure were joined by a Turkish Cypriot – who became known as the 'Thirteenth Greek'.[12] The measure was nevertheless imposed by an Order in Council, and agitation began. The Bishop of Kition even declared the union of Cyprus with Greece, and on 21 October there were major riots in which Government House was burned down. This led to the suspension by Britain of the Colonial Constitution, and the introduction of various repressive measures, including the deportation of two bishops and two Communist Party leaders.[13] The Communists, feared as much as the Church by the British administration for having helped to foment the riots, had not yet been openly pushing for *enosis*, but one major result of the repression was a change in policy, whereby the Communist Party now lined up with the Church on the *enosis* issue. In 1933, the British therefore banned it.[14] The years up to the end of the Second World War in Greece were quieter, with the British and Greeks in Cyprus retreating into their respective social and mental compartments.[15] After Britain declared war on Germany, some 37,000 Cypriots volunteered for the British Armed Forces (including a later president, Glafcos Clerides, who became a fighter pilot), of whom one third were Turkish. Proportionately, then, twice as many Turkish as Greek Cypriots volunteered. Interestingly, the British authorities even used the slogan 'For Greece and Freedom' in their recruiting.[16] Whether this was faintly cynical or simply desperately realistic is debatable. The fact that one third of the recruits were Turkish Cypriots is more intriguing, particularly when faced with such a slogan, although economic factors may have played some role. At all events, the end of the Second World War brought renewed and more widespread demands for *enosis*, in Greece, Cyprus, in certain influential quarters of the USA and even, as we shall see, in the upper echelons of the Foreign Office; but again, the Russian spectre was going to be wheeled out, this time in the cloak of Communism, as a reason, some would say an excuse, for preventing independence as well as *enosis*. There were, as we shall see, arguments both in favour of and against giving up Cyprus. Paradoxically, proponents of both arguments used the Communist threat as a main pillar of their reasoning.

THE RUSSIAN OBSESSION

Even before the end of the Second World War, left-wing demonstrations and strikes had begun in countries freed from the Germans. Cyprus, although not occupied by the Germans, also experienced a renewed wave of agitation for *enosis*. Along with the left-right polarisation of politics,[17] the question began to loom ever larger. During the war, the question had been in the minds of the Greek government in exile; one month before the invasion of Greece in 1941, the Greek prime minister had asked his British counterpart whether, in return for Greece's war effort, Britain would consider ceding Cyprus as a reward, but was politely rebuffed.[18]

It is fair to say that before the end of the war, the stage was set for a future concerted effort by Cyprus and Greece to push for *enosis*. The British were clearly well aware of the strength of feeling on the issue. In August 1944, the Governor, Charles Woolley, wrote in a secret telegram:

> Several factors have since combined to bring the issue of the union with Gruce [sic] to the fore. Following the announcement of proposed visit [by Cosmo Parkinson, Under Secretary of State for the Colonies], Akel [Left-wing] and National [Right-wing] parties have vied with each other in public support of *enosis*. Moreover, recent rapid progress of Allied arms has led Cypriots to believe that decision on their claims is imminent, following an early end to the war.
>
> Result is that it is now certain that in petitions to Parkinson, *enosis* will be in the forefront of all the demands of all the parties. Some local politicians are even pressing that no other request should be submitted [...].[19]

The main factors in favour of *enosis* were: the Atlantic Charter and the Universal Declaration of Human Rights, often quoted by Greek Cypriots; impending de-colonisation, for example in Transjordan, India, Burma and Ceylon; the handing to Greece of the Dodecanese Islands by Italy, via the British Military Administration (Peace Treaty with Italy 1947); and the natural feeling of Greek Cypriots that they were, in fact, Greek, just as Greek Cretans had felt Greek.

Before discussing what got in the way of pro-*enosis* recommendations by British politicians and senior Foreign Office officials, we need to look at their arguments. Immediately following the end of the war, a British member of Parliament, Noel Baker, wrote to the foreign secretary, Bevin, to propose a 'new policy in Greece', which included the cession of Cyprus. The first stage of the Greek civil war had already passed, with a tenuous and ill-fated agreement at Varkiza, and there was considerable resentment among many Greeks, particularly the left wing, towards Britain's role in fighting the Greek wartime resistance movement, EAM-ELAS. This resentment stemmed from the fact that the British Operations Executive had assisted the Greek resistance (of which ELAS was the largest part) in fighting the occupiers, but that the British army had subsequently turned against them (see pages 15–19). Baker advocated various measures, including the return of Cyprus to Greece, writing: 'There is no doubt that the people of Cyprus ardently desire to rejoin Greece, and that feeling is beginning to run high.' He added that adoption of such a policy would kill Communist hopes of attaining power by civil war, and would greatly strengthen the foreign secretary's hand in his efforts to check 'Russian imperialist plans in the border countries'.[20] Although there was some agreement in the Foreign Office, the Ministry of War and Colonial Office were not prepared to stick their necks out, particularly because of the old Russian fear, which was beginning to reappear, in the guise of the incipient cold war. Although Britain had become the USSR's wartime ally (despite the latter's invasion of Poland), immense distrust of Russian policy was ingrained, particularly in Winston Churchill and, following the latter's electoral defeat, in the new British foreign secretary, Bevin. Only two years later, a senior under secretary in the Foreign Office, Oliver Harvey, lost his battle to have Cyprus ceded to Greece. A defining year was of course 1947. It saw the ideological divide between 'East' and 'West' rapidly re-establishing itself. The Four Power disagreement on what to do with Germany, the setting up of the Cominform in Moscow and of the Information Research Department at the Foreign Office in London, the coming into effect of the 'Truman Doctrine' (mainly as a result of the civil strife in Greece) and the consequent replacement of British military and economic support for the Greek government with American all bear ample witness to the hardening of positions on either side of the future 'Iron Curtain'.[21]

Sir Oliver's arguments in favour of *enosis* were cogent:

1. We can do little materially to help Greece although it is of the first importance to maintain confidence in Great Britain and in herself. I suggest therefore that further consideration be given to the question of the cession of Cyprus.

2. The action of H.M. Government in India and Burma has enormously impressed opinion throughout the world. Our proposed evacuation policy in Palestine and the possibility that we may propose independence for Cyrenaica, when coupled with what we have done in India and Burma, makes our continued presence in Cyprus indefensible.

3. I understand that Cyprus has been rejected by the Chiefs of Staff as unsuitable for any long-term strategic purpose. We have in fact never made use of the island for military purposes, and we have spent next to nothing on its material and social betterment. We have nothing to be proud of there.

4. It can hardly be questioned that Greece, who has governed Crete effectively, and has now been given the Dodecanese, can equally well govern Cyprus. (There is a small Turkish minority whose rights would be secured.)

5. British administration in the island is meeting difficulties owing to increasing Cypriot non-cooperation. Hitherto, serious violence has been avoided but with the examples of Palestine, Egypt and Greece itself, we cannot hope that this will last long.

6. It would be tragic if Anglo–Greek relations were now to be poisoned by an E.A.M. campaign of violence in Cyprus. Moreover, we are always exposed to the risk of the Slav bloc raising Cyprus at the United Nations for our embarrassment. What convincing defence we could make there I do not know.

7. Our position for holding the United States to the necessity of assuming new responsibilities in Greece would be greatly strengthened if we ourselves had contributed Cyprus.

8. I do not know whether Cyprus would prove an economic asset to Greece but it would be the greatest possible contribution to Greek morale and British influence. (We are still living in Greece on the credit of Mr. Gladstone's retrocession of the Ionian Isles.)

9. For these different reasons I would strongly advocate that consideration be given to the very early cession of Cyprus to Greece, before the Cypriot campaign is embittered by violence and before cession can be represented as yielding to force.

10. (I had an opportunity of discussing this with Sir Clifford Norton [British Ambassador in Athens] in Switzerland in August. Although he has not seen this paper, I know he shares these views.)[22]

In essence, Sir Oliver was saying that it would be sensible to give up gracefully, gain respect and help to combat the perceived (by some) threat of the spread of totalitarian ideology in Greece, all in one fell swoop, thereby preventing the inevitable strife in Cyprus and anger at Britain's rigid attitude that would otherwise follow. A senior Foreign Office counsellor, Wallinger, responded:

> In more normal circumstances, the early cession of Cyprus to Greece might well be a wise policy, justified by considerations not only of justice, but also of expediency. But present circumstances are not normal.[23]

By 'not normal,' Wallinger of course meant the Greek civil war (see pages 15–19) that followed the Second World War, fought mainly by the extreme left- and right-wing, with Britain and the USA supporting the latter (although she had supported the mainly left-wing Greek resistance during the Second World War).

Thus, despite Wallinger's lip service to justice and expediency, he was paradoxically using the perceived Communist threat as a reason to *hang on* to Cyprus, in stark contrast to Sir Oliver, who was using the Communist threat as a reason to *give up* Cyprus. Conflict of argumentation seemed to be the order of the day: emotive political ideology tends to undermine rational thinking. Nevertheless, it has to be said that the combination of British fear of the Soviet Union, growing East–West distrust and the Greek civil war helped those who were opposed to independence, particularly at the Colonial Office, to present compelling counter arguments:

> So long as the internationally supported bandit war continues on its present scale, Greece's independence must remain to some extent doubtful [...] control of the island by a foreign power (USSR) would be a danger to us. Various telegrams from Athens in recent weeks have given very pessimistic estimates of the Greek Government's chances of victory.[24]

Another official was more specific:

> Cyprus is in fact the only firm bit of ground in the Middle East left to our strategic planners. From the purely strategic point of view, to sacrifice this one remaining asset at a time when it is not even certain that we shall get any strategic rights or facilities in any part of Libya would seem inconsistent with the policy of the firm hold on the Middle East which has been endorsed by the Prime Minister and Secretary of State, as well as by the Chiefs of Staff [...] with Cyprus ceded to a Greece gone Communist, we should not only have created a vacuum in the Middle East, we should have gone halfway towards letting the Russians fill it.[25]

With the impending British pull-out from Palestine and the failed Soviet attempts to be granted naval facilities in the Dodecanese following the handover of the islands to Greece by Italy, British fear of Soviet naval competition in the Eastern Mediterranean was palpable. Yet these arguments did not budge Sir Oliver, who riposted:

> I confess I remain quite unmoved by the arguments in the minutes. The Chiefs of Staff will always object to evacuating anything where they have been for some time, just as they will always object to occupying anything where they have not hitherto been. The views of the Colonial Office are, of course, not worth having on the subject, which is essentially foreign affairs. When the Greeks in despair turn to the methods of the Irish, the Jews, the Hindus and the Egyptians, then, I suspect, the British people will rise and compel the Government to evacuate.[26]

The Greek Cypriots and Greek government were beginning to feel that the British government was being somewhat intransigent. Certainly, the Colonial Office was obdurate in the extreme, refusing even to acknowledge, let alone reply to a letter from the Cyprus Ethnarchy (church) to consider *enosis*:

> Colonial Office was taking no action whatsoever on this letter. [...] There is a long standing tradition at the Colonial Office that no letters or petitions asking for the union of Cyprus with Greece are ever answered; experience shows that to answer them gives rise to endless controversial correspondence. It is undesirable that the 'Ethnarchy' of Cyprus should receive any official recognition as a body.[27]

How intrinsically valid were the claims that ceding Cyprus to Greece would weaken, rather than strengthen the resistance to, Soviet influence? Clearly, the perceived Communist threat was played on as an argument, and connected almost automatically to the Soviet Union. Thus, the Greek civil war played a major role in British calculations, and was used as a lever to rebuff the *enosis* argument.

THE GREEK CIVIL WAR

In Greece today, the civil war is still a sensitive subject: in schools, the history curriculum stops abruptly at 1944, with most school-leavers blissfully unaware that anything happened other than a victory against Nazi Germany and then against Communism. The conventional and oversimplified picture that many have today is that the wartime Greek Resistance ended up as a tool of the Communists who, with Soviet support, wished to take over in Greece. The ensuing war, in this scenario, was a battle between the forces of freedom, represented by those who supported the return of the King, supported by the British Army, against the dark forces of totalitarian Stalinism.

The evidence to date suggests that this is an overly broad-brush view. The situation was complex, involving British (the 'Russian obsession') and later US (the 'Truman Doctrine') interests. That during the war the British supported the main resistance parties, the anti-monarchist ELAS and EDES (a mixture of pro-monarchists and 'neutrals') is well known, as is the fighting between the two organisations which had pushed EDES into the mountains of Epirus by early 1944.

What is not so well known is that the head of the British Military Mission, Myers, was removed from his position in 1943 for revealing the extent of feeling in Greece against the return of the king.[28] Although he was removed on Foreign Office advice, Winston Churchill may have been the likely instigator, as he was 'closely wedded to the king's cause'.[29] After the war, Myers had considerable trouble getting his book on the causes of the Greek civil war published. It was not until 1985 that a full edition was published, the original script having been 'lost' in the Foreign Office in 1945.

The question of the king was indeed to sow great division in Greece, and the British (not only Myers) were aware of this. In a 'Most Secret' telegram, in December 1943, the British ambassador to Greece recorded that the Greek prime minister in exile's (Tsouderos') secret analysts in Greece had said that the return of the King at the moment of liberation 'was not in Greece's best interest'.[30] Early the following year, there was an anti-monarchist mutiny among the Greek forces in Egypt, followed by Tsouderos' resignation. There was little enthusiasm in Greece for the return of the King.[31]

The British, apart from supporting the king (who was to return in 1946, following a controversial plebiscite), had more immediate concerns, namely to ensure their interests in the Eastern Mediterranean as a whole. As the Soviet armies approached Germany, Britain started to get the jitters and British policy in Greece began to get somewhat confused. In a top secret memorandum in June 1944, the foreign secretary, Eden, wrote:

> In recent months I have become disturbed by developments which seem to indicate the Soviet Government's intention to acquire a dominating influence in the Balkans [...] We should not hesitate to make our special interests in the Eastern Mediterranean and therefore in Greece and Turkey, and indeed our interests elsewhere in the Balkans, clear to the Russians: but in any step we take to build our influence we must be most careful to avoid giving the impression of a direct challenge.

An annex to the memorandum stated:

> Furthermore, if anyone is to be blamed for the present situation in which the communist-led elements are the most powerful elements in Yugoslavia and Greece, *it is we ourselves*. The Russians have merely sat back and watched us doing their work for them [...] as a result of our approach to the Soviet Government, however, *the latter have now agreed to let us take the lead in Greece* [my italics].[32]

In October 1944, Winston Churchill and Stalin agreed that Greece 'would be 90% British', in the infamous 'percentages agreement'.[33] By now, Britain was hoping that the EAM (the political organisation behind ELAS) would be absorbed into a Greek National Unity government, obviously initially 'with British help'.

Instead, political chaos and partisan government were the result. Matters came to a head when the British Commander in Greece, Scobie, ordered the ELAS forces and the army to disband, whereupon EAM's nominees (five out of fifteen in the Cabinet) resigned. On 3 December, 'ill-disciplined police' shot dead fifteen EAM demonstrators in central Athens, whereupon ELAS took over a large part of the city. Fighting then began between the British and regular Greek army on the one hand, and ELAS on the other, which resulted in the controversial and unpopular British bombing of Athens. Britain's image was not helped, with moderate newspapers joining the fray against the British. The moderate *To Vima* wrote:

> Greece, like Cyprus, is needed as a base on the road of British imperialism [...] the danger to Greece does not come from the North [...] these were massacres instigated, encouraged and directed by Scobie [...] Future historians have already placed Churchill with Xerxes, Mussolini and Hitler [...] Plastiras [former titular head of EDES] was made a British puppet Prime Minister because Churchill wanted him to fight social justice, progress and democracy [...] The Scobie-Plastiras dictatorship protects war criminals [...] The Tory war against the Greek people is part of a general Balkan Tory plan [...] British troops were sent to Greece to guarantee law and order. Instead they started civil war. [...] Yet even the Germans themselves, even the Nazi beasts, never went so far as to bombard the popular quarters of Athens. Today it is the British who are murdering the poor people of Athens; it is General Scobie's aircraft which are burning them up.[34]

Churchill visited Athens in December 1944, but failed to halt the fighting. One of his central aims was to strengthen the Greek monarchy. He met Archbishop Damaskinos, whom he had previously described as a 'pestilent priest, a survival from the Middle Ages', and persuaded the king in exile to support the archbishop as regent, thus further fuelling the controversy in Greece about the monarchy.[35] The prime minister, George Papandreou, resigned, to be replaced by the more pro-British above-mentioned General Plastiras. Eventually, a ceasefire was agreed, followed by the Varkiza agreement in February 1945, which gradually broke down when the right wing took revenge.[36] A British Foreign Office official, in a typical understatement, wrote that a number of EAM complaints about the activities of the National Guard and right-wing organisations had 'considerable justification'.[37]

Matters were confusing. Following the landslide Labour victory in Britain in July 1945, a leader of a Labour Party delegation said that in Greece, 'the aim was to have elected a truly democratic government, even if that meant the rise of EAM and ELAS. In no circumstances would a Labour government help to uphold royalist or other regimes that did not enjoy the support of the people.'[38] The opposite was in fact the case, as Britain's obsession with Russian influence was maintained, and political polarisation leading to the Greek civil war proper was taking place. The British ambassador, Leeper, wrote that the Greek problem during 1945 'became largely one of Anglo–Russian relations'.[39]

What exactly were Britain's interests, in the knowledge that the British government was aware that the Soviet Union had no designs for taking over Greece? A report by the Joint Planning Staff sums them up rather coldly:

> Our strategic interest is to ensure that no unfriendly power, by the acquisition of Greek bases, can threaten our Mediterranean communications. On the other hand, we wish to liquidate our present military commitment as soon as possible.[40]

This was not as contradictory as it sounds: the British had been working hard on the Americans to convince them of the necessity of combating Communism, wherever they thought it was rearing its head, but particularly in the Balkans, because of their desire to maintain military control in the Eastern Mediterranean. Although the USA had been highly critical of British entanglement in Greece,[41] it took over from the British in 1947, just as the 'Democratic Army of Markos' (Vafiadis) had begun to score successes against the regular Greek army. Thus began the 'Truman Doctrine' and massive military supplies to Greece (and Turkey), while the British set up the Information Research Department in the Foreign Office, to promote anti-Communist propaganda.

The end of the war was now only a matter of time: the original ELAS forces were by now essentially led by Communists, and when some of the Greek Communists who were Slav speakers began suggesting autonomy for the Yugoslav part of Macedonia, Tito was angered. Add to this Stalin's annoyance at Tito's previous support for the Greek Communists and the ideological debate between Belgrade and Moscow, and the result was inevitable: a closure of the border with Greece, which cut off most of the supplies for the 'Democratic Army'. There was an end to the fighting, if not to the recrimination, in 1949. An expert historian provides us with a telling epithet: 'The persecution of the Left, combined with a leniency towards former collaborators unprecedented in Europe, alarmed observers at the time.'[42]

THE CYPRUS CONNECTION

As we have seen, there had been strong arguments within the British government to cede Cyprus to Greece to strengthen the fight against Communism, since Greece and Cyprus together would be in a stronger position to ward off Communism than Greece alone. As we have also seen, the arguments were rebutted with claims that *enosis* would help Communism. Indeed, one official had argued in 1947 that were the Americans to withdraw from Greece, there was a danger that a Communist regime could be in power by Christmas 1948.[43]

Perhaps curiously, the Cyprus Communists, in the form of AKEL, had been ready to cooperate with the colonial authorities in recreating a colonial constitution; but at the climax of the Greek civil war, the Greek Communist Party had purged AKEL in annoyance at this 'collaborative' approach, and thereafter AKEL was never to 'undermine' the *enosis* movement again.[44]

In any event, the disorganisation in Greece helped the British government to justify its claims in Cyprus. One view is that the civil war suited the British government in its efforts to distract attention from Cyprus and at the same time use it as an excuse to hang on to the island to counter the Communist threat.[45] In the words of one authority, 'the slippery relationship between strategic utility and political policy which took root in the framework of post-war instability in the Eastern Mediterranean was profoundly to shape the evolution of the Cyprus issue.'[46] The suspicious mind might construe that it was not in Britain's interests to nip the civil war in the bud.

HARDENING OF POSITIONS

Following the defeat of the Communists in the Greek civil war, the dispassionate observer might feel justified in asking whether, with Greece now firmly entrenched in the western camp, it would not be a good idea to accede to Greek and Cypriot requests for *enosis*, since a stronger Greece would aid the fight against the 'Red Devil'. Britain, however, took the opposite course, despite a referendum by Christian (Greek) Cypriots resulting in a resounding 96.5 per cent vote in favour of *enosis*.[47] The reaction of the British government was to call for a Chief of Staff report on Cyprus. This described Cyprus as having a 'positive and increasing strategic role as an air base and a garrison' yet, ominously, concluded that 'we must resign ourselves to the position of being primarily an occupying power.'[48] The British position began to go slightly 'over the top': when the municipal council in Limassol changed the name of 'Churchill Street' to 'October 28th Street', the offending Council members were imprisoned and replaced with the governor's appointees.[49]

The most important Greek national holiday was 28 October. This is the day, in 1940, when the Greek leader, Metaxas, is reputed to have said 'No!' to the Italian ambassador's request to allow Italian troops into Greece, purportedly to prevent the British from setting up in Greece. In fact, he said: 'C'est la guerre, alors!' At any event, the Italians invaded (indeed, they were already marching over the border from a compliant Albania when the ambassador was seeing Metaxas) and were beaten back, thus triggering the German 'rescue'.

At any rate, Britain's intransigent and uncompromising stance was leading to considerable frustration, and British–Greek relations were beginning to be adversely affected, despite Greek efforts not to play up the tension.[50]

The election in October 1950 of Michael Mouskos as Makarios III, Archbishop of Cyprus, marked a major development in the gathering storm. Armed with the results of the plebiscite, he began to pressure the Greek government into taking a more active stance. The Greek prime minister duly obliged, and the semantic ping-pong between the British and Greek governments that was to end in bloodshed (predicted, as we have seen above, by Oliver Harvey), began. When a British minister, in November 1950, made a distinction between the 'long-term thoughts or intentions of Greece and Britain and the immediate position being influenced by the strategic situation in the Eastern Mediterranean',[51] the Greek press interpreted this as flexibility, when it was really semantic swordsmanship masking rigidity. The Greek government even submitted a proposal in June 1951 for an Anglo–Greek condominium, with rights to a British military base, but this was rejected as 'ill-conceived and ill-timed'.[52]

The Cyprus question thus began seriously to bedevil Anglo–Greek relations. When the foreign minister, Eden, told the Greek prime minister, in September 1953, that there was no Cyprus question to be discussed, the Greek government issued a statement claiming entire liberty of action in promoting *enosis*.[53] In July 1954, a Cabinet paper concluded:

> We must, therefore, act on the assumption that deterioration in our relations with Greece is the price we must pay if we are to keep Cyprus. A point may even come at which we should have to decide whether Cyprus is strategically more important to us than Greece.[54]

More brutally, Eden put the question thus: 'No Cyprus, no certain facilities to protect our supply of oil. No oil, unemployment and hunger in Britain. It is as simple as that.'[55]

The diplomatic squabbling had now become a diplomatic war.

2 Watershed Year: 1955 and the Aftermath

I should not produce any British plan or proposal until a Greek–Turkish difference has been defined [...] until the Greek–Turkish difference has been exposed.[1]

INTRODUCTION

By 1955, a combination of Britain's perceived inflexibility, Greek lobbying and the exigencies of the cold war were bringing matters to a head. The US government was increasingly concerned that British intransigence could lead to instability in Cyprus and the region, in the form of problems between Greece and Turkey who, ever since the Friendship Treaties of 1930, had enjoyed reasonably correct, if cool, relations.[2]

America's stance was still somewhat ambivalent. On the one hand, it was bound by its post-war commitment to the self-determination of peoples – in other words decolonisation – while on the other it was committed to balancing this against safeguarding strategic global interests.[3] Moralising apart, America's main objective in encouraging decolonisation was to gain unfettered access to new markets, breaking in the process Britain's 'imperial preference'.[4] Cyprus hardly had the market potential of India. At the same time, however, the cold war meant that the USA was seeking to combat perceived Soviet expansionism and to strengthen its presence in the Middle East, including the Eastern Mediterranean. Economic interests, particularly those in the form of oil, were also considered crucial.[5]

Importantly, Turkey was assuming an increasingly significant role in US military planning, which meant that Cyprus, as a British-controlled island, was becoming important to America's growing cold war role worldwide. In April 1955, Turkey signed the Baghdad Pact with Britain. The pact, also comprising Iran, Iraq and Pakistan, was designed to contain perceived Soviet influence in the Middle East. As problems with Egypt, especially over Suez, loomed, Cyprus became little more than a British chess piece in a rapidly developing cold war game.

As we have seen, the British were worried about the strength of American public opinion favouring the Greek position, mainly media-led, and began to do what they could to combat this. The government feared internationalisation of the dispute above all and had managed only with some difficulty to obtain US government support to ensure that the UN General Assembly did not place the Cyprus problem on its agenda at the end of 1954.[6] So important was Cyprus to Britain that relations with Greece had even begun to take second place.

SECRET COLLUSION

Faced with a deteriorating situation in Egypt, an increasingly indignant Greek government and worries about the influence of the US media, Britain turned to clandestinely supporting the Turkish position, which was essentially to ensure that Britain did not relinquish Cyprus. Thus far, Greek–Turkish bilateral problems had remained largely a private matter, with no public crises. This was to change, as Britain began actively – but secretly – to help the Turkish government over Cyprus. In February 1955, the British ambassador to Ankara, Bowker, wrote to the Foreign Office, suggesting ways of helping the Turkish government over Cyprus; extracts from the letter are revealing:

> [...] First, Turkish representatives abroad, particularly in London and Washington, might be more active in their publicity about the Turkish attitude to Cyprus. In the United Kingdom, their efforts might be directed (in this order) to: a) Members of Parliament, b) the weekly press (they have already been helped by the journalists' visit last year). The same appears to be true in the United States and other countries. Turkish propaganda should however be presented with tact. For example, the Turkish Press Attaché in London has done no good by distributing leaflets of the 'Cyprus is Turkish' Association.
>
> This has already been discussed in general terms with officials of the Ministry of Foreign Affairs [...] Secondly, the Department might be able to encourage a few selected Members of Parliament to come here on their own initiative, to learn something of Turkey generally and the Turkish attitude to Cyprus in particular...the Turks will no doubt be glad to know in due course what policy H.M.G. propose to follow between now and the next meeting of the United Nations General Assembly and Turkish policy is likely to be influenced by British views.[7]

Anglo–Greek relations were by now at an all-time low. A Foreign Office under secretary recorded that according to the British ambassador in Washington 'the Greek Ambassador in Washington was a snake who, despite fair words, was known to be working actively against us over Cyprus.'[8]

By this time Sir Oliver Harvey's warning (see previous chapter) that, if Cyprus were not ceded to Greece, the Greeks would in despair turn to the methods of the Irish, Jews, Hindus and Egyptians, was proving correct. On 1 April, Colonel Grivas' EOKA campaign on Cyprus began with bomb explosions all over the island. The '*enosis* war' had now begun in earnest, and would finally result in qualified independence and a botched constitution for Cyprus.

Despite the increasing internationalisation of the problem, the British government was still bent on maintaining sovereignty at all costs, using secret collusion with Turkey if necessary. One way of trying to justify British control of Cyprus was to help promote, at worst, or at least condone, at best, Turkish Cypriot opposition to Makarios. The evidence is compelling. For example, at a time when all Greek-speaking political parties were banned, the British authorities allowed the Turkish Cypriots to establish a political party called 'Cyprus is Turkish'. Although many members of EOKA were hanged and imprisoned, very few members of Volkan, a Turkish Cypriot terrorist group, were ever tried.[9]

It was the 1955 conference that really brought into relief the behind-the-scenes British collusion with the Turkish government. The idea of the conference was itself a clever ploy to forestall Greek pressure to push for a full discussion and vote on the Cyprus question at the United Nations General Assembly. The British government was fully aware that the UK would be outvoted at the United Nations: a Foreign Office memorandum in June 1955 stated:

> We were able to outflank the Greeks at the United Nations last year by means of a procedural device, which we could not hope to repeat. The Americans have already warned us that, unless we do something publicly to meet the Greek point of view, they will find it difficult to give us even as much support as they did last year. Without American support we shall almost certainly be faced with an adverse vote, not only this year, but in succeeding years.[10]

American support was indeed crucial: worryingly for the British government, the US delegation to the first International Congress of Jurists – fortuitously held in Athens – worked on and pushed through a declaration that reaffirmed their faith in the rights of the individual, including freedom of speech, freedom of the press, of worship, of assembly, and of association, and the right to face election, rights that were severely limited in Cyprus by the non-elected British administration. Even more embarrassingly for the British government, in an address to the United Nations' tenth anniversary event, President Eisenhower made a strong plea to all member nations to reaffirm the principles on which the United Nations had been founded. This naturally focused attention on the UN Charter, which stated, inter alia:

> That on every nation in possession of foreign territories there rests the responsibility to assist the peoples of those areas in the progressive development of free political institutions so that ultimately they can validly choose for themselves their permanent political status.

June was indeed a vital month, and Britain considered all manner of options, bar granting independence to Cyprus, or considering *enosis*. A deputy under secretary of the Foreign Office asked the ambassador in Turkey to discuss informally with the Turkish government various options, which might be announced in Parliament, adding:

> The Turkish government would be given advance warning of this statement, with an explanation of our motives, notably to deprive the Greek government of a pretext for further reference of the Cyprus question to the United Nations, or alternatively to ensure their defeat if they did raise it.[11]

It is little wonder that some diplomacy is essentially a secret backstage activity.

DIVIDE ET IMPERA

This example of how clearly the British and Turkish governments were colluding was followed by the British proposal for a tripartite conference, the motives for which were not entirely altruistic. The main instigator of the idea appears to have been the permanent under secretary of the Foreign Office, who minuted on 26 June:

> I have always been attracted by the idea of 3 Power Conference, simply because I seriously believe that it would seriously embarrass the Greek Government. And if such a conference were held, I should not produce any British plan or proposal until a Greek–Turkish deadlock has been defined [...] a Conference could be spun out for some time and tempers would have time to cool. It is always difficult to restart a war after an armistice.
>
> The plan I like least is that alleged to be reiterated by Mr. Selwyn Lloyd [Minister of State] viz. an enquiry of the Greek and Turkish Govts. whether – if the island reverts to them – they would guarantee us the necessary military facilities. This seems to imply that we are reconciled to handing over the island to one of them – and that it is up to them to decide on the future of the island.
>
> And I repeat: I shall not produce any British plan until a Greek–Turkish difference has been exposed.[12]

This extraordinary minute suggests an uncharacteristic degree of suppressed emotion and a negative approach to what was becoming a problem serious enough to endanger the cohesion of NATO's southern flank. Certainly, the USA was now taking the problem seriously. The American secretary of state, Dulles, expressed interest in resolving the problem and in any British proposals, while Macmillan told him that he had a plan that he could not reveal before consideration by the Cabinet, adding that he hoped that it would 'relax the tension'.[13] This was the idea of holding a conference.

On 27 June, the prime minister, colonial secretary, and secretaries of state for defence and foreign affairs agreed to invite the Greek and Turkish governments to a conference in London, and the following day the Cabinet agreed.[14] The next day, the chiefs of staff put down their standpoint in no uncertain terms:

> British influence and prestige in the Middle East could not be maintained without the retention of our present military position in Cyprus, which was

therefore essential. The denial of our present facilities in Cyprus would mean the complete breakdown of all plans for the development of any Middle East defence organisation and would prevent us from fulfilling our Treaty obligations towards Iraq and Jordan.[15]

On 30 June, invitations were sent to the Greek and Turkish governments to attend a conference in London on 'political and defence questions, as concerning the Eastern Mediterranean, including Cyprus'. This semantic chicanery, designed to suggest that Cyprus was not the prime focus, when it obviously was, was used as a somewhat specious attempt to skirt around Article 16 of the Treaty of Lausanne, which stated:

> La Turquie déclare renoncer à tous droits et titres, de quelque nature que ce soit, sur ou concernant les territoires situés au delà des frontières prévues par le présent Traité et sur les îles autres que celles sur lesquelles la souveraineté lui est reconnue par ledit Traité, le sort de ces territoires et îles étant réglé ou à régler par les intéressés. Les dispositions du présent Article ne portent pas atteinte aux stipulations particulières intervenues ou à intervenir entre la Turquie et les pays limitrophes en raison de leur voisinage.

Thus, although it was clear that Turkey had no rights whatsoever on Cyprus, the Turkish government accepted the invitation with alacrity on 2 July. Not so the Greek government, which took a further three days to accept. What happened during these three days was going to strongly influence at least the following fifty years. The initial reaction of the Greek government was one of suspicion. On 1 July, the Greek ambassador in Washington, Melas, went to see Dulles to say that he was resigning his post since he 'did not wish to have anything to do with what would turn out to be the funeral of Greek–Turkish friendship'. Dulles told him that it had been agreed with the British that Cyprus would be handed to Greece, and that Turkey was only being invited as a witness. Melas informed the Greek government which, apparently in good faith, then accepted the invitation,[16] albeit with 'certain reservations about the rights of Turkey on the subject of self-determination'.[17]

As regards the US record of Melas' visit, Dulles wrote that the former was in an emotional state and that he criticised the UK for 'once more following its policy of divide and rule'.[18] The available papers lend evidence to Melas' criticisms, as secret British 'cooperation' with Turkey intensified. On 7 July, the British prime minister's private secretary wrote to a senior Foreign Office official:

Dear Tony,

On Ankara telegram number 479, the Prime Minister has minuted: Foreign Secretary – Turks are behaving well. If we keep friendly with them, the Greeks will have to come along in the end. Therefore we must not be parted from Turks, though we need not be ostentatious about this. – A.E. [Antony Eden].[19]

The British government's method of keeping Cyprus was simply to do what it could to undermine Graeco–Turkish relations. On 27 July, the foreign secretary told the Cabinet, 'Throughout the negotiations our aim would be to bring the

Greeks up against the Turkish refusal to accept *enosis* and so condition them to accept a solution, which would leave sovereignty in our hands.'[20]

The US government was by now well aware of British cooperation with Turkey. The US ambassador in London wrote on 10 August: 'Since British undoubtedly know what position Turkey will take at Conference their tactics are obviously designed to force Greece to define its attitude.'[21]

Given all this backstage manoeuvring and 'frontstage' acts such as the creation of an auxiliary police force made up exclusively of Turkish Cypriots, it seems clear that the British government's objectives were to divide the Greeks and Turks, so they could claim that they were the only power capable of preserving some element of stability, and at the same time to try to prevent the Greek government from taking the Cyprus issue to the United Nations. In the first, British tactics certainly succeeded with a vengeance.

The conference opened on 29 August, and proceeded quickly to dramatic failure, as the British government had wished. A British briefing paper reveals and under-lines the government's tactics:

> The Turkish Government [...] are opposed to any change in the sovereignty of Cyprus, and consider that if the British Government were [sic] ever relinquished the island should revert to Turkey [...] consequently the British delegation proposes that the Conference should record that it is unable to agree upon the problem of the future international status of Cyprus, including the question of self-determination.[22]

The former counsellor at the Greek Embassy in Washington, Themistocles Chrysanthopoulos, wrote recently:

> The Cyprus question began in 1955. In the summer of that year the British Government convened a conference in London with Greece and Turkey on the subject of Defence of the Eastern Mediterranean and Cyprus. It was the first time Turkey was brought into the Cyprus affair [since 1878], contrary to article 16 of the Lausanne Peace Treaty with Turkey in 1923, by which Turkey waived all rights in territories ceded to other countries, including, of course, Cyprus. To the Greek objection to involving Turkey in Cyprus the British side replied that Turkey was being invited as a witness. During the conference, Turkey demanded that, were the United Kingdom to withdraw from Cyprus, the island should of course, be returned to its former owner (Turkey). This claim, of course, blew up the conference. The terrible riots in Istanbul and Izmir followed on 6 September, as 'proof' of the interest of the Turkish people in Cyprus. Consequences: 1) The end of Greek Turkish friendship dating from 1930. 2) Turkey became an active party in the Cyprus question.[23]

As regards the riots, although some Jewish and Armenian properties were attacked, it was the Greek community of around 100,000 that bore the brunt. The British Embassy in Ankara noted that, in Istanbul alone, twenty-nine Greek Orthodox churches were completely destroyed, thirty-four badly damaged, tombs opened and a monk burned to death, and that 'neither police nor troops made any effective effort to protect property and restrain looters.'[24] The riots were immediately preceded by a dynamite explosion at the Turkish consulate in Thessaloniki, but there was a clear pattern of organisation.[25] The US State Department wrote: 'US Government shocked over these events, especially over apparent lack effective police intervention in what appears to be result coordinated planning.'[26]

There is unfortunately more to this story than meets the eye: the British government was aware of the possibility of riots. Although Grivas had taken care not to attack the Turkish community on Cyprus, limiting his operations to the British and to those whom he considered to be Greek Cypriot collaborators, the British government jumped at the opportunity to exploit activities with the Turkish government. When the Foreign Office heard about a Turkish campaign to implicate the Christian Orthodox Patriarchate of Istanbul in the Cyprus dispute, an official noted that this had 'interesting possibilities'.[27] The embryo of this sentiment had already been exposed by a Foreign Office official the previous September with the words: 'A few riots in Ankara would do us nicely.'[28] Although the Greek community in Ankara was small, anti-Greek riots in the Turkish capital could be expected to spread almost automatically to Istanbul. More damningly, during the London conference, the Turkish foreign minister, Zorlu, telephoned Istanbul to say that 'a little activity will be useful.'[29] One respected authority writes that the similarity in language ('do us nicely' and 'be useful') is transparent.[30] More ominous was the growing involvement of MI5 in Cyprus, which included the successful 'placement' of a probe microphone in the Greek embassy in London.[31]

It is clear that the Greek government's decision to accept Britain's invitation and participate in a conference that was expressly designed to fail was a naive blunder. Former Greek prime minister Constantinos Mitsotakis describes the decision as a 'tragic mistake'.[32] The question of Greece's acceptance is so embarrassing (and perhaps murky) that the Greek government still refuses to release the pertinent papers.

BRITAIN LOOKS TO THE USA

The British government had of course been able to claim, with considerable justification, that it would not negotiate under the threat of terrorist acts, which had begun with the EOKA bomb explosions across the island on 1 April 1955. The failure of the conference gave the British further cause to clamp down, just as the Greek government decided to lobby to get Cyprus on to the UN agenda. Now the British began to exercise full pressure on the USA. The prime minister wrote an almost pleading letter to the US secretary of state, Dulles, ending:

> I must ask you to use your great influence against the inscription of this item. The present indications are that the vote will be a close one and that the attitude of the United States will probably be decisive. Acting in harmony, we could, I believe, prevent further discussion of this vexed problem in an atmosphere which is full of such explosive possibilities.[33]

The former counsellor at the Greek embassy in Washington recalls how, after South American countries had assured the Greek embassy that they would vote in favour of including the Cyprus question on the agenda of the UN General Assembly, they subsequently telephoned the embassy to inform the Greeks regretfully that they would not after all vote for inclusion, but rather for exclusion. Last-minute lobbying by the Americans and British must have been intense.[34] The item was not included.

At any event, Anglo–Greek relations were at a low point, with propaganda now assuming a more important role than hitherto. Even before the fateful conference, the colonial governor, Harding, had written to the secretary of state for the colonies:

> I have considered that this task would be better performed by the selection of an officer from outside Cyprus possessing expert knowledge of propaganda methods, including clandestine or 'Black propaganda'.[35]

Under the stern governor, (who had recruited large numbers of Turkish Cypriots into the police, thus antagonising the Greek Cypriots),[36] the danger of a general uprising was growing. Peter Wright wrote in his notorious *Spycatcher*:

> Britain, anxious to retain Cyprus as a military base, was resisting, and by 1956 a full-scale military emergency was in force, with 40,000 British troops pinned down by a few hundred Grivas guerrillas.[37]

Britain's next major move was to arrest Makarios and three close associates on 9 March and deport them to the Seychelles. Anti-British riots broke out in Greece, the British consulate in Crete was burned and Greece recalled its ambassador in London.

The British government reacted by increasing its secret cooperation with Turkey. A Foreign Office official wrote to a British embassy official in Bonn in July 1956:

> Our attitude to this [Cyprus] question is that we wish to assist the Turks as much as possible with the publicity for their case, but must at the same time be careful not to appear to be shielding behind them and to be instigating the statements.[38]

This was not exactly straight bowling.

Although in public, the British government wished to underline impartiality, the reality was entirely different, and this backstage cooperation with Turkey exacerbated the problem and fuelled extremism. In the meantime, the British government expended considerable energy on the information war. Following the international – especially US – criticism that followed the arrest and deportation of Makarios and his associates, the British Information Services Office in New York wrote to the Information Policy Department of the Foreign Office:

> The Americans dislike the fact that we are having to use force in Cyprus... needless to say we are plugging the constitutional proposals [these were largely unacceptable to the Greek government]. We are explaining that the opposition of the Church is largely based on fear, lest political power in Cyprus shall pass from the Church oligarchy to democratically elected Cypriots.[39]

This was a little over the top, since the Church of Cyprus was simply opposed because the elected majority principle was 'strangled by the almost unlimited power of the governor', and because it did not envisage the right of self-determination in accordance with the UN Charter.[40]

In private, some British officials were admitting that the Turkish case was weak. A note from the Government Statistical Department stated: 'report [...] shows the decline of the Turkish population [in Cyprus] from about one quarter to about one fifth –which does not really help the Turkish case very much.'[41]

Particularly revealing of the rigidity of the British view, and that of the more rigid Colonial Office, was a pompous letter from the latter to the Foreign Office:

> We, the British, are not enamoured of plebiscites because it is impossible for all the various aspects of a problem to be included in the question which is posed of a plebiscite [...] now it may well be (and personally I think it would be) that if all this had been discussed by the Cypriots in a quiet and objective manner in the Legislative Assembly (free from physical intimidation, spiritual blackmail and mass hysteria), the result would be that the Cypriot people would formally go on the record as demanding *enosis*.[42]

This rather specious semantic irony hardly provided a coherent argument against a free plebiscite in Cyprus, which the British government was naturally desperate to avoid, particularly since most of world opinion, particularly in the USA, was by now critical of Britain. It was the United States government's involvement and pressure on Britain, which was to lead to some British backtracking.

In August the State Department produced a paper that was to get the ball rolling.[43] Its intermediate goals included:
– a solution that could be presented as a tangible accomplishment of NATO; and
– to strengthen the Allied position in the area and to free the British forces now tied down in Cyprus for general defence operations in the Middle East.
Its eventual goals included:
– guaranteeing that the bases in Cyprus will be at the permanent disposal of Great Britain for protecting its interests to the East; and
– to provide the inhabitants of the island with guarantees of their rights of self-
 determination with full protection of minorities.

The plan included the calling of almost immediate elections and a plebiscite ten years later permitting union with Greece, local autonomy under the Greek crown, and full independence or self-government within the Commonwealth. It also included provisions for Britain to hold on to specified areas in perpetuity for maintenance of military bases. Although at this stage the USA was still openly in favour of 'decolonization', its private stance began to modify as it took over the safeguarding of more and more British interests worldwide. The Suez crisis, in particular, caused the USA to put pressure on Britain for a Cyprus settlement. The USA, fearing the possibility of a wider outbreak of hostilities, even a world war, as a result of the Anglo–French attempt to oust President Nasser of Egypt, was to insist on British and French withdrawal from Suez.

Cyprus was now Britain's main Middle East headquarters, and housed important British electronic spying stations and early warning radars. Intelligence gathered was shared with the USA under the UK/USA pact of 1947. A former press counsellor of the embassy of Cyprus in Washington wrote:

> In Cyprus, at any rate, the US global intelligence collation machinery was well ensconced by the fifties through a number of signal monitoring stations run by the CIA and various other cooperation intelligence ventures with the British, all in the name of anti-communist sentiment. This basic objective guided US foreign policy at crucial junctions in the evolving Cyprus problem...[44]

The USA continued to apply pressure, the most obvious result of which was to be the release of Archbishop Makarios on 6 April 1957. Three weeks previously, President Eisenhower had written in his diary, following a meeting with the British prime minister:

> The Prime Minister outlined the major factors in the whole Cyprus problem. They are quite complicated and he asserts that Britain wants nothing more to do with the island except to keep its base there, but any action that the British can suggest up to this moment antagonises the Greeks or the Turks. The British believe that the antagonisms that would be created by dropping the British responsibility in the island might even lead to war between the Turks and the Greeks.
>
> I told them that I had certain important messages, particularly from the Greeks, asking me to urge upon Macmillan the importance of freeing Archbishop Makarios. I told them that in my opinion I didn't believe they were gaining much by keeping him prisoner, so I would just turn him loose on the world...[45]

In the manic secret negotiations that followed, Britain agreed that Archbishop Makarios would be freed, but would return to Greece rather than Cyprus, for the time being. The Greek government asked Elias Demetracopoulos, a Greek journalist and then correspondent of *Kathimerini*, to travel to the Seychelles and accompany Makarios to Greece, which he did.[46]

The scene was now set for the run-up to the qualified independence that Cyprus was set to achieve.

3 The End of *Enosis* and the Road to Partition

Well, thank heavens the [Greek] bastards are getting it now.[1]

INTRODUCTION

The years up to qualified independence were characterised by a continuation of Grivas' EOKA campaign; increasing Soviet Union influence in Iraq, thus making instability in Cyprus more poignant for the US and Turkish governments; the involvement of the NATO secretary general, Spaak, in seeking, with strong US support, a NATO-friendly solution; and, crucially, a temporary rapprochement between the Turkish and Greek governments, particularly between their respective foreign ministers, Zorlu and Averof. As so often in the past, the people of Cyprus seemed to have the least say in the matter, although Makarios had certainly done his best to achieve *enosis*.

The Suez débâcle, when America had shown Britain (and France) that she (the USA) was now the main western policy-maker, also had an effect on a Cyprus 'solution', as for example when Britain was obliged to release Makarios in the Spring of 1957 (but not yet to allow him back to Cyprus). It was becoming increasingly obvious that *enosis* was a non-starter, since the British had fully succeeded in dividing both the Muslim and Christian Cypriots and, especially since the cynically planned conference in 1955, had brought to an end the reasonable correctness in Graeco–Turkish relations that had subsisted since 1930.

Now that the problem had been fully internationalised and with the cold war in full swing, it was clear that some form of external involvement would be required to bring about an end to the impasse.

Britain had by now come to understand that hanging on to the whole island was just a colonial dream: keeping some bases while letting the rest go was becoming a more realistic proposition. The end of 1957 marked some key developments: a UN General Assembly resolution supporting self-determination for Cyprus mustered a simple majority; the Foreign Office permanent under secretary, Kirkpatrick (of 'embarrass the Greek Government' fame), retired; and a liberal-minded Cyprus governor, Hugh Foot, replaced the rigid 'little Englander' Harding.

Shortly thereafter, the ill-fated 'Macmillan Plan' for a 'tridominium' (tripartite condominium of Britain, Greece and Turkey) on Cyprus was introduced. It in fact originated with a member of the governor's staff, Reddaway, and was presented to Macmillan via Foot.[2] Essentially, the plan, despite being a 'tridominium,' envisaged that the colonial administration should remain in control of the island for fifteen years – hardly realistic, given the push for *enosis* and Greek misgivings about the official involvement of the Turkish government. NATO was now also involved in the search for a solution, with the support of the US government.

The summer of 1958 was tense in Cyprus, the Middle East and, therefore, internationally. The increasing radicalisation of the Turkish Cypriots helped to bring matters to a head. On 6 June, Denktash, the Turkish Cypriot deputy-leader, returned to Cyprus from a visit to Turkey and delivered a 'highly incendiary' speech, leading to Turkish Cypriot anti-Greek rioting, causing many Greeks living on the edge of Muslim areas to flee their homes. The British authorities were excruciatingly slow to react and, when they did, some two days after the rioting had begun, arrested more Greeks than Turks. Tellingly, British Intelligence was aware that the spark for the riots had been an explosion at the Turkish Information Office, caused by a bomb planted by a 'Turkish hand', just like the bomb which had triggered the anti-Greek riots in Istanbul during September 1955.[3] One authority concluded that the violence was 'Turkish-inspired and executed *pur et simple*'. A comment by the wife of the deputy-governor, Mrs Sinclair, was not overly tactful: 'Well, thank heavens, the [Greek] bastards are getting it now.'[4] To make matters worse, on 12 June the British arrested thirty-two Greek Cypriots, crouching in a riverbed, armed with sticks and stones, drove them to a Turkish Cypriot village and left them to walk home. Four were hacked to death; four died afterwards of their injuries, and the rest were injured.[5]

This increasing radicalisation of the Turkish Cypriots, fuelled by Denktash, helped to bring matters to a head, linked as it was to increased American fear of the Soviet Union in the wake of major developments in the Middle East. The Iraqi revolution in July 'sent a thunder-clap through the entire region',[6] a region already shaken by Nasser's 'pan-Arabism'; and the Soviet Union increased its support for the radical regimes in Egypt, Iraq and Syria. The Greek government, furious about the riots, withdrew its contingent from NATO's South-East Headquarters at Izmir, while negotiations over the Macmillan Plan continued. Grivas' EOKA continued to kill British personnel, as well as Greek Cypriots deemed to be collaborators.

Behind-the-scenes US pressure increased. A large economic aid programme for Turkey (shades of today) was announced by the USA, the International Monetary Fund and the Organisation for European Economic Cooperation. The USA also rejected the Macmillan Plan.

December 1958 was the defining month: something had to give, and it was the unstable Greek government which, having wholly rejected the Macmillan Plan, introduced a motion at the UN calling for a period of self-government for Cyprus, leading to independence, with guarantees for the Muslim community. The USA, rather than reject the motion, supported an Iranian one calling for talks between the British, Greek and Turkish governments and representatives of the Cypriots, which was passed, to the chagrin of the Greek government.

Shortly after the resolution was passed, the Turkish foreign minister, Zorlu, approached his Greek counterpart informally and suggested direct talks, which began on 6 December. These were consolidated at Zurich in February, without the British even being overtly involved, although the USA was almost certainly in the background.[7] The compromise agreement was that Britain, Greece and Turkey would jointly guarantee an independent Cyprus. The president would be Greek Cypriot, the vice-president Turkish Cypriot, with separate communal assemblies, but a joint national assembly, while 950 Greek and 650 Turkish troops would be stationed on the island; Britain would retain two military bases.

These direct Greek–Turkish contacts led to the London Agreements, and were helped by the fact that Makarios agreed to forget *enosis* and accept 'independence' instead, while Grivas, albeit furious, gave up his EOKA campaign. The momentum provided by the direct contact between the Greek and Turkish governments, strongly supported by the USA, was the decisive factor. Nevertheless, there was a residue of anger among sections of the Greek government, which had never wished for Turkish involvement. Even when the Greek government had poured cold water on the Macmillan Plan, the main reason had been the question of Turkish intervention. The British ambassador had written:

> The Greeks are angry at the UK plan to involve the Turks [...] on the grounds that it introduced an element of Turkish governmental intervention [...] and since it must lead to further antagonism and eventually to partition.[8]

Thus, the Zurich and London Agreements can be presented as a Greek caving-in, given their previous policy of support for *enosis* and the non-involvement of Turkey. On the other hand, it is also true that the Turkish government rejected – at least nominally – its policy of partition. Makarios was not allowed to play a role in Zurich, remaining at his hotel in Athens.

PAPERING OVER THE CRACKS

When it came to the London Conference, Makarios delayed signing for two days, during which he strongly objected to a clause giving Turkey (along with Britain and Greece) a veto over changes to the constitution. During these two days, even Queen Frederica of Greece telephoned him to beg him to sign,[9] which he eventually did. Although he signed, he was able to delay official 'independence' until August, by driving as hard a bargain as he could on the question of the British bases, which he managed to get whittled down in size from 160 to 99 square miles of 'sovereign British territory'. Makarios' other main feat was to persuade Grivas to drop his EOKA campaign, and disband the organisation. Later, he described the negotiations at the London Conference thus:

> In London, I tried hard to get some changes made, but there was not enough time to study the agreement. But at the very first reading I singled out thirteen points which were the thirteen points which I raised again in 1963 [see below]. I tried hard and failed [...] I am sure that if I did not sign the agreement, there might be partition. Cyprus would be divided as a colony and we should not be able to raise the question again. The less bad thing was to sign.[10]

Three crucial documents were signed. First was the 103-page Treaty of Establishment, between Cyprus and Britain, providing for the transfer of sovereignty (apart from the bases). Fifty-six pages of this document were devoted to Britain's continued use of military and intelligence facilities on Cyprus. Second was the Treaty of Guarantee, signed by Britain, Greece and Turkey on the one hand, and Cyprus on the other. Its most tricky clause was Article IV, which stated:

> In the event of a breach of the present Treaty, Greece, Turkey and the United Kingdom undertake to consult together with respect to the representations or measures necessary to ensure observance of these provisions. In so far as common or concerted action may not prove possible, each of the three guaranteeing powers reserve the right to take action with the sole aim of re-establishing the state of affairs created by the present Treaty.

Ominously, this second sentence was inserted at the insistence of Turkey.

Finally, a Treaty of Alliance was signed between Cyprus, Greece and Turkey, establishing a tripartite headquarters and the presence of 950 Greek and a disproportionately large Turkish contingent of 650 troops.

To claim that Cyprus gained independence or sovereignty in 1960 is going rather far. The major external trappings, such as membership of the UN and other organisations were there, even membership of the Commonwealth; but no member of the Commonwealth had its hands tied to the extent that Cyprus did. The fact that both *enosis* and partition were expressly forbidden speaks for itself. The role of outside powers went against the grain of the UN Charter. The number of British listening posts dotted throughout the island – quite apart from the establishment of British sovereign territory on Cyprus – detracted from any notion of serious sovereignty.

The constitution itself could be described as a blueprint for further partition, which is in fact what began to occur almost as soon as the 'novelty' of 'independence' began to die down. The constitution was an extremist's paradise. Despite the fact that the Turkish Cypriots constituted less than twenty per cent of the population, they held thirty per cent of the seats in the House of Representatives and main Cabinet posts, and could exercise a veto, as could the Turkish Cypriot vice-president; finally, the ratio of Greek to Turkish soldiers was clearly weighted in favour of the Turkish Cypriots.

Wrangling began, mainly over the ill-defined boundaries of the Turkish-speaking municipalities in the five largest towns; over the sacking of hundreds of

Turkish Cypriot policemen who had been auxiliaries during the EOKA campaign; over taxation; and over the setting-up of integrated armed forces. When the vice-president, Kütchük, vetoed the latter, Makarios simply refused to create an army at all: this resulted in the setting up of para-legal forces on both sides.

The actual characters in the whole scenario hardly inspired confidence: some of the government ministers had been EOKA commanders, while Denktash had also been very active in subversion. Makarios began to irritate the anti-Soviet USA by visiting the pro-Soviet Nasser and by attending a conference of the non-aligned nations in Belgrade. The strength of the left-wing party in Cyprus, AKEL, also worried the USA, particularly since the latter had retained a fair number of listening posts on Cyprus outside the terms of the London Agreements. The Cuban Missile Crisis added poignancy to these concerns.

MAKARIOS' THIRTEEN POINTS

As the extremists on both sides made their plans, negotiations on the municipal law broke down. The British high commissioner, Clark, blamed the Turkish side, particularly Ankara, while two Foreign Office officials put more of the blame on Makarios.[11] The Cyprus government then began secret negotiations with the Foreign Office and British high commissioner over changes to the constitution.[12] News slipped out over the summer, and Makarios began to make press statements questioning the Treaty of Guarantee and suggesting amendments to the constitution. Clark helped the Cyprus government with its proposed amendments, even redrafting some of the points.[13] On 30 November 1963, Makarios delivered his thirteen points to Kütchük. Although the Foreign Office helped and encouraged Makarios, and Clark had considered these proposals reasonable,[14] Ankara rejected them (they had been given the proposals for information) before Kütchük had a chance to do so. The amendments included: the revision of the ratio of Greek to Turkish Cypriots in the public services and armed forces, to reflect reality; abandonment of the right of veto of the president and vice-president; and the unification of the administration of justice. Several of the points were clearly objectionable to Turkey and to the gung-ho element of the Turkish Cypriots, but Makarios was emboldened by the British high commissioner's help.

'THERE'S ONLY ONE SOLUTION: PARTITION'

The civil strife and 'ghettoisation' of much of the Turkish Cypriot community that resulted from the abortive submission of Makarios' Thirteen Points are still a controversial question. Few, however, could nit-pick with the evaluation that it was the result of pent-up frustration on both sides of a divide that had only been papered over in the London Agreements, fuelled by extremism and simultaneous political crises in Greece and Turkey.

The British government was now happy to let the USA make the running, in securing NATO's southern flank, since this would ensure the retention of the British bases. Although, as we shall see, the Foreign Office was not to become as averse to Makarios as was the USA, it appears that, at the highest level, there was concurrence between Britain and the USA that Cyprus was of crucial strategic importance, essentially because of the Soviet bogeyman. Credence is lent to this conclusion by the sudden withdrawal of Lieutenant Commander Martin Packard, who had been sent to help arrange a truce, but then began to plan the reintegration of Turkish Cypriots into their villages. Further weight is given by Packard's report on his mission to 'reintegrate' the communities, which included the statement:

> The maintenance of the Sovereign Base Areas and other military facilities was deemed of paramount importance by the British and American governments, and their advisers certainly thought that this aim would more easily be achieved in a divided Cyprus than in a cohesive, unitary state.[15]

The US assistant secretary of state, Ball, had, after all, told Packard; 'You've got it wrong, son. There's only one solution to this island, and that's partition.'[16]

During the troubles, which included 'limited' Turkish bombing, Ball tried to persuade Makarios to allow partition of Cyprus between Greece and Turkey and permit a NATO force to enter. Grivas, now a general, had returned to Cyprus, and the Americans quickly established contact with a lieutenant of his, Iliades.[17] As Grivas and Makarios were now falling out, Ball hoped that by supporting the former, it might be possible to get rid of the latter. This was diplomacy at its most unsubtle, and was divisive into the bargain.

By this time, it was clear that Cyprus was no more than a chess piece for NATO, albeit a difficult one, since Makarios was playing a skilful balancing game to maintain what independence he could for the island. A senior British diplomat wrote:

> It follows that our international aims over the Cyprus problem should be not only to preserve the NATO alliance and retain our bases in Cyprus, but also to secure the establishment of British bases elsewhere (Turkey, Malta) if this should eventually prove necessary.[18]

Britain and the USA both agreed that war between Greece and Turkey would be fatal for NATO's southern flank, would benefit the Soviet Union and even lead to a wider conflagration. Thus, a speedy solution was considered necessary, in the shape of Ball's plan to involve American and NATO troops in Cyprus, which Makarios rejected, to Ball's fury.[19] Makarios proposed instead a UN solution, which he achieved, despite Ball's quest for a NATO solution. This of course had the effect of keeping the dispute internationalised, and increased Soviet leverage. The Soviet Union was indeed opposed to putting this small neutral state under the control of NATO, and made diplomatic representations. This had an obvious affect, resulting in US pressure on Turkey not to overstep the mark.

However, it is probable that America was nevertheless still hoping for a 'limited invasion', provided that war between Greece and Turkey could be avoided. Some available documentation lends credence to this scenario: in January 1964, the British prime minister told the Cabinet: 'If the Turks invade or if we are seriously prevented from fulfilling our political role, we have made it quite clear that we will retire into base.'[20]

Even more pertinently, the British embassy in Washington reported to the Foreign Office, at the height of the crisis in July 1964:

> The Americans have made it quite clear that there would be no question of using the 6th Fleet to prevent any possible Turkish invasion...We have all along made it clear to the United Nations that we could not agree to UNFICYP's [by now, UN forces were stationed in Cyprus to prevent further bloodshed] being used for the purpose of repelling external intervention, and the standing orders to our troops outside UNFICYP are to withdraw to the sovereign base areas immediately any such intervention takes place.[21]

The Greek chief of staff, Pipilis, naively believed that the USA would forcibly prevent a limited Turkish invasion. The British ambassador to Athens met him and repeated:

> I said I was speaking on a purely personal basis and hoped that the Greeks now believed that the Americans did not intend to use the Sixth Fleet to stop Turkish intervention. To my surprise they still seemed incapable of believing that if Makarios pressed the Turks too far [...] and the Turks in consequence intervened, that the Sixth Fleet would be so anxious to avoid the inevitable war between Greece and Turkey which would follow Turkish intervention that they were bound to stop Turkey, using the Sixth Fleet.[22]

The idea of the USA permitting, even instigating, a limited Turkish invasion, to achieve Ball's plan, if this could be done with impunity, is, therefore, compelling. It certainly worked ten years later, and was, indeed, never entirely off the agenda.

At the end of the day, however, a firm Soviet stance appears to have prevented a Turkish invasion and the unwelcome (to the Soviets) spectre of a Cyprus divided by two NATO powers, Greece and Turkey. The USA, worried about Soviet intervention, even warned Turkey that were the Soviet Union to invade her if she invaded Cyprus, NATO might not be able to help her.[23] The Soviet leader, Kruschev, must have made a considerable impact on the US government when he had stated:

> The Soviet Government hereby states that if there is an armed foreign invasion of Cypriot territory, the Soviet Union will help the Republic of Cyprus to defend its freedom and independence against foreign intervention.[24]

The USA also used some particularly tough diplomacy on the Greeks (see Introduction).

DIPLOMATIC INCONSISTENCIES

Interestingly, however, only one month before the Americans had told the British that they would not use the Sixth Fleet to prevent a Turkish invasion, and in the middle of the efforts of Ball (and Dean Acheson, the former US foreign secretary) to partition Cyprus, the US secretary of state, Dean Rusk, told the British ambassador to Washington that they would tell the Turks that they:

> had no right under the Treaty of Guarantee to take the action they now contemplated [to invade Cyprus and declare part of it Turkish]. Under Article III, they were bound to consult with the other guaranteeing Powers, and this they had not done. Under Article II both partition and *enosis* were excluded, yet they were basing their action on the declaration by Kütchük of the partition of the island.[25]

This suggests that overtly, the Americans were trying to go along with international agreements and prevent a Turkish invasion, at least in June 1964. It also suggests that their policy formulation was rather volatile, given their assurance to the British the following month that they would not intervene if Turkey invaded.

The British government was by now considering all manner of options, with particular consideration given to *enosis*. A brief prepared at the request of the Ministry of Defence for the Defence and Overseas Policy Committee stated, inter alia, the views of the British high commissioner in Cyprus:

> There is no hope of re-establishing the constitution, which was destroyed at Christmas. A radical change is inescapable.
>
> None of the solutions favoured by the Turks is within the realm of practical politics. Somehow, the Turks must be induced to understand this.
>
> The only two solutions which could bring peace and order to Cyprus are *enosis* or the establishment of a unitary republic dominated by its Greek–Cypriot majority.
>
> [...] although *enosis* is in some respects more attractive than the unitary state, Turkey's objections to it are so strong that it may not be a practicable solution at present. He [the high commissioner] suggests, therefore, that effort should be concentrated on easing the path to the unitary state, e.g. by providing UN safeguards for the minority and by giving financial and other assistance to the resettling of those Turkish Cypriots to whom Cyprus may no longer appear a tolerable home.
>
> From the defence point of view, *enosis*, notwithstanding its obvious difficulties, has certain advantages over the unitary state. It seems more likely to achieve real stability in the island since the civil authority might be stronger and better able to check vendettas; the risk (a real one with the unitary state) of Cyprus falling under Russian or U.A.R. influence would be largely eliminated and the retention of our Sovereign Base Areas and other defence facilities might be easier with Cyprus as a province of a NATO ally than with a Cyprus tempted to cash in on the benefits of neutralism [...]
>
> For these reasons we hope that the possibility of achieving *enosis* will not be too readily set aside.[26]

The brief was followed by an appendix listing eight different solutions to the Cyprus problem, 'not in any order of preference', listing their pros and cons: *enosis* with Greece; two-way *enosis* (i.e. partitioning Cyprus, giving one part to Turkey and one part to Greece); condominium between Greece and Turkey; trusteeship; population exchange (essentially, removal of Turks from Cyprus and replacement by Greeks from Turkey); status quo; unitary state (with untrammelled majority rule); and separation of the two communities (partition/federation/fragmentation into cantons).

The documents are remarkable in that they suggest that Britain was at least considering *enosis*, but also because they showed that at the same time, it was prepared to ignore the Treaty of Guarantee, which forbade both *enosis* and partition.

Thus, from the British government's (backstage) viewpoint, the 1960 arrangements no longer figured in policy formulation, and *enosis* was seriously considered. Only two months later, the NATO secretary general, Dirk Stikker, told the British prime minister that the Greeks were now talking of the 'Natofication' of Cyprus, while the Turks were talking about double *enosis*, which meant partition.[27] As for the Cypriot government, it was considering *enosis*, an element of 'Natofication' and concessions to Turkey, or so the British military attaché in Cyprus reported to London, following a lunch with the Cypriot labour minister, Papadopoulos, in August:

> In the same conversation, Tassos Papadopoulos also said with emphasis that whatever his views two or three months ago, Archbishop Makarios was now definitely in favour of *enosis*.

> Although his remarks were very informal, he did appear to be indicating that the Cyprus Government might contemplate a settlement based on *enosis* [...] with the transformation of Dhekelia into a NATO base with Turkish participation.[28]

GREEKS OUT

A crucial year in determining the future was indeed 1964, and it illustrates how the Cyprus question affected Graeco–Turkish relations in a particularly negative fashion, resulting in the expulsion of most of the remaining 12,000 Greek nationals living in Turkey, and most of the 60,000 Turkish citizens of Greek stock in Istanbul and the islands of Imbros and Tenedos. The former Greek consul-general in Istanbul, Themistocles Chrysanthopoulos, recalls:

> The Establishment treaty between Greece and Turkey contained a clause allowing either party to denounce it, effective after six months. On 15 March 1964, Turkey denounced the Treaty, on the spurious grounds that it was outdated, adding that she was prepared to renegotiate it. Greece immediately appointed its delegation to renegotiate the treaty, informing the Turks that they were ready. The Turks, however, claimed that they did not have sufficient time to study the treaty deeply enough, and on 15 September, the treaty died.[29]

The Turkish claim that there was insufficient time to study the treaty was clearly rather disingenuous, since it was the Turkish government itself that had denounced it. Moreover, a similar treaty with Germany was not denounced, despite being older.

Harassment of the Greek population had already begun, but now a whole plethora of measures was taken, usually, but not always, on a legalistic pretext. Many people were expelled on the grounds that their 'presence was not in accordance with public order'. According to Chrysanthopoulos, six dead people were expelled (computers were in their early days). Other measures included the setting up of an all-male teacher training college on Imbros, which resulted in Christian fathers sending their daughters to Greece post-haste; the closure of Greek schools on Imbros and Tenedos, on the grounds that they 'offended the national educational principles of Turkism and Laicism' [in contravention of Article 14 of the Lausanne Peace Treaty]; and the removal of Greeks from jobs 'reserved by law for Turks'.[30] The British ambassador wrote that the Turks had prosecuted two headmasters for showing a film in the Greek school in Istanbul depicting the patriarch in 'Byzantine robes'.[31]

One particularly tawdry, yet indicative, story of the treatment of the Greeks of Istanbul is that of the Turkish teacher in one of the few remaining Greek schools of Istanbul (by law, the schools had to employ Turks to teach Turkish) who set his class a composition about 29 May 1453 (the day the Ottoman Turks captured Constantinople). When they had ended the composition and were expecting to submit it to the Turkish teacher for marking, he simply told them to keep it as a reminder.[32]

More telling is a letter from the British consul-general in Istanbul:

> The Turks are simply getting their own back for the sufferings of their compatriots in Cyprus. Apart from the measures and deportations [...], the currently favourite form of vexation is to exact from Greeks income tax payments in advance of deportation for the year ahead instead of the year in arrears as is customary. Failure to comply means confiscation and/or immediate deportation. Sometimes Greeks are made to pay twice before being deported. This is little more than organised robbery and there are I am glad to say a few, but only very few, Turks who are ashamed of the Government in this regard.
>
> There is no sign yet that the campaign is abating. It is undoubtedly organised from Ankara and it reveals an ugly side to the Turkish character [...] There has always been an element in any Turkish Government, which wants to get rid of the Greek minority here. Cyprus is an excuse but only an excuse for prosecuting such a campaign. Secondly, and also independently of Cyprus, the Turkish Government find it convenient for home political purposes to encourage the latent chauvinism of their people.[33]

The Turkish government was at any event clear in its objective of using the Greeks of Turkey as a hostage to exert pressure on Makarios, telling the British embassy that it was taking these steps 'with the object of inducing the Greek government to restrain Makarios'.³⁴ According to a Greek Foreign Ministry official:

> The Turks [...] were behaving in the classical manner. Whenever Turkey had any difficulty with Greece, as now with regard to Cyprus, the Turkish government invariably took action against the Greek minority in Turkey. Their aim was always threefold. In the first place, they wished to put pressure on the Greek Government. Secondly, they wished to satisfy Turkish public opinion. Thirdly, they aimed at weakening the Greek minority economically and otherwise at getting rid of them altogether in the long run.³⁵

Today, there are few Christians of Greek stock left in Turkey. It has to be said, notwithstanding the Turkish government's behaviour, that the Greek government's infiltration of thousands of Greek irregulars into Cyprus was counter-productive, and gave Turkey a valid excuse to infiltrate its own 'irregulars', with a view to claiming part of the island.³⁶ It must be said that the Greek government's clandestine operation of sending troops to Cyprus was not a success. On the other hand, it is equally true that the Greek government did not harass the large Moslem population of Western Thrace, most of whom were of Turkish stock (the rest being Pomaks, i.e. Slav Moslems, or gypsies).

THE UN FACTOR

Throughout 1964, Acheson tried his hardest to persuade Greece and Turkey to accept partition, with various options, including double-*enosis*, confederation and federation. By this time, Makarios was, perhaps understandably, courting the Soviet Union to preserve what little was left of his once quasi-independent state, and fighting off efforts to impose a purely NATO solution. Although he was considered by many cold war warriors in the West (particularly by Ball, who favoured the anti-communist Grivas), as a destabilising and pro-Soviet force, the testimony of the British high commissioner to Cyprus, Hunt, re-establishes some balance:

> Makarios has the intellectual abilities, which would enable him to make his mark in a country of a hundred times the population. His mind is both clear and agile. He is a good psychologist and, although he sometimes cannot keep back a trace of arrogance, he is good at managing men [...] For a Greek, he is astonishingly undevious [...] I do not believe that he ever told me a deliberate lie [...] perhaps because he thinks such a thing beneath him.³⁷

Makarios' greatest 'success' was in involving the United Nations, whose troops moved into Cyprus and have been there ever since (having been unable, nevertheless, to prevent the Turkish invasion of 1974). By the end of 1965, the UN General Assembly had adopted a resolution recognising that the Republic of Cyprus should enjoy *full sovereignty and complete independence without any foreign intervention or interference*. This was a boon for Makarios.³⁸ He also received a moral boost from the report of the UN mediator, Galo Plaza, which came out against partition, and, *inter alia*, called for the people of Cyprus to vote for or against any settlement in total and not accept or reject the settlement partially. This settlement would include autonomy for Turkish Cypriots in 'national' tradition, religion, education and personal status. Significantly, the report stated that the Turkish Cypriots should not expect the same privileges as those granted them by the 1960 Agreements.[39] This last point, combined with the weakness of a caretaker government in Turkey, resulted in outright Turkish rejection of the report, while the Greeks and Cypriots cautiously welcomed it, and the Political Committee of the General Assembly noted it.[40] Makarios was now free to exploit this resolution legitimately and seek independence of action. The next major crisis would not be until the end of 1967, some six months after a military coup in Greece, that some suspect was supported clandestinely by certain US agencies. The years 1965 and 1966, while not overtly 'critical', are worthy of some analysis in order to understand better both the climate of instability in Greece, which helped Makarios to stay on the tightrope, and the double-dealing surrounding the Cyprus question.

4   Makarios Between East and West

It would obviously be a major triumph for Russia, if she could gradually detach Turkey from her unquestioning allegiance to NATO and support for Western policies.[1]

INTRODUCTION

The period between 1965 and the military coup in Athens on 21 April 1967 was characterised by the following factors. First, the legitimacy given by the UN to the Cyprus government increased Archbishop Makarios' room for manoeuvre; second, the Turkish government, angered and frustrated, began flirting with the Soviet Union to put pressure on the USA; third, the Greek government was going through a major political crisis; and fourth, the covert involvement of the US government in Greek affairs increased dramatically. Nevertheless, the period can be characterised, outwardly at least, as one of uneasy calm in Cyprus.[2] Backstage, however, matters were fairly frenetic, with the leading players jockeying for position in a race that would lead to the military coup in Athens and another major crisis in Cyprus and near-war between Greece and Turkey in November 1967.

MAKARIOS AND THE SOVIET BUGBEAR

The Plaza report (see page 41), rejected by Turkey, had ruled out both *enosis* and partition. This irritated the Turkish government, and also the US administration, since the Turks were pressing for partition, and the Americans were still pressing – behind the scenes – for the Acheson plan of 'double-*enosis*', while the Soviet Union was delivering arms to Cyprus.[3] The Turkish Cypriots, for their part, further consolidated their enclaves. While the 1964 troubles had certainly provided both the Turkish government and Turkish Cypriot leaders with a valid excuse to consolidate their de facto autonomy, it was pressure from the Turkish Cypriot leadership rather than from the Greek Cypriots, which cemented physical divisions:

> The isolation in which the Turkish Cypriots live in the enclaves is due much more to the refusal of their leadership to allow them to move out than to any Greek Cypriot blockade keeping them in.[4]

Behind the façade of UN involvement, Makarios skilfully balanced the forces around Cyprus, by ensuring that the Soviet Union gained increased leverage, which worried the unstable Greek government. March 1965 was a particularly poignant month, when a Soviet freighter delivering sophisticated ground-to-air missiles to Cyprus was turned back, following intense pressure on Makarios by the Greek and US governments. Makarios was now a force to be reckoned with, more than ever before. It would be naive to assume that he wished Cyprus to be subject to Soviet – or Communist – control, or that he was in 'Moscow's hip pocket'. Rather, he was reacting to Moscow's – and the UN's – emphasis on political self-determination for the island,[5] a factor which began to drive a wedge between him and the purely *enosis*-minded – and US-supported – Grivas. Washington's depiction of Makarios as the 'Castro of the Mediterranean', although convenient for sloganising media purposes, was way off the mark. His essential medium-term objective was simply to neutralise Anglo–American–Turkish efforts to involve NATO in Cyprus. This clearly entailed the maintaining of good relations with Moscow, since the primary US goal remained the 'NATOisation' of Cyprus, while the Soviet objective was the maintenance of a non-aligned Cyprus friendly to the Soviet Union. In the middle of these two conflicting policies was Makarios, playing 'tightrope diplomacy' to balance conflicting Greek (and Grivas') and Turkish claims on the one hand and, on the other, East–West tactics and goals.[6] By keeping the UN in and NATO out, Makarios ensured that the USSR had a role.

TURKISH FURY AND FLIRTATION

If Cyprus was the major foreign policy headache of an unstable Greek government, this was even more true in the case of an unstable Turkish polity, where Cyprus was the dominating factor.[7] The Turkish government pursued a three-pronged policy of continuing to harass those of Greek stock in Turkey, to threaten Greece verbally and to increase contacts with Moscow, in order to put pressure on the USA.

The fact that the Greek government did not reciprocate Turkish actions against the Greek-speaking Christian minority, by moving against its own large Turkish-speaking Moslem minority in Thrace and the Dodecanese, did nothing to alleviate Turkish zeal.[8] The Greek schools of Imbros and Tenedos (see p. 40) were closed, while the expulsion of Greek nationals continued, including that of many Greek-speaking Christians of Turkish nationality (for example, children born in Turkey). The Turkish government also afforded recognition to the 'Turkish Orthodox

Church', while the prime minister, Ürgüplü, refused to meet a delegation from the Ecumenical Patriarchate.[9] The British ambassador to Turkey wrote that the governor of Istanbul had invited the leader of the 'Turkish Orthodox Church' to a reception also attended by the Ecumenical Patriarch.[10] The former, Efthim II's, father had actually occupied the Patriarchate for a time in 1923. History appeared to be repeating itself. There was even speculation that if the Patriarchate were expelled, the Russians might try to establish themselves in Istanbul.

The anti-Greek anger was exploited by extremist politicians. At the end of 1965, Alpan Turkes, leader of the Peasant Party of Turkey, said that the time had come to 'indicate to Turkish youth as their goals Salonika, Moslem Thrace and the islands of the Aegean, which are part of Anatolia'.[11] Greek politicians were not impervious to extreme rhetoric either: Greek prime minister George Papandreou told the Greek Officers' Club in Thessaloniki that *enosis* was coming, and that with Cyprus as a stepping-stone, Hellenism would continue its advance into the Middle East in the steps of Alexander the Great.'[12]

At the same time, Ankara pushed for a warming of relations with Moscow, its historic enemy, Communism or no Communism, to exert pressure on the USA to support its aims for Cyprus. This, of course, suited Moscow's aims of irritating NATO's south-eastern flank and maintaining the independence and non-alignment of Cyprus.[13] A Soviet delegation visited Turkey in January 1965 and this was followed by an exchange of visits in June and August by the Soviet and Turkish leaders respectively. This extra pressure worried the USA and Britain, who initiated secret negotiations between the Greek and Turkish governments in the hope of achieving *enosis*, with compensation for Turkey. The latter, however, was insisting on 'double-*enosis*', which was particularly galling for Makarios and unacceptable to the Soviets, and the talks came to nothing, unsurprisingly.[14] The historic 'Russian factor', already evidenced in the 1964 crisis, was again increasingly prevalent in the corridors of London and Washington, as we shall see later.

GREEK CHAOS

It is no exaggeration to say that Makarios dealt deftly with the succession of Greek governments and political instability in Greece to consolidate his position internationally. Unlike leading sections of the Greek government and Grivas, whom Greek prime minister George Papandreou (elected in February 1964) had sent back to Cyprus, Makarios had put *enosis* on the back-burner, to such an extent, that some British officials even fretted about a possible rapprochement between Makarios and the Turkish government. The ambassador in Ankara referred to a 'need for caution in urging the Turks actively, against their own judgment or inclination, to make a deal with Makarios. For such a deal may pay scant attention to our own interests.'[15] He also referred to 'trendy' new intellectual views in Turkish foreign policy. Apart from Makarios, the less subtle and more worldly Grivas was the other major figure who could exploit matters. The two had enjoyed an uneasy alliance during the *enosis* campaign of the 1950s. Now, however, with the out-and-out *'enosists'* growing suspicious of Makarios, Papandreou relied more on Grivas than on Makarios, and did not trust the latter's commitment.[16] He also told him that 'no decision shall be taken in Cyprus that may lead directly or indirectly to hostilities without our approval.'[17]

To add confusion to a tense Greek political situation, Grivas, as commander of the Cypriot National Guard, took his orders from Athens rather than from the Cypriot government.[18] There were already at least 12,000 illicit Greek troops stationed on Cyprus. Makarios failed to have Grivas replaced as commander, with the latter declaring that there was only one army in Cyprus – the Greek one.[19] By this time, Grivas was Makarios' biggest bugbear, not only because his virulent anti-communism made Makarios' relations with Moscow more difficult, but also because of Grivas' relations with covert sections of the US government. He is reported to have once told Makarios: 'You could not replace me as a soldier, but I would make a better archbishop than you any day.'[20]

Tensions between the ideological left and right were particularly poignant during this period, with memories of the civil war (see Chapter One) still part of the emotional pattern of politics; it was the liberal-minded George Papandreou's decisive election victory in February 1965 and his clash with the new king, Constantine II, that underlined the inherent instability in Greek political life. Eleven years of right-wing government had ensured that most of the senior officers in the armed forces would have right-wing sympathies, some of them extreme. The murder of a left-wing deputy, Grigorios Lambrakis, in May 1963, had inflamed left-wing passion against senior army and police personnel, some of whom were eventually convicted of culpable homicide. Papandreou tried to replace senior right-wing military men with his own nominees, at the same time seeking evidence of a right-wing army conspiracy against him. This rebounded on him when a left-wing army conspiracy, known as 'Aspida' (shield) was discovered, and quickly associated with his son, Andreas, who had recently returned from exile in the USA (he had left in 1939, having betrayed a list of left-wing friends to the Metaxas dictatorship, and had become a respected professor of economics).

The whole affair resulted in the young and inexperienced king (or, rather, his advisers), who was head of the armed forces, dismissing George Papandreou, thus starting a serious constitutional crisis. A British Cabinet paper sums up the situation succinctly:

> The Foreign Secretary informed the Cabinet that the current constitutional crisis in Greece had its origins in a dispute between the King of Greece and the former Prime Minister, Mr. Papandreou, about the action to be taken as a result of the discovery of a left-wing political faction within the armed forces. Mr. Papandreou had objected to a proposal by the Minister of Defence to conduct an enquiry into this incident and he had proposed to dismiss the Minister and to assume the defence portfolio himself. The King had been unable to accede to this arrangement and he had therefore dismissed Mr. Papandreou, and, if a general election proved unavoidable, Mr. Papandreou would decide to campaign on an anti-Royalist platform. If it became clear

that, in so doing, he had the support of the [outlawed] Communist Party in Greece, the crisis would develop on lines unfavourable to the West, and Greek support for the North Atlantic Treaty Organisation might be called into question.[21]

The clash between the king and Papandreou precipitated a shaky period which saw several governments come and go, although the government led by Stephanos Stephanopoulos managed to last almost eighteen months, 'at the price of remaining entirely ineffectual'.[22]

THE GREEK ARMY COUP AND AMERICAN 'ACQUIESCENCE'

Although the Soviet Union, like Britain and to a lesser extent France, had their spying networks well ensconced in the Eastern Mediterranean by the mid-1960s, with occasional embarrassing results, such as when the Aeroflot representative and a Soviet embassy attaché were expelled from Cyprus in early 1967,[23] it is obviously not easy to assess the impact of covert government work in Greece, Turkey and Cyprus, since such documents as were filed are still mainly under lock and key. Particularly unfortunate was the US government's decision (see Preface page xix) to block for a while release of the already edited and printed 'Foreign Policy of the United States' volume for 1964 to 1968. This naturally leads one to wonder what recent events have embarrassed the US government into issuing a tardy and re-edited publication. The same can be said of certain documents that should have been released, under the Thirty Year Rule, by the Foreign and Commonwealth Office.

America's stance vis-à-vis Greece and Cyprus between 1965 and 1967 has been well documented, and was well summed up, albeit succinctly, by a US congressional mission:

> The United States, despite an official policy of neutrality and non-intervention in Greece's domestic affairs, appears to have sided, throughout 1965–1967, with King Constantine (and the conservative forces which coalesced around him) and against George Papandreou. Apparently, the conservatives were expected to take a more moderate (i.e. pro-NATO line) vis-à-vis Turkey on the subject of Cyprus.[24]

Moscow, conversely, supported Papandreou and criticised anti-Papandreou figures such as Stephanopoulos. As regards Cyprus, *Pravda* wrote:

> The support given to Grivas by the government of Athens has aroused justified fears, both among the Cypriots and the Greek people about the true aims of the ruling circles of Greece over the Cyprus question. As is well known, Washington, for the sake of strengthening the South–East flank of NATO, has more and more insisted that Greece should agree to the Acheson plan, which envisages the elimination of the Republic of Cyprus and the conversion of its territory into a military strategic base in the Mediterranean for the North Atlantic bloc.[25]

It appears, from the scanty evidence available, that the Central Intelligence Agency was heavily, even manically, involved in all manner of schemes in the frenetic period of the mid-1960s, and, of course, probably still is. A quote from the CIA escapee Philip Agee's book *On the Run* provides us with an entrée:

> The Left had been the principal resistance movement during the Nazi occupation [of Greece]. After the war, first the British, then the Americans, intervened to install and sustain corrupt, conservative regimes. Through savage political repression, as in Chile, they tried to exterminate the Left. The CIA was the main instrument, working through the police and security services. They set up the Greek CIA, the KYP [now the EYP], trained its people and gave it money and equipment. Then in 1967, when it looked like a moderately reformist government might come to power through elections, the 'colonels' staged a coup using a sham 'communist plot' as pretext. Echoes of Latin America.
>
> For the next seven years Greece lived under a fascist military regime, led almost to the end by the colonel who had been the KYP's chief liaison officer with the CIA.[26]

The US stance on the whole Cyprus question makes the possibility of CIA involvement in the military coup of 21 April 1967 look like a probability, in the light of further evidence. A former confidant of President Johnson, Eliot Janeway, told the authors of a book on Cyprus that when Johnson visited Greece in late 1966, he was surprised to discover that the 'visit coincided with the preliminaries for the Greek military putsch, and the undercover Defence Intelligence Agency',[27]

The Boston Globe, for its part, wrote:

> The Greek military coup may have come as a surprise to King Constantine, but if it also came as a surprise to the US government (which is hard to believe) there is something radically wrong with our intelligence system.
>
> First of all, many informed foreign correspondents and diplomats have been warning for months that the military (with the approval, passive or otherwise, of the throne) was prepared to seize the government if democratic forces won the May 28 election, or even if they appeared on the verge of winning. [...] At first glance, it appears that, as with the King, the United States may not have known when or how the army intended to strike, but, as is now obvious, the planning was elaborate and must have been worked out with many people over considerable time, for the coup was synchronised all over the country. [...] *for twenty years the Greek army has almost been a branch of the US armed forces*. [my italics][28]

Remarks about covert American involvement were not, of course, new: in August 1965, Greek newspapers accused the CIA of causing an explosion, killing thirteen and wounding fifty, at a Second World War commemoration ceremony. One newspaper even published a document purporting to be from the US embassy military attaché to the assistant chief of staff of army intelligence, discussing the aftermath of the operation. The US embassy denied the veracity of the document, saying that it was a fabrication.[29]

One can perhaps conclude with safety that it was not so much a question of whether certain sections of the US government were covertly involved in Greek political life, but, rather, how and to what extent. At any event, the US government did not condemn the coup, as did the Soviet government, but merely expressed reservations, and Vice President Agnew visited Greece. A final epithet to the question of US interference comes from Andreas Papandreou, who was reported by the head of the Southern European Department of the FCO to have said that the Pentagon/CIA had done in Greece what the Soviet Government had done in Czechoslovakia, and that he could document this. (Interestingly, Papandreou also said that the Junta members were all corrupt, apart from Brigadier Pattakos.)[30]

When the Junta took power, General Grivas was enthusiastic. Shortly after the coup he sent King Constantine (who almost immediately recognised the Junta) an enthusiastic message saying that 'now was the moment to polish off the Communists in Cyprus' and asking permission to go straight into action. The King told him to do nothing of the sort and to abide by the orders of the Greek General Staff.[31]

BEHIND THE SCENES

There was a strong possibility of a renewed push for *enosis* in the anti-Communist euphoria that followed the coup, which could well have led, provided that Turkey agreed, to a 'NATO solution' for Cyprus. Behind the scenes, it should be remembered that Britain's essential aim was to preserve its military bases on Cyprus, rather than have Cyprus as a member of NATO. Even David Hunt, the high commissioner, who favoured *enosis* with Greece as a solution, made it quite clear that the bases would be 'even more secure if Cyprus were united to Greece'.[32] More to the point, and worrying for the British government, had been the conclusion of a 'Gentlemen's Agreement' between Greece and Turkey, initialled on 11 February 1959, in which they agreed to support the entry of the Republic of Cyprus into NATO.[33] It was not only the USSR which was against the NATO connexion, but also the British Ministry of Defence, albeit for different reasons:

> Membership of NATO might make it easier for the Republic of Cyprus and possibly for the Greeks and Turks to cause political embarrassment should the United Kingdom wish to use the bases [...] for purely national ends outside Cyprus [shades of Suez!]. [...] The access of the Cypriot Government to NATO plans and documents would present a serious security risk, particularly in view of the strength of the Cypriot Communist Party. [...] The Chiefs of Staff, therefore, feel most strongly that, from the military point of view, it would be a grave disadvantage to admit Cyprus to NATO.[34]

A ministerial brief for the Cyprus Ministerial Committee on Membership of International Organisations also provides further arguments against membership:

> If Cyprus becomes a member of NATO, any dispute that may arise between Cyprus and either Turkey or the United Kingdom could be represented by the Russians as dissension within the NATO alliance.[35]

In other words, Cyprus was not to be treated as an equal as regards NATO membership. Its membership of the Commonwealth was quite troublesome enough.

The British government was fully aware of the possibility of the Athens coup being extended to Cyprus, as a senior FCO official wrote in a top secret memorandum in May 1967:

> Ever since the Army coup in Greece there have been repeated rumours of an attempt to extend the military regime through the Greek regular officers in Cyprus, in such a way as to bring about *enosis* quickly by encouraging the right-wing elements in Cyprus and if necessary displacing President Makarios. The move would probably, though not necessarily, be made through General Grivas on orders from Athens [...] the report makes the present crop of rumours more plausible than any others hitherto.[36]

In the event, rather than charging in like a bull, the Junta reopened secret talks with Turkey, in the hope of achieving *enosis* in exchange for territorial concessions to Turkey – roughly, in fact, what the USA wanted. Turkey, however, demanded far more territory than Greece was ready to accept, which would have amounted to double-*enosis*. Moreover, Makarios was not invited to the summit meeting, which led to a further deterioration of relations between Makarios and the Junta.[37]

The Soviet factor in the secret negotiations between the Junta and Turkey that began in June 1967 and ended in failure cannot be ignored, particularly since it went hand in hand with Makarios' then policy of independence. A Tass statement in July 1967 made matters plain:

> The 'Acheson Plan', liquidation of the Republic of Cyprus and actual partition of the island, depriving the Cypriots of their statehood, has now emerged at NATO once again. It is reported that implementation of this plan is a matter of the next few days. The 'Acheson Plan', like other similar projects for a NATO solution to the Cyprus problem, is intended in the long run to convert the island into a place d'armes for the aggressive North Atlantic bloc against the Socialist States, the Arab countries and the national liberation movement [...] no one may interfere in the internal affairs of the Republic of Cyprus. Only the Cypriots themselves, both Greeks and Turks, have the right to decide their destiny.[38]

The day after the statement, the Soviet ambassador called on the British secretary of state to warn against foreign intervention in Cyprus. The FCO brief prepared for the 'encounter' alluded to the possibility that Makarios had asked for Soviet intervention, stating that he had been reiterating and strengthening public opposition to the establishment of any Turkish base on the island, and indeed to any *enosis* constitution which did not bring about pure and complete *enosis* (to which the Turks would never agree).[39] The Soviet Union was, of course, particularly incensed by the defeat of the Arab states in the June Six Day War and must have begun to see a connexion between Cyprus and Israel in US military strategic thinking, particularly since Turkey and Israel had signed a secret military pact in 1958.[40] Significantly, following the war, Makarios declared his support for the Arab states.[41]

To say that Makarios was in the middle of a murky diplomatic jungle is an understatement, particularly since matters were confused, at least as regards policy formulation. On the one hand, he had to continue publicly to support the idea of eventual *enosis*, while on the other he saw *enosis* as a NATO weapon to further erode the independence of Cyprus. While Grivas commanded support in the Cypriot National Guard and extreme elements of the Junta in Athens, Makarios had to tread a tightrope between Grivas and his own auxiliary forces. Unlike the USA, Britain clearly saw Grivas as a threat, as did Makarios. The Soviet Union, too, saw Grivas as dangerous to their objective of ensuring an independent, non-aligned and, presumably, Soviet-friendly Cyprus. This unwitting 'unholy alliance' against the virulently anti-communist Grivas nevertheless betrays how Grivas' role helped the British government in irritating Makarios and angering Turkey vis-à-vis Greece and Cyprus.

The crisis of November 1967 was to throw into full relief the forces that were at work behind the scenes. In some ways, it was almost a dress rehearsal for the Turkish invasion of 1974, indeed, might well have been, had Grivas taken it into his mind to launch a military coup in Cyprus. As yet, however, despite extreme elements in the Junta in Athens, its leader, Papadopoulos, was not prepared to countenance the kind of adventurism that would occur in July 1974, and Grivas had his wings clipped. It was nevertheless a tense time. Intercommunal problems had again flared up. At the village of Agios Theodoros, (Greek) Cypriot police had insisted on resuming patrols on 15 November (as they were entitled to do, particularly since it was a mixed village). According to an UNFICYP report, three shots and a burst of automatic fire had come, 'from the evidence at hand', from the Turkish Cypriots.[42] This resulted in a massive reaction from the Grivas-controlled forces, which retook control of two villages, resulting in the killing of twenty-four Turkish and two Greek Cypriots. Turkey reacted immediately by flying fighters over Cyprus, making preparations to invade the island and massing troops on the Greek–Turkish border. Rather than risk a full-scale war, and following pressure from the USA, the Greek government agreed to the withdrawal of Grivas and the 12,000 or so illegal Greek troops stationed on Cyprus (see page 41). The Soviet government realised that whether the Greeks or the Turks had won, it could have resulted in Cyprus becoming an (official) NATO base, as a result either of double-union with Greece and Turkey or of outright conquest by Turkey. Either option would have sidelined Makarios, who certainly saw eye to eye with Moscow on the need for independence. Thus, they did not take sides, other than to stress their usual support for Cyprus' integrity and independence.[43] This support, however, was not to be sneered at, and must have been an additional factor in Turkish and US considerations. The situation was also less clear-cut than in 1964, when the Soviet Union had been more forthcoming in its opposition to Turkish intervention: then, it had supported both the Greek government (George Papandreou) and Makarios, whereas now it was the USA which supported the

Greek government. The latter was not prepared to risk all-out war. The climbdown by the Greek government averted war, and at the same time emboldened Turkey and the Turkish Cypriot leadership, which was able to consolidate its position and offer the resumption of intercommunal talks. Its aim was to strengthen the Turkish – and US – aim of partition, initiated originally, of course, by Britain.

At any event, Archbishop Makarios remained in the middle of the mess, ever-popular with the Greek Cypriots, disliked by the Americans, distrusted by the British, supported by the Soviets, and feared by the Junta and the Turkish government, all in their own way and for their own reasons. The British government, while following the whole Cyprus affair with great concern, was by now letting the USA make the running, since this was a reasonably stress-free way of safeguarding its only real foreign policy concern regarding Cyprus, namely its ninety-nine square miles of sovereign territory. It was, after all, the British government which had devoted so much energy to ensuring that the bases remained outside Cypriot control, or indeed that of any foreign power.

BRITISH POLICY FORMULATION

Two strands emerge from a scrutiny of Foreign Office documents for 1967 and 1968: the atavistic fear of Russia and, therefore, the Soviet Union, which was one of Britain's main motives for acquiring Cyprus in 1878; and to hang on to what it could of Cyprus, shielding itself, if necessary, behind America's cold war stance. Apart from a curious episode in November 1966, when the prime minister, Harold Wilson, had offered King Constantine the transfer of one of the sovereign base areas 'if a generally acceptable solution to the Cyprus problem could be worked out'.[44] Britain's essential position was not overtly active.

One week after the military coup, Wilson wrote a personal memorandum to the foreign secretary setting out his views on Greece, of which it is worth reproducing the bulk:

> [...] I don't think we can treat Greece (however lunatic its politics have been traditionally) on a par with Sierra Leone or Paraguay. Greece is a NATO ally and a fairly key spot in the Mediterranean, to say nothing of its involvement in the Cyprus problem.
>
> Am I right in thinking that
>
> a. the crew of colonels have [sic] produced an unimpressive Government and, with no recognised politicians, very few generals and apparently no King behind them, their situation looks precarious;
>
> b. popular acceptance of their regime depends largely on their bluffing successfully in claiming more political, military and Palace support than they have; and

c. if they can survive and consolidate their hold their political base will be so narrow that they can only maintain themselves with open fascism; in which case

d. the only gainers can be the Communists.

If all of this – or part of it – is right then, at the end of the day, Greece will once again be in a mess. Ought we not to be thinking (no doubt in consultation with the Americans, the French and other NATO allies) about how to strengthen the resistance of the King and, in particular, see what measures might conceivably tip the balance amongst Greek conservatives against co-operation with the Putschists and try to bring about a return to some form of non-Communist constitutional Government before resistance becomes an exclusively Communist prerogative? Difficult, I know. But we already have one dictatorship in NATO. I doubt whether the Alliance can survive many more and still retain the kind of support it needs within this country.[45]

Apart from the curious reference to France as a NATO ally (when it had left the integrated military structure the previous year), and the reference to there 'apparently being no King behind them' (when the King had already exchanged formalities with the new government and posed for photographs with it the previous day),[46] the mention of the Cyprus problem is significant in that it shows how NATO, Greece, Cyprus and Communism figured high in the prime minister's thinking.

The FCO immediately drafted a reply from the foreign secretary to the prime minister urging caution over supporting 'the King's resistance' and advising a policy of non-interference, for fear of isolating the regime and making it more dictatorial and fascist.[47]

So much for the Foreign Office's initial reaction to the coup, which was understandably cautious. According to the British ambassador in Turkey, the US government was likely to 'support Turkey in relation to Cyprus'. He added that this was a 'Pentagon' idea.[48] Adding a note of caution, the Ambassador also added that such courses of action should not be embarked upon without 'clear ideas being formed as to how far we were prepared to take them'.

The FCO's main concerns seem to have been the Soviet Union and Makarios. The ambassador in Ankara noted:

Makarios, of course, knows that he has the Russians behind him (for what that is worth) in the United Nations and in the international field generally [...]. One thing the Russians have not wanted to see is agreement between Greece and Turkey which would result in the elimination of Makarios from his present position and a long term settlement of the Cyprus problem, giving Greece a degree of control over Cypriot policy. Still less do they want it now, in view of the anti-Soviet character of the present Greek Government.[49]

The November crisis prodded the FCO into scrutinising British policy on Cyprus, with some curiously inconsistent results. On 22 November, the foreign secretary told the Cabinet that:

If Turkey invaded Cyprus she would probably invade Greece as well. The attack on Cyprus would not be against the Cyprus Government but against the Greek forces on the island, of whom the Turks alleged that 12,000 were there illegally. We had no defence treaty with Cyprus and were therefore under no obligation to respond to any appeal, which the Cyprus Government might make to us for assistance in the event of a Turkish invasion.[50]

Legally, this was somewhat simplistic in view of the Treaty of Guarantee, and led to an extraordinary, but significant, exchange of memoranda in the Foreign Office. While the foreign secretary appeared to be avoiding or overlooking the Treaty of Guarantee, the Foreign Office appeared to be clinging on to it for dear life, provided that it could be interpreted in such a way as to preclude Britain from preventing a Turkish invasion. It was a case of attempting legally to justify inaction.

The Foreign Office asked the Law Officer's Department whether, under the Treaty of Guarantee, Britain was under any obligation to take unilateral action in the 'current situation', i.e. the threatened invasion of Cyprus by Turkish forces, to protect the Republic of Cyprus from such aggression. On 24 November, at the height of the crisis, the law officers stated that no such obligation was *imposed* by the Treaty.[51]

Use of the word *imposed* is significant: it implies that the Treaty did at least suggest that such an obligation *existed*. Before looking more piercingly at the argumentation of the law officers and within the FCO, let us quote Article IV of the Treaty:

> In the event of a breach of the present Treaty, Greece, Turkey and the United Kingdom undertake to consult together with respect to the representations or measures necessary to ensure observance of these provisions. In so far as common or concerted action may not prove possible, each of the three guaranteeing powers reserves the right to take action with the sole aim of re-establishing the state of affairs created by the present Treaty.[52]

The law officers' argumentation was occasionally contradictory and obtuse. They justified their opinion that the Treaty did not *impose* an obligation on Britain to intervene if Turkey invaded by saying that if Article IV were breached, the three powers would be obliged to *consult*; however, they also added that Article IV did not purport to impose any obligations on any of the guaranteeing powers to take unilateral action, if such concerted action did not prove possible, since it merely *reserved* the right to do so.

If we attempt to interpret simply this slightly contorted language, it appears that the law officers were saying that *reserving* the right to act unilaterally did not automatically entail the right actually to do so, and that therefore no guarantor power, whether Britain, Greece or Turkey, had this right. This is contradictory, since for practical purposes it appears to render the article and, by extension, the Treaty, otiose, even meaningless. However, the law officers had an answer: the Treaty had been concluded between the Republic of Cyprus, on the one part, and Greece, Turkey and the United Kingdom on the other. The essence of the Treaty was, therefore (they claimed), the undertaking by the government of Cyprus to refrain from certain kinds of activity (namely, promoting *enosis* or partition) and to respect the contractual arrangement. In this way, the law officers played down the obligation to prevent a putative invasion. This reduced Cyprus' legal position to that of a second-class citizen, or a de facto protectorate.

More ominously, they then 'dealt with' the arguments as to what Britain's obligations would be if Cyprus itself were to invoke the Treaty of Guarantee and ask the United Kingdom to protect it against a Turkish attack. They said that the British government would be entitled to reject such a request, because of numerous breaches of the Treaty already committed by the Cyprus government.[53]

Here, they were treading on thin legal ice. First, two wrongs do not make a right, even less a legal one; second, some of the alleged breaches, such as appointing Greek Cypriots to ministerial posts reserved for Turkish Cypriots, were necessary, because of the refusal of Turkish Cypriots to participate in the government, which had become the victim of an unworkable constitution in the first place.

Yet despite this legalistic manoeuvring, the law officers did say that 'on the assumption that an invasion would in fact constitute a breach, it would then be the duty of the United Kingdom and also of the other guaranteeing powers to consult together, as provided for by the first paragraph of Article IV.' They added, significantly, that the language of Article IV could 'reasonably support the argument that such a duty arose even when there was merely a threat of an imminent invasion'.[54]

Most significantly, the law officers also noted that the Cyprus government's contention that the Treaty of Guarantee was *contrary* to Article 2.4 of the United Nations Charter and *completely overridden* by Article 103 was *'not without force'*. Article 2.4 states:

> All members shall refrain in their international relations from the threat or use of force against the territorial integrity or political independence of any state, or in any other manner consistent with the purpose of the United Nations.

Article 103 states:

> In the event of a conflict between the obligations of members of the United Nations under the present Charter and their obligations under any other international agreement, their obligations under the present Charter still prevail.

The law officers concluded their answer by stating:

> The threatened invasion of Cyprus and any forcible intervention in Cyprus undertaken by the other guaranteeing powers without the consent of the Cyprus Government might well be held to be forbidden by the Charter and thus to be unlawful even though committed in reliance on the Treaty of Guarantee. But forcible intervention in Cyprus by the United Kingdom or Greece at the request of the Cypriot Government and to protect it against Turkish invasion would not be contrary to the Charter.[55]

From the somewhat tortuous reasoning of the law officers, three pieces of advice seem to emerge: first, that no obligation was imposed to intervene in order to protect Cyprus from a threatened (Turkish) invasion; second, that the United Kingdom was obliged to request consultation without waiting for an invasion to take place, and third, that the Treaty of Guarantee was contrary to the UN Charter because it envisaged forcible intervention in Cypriot affairs without the consent of the Cypriot government.

All this may seem rather convoluted, but it does suggest that the law officers regarded the Treaty of Guarantee as invalid or at least overridden by the UN Charter. It also strengthens the argument that the Treaty of Guarantee was drawn up hurriedly on a 'take it or leave it' basis, with Turkey insisting on inserting the second sentence of Article IV, namely of reserving the right to intervene unilaterally, thus further muddying already muddied waters.

The Foreign Office's reaction to the law officers' advice was somewhat cursory, and betrays considerable disagreement, with the chief legal adviser, McPetrie, apparently keen to sweep the whole issue under the carpet, and 'let sleeping dogs lie'. An assistant under secretary of state, John Moreton, was clearly not satisfied with the law officers' opinions, and wanted more precision. He wrote to McPetrie:

> While it is true that the immediate threat of an invasion is past, it is far from inconceivable that it will be revived. We should then be faced, again at short notice, with the need for definitive advice on the interpretation of the Treaties and again the Law Officers might feel they had insufficient time to consider the matter properly. I therefore wonder whether you would feel it wise to put these issues to them now.[56]

Far from seeking immediate precision and clarity, McPetrie waited ten weeks before replying, something normally considered bad manners, not to say unprofessional, at least in the FCO. He wrote: 'We were under no obligation to take unilateral action in the situation then obtaining.'[57] He also wrote that the law officers had been very reserved as to whether forcible intervention under the Treaty without the consent of the Cyprus government would be a breach of the [UN] Charter. Since the law officers had at least been clear that any forcible intervention without the Cyprus government's consent would be forbidden by the Charter and be unlawful (see above), one is left to wonder what was going through McPetrie's mind when he wrote so irrationally. He was either attempting – unsuccessfully – to reinterpret tactically the advice; had expressly mis-understood it; or could simply not cope with the intellectual challenge of taking the law officers' advice seriously. He concluded by suggesting that the advice be put on file. Moreton, curiously, simply wrote: 'Very well.' Again, one is inclined to wonder whether Moreton could simply not be bothered to react to the flaws in McPetrie's argumentation, or whether he was just not prepared to put up a fight.

A final epithet to this bizarre yet revealing story lies in the Foreign Office briefing to the foreign secretary about how to handle difficult questions about Cyprus from a member of parliament, Mr Gardner:

> It is important to avoid becoming involved in questions about the effects of the provisions of the Treaty of Establishment and Guarantee, and the extent of our obligations under them.[58]

To conclude, British foreign policy formulation concerning the Cyprus question appears to have been beset by a certain amount of dilatoriness, disagreement and contradiction. Very few people know today what informal, high-level, unrecorded meetings might have taken place in the ten weeks it took McPetrie to respond to Moreton's memo. As we saw in Chapter Three, the British had already decided in 1964 to 'retire into base' were Turkey to invade Cyprus. Given the beating about the bush during the crisis of 1967, it is not unreasonable to assume that this was still British policy, even in 1974. It may well be today.

CLOAK AND DAGGER

Whether the man in the middle, Makarios, was wholly aware of the above is a moot point, but the evidence to date suggests that the British government was keen to avoid taking an overt leading role, to the point of avoiding its responsibilities, knowing that it could when necessary shield behind the USA on the question of its sovereign base areas.

It is difficult to locate precise documentation on the various conspiracy theories that abounded in Greece during the late 1960s, but it would be irresponsible to avoid mentioning them. For example, there was a story, reported by the British embassy itself in an internal memo, that Britain had engineered the November 1967 troubles in Cyprus to force the Greeks to withdraw their troops from Cyprus under the threat of a Turkish invasion (the Turks may have been bluffing about war with Greece), thus humiliating the Junta and bringing about its fall and the restoration of rule by 'King and Parliament'.[59] This certainly makes sense, given Harold Wilson's wish to support the king, but it may be stretching credibility to think that Wilson ignored the advice of the Foreign Office (see above). Significantly, some Foreign Office files concerning the king have still not been released under the Thirty Year Rule. At any event, the head of Greek intelligence, Hadjipetros, told a French journalist that the Junta was convinced of British involvement. In the event, when the king attempted his counter-coup in December 1967, he found insufficient support, and fled, although the Junta still considered him king.[60] It is possible that Spandidakis, the defence minister, had helped the king, but that the latter had got cold feet at the last minute.

The question of the king had always been laden with a degree of controversy. Greece's first king, Otto, was exiled and replaced by George I, who was assassinated in Thessaloniki in 1913. George's son, Constantine I, quarrelled with Venizelos, leading to two governments in 1916, in Thessaloniki (Venizelos) and Athens. He was forced to leave following Venizelist, British and French pressure, to be replaced by his second son, Alexander, who died from a monkey bite in 1920. Constantine returned, only to be overthrown by a coup and succeeded by his first son, George, who nevertheless had to live in exile when Greece declared a republic in 1924. Returning to Greece in 1935, following a rigged plebiscite,[61] he then sanctioned the Metaxas dictatorship, which, as we have seen in Chapter One, did not endear him to the majority of the population. British 'Churchillian' pressure and another somewhat curiously organised plebiscite ensured his return to Greece in 1946, where he died almost immediately, to be succeeded by his brother Paul.

When Paul died, his son, Constantine II, inherited not only a history of controversy about the powers of the monarchy, but found himself embroiled in political controversy, leading, as we have seen, to his dismissing the prime minister in 1965. It seems that the young king relied to a considerable extent on his advisers. His chief of cabinet, Bitsios, told an American diplomat in early 1967 that if a dictatorship were decided upon, 'Andreas Papandreou would not be around,' and that 'for the present, the loyalty of the army could be counted upon to support a temporary dictatorship.'[62]

Only twelve days before the military coup, the king himself told the American ambassador, Talbot, that only a near miracle could save him from the final choice of yielding his country to Andreas Papandreou, or establishing a dictatorship either before or just after the May elections.[63] Any idea that the king and his advisers had about their own coup was however thwarted by the colonels' coup. The king was surprised enough to ask the American military attaché to 'get word to the Sixth Fleet' and have Washington 'send in the army'.[64] One of the members of the coup triumvirate, Pattakos, confirmed to Talbot that the king had known nothing about the coup.[65] At any event he was quick to sanction the new regime, albeit with some initial reluctance, while keeping in constant touch with the American government, to the point of revealing his plans for a counter-coup. In September, he even asked President Johnson if, in the case of a confrontation with the coup leaders, the USA would 'land marines as a show of force, position the Sixth Fleet in Greek waters and issue a public statement supporting his efforts to return the country to constitutionalism.'[66] Johnson refused politely. Pattakos himself told the king that a counter-coup would fail, since the army would not support him.[67]

On 13 December, the king informed Talbot that he was moving against the Junta that day, and asked for the USA to endorse his action.[68] He flew north to Kavala where he had some support from military commanders. The same day, when the Junta leader asked Talbot whether he had any knowledge of the king's action to 'overthrow the revolution', the ambassador was somewhat economical with the truth in saying that 'there was certainly nothing he could tell him.'[69]

Throughout the day, there was a frenetic exchange of telegrams between Washington and the Athens embassy, with the essential object of trying to ascertain the degree of support the king had, followed by a meeting early the next day between Talbot and the Junta leaders, at which it became apparent that the Junta was not to be overthrown. The king and his family flew to Rome, obviously with the acquiescence of the Junta.

Martin Packard (see Chapter Three) provides us with a final epithet to this tale. At the time, he was on paid leave from British naval intelligence to learn Greek, not long before his rather early retirement. He visited King Constantine in Rome. The king told him that he had followed British and American advice, but that they had then 'dumped him'.[70]

It seems clear that, at the end of the day, the USA was more interested in ensuring the maintenance of the regime than in indulging in risky moral enterprises, which could have led to civil strife. As for the British, some of the (obviously most pertinent) Foreign Office files have been withheld, which renders a precise description of policy vis-à-vis the king rather risky.

The US government would probably have been irritated by strong British support for the king, since it was increasingly supporting the Junta, and slowly resuming supplies of heavy arms.[71] The most obvious manifestation of this support was in 1969, at Eisenhower's funeral, when President Nixon received Stylianos Pattakos, the Junta's number two, but not King Constantine, who also attended the ceremony.[72] As we shall see in the following chapter, the USA increasingly saw the king as a problem, even to the point of allowing this to affect relations with Britain.

THE PAPANDREOU MYSTERY

Even after his death, suspicion still abounds in Greece about Andreas Papandreou and his 'Jekyll and Hyde' relationship with the USA. It is clear that both the king and those politicians whom he supported, such as Kanellopoulos and Stephanopoulos, were prepared to accept a dictatorship rather than allow Papandreou to win the election in May.[73] Talbot's views of the danger Papandreou posed were nothing like as extreme as those of the king and politicians like Kanellopoulos. Commenting on the possibility that he would transform the military high command into a party-controlled instrument and effectively break the king's authority, he wrote:

> The United States would not necessarily find that and various domestic programs projected by Andreas so damaging except that they would give him a springboard for foreign policies that sound like a Mediterranean Bhutto's [...] we could live for a while with his abrasive if not defiant policies.[74]

Washington's view was to suggest that Talbot suggest to George Papandreou that if he were to win the elections, he would, in return for his son not being arrested for his alleged role in the Aspida affair (a conspiracy of left-wing officers), appoint only ministers of 'mutual confidence'.[75]

This was a clear case of political meddling.

Andreas Papandreou was arrested when the coup occurred, but released at the end of the year. In January 1968 he had a long talk at Talbot's home, in which he explained, *inter alia*, that he had never advocated the departure of the king from Greece, but merely wished to delimit his powers. He also said that he was never in favour of Greece departing from the Western Alliance, and that he had not attacked US policies as an enemy but as a member of a family.[76] Even if Papandreou was being ingratiating (because of the US visa being prepared for him), when he did eventually come to power in 1981, he did not take Greece out of NATO, restricting his activities to closing down the Hellenikon airbase and indulging in populist rhetoric. His policy on US bases was in fact little different from that of his predecessor, Karamanlis.[77]

It is difficult to make any firm conclusions about Andreas Papandreou's precise relationship with the US administration (and its undercover elements), perhaps because some descriptions of papers in the volume of American diplomatic papers released for the years 1964–1968 are peppered with the phrase 'not found'. This probably means that they have been retained on 'security grounds'. Another method of retaining documents without the casual researcher being aware is simply to omit them. For example, in the volume on 'Breakdown of Constitutional Government in Greece, November 1966–April 1967', there is apparently no correspondence between 15 and 19 April. This is ludicrous, as there must have been several important telegrams.

To even try to point a dark finger at Papandreou, we have to turn to a later record of a meeting of 20 March 1974 at the State Department, chaired by Henry Kissinger. We need to remember that Papandreou had been a prominent US academic, from when he left Greece in 1939 until his return twenty years later. At the meeting, Kissinger, addressing the intelligence director of the Department of State, said:

> The Papandreou situation is a possibility – that's one thing. We've worked with him before. And, if we can work with him, obviously, from our point of view, it would be best to have a government that protects our security interests [...] If you could produce a Papandreou tomorrow in a state government, I wouldn't even want to know how you did it.[78]

Apart from the cynicism and dark possibilities at the end of this statement, Kissinger, in referring to the fact that 'we have worked with him before' could only have been referring to Papandreou's having been used by the CIA as a source of information in the 1950s, during which time he was 'co-opted by the CIA into a covert study group for Mediterranean policy-making'.[79]

While there are Greeks who have studied in the USA and who even today subtly promote US policies in Greece (particularly certain academics, whom it would not be judicious to name), one cannot be sure that Papandreou was 'a deep-cover agent' of US interests, unless some specific and revealing document comes to light. One can however be sure that Papandreou wrote in January 1972 to the British prime minister that the Greek people were 'entitled to combat in Greece the brutal usurpers of power – an occupation force emanating from the Pentagon – in exactly the same way they combated the Nazi and fascist invaders of the 40s'.[80]

What one can conclude with confidence is that the main reason for the military coup was to keep Papandreou out of office, at least for a number of years.

MORE CLOAK AND DAGGER

The Junta's first year in power was not successful from Greece's foreign policy viewpoint, mainly because of the climbdown over Cyprus – the withdrawal of Grivas and the twelve thousand mainland troops. An element of instability was evident in the links between elements of the Junta and pro-*enosist* activists in Cyprus. One example of dark forces at work in Cyprus was the attempted assassination, in August 1968, of the Junta leader, Papadopoulos, by a zealous young officer, Panagoulis. There was even speculation that the British Secret Service had been involved. According to the British high commissioner in Cyprus, in a top secret and personal letter to the permanent under secretary (whose department is responsible for the Special Intelligence Services), Polycarpos Georgkadjis, a former EOKA commander and Cyprus minister of the interior, was possibly involved. Whoever was behind the plot, it appeared that the Cyprus authorities had issued a passport to Panagoulis, although there was also speculation that it was forged.[81]

A more credible story that preoccupied British diplomats was the influence of the independent-minded General de Gaulle, who had of course taken France out of the integrated military structure of NATO in 1966 and kicked the NATO Headquarters out of Fontainebleau. According to the US embassy, an emissary of General de Gaulle had given the head of Greek intelligence an undertaking that France would back Greece, if the Junta leader, Papadopoulos, were to follow the French line in relation to NATO.[82]

Whatever plots and counter-plots existed around Greece and Cyprus, Papadopoulos appears to have been a shrewd operator, and not regarded as an extremist. A Foreign Office working paper of June 1968 stated:

> If Mr. Papadopoulos goes, his government will probably be replaced by a tougher and more extremist regime. So the right course is to try to move the Papadopoulos Government in the right direct [sic] we want, not to topple it [...]. The King does not command a wide and enthusiastic following inside Greece. But he has some support [...]. Mr. Papadopoulos and the moderate leaders are known to envisage his return.[83]

The British ambassador in Greece commented that King Constantine was 'rash, not a good conspirator, and not discreet'.[84]

At any event, it was fast beginning to look as if, despite their bad relations (as we shall see), Makarios and Papadopoulos shared one thing in common: they were both men in the middle.

5   Foreign Policy Distortion

It is absurd for democrats to reserve their blows for the Junta. They ought to attack the problem at its American root and not confine themselves to its external manifestation.[1]

INTRODUCTION

Following the Cyprus crisis at the end of 1967 and the beginning of inter-communal talks, the period to the end of 1972 was on the surface reasonably 'crisis-free'. The Cyprus talks continued intermittently, with little expectation of a serious breakthrough, despite 'good relations between Greece and Turkey',[2] and notwithstanding President Makarios' willingness to accept separate electoral rolls, an increase in the number of Turkish-speaking members of the House of Representatives and the right of Turkish Cypriots to be tried by a judge 'of their own language' or by a Turkish Cypriot judge.[3] In Turkey, foreign policy was dominated, even distorted, by the Cyprus issue.[4] So was it in Greece, although this was more in evidence behind the diplomatic scenes than 'frontstage'. The Greek government appeared to consolidate its position with British and US support, while Makarios and Papadopoulos both tried, with some success, to hold off the extremists, as did the Turkish establishment. Other factors in evidence – essentially 'backstage' – were the FCO's continuing preoccupation with Soviet policy, the growing rift between Makarios and the government in Athens, US–British tension over the king, conspiracies – both theoretical and actual (an assassination attempt on Makarios) – and, perhaps significant for the future of Cyprus, the increasing involvement, more covert than overt, of the USA in Greek and Cypriot affairs, and its distaste for Makarios.

US POLICIES

Although the USA was markedly in favour of double-*enosis* through partition, it was not obvious about this, preferring to adopt a low-key crisis-avoidance policy for the time being. A secret State Department paper of January 1969 is revealing of the country's 'slowly slowly' approach and its concern about the Soviet Union:

> Resolution of the Cyprus problem is a major objective in a regional goal of maintenance of peace in the Eastern Mediterranean. Eruption of another crisis would run the very strong risk of conflict between Greece and Turkey and incalculable damage to the Southeastern flank of NATO. The recently increased Soviet naval presence in the eastern Mediterranean has further complicated the situation.[5]

The paper then looked at, and dismissed, the following options:

> *enosis*; partition of the island between the Greek–Cypriots and the Turkish–Cypriots; 'compensated *enosis*' – secession of part of Cyprus or a military base or some portion of Greek national territory to Turkey, in recompense for union of Cyprus with Greece; and various other more or less drastic solutions involving population exchanges, forced or compensated resettlement, condominium with Greece and Turkey, etc. These permanent solutions, having been rejected by one or more of the parties, do not appear viable under current circumstances.

In effect, the State Department, unlike Britain five years earlier, was not now considering any kind of *enosis*, at least not as an immediate option. It in fact opted for what it termed 'a long term *modus vivendi*'.[6] The paper also listed three different US 'attitudes': a unitary state protected against Turkish intervention and with freedom to opt later for *enosis*; favouring the Turkish Cypriots in their desire for full autonomy under the protection of Turkey (a federated state with complete equality for the two communities); and a compromise between these 'extreme' views. These alternative 'attitudes', however, took second place to the '*modus vivendi*' objective – in other words the 'slowly slowly' attempt to achieve a climate for a more permanent solution.

Some harsh realism, if not cynicism, also emerged: in a covering memorandum explaining the terminology used in the secret papers, the State Department wrote:

> No solution is permanent. A glance at the last 3,500 years of Cypriot history demonstrates that the Phoenician, Greek, Assyrian, Macedonian, Egyptian, Persian, Roman, Byzantine, Saracen, Frankish, Venetian, Genoese [sic], Turkish and British solutions were not permanent, regardless of how permanent they may have been at one time.[7]

This 'analysis' was somewhat simplistic and superficial, since the Macedonians (Alexander), Egyptians (Ptolemaic dynasty) and the Byzantine leadership were essentially Greek; but it also seemed to imply justifying outside intervention. Thus, the paper concluded:

> The question of timing and nuance in use by the United States Government of diplomatic persuasion and *pressure*[8] is more important. It is undebatable that

the United States Government must maintain an active interest in the Cyprus problem and be prepared to expend diplomatic resources on behalf of a solution.

US PRESSURE AND THE KISSINGER FACTOR

Diplomatic pressure can take many forms, particularly since diplomacy is still essentially a secret activity. By 1969, the German-born Henry Kissinger was influencing President Nixon. Kissinger's brand of power politics was not to everybody's taste. His own words in 1957 provide a foretaste of what was to come, particularly for Cyprus:

> But for the foreseeable future we should be able to count on Okinawa or perhaps the Philippines as staging areas for the Far East, on Cyprus or Libya as staging areas for the Middle East, and on Great Britain as a staging area for Europe. And if our policy is at all far sighted we should be able to create or hold other friendly areas close to likely danger zones.[9]

Such broad-brush and simplistic 'vision', which is interesting to read in tandem with that of geopolitical 'gurus' such as Kjellen, Haushofer, Mackinder and even Hitler, and connected – even if not directly – to Metternich's obsession with controlling the Danube basin and respecting the Ottoman Empire – but on a worldwide scale – may have underpinned Kissinger's methods of dealing with the intricacies of diplomacy. Kissinger's lack of professional diplomatic training (he was never a career diplomat) appears to have detracted from a tactile approach. Certainly, by the end of 1971, the German government was beginning to worry. Its state secretary, Frank, appears to have had a worrying impression of Kissinger:

> [...] Frank turned to the subject of Kissinger, with whom he had spent some time [...] he [Kissinger] saw himself as a policy-maker on the grand scale and whatever the degree of co-operation between the working level of the State Department in the White House might be, this made for considerable difficulties. He had said after making one statement that this represented his (Kissinger's) personal view, but added 'I can assure you that in two weeks time it will be White House policy [...]' Frank regarded Kissinger with considerable misgivings. He thought he was far more in the mould of Metternich than a man with a full understanding of the inter-dependence of a modern world. He was interested in where power resided and the exercise of power. Frank clearly feared that this 19th century approach was affecting White House thinking and perhaps the attitude of the President in particular.[10]

These misgivings were shared by the British embassy in Washington:

> As you know, we share Frank's misgivings about the rôle of Dr. Kissinger. [...] But it is not as a rule so much the direction of Kissinger's foreign policy ideas that upsets us [...] It is rather his manner of conceiving and conducting foreign policy without reference to, or knowledge of, the State Department

or anyone else which is most worrying. It leaves one with the fear that any day *something could go seriously wrong because the normal sources of advice, restraint and execution are by-passed* [my emphasis].[11]

Thus it is not only the Hitchenses of this world[12] who have criticised Kissinger adversely, but senior British and German diplomats, to mention but some. At any event, in the case of Greece, US policy was certainly somewhat intrusive. Another insider wrote:

> It seemed the Agency's (CIA) hands were into everything in that country [Greece]. And apparently it hadn't changed much, because a recent mission directory showed an enormous CIA contingent for a nation the size of Greece [1987].[13]

Then, as now, the CIA in Greece (as elsewhere) operates using a network of non-diplomatic US and local personnel, the latter usually working for money, ideology, or both. This is of course the way that the intelligence organisations of most countries operate, and is understandable. What differentiates matters, however, is the breadth and depth of US involvement in Greece in the 1960s and 1970s, and, almost certainly, today. The Junta leader, Papadopoulos, had been the Greek Intelligence Agency's chief liaison officer with the CIA.[14] He and many of the Junta had close links with the CIA, according to one of the Junta leaders, Brigadier Pattakos.[15]

Andreas Papandreou, visiting Britain after he was freed by Pattakos, put US influence in Greece another way, by saying that there was a close parallel between Greece and Czechoslovakia: the 'Pentagon and CIA had done in Greece what the Soviet Government [presumably the Defence Ministry, KGB and GRU] had done in Czechoslovakia. His father, in this sense, was the Dubcek of the Greeks.' (Interestingly, Papandreou added that Pattakos was the only member of the Junta who was not corrupt.)[16]

It would not be parodic to state that a fair proportion of the leadership of the Greek armed forces, particularly the army, was virtually a branch of the US armed forces, at least according to The *Boston Globe*.[17] It was these Manichean ideological children of the Truman Doctrine, the Greek civil war and surrogate McCarthyism who influenced matters. It is significant that the KYP, Greece's new intelligence service, had been established in 1953 with the close involvement of the CIA.[18]

BRITAIN'S LOW PROFILE

Britain's main preoccupation, then and now, was to avoid any discussion, let alone debate, about its sovereign territories on Cyprus, and its policy towards the Greek government was predicated on this to a large extent. It was a relief for the British government that Papadopoulos' relations with Makarios were tense, and deteriorating, as we shall see, since the latter had made his negative view on the bases clear. The British had not forgotten how he had managed to whittle down the agreed size of the bases at the London negotiations, even though he was only brought in towards the end of the negotiations. Towards the end of 1968, Makarios had worried them by telling the Soviet *Pravda* that his readiness to declare the demilitarisation of Cyprus included the 'liquidation' of the military bases.[19]

The fear of Soviet power loomed large and, in combination with fear of Makarios' immediate objective of an independent, NATO and British-free Cyprus, certainly determined the British government's stance, as it did America's, towards the Athens Junta. The British foreign secretary wrote:

> The coup of last year had one good result. It left in control of Greece a government, which unlike its predecessors, could take a relatively independent line over Cyprus and pay more regard to Greece's national interest than Greek emotions.[20]

The same paper listed a number of objectives, including the preservation of Greece's military effectiveness as a NATO ally, the pursuing of British commercial interests and the retention of the 'ability to influence the Greek government in matters of foreign policy, e.g. Cyprus'.[21]

The British government was therefore sensitive to anything that might upset the apple cart. Certainly, the Junta, with its respected civilian foreign minister, Pipinelis, served British interests in Cyprus in a more consistent way than the series of unstable – albeit more democratic – governments that had preceded it.

The Soviet attitude towards Cyprus further fuelled British support for the Greek government, and its keenness to support partition. The Soviet position was well summed up in a diplomatic memorandum reporting the views of a Soviet diplomat:

> His government had made their position clear: they wanted a peaceful settlement and the withdrawal of all foreign troops, including the bases and direct talks between the parties on the island. If Britain insisted on maintaining the Zürich and London Agreements, talks could not begin. He suggested that we were using Turkey to maintain these Agreements. He [...] understood that we, and particularly the Americans, were giving very substantial aid to Turkey. Why, he asked, should Turkey go, from her own meagre resources, spending so much on aid to the Turkish Cypriots? Mobilisation had cost them a lot. They could not afford this without our aid [...] He laughed at the idea of Turkey having any really sincere regard for their minority, and seemed convinced that Turkey would abandon them if she were not 'kept up to it'.[22]

The British diplomat finished by alluding to the Soviet's conclusion that Turkey's intransigence was being backed by Britain and the USA for the purpose of maintaining the Zurich and London Agreements, in order to hang on to the bases. The Soviet's views of Turkish intransigence were not wide of the mark: the following year, the view at Anglo–Canadian–US talks on Cyprus was that the Turkish Cypriots had not responded 'to the significant moves made by the Cyprus Government towards normalisation and that the momentum had been halted'.[23]

In this connexion, the British High Commission in Nicosia had a poor opinion of the Turkish Cypriot leadership:

> There is a feeling on the part of many that the present leadership is insensitive to the sufferings of the community and has even profited from the intercommunal strife. This is at least partly true [...] most of the leadership are so closely identified with the 'siege' policy of the Turkish Cypriot community and, in some cases, so discredited by their personal financial dealings over the past four years, that it seems doubtful whether many of them could continue in office following an intercommunal settlement.[24]

Despite this astute British diplomatic reporting, Britain was happy to play a backseat role to that of the USA, worrying nevertheless about Soviet intentions, as had been its atavistic wont, at least ever since Russia had begun pressuring the Turks (namely the Crimean War) and extending its influence to the Mediterranean. The Soviet espionage apparatus was at least as involved as America's and Britain's, to the extent that the Soviet government even warned Britain about '*enosist* links' between the Cypriot and Greek governments. Although the FCO actually gave some credence to Soviet concerns about 'terrorist links' between the Athens Junta and the Cyprus government, the assessment of the British ambassador in Athens was that the Soviets were simply asserting their claims 'to be a Mediterranean power', trying to distract attention from their problems in the Middle East, and perhaps 'genuinely believing that there was a risk of a Greek takeover in Cyprus which would make the island a "NATO springboard"'.[25] In this they were obviously correct, given Kissinger's views enunciated above.

British worries about the sovereign bases becoming a major issue were always in evidence, especially when Makarios' views were publicised by the Soviet media, and even led to the distribution of a clandestine paper on the Soviet attitude to Cyprus, in the Information Research Department's 'Communist Policy and Tactics' series.[26] Concern about Soviet motives even worried the FCO sufficiently to ask the MoD to produce a study of Soviet military capabilities vis-à-vis Cyprus, and 'the most likely form such intervention would take'.[27] The MoD, however, replied that 'it would be wrong to provide a definitive answer to the military questions posed unless a more sophisticated political situation were depicted.'[28]

Perhaps somewhat disingenuously, the departing British high commissioner to Cyprus wrote in 1969:

> The Russians, often more logical than ourselves, think that our concern for our interests here must mean that we want to keep Cyprus divided, since a settlement of the Cyprus problem could and probably would lead to the development of Left-wing pressure on us over the bases. We are in fact perhaps less logical and certainly more altruistic than the Russians give us credit for. We regard the importance of good Greek–Turkish relations as of more importance to the defence of Europe through NATO than our interests in Cyprus. But it may be that the Russian thinking is right to the extent that it would be a wiser policy for us to be less active than we have been at various times in the past about promoting a settlement.[29]

This curious statement (curious because the British bases were obviously considered to be more important than Graeco–Turkish relations) nevertheless epitomises Britain's then rapidly developing policy of taking a back seat to the USA, by 'being less active'. From the British viewpoint, this apparently bore fruit, as the high commissioner noted:

> As you know, we have been particularly careful to avoid comment and activity that could be (mis)construed locally as appearing to support any of the political parties, although we have continued with our usual IRD[30] activities. This policy has so far been justified in that both the Americans and now the Greeks have been attacked in recent weeks for involving themselves in the internal affairs of Cyprus, while we have been exempt from criticism.[31]

ANGLO–AMERICAN COLLABORATION

Although the USA and Britain clearly saw eye to eye on the bases, particularly since the USA had its network of listening posts, there were other areas of disagreement, to the extent that, in the second half of 1970, there were only low-level contacts between the British and US embassies in Athens, because the US ambassador, Tasca, was 'annoyed at British support for the King'.[32] In this connection, it is significant that the FCO has retained the files on 'The King's Position'.[33] As a sign that the USA was the Junta's staunchest supporter, Tasca issued an 'almost passionate appeal' that the new government [Heath's, who tended more towards cooperation with Europe than the USA] should give Papadopoulos a 'helping hand for fear of something worse'. The USA was clearly also irritated by Britain's failure to vote for Greece at a Council of Europe meeting, which essentially tipped the scales, forcing Greece to withdraw from the organisation, rather than face the ignominy of expulsion. Certainly, by this time, although Tasca did suggest that the UK and USA 'work together on Greece and Cyprus',[34] the USA was by far the more active partner. A leading French politician even claimed that the CIA and American military were the masters of Greece.[35] Given the support for Grivas by extremist elements of the Junta and covert elements of the US establishment, there was an element of credibility in the politician's statement.

At any event, the British were worried about extremist elements, which 'appeared to be pressing Mr. Papadopoulos hard'.[36] Judging by Kissinger's support for the military coup in Cyprus that led to the Turkish invasion (see Chapter Six), it does appear that certain parts of the US establishment were, perhaps because of their deep distrust of Makarios, maintaining links with extremist groups, which would have been troubling for the British, notwithstanding the US ambassador's wish that the British support Papadopoulos.[37] The British were constantly worried about assassination attempts, particularly after the one against Papadopoulos (see Chapter Four): 'But there is always the possibility of a successful assassination or of a coup led either by an extremist group of the Right or by a respected senior army officer.'[38]

Such 'gossip' was not idle. Extremism was building up behind the scenes, leading to an assassination attempt against Makarios in March 1970, following which the very same Georghadjis, who had resigned over accusations of involvement in the assassination attempt on Papadopoulos, was himself assassinated. A secret British telegram analysed speculation as to the assassination theories. One was that Georghadjis had indeed been involved, along with the extremist National Front 'enosist' party; another was that the CIA had been involved.[39] At any event, Makarios expelled the CIA station chief in Nicosia.[40] The Turkish and Soviet governments believed that a military coup in Cyprus was imminent. It is likely that one was in the offing, but that the failed attempt on Makarios scotched it. It was only a matter of time. One rather distasteful element (with the benefit of hindsight) was an unfortunate quote by former Acting Secretary of State Ball: 'That son of a bitch Makarios will have to be killed before anything happens in Cyprus.'[41] Makarios had of course frustrated Ball's plan to formally partition the island, hence the emotion.

FRONTSTAGE AND BACKSTAGE

On the surface, and thanks to a considerable extent to the Greek foreign minister, the civilian Pipinelis, the Greek–Cyprus boat sailed through rocky waters, with Pipinelis and Papadopoulos at the Greek end, and Makarios himself at the other, playing the Soviet card when necessary and thereby antagonising the USA, but particularly the CIA. Two major events were to mark the beginning of the rise of hidden extremism in Greece and Cyprus: the death of Pipinelis and the arrival (again) in Cyprus of Grivas, the latter occurring with almost indecent haste two months after the foreign minister's death. The Turkish government, already worried by extreme Greek elements, had made it plain that Mr Pipinelis' disappearance would be a very serious matter indeed.[42] This was hardly surprising, given the assessment of the British ambassador to Athens that 'in the firm hands of Pipinelis Greece followed a policy of complete and rigorous loyalty to NATO, reconciliation with Turkey and a sustained and imaginative effort to find a permanent solution to the problem of Cyprus.'[43]

Plots to assassinate the moderate Pipinelis abounded. The British ambassador wrote that they were the work of 'undisciplined elements' or, less likely, anti-monarchists (Pipinelis had kept in touch with the king).[44] He added that 'contrary to their normal political tradition, the Greeks may be acquiring a taste for political [sic] assassination.' Pipinelis in fact died only six days after the ambassador wrote, but by the hand of cancer, rather than by the hand of a human assassin. Pattakos, for one, bewailed his demise.[45]

While Pipinelis lay dying, Papadopoulos sent Makarios a subtly threatening letter, in which he accused the latter of going against a Greek proposal for a solution in Cyprus, denied that there had been collusion between Athens and Ankara and suggested that going against the proposals would mean 'splitting our common front'. The letter was leaked, probably by Makarios, according to the British High Commission in Nicosia.[46]

Makarios' response was acerbic:

> This sentence gives the impression of a threat, although it is difficult for me to accept this impression as correct. [...] If there is indeed a threat, then I am sorry to have to say that an inadmissible situation is being created thereby, which I, the representative of Cyprus Hellenism, cannot accept.[47]

With another moderate gone, the behind-the-scenes power of the extremely nationalist and fervently *enosist* Head of the Military Police, Ioannides, increased. As it is, he had always had considerable power[48] in the Junta. The result was that Grivas was sent back to Cyprus, clandestinely, in September. According to a former Greek foreign minister, Averoff-Tositsas, some senior members of the Junta, particularly Ioannides, were also considering reorienting Greece's historical position vis-à-vis the West, and the more moderate Papadopoulos and Pipinelis were excluded from this scheme of things.[49] Certainly, with Pipinelis gone, Ioannides was able to influence Papadopoulos more than before. Greek foreign policy appeared to undergo a certain realignment, with the objective of convincing NATO that Greece mattered; this actually worried the FCO. First, Greece recognised Albania.[50] This was particularly annoying to the British government, which had broken off relations in 1949, following the sinking (by a mine) of a British naval vessel. Greece also began improving relations with Romania, Bulgaria and Yugoslavia. Pattakos even told the British ambassador that 'the Greeks were at once cold-shouldered and taken for granted by some members of NATO, and that it might be no bad thing if the impression were created that she had something else to fall back on.'[51]

THE GRIVAS FACTOR

To say that Grivas was simply an extreme nationalist who would stop at nothing to achieve *enosis*, and that he was a puppet of the extreme elements of the Junta, is to paint too simplistic a picture. He had always tended to pursue an independent line, and was a strong and overt supporter of the king; but there is absolutely no evidence that he colluded in attempts to assassinate Makarios.[52] The most he had in common with the Junta as a whole was his anti-communism and (with parts of the Junta), his wish for complete *enosis*. Certainly, he wished to remove Makarios from power, if he could not persuade him to toe his line.

Conversely, Makarios was apparently even prepared to work with Grivas and give him a place in his government, provided he had him 'under his thumb'.[53] When Grivas landed in Cyprus, Makarios' principal concern was to ascertain Grivas' precise aims and intended methods. Were Grivas to engage in a campaign of clandestine activity, Makarios made it plain that he would hit back hard, since such activity would 'give the Turks a perfect card of entry'.[54] Two months later, it was clear that Grivas was a problem, when Makarios told the British high commissioner that money from Greece was being used to finance *enosist*, pro-Grivas newspapers, and that Greek officers in Cyprus were openly taking a pro-Grivas line. Significantly, Makarios added that the Greek government's ambivalence had put him in a very delicate position.[55] Makarios' major concern was that Grivas' policy had become double-*enosis*/partition; but that even if this were not so, what Grivas did would in practice lead in that direction.[56] Makarios' medium-term aims were in direct conflict with those of Grivas: an independent, unitary state under his own ultimate control, with *enosis* postponed indefinitely. Double-*enosis* was anathema to him, and in this, he was supported not only by the Soviet Union and the United Nations, but, interestingly, by France.[57] France had angered Britain by giving Cyprus permission to set up a powerful relay station.[58]

While Grivas was strongly anti-communist, so, it must be recalled, was Makarios.[59] The big difference was that Makarios was a skilful politician, who needed the support of the Cypriot left-wing parties and of Moscow. Although Grivas had the strong support of a hard core of nationalist *enosists* and the leadership of the National Guard, who were Greek nationals, Makarios' support was far more widespread.[60] From that viewpoint, Grivas was more of a thorn in the side – albeit a dangerous one – than a serious political challenge to Makarios. The British government was not by now as hostile towards General Grivas as is often thought. Instead, the Foreign and Commonwealth Office was keen to keep its options open, should he actually come to power overtly in Cyprus. Grivas in fact communicated secretly with the British High Commission. He even sent a message via a right-hand man, Eliades, which stated that should Britain help him achieve *enosis*, the British bases 'would be safe because they would be used for the defence of the free world'.[61] The British high commissioner's attitude towards the secret contacts with Grivas are revealing of the British backstage approach:

> We are confronted with a potentially violent situation in Cyprus, which could have a direct effect on British interests here. Not only is it possible that we may one day find ourselves obliged to deal openly with Grivas, but it is already important at this stage to encourage him, so far as possible, to keep a relatively open mind about the future of the Sovereign Base Areas.[62]

THE 'RED FACTOR'

It can safely be said that, by 1971, most of the Greek government, the Turkish government and the US government were virulently against Makarios. British policy was still to 'keep out'. This was even justified by a private admission that British 'direct involvement' in helping Makarios present his 'Thirteen Points' in 1963 had contributed to the intercommunal troubles.[63]

The British high commissioner suggested to the FCO that there were three options:

> a. to pursue an active diplomacy to preserve the Cyprus Republic, but not necessarily Archbishop Makarios as president;
> b. If you can't beat them, join them. That is to say, if there is to be a carve-up, we could at least make sure discreetly that the job is done in a way that does not jeopardise our interests on the island. The danger is that someone like Grivas might try to use our interests (particularly the Eastern SBA-Dhekelia, and Agios Nikolaus-complex) as a pawn in the very process that would ensue;
> c. Stand back and hope for the best.[64]

British policy by now appeared to be tending towards the third option, just as a military-inspired change of regime had taken place in Turkey, leading to a sudden superficial temporary warming of Graeco–Turkish relations. The Turkish prime minister even stated that the Cyprus problem was insignificant compared with the importance of Turko–Greek relations.[65] The Turkish polity however was not wholly rational, and despite the assurance given by the prime minister to the Greek ambassador in Ankara that the Greek Orthodox seminary on the island of Halki (Heybeli) was safe, the education minister closed it down a few days later. It was significant that the education minister was a former army colonel closely associated with the Turkish military coup in 1960.[66]

Makarios by now realised that the pressure was mounting at an increasing tempo, and he again played the Soviet card by visiting Moscow for eight days in June, to appeal for help, whereupon the Soviets called for, *inter alia*, the removal of all foreign troops and the abolition of all foreign bases. Crucially, Makarios backed this position, thereby sending cold war shivers down British and American governmental spines. It would not be unreasonable to think that, perversely, the British Secret Service, not to mention the CIA, might by then have been happy with Grivas' activities.

In the meantime, the intercommunal talks dragged on: on the one hand, Makarios refused Greek demands to make more concessions to the Turkish Cypriots while, on the other, the Turkish side continued to insist on complete autonomy.[67] Perspicaciously and, as it turned out, accurately, the British high commissioner wrote:

> Although Makarios remains supremely self-confident and believes that time is on his side, the threat of a Turkish invasion remains. The backdrop of the intercommunal talks, which have been the symbol of the benign stalemate which has suited our interests so well for the past three years, obliges us to face the prospect that this stalemate may now be turning malignant.[68]

It was clearly the Soviet factor which helped Makarios to fend off the pressure on him to agree to a solution, which he believed would be tantamount to double-*enosis*, and thereby be the end of the independent, unitary state that he so cherished. Another, perhaps unwelcome factor, was Soviet activity in Egypt where, following the death of Nasser, the Soviet Union was trying to maintain and further increase its influence. This led to speculation that the Soviet Union might try to conclude a treaty with Cyprus (as well as with Malta, which had already started pressuring the British to remove their naval base). With US worries about the defence of Israel, Cyprus was becoming increasingly important, as was Turkey, which had, under US guidance, built up secret military intelligence with Israel in the 1950s, culminating in a secret military pact in 1958.[69] Despite the vicissitudes of anti-US and -Israel agitation among Turkish radicals in the 1960s, the 'strategic axis' remained in place, and in 1971, the Turkish prime minister even issued a statement that Greece and Israel were its only valid allies in the region![70] The cold war tension was rising in the region, while Greece was cultivating better relations with Libya and Egypt, both avowed enemies of Israel.[71]

BEFORE THE SECOND TURKISH INVASION

The evidence examined thus far, gleaned mainly from government documents released up to 1973, strongly suggests that by the end of 1972, the situation under the surface was volatile, and that it was only a question of time before a serious crisis occurred. The Turkish Cypriot response to the return of Grivas, for example, had been to speed up the creation of an 'irregular' army, of whom there were estimated to be some 10,000 by the end of August 1971. There were occasional flare-ups, such as the detention of a busload of Turkish Cypriot fighters, and the taking of Greek Cypriot hostages as a reprisal.[72] The British high commissioner to Nicosia concluded in 1972 that the 'unconstitutional administration had many of the characteristics of a Government responsible for something very like a state within a state', and that its consolidation had accelerated in 1972. He added, ominously, that if the intercommunal talks failed, a Turkish Cypriot attempt to achieve international status for the administration and Greek Cypriot reactions could lead to a major crisis.[73] The death of Pipinelis, respected by all, had been a severe blow to stability, leading to more behind-the-scenes radicalisation in the Junta. The British ambassador to Greece wrote in 1972 that the possibility of a further coup by junior officers on 'Nasserite' lines could not be altogether discounted.[74] Meanwhile, the volatile nature of Turkish politics and military interference in political life also detracted from cohesion of policy. Nor was the influence of Kissinger a stabilising factor, as was to be shown.

The immediate parties, the Cypriots themselves, also had their hands tied, the Greek Cypriots by Makarios and the Turkish Cypriots by the Turkish establishment:

> Undoubtedly the most able and dove-like leaders to emerge are Glafcos Clerides on the Greek side and Rauf Denktash on the Turkish side. If the negotiations were left to these two men, it is probable that an early solution or at any rate a modus vivendi, could be reached [...] In the last resort the authorities in Ankara undoubtedly run the Turkish–Cypriot Administration in both its civilian and military aspects (though these may not always pull the same way). The Turkish Government underpins the Turkish Cypriot administration

by supplying armed forces and subsidies of about 7 million pounds a year. The key to a continuation of the benign stalemate probably lies more in Ankara than in Athens or Nicosia [...] The division between Greeks and Turks in Cyprus is historical, religious, linguistic, but not racial. To the outside observer it is difficult on sight to tell a Greek from a Turk. The division is unhappily also becoming geographical and economic. The *de facto* partition of Cyprus now in its sixth year means that there is a danger of perpetuating the segmentation of Turkish Cypriots into urban ghetto areas and rural slums as second-class citizens politically and economically, with the minimum of intermixing. This in turn means that the younger generation of Greeks and Turks are educated separately and brought up to regard one another as enemies waiting to commit genocide.[75]

6 Invasion and Cementing Division

The first fact that needs to be grasped about Cyprus is that although there is a Cyprus state and a government of Cyprus, which is a member of the United Nations and of the Commonwealth, there is no Cypriot nation and there are in fact two Cypriot administrations.[1]

INTRODUCTION

By the end of 1972, there was no love lost between Archbishop Makarios on the one hand, and Washington, Athens, Ankara and, to a lesser extent, London, on the other. Makarios relied to a considerable extent on his skilful exploitation of the Soviet factor (he had visited Moscow) and on the undoubted charisma and respect that he commanded, both in Cyprus and internationally.

The Junta was becoming increasingly unstable, due mainly to foreign policy differences between Papadopoulos and the chief of the Military Police, Ioannidis, described by a leading Junta member as 'having always had great influence'.[2]

The two-stage Turkish invasion of Cyprus in the Summer of 1974 was the culmination of ten years of planning by various US governmental sectors, initiated with the 'Ball/Acheson' plan for double *enosis* in 1964 (see Chapter Three), in secret connivance with the Turkish armed forces, with the British government looking on, anxious only to ensure the integrity of its sovereign territory on Cyprus.

The essential ingredients of the climate that enabled Turkey to invade with impunity were: Ioannidis himself; confusion in US foreign policy formulation and implementation, brought on by the Watergate scandal, and, crucially, the Israeli factor. These ingredients fused into a fatal cocktail, which bedevilled an unstable Greek polity.

IOANNIDIS

Brigadier Dimitris Ioannidis was one of the original conspirators of the takeover of 1967,[3] whose power increased when the moderate and urbane foreign minister, Pipinelis, died (see Chapter Five). He was an uncompromising *enosist*, known to have wanted to attack the Turkish Cypriots in the 1960s,[4] and dealt essentially with the CIA, with whom he had close links.[5] Crucially, Ioannidis controlled EOKA B, even while Grivas was still alive,[6] and was supported by CIA funding, in the hope of undermining Makarios,[7] who was to outlaw EOKA B. Grivas was thus sidelined by the rumbustious Ioannidis. Following Ioannidis' takeover (see below), the latter dealt exclusively with the CIA, causing a dysfunction in normal diplomatic procedure, since the CIA did not always inform the US ambassador, Tasca, of their clandestine dealings with Ioannidis.[8] Formally, Tasca only dealt with the front men of the regime. US policy towards Greece and Cyprus was itself becoming increasingly inconsistent and muddled.

THE US MUDDLE AND THE KISSINGER CIA FACTOR

The Watergate scandal, which broke in 1973 and increasingly paralysed the US administration, culminated in President Nixon's resignation only one week before the Ioannidis-inspired coup in Cyprus that gave Turkey the reason to invade. The period up to the invasion is particularly murky in terms of the involvement of Kissinger and the CIA, both in Ioannidis' takeover of the Junta and in the coup in Cyprus. We have already seen how German and British diplomats were worried about Kissinger's way of conducting foreign affairs, as early as 1971. As matters became increasingly confused in Washington, Kissinger was becoming a one-man band in crucial foreign policy questions. Significantly, on becoming secretary of state in 1973, he decided to retain his position of national security adviser, thus retaining his chairmanship of the 'Forty Committee', which considered and approved covert actions by the CIA.[9] According to Pattakos, it was Kissinger who encouraged Ioannidis to try and get rid of Makarios, through the coup.[10]

At any event, apart from the 'Watergate-Kissinger' factor, the US embassy in Athens itself, with its huge CIA contingent, did not seem to be functioning smoothly. As we have seen, Tasca was not fully informed about all important developments in the Junta, but there was also considerable disagreement between Tasca and a political officer, Keely, who was later to become ambassador. Tasca was a political appointee, while Keely was a career diplomat. The former supported the Junta, at least until Ioannidis took control, while Keely disagreed with him. Thus the State Department in Washington received conflicting reports about the obviously volatile situation in Greece.[11]

As so often in public diplomacy, everything superficially was satisfactory, with the US government publicly encouraging the Junta to return to democracy, but with Kissinger 'in no hurry' to get rid of the Junta,[12] in a country where the CIA 'were into everything'.[13] While America's grand strategy was to restore democracy, the tactics employed tended to favour the Junta, which was of course ideologically, and rather naively, as anti-communist as the army of CIA operatives and their Greek informers, who were more concerned with America's immediate interests. The former prime minister, Karamanlis, in exile in Paris, summed up US foreign policy towards Greece in a letter, where he referred to confusion in US policy replicating itself in Greece:

> I don't know whether there is an American policy vis-à-vis Greek affairs; but if there is, it is incoherent enough to enhance the confusion in which our country is in danger of drowning.[14]

THE ISRAELI CONNECTION

America was becoming increasingly concerned with Israel's security, as the Soviet Union was re-arming Israel's enemies, and Dom Mintoff, the independent-minded Maltese leader, was having the British bases on that island removed. Thus far, the Junta had been cooperative vis-à-vis American defence strategy, signing a five-year agreement in January 1973 for port facilities for the Sixth Fleet. This annoyed the Arab countries, which Greece placated by assuring them of their traditional ties of friendship and continuing to refuse to recognise Israel. (Greece had never fully recognised Israel.)

A crucial point was reached with the Yom Kippur war, when Egyptian forces attacked Israeli forces on 6 October 1973. America asked the Greek government for permission to use the facilities at Elefsina Air Base to fly military supplies to Israel, but were politely rebuffed on the grounds that such action was 'incompatible with NATO's purpose'.[15] Although other European countries also denied the USA the use of facilities, the proximity of Greece to Israel made matters more poignant in terms of US–Greek relations, particularly since Britain (Edward Heath) had denied the use of its bases on Cyprus to the USA. Kissinger was apoplectic.[16]

Cyprus was by now of major strategic importance to the USA for the defence of Israel, as was Turkish–Israeli military cooperation, and Kissinger was clearly trying to engineer the removal of Makarios and the installation of a NATO/US friendly government in Cyprus, whether by a US-friendly government in Athens forcing union with Cyprus, or by a Turkish invasion of sufficient territory to ensure facilities for protecting Israel. This was very much in line with Kissinger's pro-Israel and -Turkey strategy of using Cyprus as a 'staging area for the Middle East'.[17] The situation is the same today. Former Greek prime minister Constantinos Mitsotakis agrees that the USA wants Cyprus to play a role in Israel's defence;[18] journalist Elias Demetracopoulos also says that Cyprus is important to Israel's defence.[19]

17 NOVEMBER

While Makarios was infuriating Ioannidis by outmanoeuvring EOKA B, the political sands were shifting dangerously in Athens. In the summer of 1973, Papadopoulos was already attempting, perhaps desperately, to pave the way for free elections by declaring a republic, becoming president, appointing a new government, under Spiros Markezinis, and announcing elections, to be held early in 1974. To this end, on 8 October 1973, the Junta resigned pending elections. The Yom Kippur war ended on 11 November, and six days later the infamous anti-Junta riots took place, resulting in the killing of several Greek students by the Greek army at the Athens Polytechnic, facilitating the backstage takeover by Ioannidis, and the end of any chance of a return to democracy for the foreseeable future.

Some comment on recently released documents is useful here, to give some of the flavour of the vexed year 1973. One factor was the increasingly intrusive US policy towards Cyprus. In February, the US embassy in London expressed their displeasure that the British ambassador in Athens, Hooper, had spoken to the Greek government about Cyprus without consulting the USA. The Foreign Office actually apologised for not following previous practice.[20] Betraying a slight hint of tension in the UK–US 'special relationship', particularly over arms sales, the FCO wrote:

> b) Co-operation between British and Greek armed forces is good though inevitably overshadowed by the US/Greek military 'special relationship;'
> c) Our prospects for major arms sales remain poorish. The Americans still remain the major suppliers [...][21]

There were also considerable tensions within the Junta, particularly following Papadopoulos' liberalisation measures, which make the Ioannidis coup at the end of November look odd, especially since the US and British governments appeared to support the Markezinis government,[22] as did even the 'exiled' Karamanlis. Indeed, the latter even told Tom Pappas (a Greek–American tycoon who had the ESSO concession and a number of other very profitable franchises in Greece, subscribed heavily to Nixon's campaign fund and was the hate-figure of the anti-American left) that he entirely approved of Markezinis' accepting office, and wished him luck.[23]

The 17 November riots, curious in view of the impending elections and the release of political prisoners, and the subsequent Ioannidis coup, certainly put the cat among the pigeons. The British ambassador takes up the story:

> 2. When the violence started late on 16 November, it was centred around the Polytechnic University and the majority of the demonstrations were students. They were joined from early on 17 November by other, probably tougher, elements from outside with more extreme political views, described by the government as 'anarchists.' It is believed that there was a split among the students, the more militant favouring a break-out from the Polytechnic and its immediate vicinity, the occupation of public buildings, joint action by students and workers, and so on. This view prevailed, and the confrontation escalated and became more violent. The police were apparently unable to control the situation. The army was called in and martial law declared.

3. It is not clear what part if any the former parliamentary opposition has taken in the organisation of the demonstrations or to what extent they are responsible for the direction they have taken. However they have openly encouraged the students, well knowing that this could lead to violence, and in private claim credit for what has happened. They have made use of the students in pursuing a deliberate policy of trying to provoke the government into repressive action which would put an end to the Markezinis programme. *They have in large measure got what they wanted: and they must now – as the president has said – accept responsibility for their actions* [author's italics].
4. There is little doubt that what began as primarily a student movement was later to a large extent infiltrated by non-student elements, some of them of the extreme left.[24]

At any rate, the Ioannidis coup resulted in the hurried formation of a mediocre government on 26 November. At lunch with the British ambassador, the ousted Markezinis described the new prime minister, Androutsopoulos, as a 'third rate Chicago lawyer',[25] while the ambassador wrote that according to Athenian gossip, he 'is or was an agent of the CIA' and that there was predictable speculation that the Americans were in some way connected with the coup.[26]
 Whatever the gossip, Markezinis' prediction that discontent would find expression in violent anti-Americanism and that 'the Army's cohesion and discipline would go'[27] was proven accurate. Towards the end of the year, the American and British governments were troubled by dissension and instability in Greece affecting NATO interests. According to the British ambassador, the regime was 'not yet settled in and xenophobic elements in the new group of officers thought to be in charge and in the higher ranks'[28] might well overreact to hostile declarations from abroad. Significantly, the British ambassador wrote:

There is strong anti-American feeling here. This is not confined to the regime and for most Greeks NATO is loosely identified with the United States. *If the new regime reacted against criticism by asserting Greece's national independence and threatening to reduce the facilities enjoyed by NATO and the US here, they might get considerable support which they badly need* [my emphasis].[29]

For the USA, it was, at least overtly, 'business as usual' with the new government, but matters became more confused than before. Ioannidis began his more overt role as Greece's strong-man by questioning the value of Greece's defence ties with the USA and suggesting an aid programme in exchange for the USA maintaining its Greek bases.[30] As head of the military police, he did not deal with the US ambassador, who had, under diplomatic protocol, to deal with the government under Ioannidis' de facto control. This hardly facilitated matters, and gave a freer hand to the CIA's covert dealings with the strong-man. As the Watergate crisis rumbled on and Kissinger silently flexed his geopolitical muscles, the State Department, Pentagon, CIA, Congress and Senate vied with each other in the crisis-solving stakes.[31]

Elias Demetracopoulos (see above) says that Washington allowed Papadopoulos to fall. It appears, however, that the Americans then began to worry about the new behind-the-scenes strong-man. At a meeting called by Kissinger on 20 March 1974, the US ambassador, Tasca, made his concerns about the new government clear, and pushed for his government to make a public statement expressing the hope that democracy would be restored in Greece. Kissinger expediently but cleverly left the meeting open-ended, with no final decision.[32] He was quite happy to sit and await the impending chaos, probably having his own agenda.

THE INVASION

Since the vital documents are unavailable, it cannot at present be stated with certainty that Kissinger colluded with the Turkish government to occasion an invasion of Cyprus or, possibly, an agreement between Greece and Turkey following the removal of Makarios by Ioannidis. Nevertheless, the ingredients for the division of Cyprus were already being mixed. The Turkish government was undoubtedly aware of Ioannidis' intentions to get rid of Makarios and to achieve *enosis*, and a Greek–Turkish crisis soon occurred over oil exploration rights, which overlapped with the Turkish invasion.[33]

Following the death of Grivas in January 1974, which gave Ioannidis a more direct entrée into Cyprus, Makarios sensed that it would not be long before a coup was mounted against him.[34] The US government – and Kissinger – were certainly aware of the likelihood of one, as a report in the (US) *National Intelligence Daily* in June 1974 made clear.[35] Kissinger waited three weeks before responding, by approving an instruction to Tasca to tell Ioannidis that the USA opposed any 'adventure in Cyprus'. The State Department was aware that, under diplomatic protocol, Tasca could not directly warn Ioannidis, who was therefore not fully apprised of the apparent US opposition to a coup against Makarios. Kissinger, of course, as national security adviser and secretary of state, was fully aware of the impending coup, although he was extremely economical with the truth about this later.[36]

The stakes rose, while the CIA continued to finance EOKA B to get rid of the 'Castro of the Mediterranean'.[37] The Cypriot National Guard (staffed mainly by Greek officers) became the object of a tug of war between Makarios and Ioannidis, resulting in the former issuing a public letter to the Junta on 3 July, accusing the latter of plotting to overthrow him, and demanding that Athens recall its officers. Provocatively, he concluded:

> I am not a district governor appointed by the Greek government, but the elected leader of a great section of Hellenism, and as such I demand appropriate treatment from the mother country.[38]

The coup went ahead on 15 July, but, to Kissinger's fury, Makarios escaped, with British help, to the British base at Akrotiri, from where he was sent on to Malta and then London, where he arrived on 17 July. Curiously, however, on arrival in Malta, he was obliged to stay the night because of an alleged technical problem with the British military aircraft. In fact, the British high commissioner in Valletta received an instruction from the Foreign and Commonwealth Office to delay Makarios' arrival in London. A problem with the engine was concocted, and Makarios, as he was called off the aeroplane unexpectedly, to stay the night, commented: 'Another triumph for British diplomacy!'[39] *The likelihood is that the USA wanted to talk to the British before Makarios did, and that the British government complied.*

Kissinger's dual-track diplomacy now became more obvious. While the fighting between pro-Makarios and pro-Ioannidis forces continued (Nicos Sampson had been hurriedly found from a number of 'candidates' to take over as president), Turkey put the finishing touches to its invasion preparations. The US ambassador actually received Sampson's foreign minister, thus setting in motion official US recognition of the putschists.

The USA's refusal to denounce the Sampson regime strengthened Turkey's arguments for intervening. The Turkish prime minister, Ecevit, flew to London on 17 July, and suggested the landing of a token force on Cyprus to force Sampson to resign. He also asked to use the British base at Akrotiri, but was politely rebuffed. Kissinger's delaying tactics continued, with the appointment of Sisco, who shuttled between Ankara and Athens trying to prevent a major confrontation between Greece and Turkey. On 20 July, Turkey invaded, apparently to restore the constitution, setting up a bridgehead, and then beginning a creeping invasion. By the time of a UN-agreed ceasefire, initially ignored by Turkey, the Turkish armed forces had captured Kyrenia, part of Nicosia and some surrounding territory.

America was naturally anxious to avoid a full-scale war between Greece and Turkey, which would at the time have served Soviet interests by destroying NATO's southern flank; but at the same time Kissinger wished the Turks to consolidate their position on Cyprus following the ceasefire, and during the talks that followed, to prepare to take over more territory.[40]

To taste the flavour of how close all-out war was, let us turn to Pattakos' own account. The moment the Sampson coup took place, the military attaché at the Greek embassy in London, Perdikis, sent repeated warnings to the chief of the Greek armed forces, Bonanos, about the forthcoming Turkish invasion, and a Greek brigadier serving at NATO headquarters in Izmir, Sotiriadis, was warned by the Americans. He informed Bonanos on 18 July, who 'ignored the warnings', and did not reinforce the Cypriot National Guard; in fact, 700 experienced members of the Greek contingent on Cyprus were replaced with conscripts.

The Ioannidis government ordered a partial call-up to begin at 9 a.m. on 20 July, as the Turkish army was landing in Cyprus; but at 11 a.m. Bonanos ordered a general call-up, thus causing considerable confusion. On 21 July, the Greek president (Gizikis), Ioannidis, Bonanos and the chiefs of the army, navy and air force, Galatzanos, Arapakis and Papanikolau, met, and decided that the following day, under Bonanos' supervision, the Greek armed forces would

    a. begin shooting in Thrace, to divert Turkish attention;
    b. sink the Turkish landing craft outside Kyrenia and
    c. fly six Phantom jets from Crete to attack the Turkish forces in Cyprus.

All three chiefs then did precisely the opposite of what had been agreed, with the chief of the air force claiming that the Bulgarians were gathering on Greece's border, waiting to attack.[41]

Clearly, the Turkish invasion had come as a surprise to many, and one is inclined to wonder what secret reassurances may have been given to Ioannidis about getting rid of Makarios with impunity. It was the Kissinger factor that resulted in Bonanos stopping the agreed attacks. When Kissinger's envoy, Sisco, arrived in Athens on 20 July, he tried to see various members of the Junta, but was rebuffed. However, he did at least manage to find and see Bonanos and Arapakis. According to Pattakos, Sisco was heard to tell Bonanos to stop the attacks in exchange *for a promise that he would oblige the 'Turks to return to Turkey'*.[42] As regards the alleged threat from Bulgaria, the head of Greek intelligence, Stathopoulos, claimed that he had received this information 'from Anglo–US sources'. The Greek border force, however, denied that there was any Bulgarian build-up.[43]

Whatever the secret skullduggery behind the whole farrago of diplomatic double-dealing and breaches of the Greek Military Penal Code (high treason, desertion of post or mutiny), it was clear that Ioannidis had served his purpose, and lacked credibility. The Junta collapsed and the former premier, Karamanlis, returned from Paris to be sworn in as prime minister. At the same time, Sampson resigned, to be replaced by Clerides.

The US (Kissinger) attitude was to try to delay (re-)recognising Makarios, who was due in Washington on 22 July – at the invitation of Senator Fulbright. Since Sampson had not yet resigned, the State Department still only intended to describe Makarios as 'archbishop' rather than president. By the 22nd, however, Kissinger was forced to receive him in his official capacity, to his chagrin.[44]

Kissinger had had the opportunity to prevent a Turkish invasion. On 17 July, Elias Demetracopoulos had visited Fulbright, chairman of the Senate Foreign Relations Committee, and suggested that sending the Sixth Fleet on a goodwill visit to Cyprus would prevent the Turks from invading. Fulbright was impressed enough to put the idea to Kissinger, who refused to do anything, on the grounds that he could not be seen to be interfering in Greek affairs. Demetracopoulos' idea was, however, sound, since the Turkish armed forces would not have dared to invade and risk bombing an American ship, as the Israelis had done during the Six Day War, killing thirty-four sailors aboard the USS Liberty.[45] Kissinger was later to claim that he was prevented and distracted by Watergate and the death-throes of the Nixon presidency from 'taking a timely informed interest in the crucial triangle of Greece, Turkey and Cyprus'.[46] To some, Kissinger must seem to place more emphasis on power than ethics. Much credence is lent to this, when one considers that senior diplomats' misgivings about Kissinger in 1972 were replicated and indeed enhanced in 1973. For example, the minister of the British embassy in Washington wrote:

> a lot of the trouble we have run into must be attributed to Kissinger's highly idiosyncratic way of doing business [...] What I find difficult to judge is where the President ends and Kissinger begins.[47]

More was to come: in the summer of 1973, British prime minister Edward Heath actually asked to study Kissinger's books. The FCO prepared a memorandum referring to Kissinger's strange personality, in which he was referred to as a 'romantic'. The British embassy scathingly qualified this, by writing:

> If to be romantic is to admire great men who by cynical and ruthless action changed the course of history, then he is a romantic. He is also a romantic in the sense of seeing himself cutting as brilliant and successful a figure as those whom he admires. But it is quite clear for example from what we hear of his remarks in private that he enjoys making a cynical analysis of other people's capacities and motives, and is introspective and aware of the fact that he may have an incipient *folie de grandeur*.[48]

This perceived *folie* was now to wreak havoc, as the crisis continued.

FOREDOOMED CONFERENCES AND TURKISH EXPANSION

There now followed two conferences in Geneva, the first involving only the foreign ministers of the Guarantor Powers, starting on 25 July. It ended on 30 July, with agreement on a ceasefire and the dates for a new conference, to start on 8 August, and to include the Greek and Turkish Cypriot representatives, Clerides and Denktash. By the time of this second conference, Turkey had subtly further consolidated its position.

The second conference began bitterly, only the day before President Nixon resigned, leaving even more power to Kissinger in foreign affairs. Recriminations were made by both sides. Plans were put forward and rejected. The basic problem was that the Turkish side wanted far more autonomy than the Greek side was prepared to grant, the latter preferring to use the 1960 constitution as a starting point, while the Turkish side considered that it had proved to be unworkable.[49] When Clerides asked for thirty-six hours to consider a Turkish proposal, the Turkish side walked out. It was 2.25 a.m. on 14 August. The Turkish foreign minister, Gunesh, telephoned Ecevit and used the coded words: 'My daughter is going on holiday.' At 4.30 a.m., the Turkish armed forces attacked again.[50]

It would be naive not to think that Turkey had used the conferences simply to gain time to consolidate its military build-up. Certainly, Tom McNally, the British foreign secretary's political adviser, thought so.[51] Crucially, however, Kissinger was also using the time to help Turkey fulfil its objectives. On the very day that Turkey again attacked, a senior State Department official wrote to Kissinger:

> In fact, as has always been true, the only conceivable modus vivendi will have to rest on a de facto division of the island, whatever the form, [...] while the Soviets can serve as a bogey, we must keep them at arm's length. They cannot become the arbiter between US allies. Their interests differ drastically from ours: we want a modus vivendi between Greece and Turkey, they want a non-aligned Cyprus, preferably with Greece or Turkey or both disaffected from NATO. Thus, we should

– urgently try to contain Greek reaction

– bluntly tell the Turks that they must stop, today, tomorrow at the latest;

– warn the Turks that Greece is rapidly moving leftward;

– send high-level US man to exert continuing direct influence on Karamanlis;

– *assuming the Turks quickly take Famagusta, privately assure Turks we will get them a solution involving one third of island, within some kind of federal arrangement* [my emphasis];

– assure Greeks we will contain Turk demands, and allow no additional enclaves etc. [...].[52]

Apart from the obviously naive, and curiously irrelevant, remark about warning the Turks about Greece rapidly moving leftward, as if that would have figured seriously in immediate Turkish calculations, the memo is chilling in that it demonstrates that the USA was happy to condone Turkey occupying (at least) one third of Cyprus.

Turkey stopped its advance on 18 August, having achieved its objectives. The invasion was a brutal affair. There were atrocities on both sides (but more by the Turks), 200,000 Greek Cypriots were 'ethnically cleansed', leaving for the un-occupied part of Cyprus, while most of the Turkish Cypriots in the South went north, but not immediately. Today, only a few hundred Turkish Cypriots remain in the South, 'balanced' by a few hundred Greek Cypriots in the North. The final death toll was put at 4,000 Greek Cypriots killed and almost 1,000 Turkish Cypriots dead or missing, with 1,600 Greek Cypriots missing to this day.[53] Despite decades of UN-sponsored 'intercommunal negotiations', beginning in 1965, and continuing as this is being written, reunification of the island has become more and more of a pipedream, with the negotiations a necessary façade for public consumption, while the poker players continue their game.

THE SOVIET FACTOR

There has been much speculation about Soviet policy in the period up to the invasion, but until the former Soviet archives are fully opened, it is not easy to pronounce with reasonable certitude on the precise Soviet attitude. It is, however, interesting that at the UN Security Council meeting on 16 and 17 August 1974, the Soviet delegate, while blaming the Greek Junta, the USA and 'certain NATO circles' for trying to liquidate the Cypriot state and turn the island into a military base, did not criticise Turkey.[54] This of course made sense, given the USSR's policy of improving relations with Turkey so as to irritate NATO. Indeed, the USSR even delayed the Security Council resolution calling for a ceasefire immediately following the invasion, while Ecevit remarked that the Soviet Union had tried to be objective and constructive.[55]

Intriguingly, the Soviet Union, although it favoured a non-aligned, independent Cyprus, free of foreign influence, and therefore supported Makarios, also had good relations with the Athens Junta, at least according to Yiannis Marinos, former editor of *Economicos Tachidromos* and currently a Member of the European Parliament. Apart from asserting that the USSR favoured the Junta, he says that East Germany even withdrew advertising from his magazine because it was critical of the Junta.[56]

Obviously, as the other superpower, the USSR needed to maintain good relations with lesser powers, with the aim of influencing them and having a say commensurate with its power in international affairs. It probably supported Papadopoulos' rapprochement with the Bulgarians and Yugoslavs, to irritate the USA, but also wished to influence Turkey and sell it arms during the US embargo imposed after the invasion.[57] Kissinger also claimed that the Soviet Union had told Turkey to invade, much to one writer's disbelief.[58] Perhaps, however, Kissinger's claim is not as ludicrous as it seems: the Soviet Union was against *enosis*, since this would have strengthened NATO's southern flank to its detriment and have meant the end of Cyprus as an independent, non-aligned state. When it considered the possibility of Turkey perhaps letting the Sampson coup go ahead, to get rid of Makarios, and then coming to a *modus vivendi* with the Junta, it realised that one way to maintain some influence was to allow an invasion that would keep the pot boiling around Cyprus, Greece and Turkey. In this sense, although for differing motives, Kissinger's and Moscow's aims may have cynically coincided. Kissinger recently wrote that the Cyprus issue was settled in 1974.[59] That chilling revelation, perhaps a weak attempt to admit the truth about his actions, speaks volumes.

BRITISH INDIGNATION

Although the British perspective will be considered in the following section, it is important to note that the British government was at loggerheads with Turkey at the Geneva negotiations, insisting on using the 1960 Constitution of Cyprus as a starting point, to the Turkish delegation's annoyance. After the event, Callaghan admitted that Britain had had a legal obligation to take action.[60] However, we have seen in Chapter Four how inactive Britain had already chosen to be on the question of legalities, and in Chapter Three, how British troops would 'retire into base' if Turkey invaded. There is little reason to suppose that by 1974, Britain would do anything other than express public disapproval, while indulging in slipstream diplomacy, with the USA taking the lead, whatever the speculation about hypothetical British action. Thus, although British forces would have defended *themselves* against a Turkish attack, British policy was not predicated on defending the integrity of Cyprus itself, but rather to have its troops 'retire into base'. British policy had become one of keeping as low a profile as possible. Certainly, Britain was thrust into the uncomfortable limelight in 1974, but the bases were all that mattered. Had Britain – at least, publicly – expressed doubts about the Cyprus constitution, this would undoubtedly have had legal repercussions on its claim to the bases, and have been exploited by the Soviet Union. The FCO had in fact already admitted (see Chapter Seven) that anything which called into question the 1960 settlement could expose Britain to pressure on her moral right to hang on to the Sovereign Base Areas.

As for the contention that James Callaghan told an MP, 'We nearly went to war with Turkey,'[61] the former would like this author to note that 'the words in quotation marks are not his words, and should not be attributed to him either directly or indirectly.'[62]

CURRENT VOLATILITY

Although the period from 1974 until now cannot be studied incisively from a diplomatic historical viewpoint, owing to the dearth of government documentary evidence, it has been characterised essentially by the de facto consolidation of what was first mooted in 1964 by the USA, with the Ball/Acheson plan, and realised in 1974 – at least in terms of the division of Cyprus. While the intercommunal negotiations, sponsored by the United Nations, have continued for presentational purposes, the division of the island has deepened, with the importation into occupied Cyprus of 100,000 mainland settlers and the declaration of a state in the North, recognised only by Turkey. Over half the original Turkish Cypriot population has left.

Cyprus' entry into the European Union, before a serious solution to the island's division, has created frenetic behind-the-scenes activity, with the USA, Britain and Turkey believing that their interests could be threatened. These issues will be analysed in the coming pages, when we consider the standpoints of the different *partis pris*.

In conclusion, it is not unreasonable to assume that policy formulation on the Cyprus issue, with its implications for Greek–Turkish, EU–Turkish and US–EU relations, not to mention NATO's role, in the current rather unstable international climate, is not dissimilar to the double-dealing and sloppy, imprecise diplomacy of the 1960s and 1970s that led to the Cyprus invasion. Indeed, perhaps the situation is even more volatile now, given the apparent lack of a balancing superpower, and political instability in Turkey. Before embarking on our final analysis of the whole issue and the possibility of conflict, let us now turn to the divergent viewpoints of the poker players.

PART II

The Poker Players

INTRODUCTION

A leading theme of this book, which should now be self-evident, is that Cyprus has been able to exercise only minimal influence over its own destiny, particularly since 1974, even though it gained its adulterated sovereignty in 1960. Like so many former colonies – and not only British – Cyprus began experiencing political difficulties upon independence, owing to a superficially imposed constitution that simply proved unworkable.

We have seen how, despite reasoned suggestions by senior British officials for union with Greece (as happened with Crete), the island soon fell prey to cold war strategic interests and to fanaticism, fuelled by nationalist-minded political groups in Greece, Turkey and Cyprus itself. Many of the problems were caused by external factors (for example, Britain's *divide et impera* tactic and secret collusion with the Turkish government). It is telling that in Greece (Thrace) there are today more than 100,000 Turkish-speaking Muslims, living side by side with Greek-speaking Christians, while in Cyprus this was also the case, until Britain 'defined the differences'. After 1963, the Greek Cypriots themselves exacerbated a situation originally engendered by outsiders,[1] although it has to be pointed out that the British high commissioner himself helped with Makarios' 'Thirteen Points'. From then on, the US interest increased exponentially owing to cold war 'needs', the fear of upsetting NATO's southern flank and the Arab–Israel dispute.

We shall now take a look at the positions of the major poker players around Cyprus, namely Britain, the USA, Turkey and Greece.

7　Britain: Hanging in There

Leopards don't change their spots.

INTRODUCTION

Britain's position regarding the Cyprus question is inextricably linked to its past position as the world's main colonial power and to its problematic transition to that of a middle-ranking country, albeit with interests which it considers to be both important and strategic. Maintaining these interests beyond their shelf life has proved to be difficult. As long ago as 1944, Keynes said: 'All our [Britain's] reflex actions are those of a rich man.'[1] It was – and is – Britain's close defence relationship with the USA that has helped it to pursue a foreign policy that has been variously described as 'slipstream diplomacy' or 'piggy-backing the USA'. This has enabled it to portray itself from time to time as America's most important ally, while at the same time keeping its foot in the EU door.[2] Thus, a former British politician decried Britain's 'obsessive determination to preserve the Anglo–American alliance as something exclusive, wanting to keep the US to herself, like a jealous lover'.[3] Although it would be jejune and simplistic to portray Britain as a simple extension of US foreign policy, it has certainly supported the USA on a number of occasions, while the EU and Russia have been lukewarm, to put it mildly. Examples of such support include the bombing of Libya by British-based US aircraft, whereas France refused even overflying rights; the continued bombing of Iraq despite French withdrawal from the 'no-fly zone' arrangement; the bombing of Yugoslavia; and, recently, Prime Minister Blair's 'shoulder to shoulder' support for President Bush's attack on Iraq. It is significant that although most of Britain's trade is with its EU partners, it invests principally in the USA, which is itself the source of most inward investment in the UK.[4] The most obvious manifestation of British–US togetherness in military-strategic matters is their common approach to Turkey and to the question of a putative European Army, on which we shall expand in Part III, as it impinges heavily on the Cyprus question. Although there have been crises of confidence between the US and British governments, such as the British prime minister Harold Wilson's refusal to accept a huge loan from the USA in return for military help in the Far East,[5] or when, as prime minister, Edward Heath refused to allow the USA to use the British bases on Cyprus during the Yom Kippur war, the close defence relationship continues, with Cyprus as a prime example, particularly as regards Turkey's EU aspirations.

Looking for morality in international relations is like looking for a needle in a haystack. It was the Wilson government that leased the island of Diego Garcia to the USA for fifty years, and forced the 2,000 British islanders to leave. It is thus naive to assume that the interests of the Cypriots themselves played a serious role in British calculations as the UK came under pressure. Britain's objective was to hang on through thick and thin, using the strategy argument whenever it could.

HISTORICAL CONTINUITY

Britain's – or, rather, England's – first stab at the strategic game over Cyprus was in 1191, when Richard Coeur de Lion took the island, only to sell it to the French Guy de Lusignan via the Knights Templar the following year. She did not get a look-in again until 1878. Britain's fear of Russia, the Crimean War, her concomitant support, particularly under Benjamin Disraeli, of the Ottoman Empire, and the opening of the Suez Canal in 1869, all led to Britain's acquisition of Cyprus, to strengthen her control over the eastern Mediterranean. The *enosist* phenomenon had existed at least since 1821, but did not manifest itself dramatically until the riots of 1931. In contrast to Grivas' EOKA 'explosion' in 1955, however, it was the help of the Greek statesman Eleftherios Venizelos, as well as the abandonment of the 1925 colonial constitution, that pushed the idea of union with Greece back under the surface. A Foreign Office official takes up the story in 1955, by comparing the years 1931 and 1955:

> In many respects the situation was similar to the present one [1955]. Cyprus was inflamed with *enosist* propaganda put out by the nationalist party of which the Church is the effective leader. Arms and explosives appeared in Cyprus and there was evidence to show that secret organisations in Greece were planning to send saboteurs and guerrilla organisers to the island. And the Athens press conducted an anti-British campaign, which surpassed in virulence (and absurdity) even the present one. But there were some important differences. There was no broadcasting and dissemination of propaganda of any organ of the Greek Government; and the Greek Government, in particular old Venizelos, then in his last premiership, preserved a remarkably correct attitude [...]. In a statement to the press on 23 October 1931, Monsieur Venizelos repeated his declaration that the Cypriot question did not exist between the Greek and British Governments but between the latter and the Cypriots.[6]

Thus it was certainly Venizelos himself who took *enosis* off the Greek agenda, obviously to the relief of the British government. In 1955, however, matters were very different. The decolonisation movement, US pressure, the Cypriot people – at least the Greek-speaking majority – galvanised by the dynamism of Makarios, an efficient guerrilla movement supported by both Greeks and Greek Cypriots, coupled with British rigidity, meant that no self-respecting Greek leader could 'do a Venizelos'. It is perhaps rather curious that when the British ambassador to Athens was instructed in April 1955 to make representations to the Greek government about its 'behaviour' over Cyprus, he was told to 'keep in mind' Britain's relations with the Greeks during the 1931 disorders, as if nothing had happened during the intervening twenty-four years. As we have seen, British representations had no effect, and British–Greek relations continued to deteriorate. Internationalisation of the dispute and US pressure eventually led to the 1960 settlement, whereby Britain was able to keep some of Cyprus, not as a colony, but as part of Britain, with, by this time, the support of the USA and the agreement of the Greek government. Turkey had been brought into the dispute and, from then on, the die for future dispute had been cast. Britain, the USA and unstable Greek and Turkish polities danced around a smouldering powder-keg of frustration and increasing polarisation that exploded into the troubles of 1963, leading to the beginning of the de facto division that exists today. Just as with the whole island up to 1957, Britain's sole intention was to hang on to what it had kept. Since then, Britain's – and then America's – objective has been to hang on to the British sovereign territory. Even when Britain subsequently considered, but then rejected, the idea of *enosis*, there was never any question of ceding the sovereign bases. In this sense, future *enosis*, whether 'single' or double, was only considered as a way of ensuring the maintaining of its territory on Cyprus. Thus Britain's position has always been consistent, in that it involved questions of strategy and territory.

NATO

Makarios has often been accused of ensuring that Cyprus would never join NATO, but this was after the outbreak of violence, the involvement of the UN and the US attempt to engineer a double-*enosis* NATO solution, which would have meant the end of Makarios' dream of a unitary Cyprus, *enosis* or no *enosis*. *It was in fact the British government which was opposed to Cyprus becoming a NATO member.* Although Greece and Turkey had concluded an agreement on 11 February 1959, agreeing to support Cyprus' entry into NATO (see Chapter Four), a brief submitted to the Cyprus Ministerial Committee in January 1960 made Britain's position absolutely clear:

> The only question referred for the consideration of Ministers is whether Cyprus should become a member of NATO and whether a NATO headquarters might be established in the island. There are substantial military arguments against Cyprus becoming a member of NATO [...] If Cyprus became a member of NATO, any dispute that may arise between Cyprus and either Turkey or the United Kingdom could be represented by the Russians as dissension within

the NATO alliance [...] Greece and Turkey are aware that the UK opposed their own admission to NATO in 1952.[7]

This line of thinking betrays a considerable lack of confidence in the very treaties that were being imposed on Makarios, and boded ill for the future. One could equally argue that NATO membership from the beginning would have introduced an element of stability into the complex and shaky arrangement. Yet a confident and stable government in Cyprus that was a NATO member could well have questioned the necessity – and the morality – of the British Sovereign Bases, and this must also have weighed – as it still does – on British policy considerations.

THE TREATIES

The modern Cypriot state was concocted out of the imposition of three treaties, agreed by the British, Greeks and Turks, with the USA in the background. The Cypriots played only a secondary role. As we have seen, the whole elaborate but shaky pack of cards collapsed, and the Cyprus government subsequently ceased to recognise the Treaties of Guarantee and Alliance as binding.

Britain's position has appeared inconsistent. As regards the Treaty of Guarantee, we have seen in Chapter Four how the foreign secretary claimed that Britain had no defence treaty with Cyprus, and was not therefore obliged to respond to an appeal by the Cyprus government. In contrast, Turkey supported its right of invasion by referring to Article IV of the Treaty, while Britain stood by. We have seen how, in effect, following a twisted and obscure debate within the Foreign Office, the question of Britain's responsibility regarding an invasion was shelved without a clear resolution, although it was admitted that *UN law overrode the Treaty of Guarantee.*

Yet four years later, when the Cyprus government was questioning the validity of the Treaty of Guarantee, the Foreign Office legal advisers were saying that *'we would not accept that any organ of the United Nations is competent to affect the validity of a Treaty in the way apparently suggested by the Cyprus Government.'*[8] Thus, in contrast to 1967, the British were taking a firm line with the Cyprus government, but chose not to argue *why* the UN was not competent in relation to the Treaty. The Cypriot government's view, conversely, was that since the UN resolutions on Cyprus began 'pouring in', UN law superseded the Treaty of Guarantee.

The lack of firm reasoning on the question of the Treaty of Guarantee betrays the extent to which the Treaty – and that of Establishment – were concocted essentially to ensure the preservation of the territory that Britain took from Cyprus, above all other considerations. The Foreign and Commonwealth Office's legal advisers were stating in 1971 that they had 'from time to time considered whether it was necessary to maintain our stand on the Treaty of Guarantee'. They continued:

We have so far concluded that it would be against our interests not to do so. I think that our reasons were the following: a) to accept the views of the Cyprus Government would damage our general posture on the sanctity of treaties i.e. on the question of the circumstances in which Treaties can be repudiated or can be regarded as having been invalidated. b) The various 1960 agreements [...] constituted an integral settlement, in effect a package deal. The abandonment of our position on the Treaty of Guarantee would thus undermine our position on the rest of the 1960 settlement. In particular, it might one day be found to have *prejudiced our position on the treaty of Establishment* as well. c) Even though our title to the Sovereign Base Areas does not depend on the Treaty of Guarantee or the Treaty of Establishment, the express provisions in those Treaties concerning the Sovereign Base Areas may still be of value to us in ensuring our untroubled occupation and use of the Areas. *Moreover, anything which called the 1960 settlement as a whole into question could expose us to pressure on our moral (as distinct from legal) right to hang on to the Areas.* [my italics] d) Whether or not we have a direct interest in maintaining the Treaty of Guarantee, we could not openly abandon it without gravely upsetting Turkey.[9]

It is clear that Britain's underlying consideration, whatever the circumstances, was not to do anything that might be construed as impinging on the question of the bases. Therefore, any questioning of any part of any of the three treaties of Guarantee, Establishment and Alliance respectively, was simply taboo, whatever private views there were about the continuing viability of the treaties.

SITTING BACK

The British government's essential objective for Cyprus was – and is – to distract attention from its bases, and to this end it increasingly adopted a low profile policy of non-interference in Cypriot affairs in the late 1960s and early 1970s. We saw in Chapter Five how Britain avoided activities appearing to support any of the political parties, and how, unlike the USA and Greece, it was exempt from criticism.[10] When the Cypriot former minister (Kyprianos) tried to open a dialogue with Britain on the treaties, Britain refused substantive discussions, again because of its bases: the Foreign Office official responsible for Cyprus wrote in 1971:

It is interesting that Mr. Kyprianos [sic] was prepared to exclude the Treaty of Establishment from this list of invalid treaties. He presumably did so on the *(correct) assumption that we are mainly concerned about our defence facilities.*[11] [my italics]

The British position in 1971 is best summed up in a Foreign Office letter:

In the view of the Cyprus Government the two Treaties have ceased to have validity, having been overlaid by events and a Resolution of the United Nations in 1964. We disagree on legal grounds; moreover, if we were to make any concession towards the Cyprus Government's point of view, we should face a political crisis with the Turks. We see no prospect of reconciling our position with the Cyprus Government and high-level discussion between us is likely only to highlight our disagreement. If the Greek and Turkish Governments manage to reach agreement on constitutional issues in Cyprus, the question of revising the 1960 Treaties will become actual. Meanwhile, we recommend that this is an issue better dodged if possible, at any rate at Prime Ministerial level.[12]

In 1974, the Treaty of Guarantee proved to be worthless to Cyprus. The Turkish Government was able legitimately to invoke Article IV when the Sampson coup occurred. But when, after the coup had failed, Turkey continued its action and expanded its territory, it was clear that, far from restoring constitutional order, and therefore supporting the interim president (Clerides), they had decided to establish their own state. The British government, despite its anger at the continuing Turkish action, simply watched as the Treaty of Guarantee, first invoked by Turkey, was then torn up. The US government, or, rather, Kissinger, as we have seen, was dictating the terms along with Turkey. It would be correct to assume that, despite the British government's private and even moral misgivings at that time and, possibly, today, the 'special relationship' – whatever the strains – is sacrosanct. So are the bases which, through thick and thin, have remained intact, unlike Kissinger's reputation.

CONCLUSION

Britain will not be able to dodge the question of the treaties, and, hence, keep a low profile on the question of its bases, much longer, given two recent and important factors: Cyprus' entry into the European Union and the (slow) evolution of the EU's Common Foreign and Security Policy. Given its distaste for a future supra-national army and the impact that this could have on Cyprus' whole constitutional arrangement, Britain has been coordinating its Cyprus policy ever more closely with those of the USA and Turkey; hence the agreement signed between Britain, the USA and Turkey in Ankara in December 2001 – without an EU mandate – attempting to guarantee Turkey a role in the future European Rapid Reaction Force (ERRF) and deny the force any role in the Aegean or around Cyprus. This is of course connected to the whole question of Cyprus' accession to the European Union and the Annan Plan (see Chapter Fifteen), which Britain supports very strongly, since, if implemented, it would weaken the EU's role in Cyprus while strengthening Britain's and NATO's involvement. These questions will be dealt with specifically in Part III, but it is important to bear them in mind when scrutinising British and US policy vis-à-vis the Cyprus question. As we shall see, British policy towards European defence tends towards muddying the waters and blurring precision to ensure that NATO retains a pivotal role. This could well include the question of Cyprus' accession to the EU. Britain's historical aversion to precise and rigid texts,[13] particularly when supra-national aspects are involved, is of course sufficiently well known to require no further comment, other than to note the spillover effect on to the Cyprus question.

In the current scenario of an apparently uni-polar world, Britain's Cyprus policy, predicated as it is on retaining its bases, is now closely coordinated with

US military strategy. The 'special relationship' remains a central pillar of British foreign policy. Successive governments have realised that without special access to the USA, Britain would be 'reduced speedily to the rôle of a supplicant cooling its heels in the antechamber of history.'[14] This has naturally been useful to the USA, particularly in the cold war, when the US government still looked to Britain psychologically to defend the free world against Communism in the hope that it would not be 'the sole or even the principal centre of initiative and weapons in the non-communist world'.[15] As regards Cyprus, fear of Soviet power – whether justified or not – united Britain and the USA, although there were some emotional but nevertheless cosmetic strains, particularly during the Turkish invasion, when the USA gave Turkey a far freer rein than Britain wished.

Since the Gulf War and the collapse of the Soviet Union, Britain has begun to hang more eagerly on to US defence policy, as the EU has strengthened its identity. The Thatcher–Reagan syndrome has been followed by the Blair–Clinton and Blair–Bush syndromes. The first was characterised – at least presentationally – as a virtual revival of the Second World War spirit of togetherness; and the second by the 'Third Way' distraction, often criticised as a new subtle excuse for neo-liberalism[16] within the context of the 'new panacea', globalisation. The third has been presented as an apparently successful way for Britain to stand 'shoulder to shoulder' with the USA in contrast to the 'dithering' Europeans. In this way, Britain has been able to present itself as strong, rather than as part and parcel of an integrationist EU. Thus, Britain appears to be clinging to the special relationship to stress its difference from Europe, at least in strategic defence matters. Recent developments have underlined that the US–UK axis is a counterweight to the supra-national development of the European Union. The weaker the process of European integration, the stronger Britain believes it can be. The future of Cyprus, once the hostage of the cold war, is increasingly contingent on the jockeying for power between the EU and the USA, particularly as regards security. In simple terms, Cyprus, as we shall see, is now becoming the hostage of the fuzzy and altering relationship between NATO and the EU. This is where the US attitude, to which we now turn, is so crucial.

8 The United States of America: Power Projection

We are proud that America is not just another country, and we want our foreign policy to reflect our status as the globe's leading champion of freedom.[1]

INTRODUCTION

Despite America's avowed post-war policy of projecting an image of the white knight of freedom fighting the black knight of tyranny, the latter first in the guise of Communism and now in that of terrorism, Cyprus has somehow escaped the so-called New World Order. Thirty years after the occupation of northern Cyprus and the forced uprooting of close on 200,000 Cypriots – refugees in their own land – the divisions between occupied and unoccupied, legal and illegal, Greek-speaking Christian Cypriot and Turkish-speaking Moslem Cypriot have further cemented, despite the decades of intercommunal talks. Put more mildly, in public relations terms, the *'modus vivendi'* has continued. While the Soviet bogeyman provided a reason at best, and an excuse at worst, to maintain and cement the partition of Cyprus, the EU is now becoming the new force with which the USA and the UK have to contend.

US foreign policy formulation is a complex and vast field to grasp fully, particularly because of the multi-faceted power centres that lobby the Capitol, whether they be the arms industry, oil interests, deep South 'Christian' fund-amentalism, or any of the myriad of consultancies that lobby Washington. While it is not the purpose of this book to conduct a deep analysis of US foreign policy formulation, the latter needs to be sufficiently comprehended in order to recognise the enormous impact of US policy on Cyprus.

The 'micro-policy' vis-à-vis Cyprus needs in turn to be seen within the historical cold war context of the USA's post-war 'macro' strategic investment in Western and Southern Europe, with its primary focus on Greece and Turkey. It was from this that the so-called Truman Doctrine of supporting Greece and Turkey against the perceived threat of Communism emerged.

We have seen in Chapter One how Britain 'handed over' Greece to the USA, mainly for financial reasons, but also to avoid further association with the Greek civil war. Cyprus was an important exception, and bucked the trend of de-colonisation that saw the British having to leave India, and the Dutch to depart from Indonesia, with the USA encouraging the process. Despite temporarily embarrassing USA pressure on Britain to give up Cyprus, it remained a colony until 1960. By then, due very largely to pressure from Britain under Prime Minister Macmillan, the US and Britain had agreed that the latter would keep some of Cyprus for defence purposes, while the rest would remain nominally independent. As we saw in Chapter Two, the USA was already closely involved in Cyprus, wanting a solution requiring a 'tangible accomplishment of NATO', guarantees that Britain would retain bases, and 'provision to the inhabitants regarding self-determination and protection of minorities'.[2] From 1957, the USA had convinced Britain that independence was necessary to avoid disruption to NATO's southern flank. Thereafter, both countries' primary focus regarding Cyprus was military strategy. It remains so today. When the US saw this threatened by the *enosis* fervour, it introduced the 'Ball-Acheson plan', which was to provide for double-*enosis* and, therefore, partition – even though this was forbidden by the Treaty of Guarantee – as a way of strengthening NATO's southern flank. Although *enosis* did not occur, partition did, albeit without any international legal consensus. The Cyprus problem is now strictly part and parcel of US Middle Eastern strategy, with British support. The premises behind US strategy need to be pinpointed before evaluating current US policy regarding Cyprus.

ASSERTIVENESS

Even before the break-up of the Soviet Union, the Gulf War and the ensuing outburst of moralistic euphoria surrounding President Bush Senior's concept of a New World Order, the USA was sensing the opportunities – and threats – of the perceived end of the cold war, and leading pundits were arguing for the USA to 'take the lead in organizing greater international co-operation'.[3] Three years later, Bush was saying:

> The world can, therefore, seize this opportunity to fulfill the long-held promise of new world order [...] Yes, the United States bears a major share of leadership in this effort. Among the nations of the world, only the United States has the moral standing, and the means to back it up [...] our cause is just, our cause is moral, our cause is right.[4]

The same sort of bombastic rhetoric accompanied the bombing of Yugoslavia. In the cases of Kuwait and Kosovo, however, a certain element of cynicism can be detected behind the moralising. For example, a few days before Iraq invaded Kuwait, the US ambassador in Baghdad, April Glaspie, assured the Iraqi leader, Saddam Hussein, *that the USA had no interest in Iraqi's dispute with Kuwait.*[5] This was not exactly an effort to restrain Iraq, which went ahead with its unfortunate invasion, only to witness an about-turn by the USA. An interesting comparison can be made with the bombing of Yugoslavia eight years later. On 23 February 1998, the US special envoy to the Balkans, Robert Gelbard, described the Kosovo Liberation Army (KLA) as 'without question a terrorist organization',[6] thus giving overt moral and political support to the Yugoslav leader, Milosevic, to intensify his actions against the group. Gelbard was then given 'French leave'. Yet only four months later, the new envoy, Richard Holbrooke – who, perhaps ominously, has also been involved in Cyprus – was photographed, smiling, with a Kalashnikov-toting KLA terrorist. US policy had transmogrified, and the bombing began, following Yugoslavia's refusal to accept a clause in the so-called Rambouillet agreement – NATO's attempt to draft a peace document acceptable to the Serbs and those of Albanian stock in Kosovo. That clause, as Lord Carrington, former British foreign secretary and NATO secretary general later observed, would have allowed NATO to use Serbia as a part of the NATO organisation, a loss of sovereignty that was clearly unacceptable.[7] In fact, the USA was clearly 'determined to prevent the emergence of an alternative Europe-wide security structure that could challenge its authority',[8] and used NATO's fiftieth anniversary – when the NATO treaty was due to expire – as the occasion to re-assert NATO's influence over and above that of the UN.

Lest the reader begin to suspect that the whole question of conservative American foreign policy is only tangential to the future of Cyprus, he needs to consider that it is in America's 'strategic interest to keep Europe weak and subservient'.[9] It follows that a Cyprus solution (if indeed there can be a clear-cut one) is unlikely to fit in with the European Union's security requirements, since Cyprus overlaps with America's security interests in Turkey, Israel and the Middle East in general. Thus the south-eastern edges of the EU are likely to remain distinctly frayed and subject to American, rather than EU interests.

SYSTEMS CONTROL

Under Bush's son, the current US penchant for a somewhat unilateralist policy has developed. Terms like 'globalisation', 'free markets', 'democracy promotion' and 'humanitarian intervention' are used liberally, but betray a hard-nosed pursuit of perceived national interest. This trend, wholly apparent before the 11 September 2001 outrage, was given added impetus by the destruction of the World Trade Center. The USA had been able to justify a policy of unilateralism, not-withstanding mounting criticism, owing to its industrial pre-eminence and taking over of new markets enhanced by the collapse of the Soviet Union. This is particularly evident in military spending and arms sales. Russia lost huge markets to the USA: where before there had been approximate parity (depending on how one values the equipment sold), by 1998, the USA accounted for half of all global arms sales, $55 billion, while Russia was in fourth place, behind Britain and France. Since 1992, the USA has accounted for almost forty per cent of the world's military expenditure and is currently increasing its own expenditure.[10] From the American point of view, then, 11 September has its positive business side. The 'American urge to remain number one'[11] has been reinforced.

Criticism has been harsh and widespread. Even two years before 11 September, the USA was being criticised for misusing its acclaimed moral superiority. Since the end of the cold war, its aid to the poorest countries had halved; it had marginalised the United Nations over Yugoslavia, violated international law and refused to ratify the treaty establishing the International Criminal Tribunal.[12] Since then, the USA has annulled the 1972 ABM Treaty, is developing its own missile defence and has refused to sign the Kyoto Agreement on environmental protection. These are but some of the complaints. One expert has written:

> The war on terrorism is simply a euphemism for extending US control in the world whether it is by projecting force through its carriers or building new military bases in Central Asia.[13]

Well-known critics of US policy such as John Pilger have lambasted the USA in harsh terms:

> This [the Bush 'doctrine'] means controlling the oil and fossil riches in Central Asia. It means attacking Iraq, installing a replacement for Saddam Hussein and taking over the world's second largest source of oil. It means surrounding a new economic challenge, China, with bases, and intimidating the leaders of its principal economic rival, Europe, [...] democracy means nothing if its benefits are at odds with American 'interests,' a world where to express dissent against these 'interests' brands one a terrorist and justifies surveillance and repression.[14]

This critical language is not confined to well-known detractors of American foreign policy; it has also come from the likes of Lord Carrington (see above), French politicians and the moderate former (British) EU Commissioner, Chris Patten (see Introduction). The former secretary general of the UN, Boutros Boutros-Ghali has written: 'It would be some time before I fully realised that the United States sees little need for diplomacy; power is enough.'[15]

Boutros Ghali shows in his book *Unvanquished* how the USA has tried to weaken the United Nations, which it often finds a stumbling block to its plans. It is not surprising that the USA refused to support Boutros-Ghali for a second term, finally accepting the more amenable Kofi Annan. Certainly, the USA has tended to use NATO, especially in the bombing of Yugoslavia, to circumvent, or even ignore, the UN Security Council.[16] Whatever lip service is still paid to the UN, US policy has clear implications for Cyprus, where the UN peacekeeping force has to be renewed on a regular basis. The USA's 'red bogeyman', Makarios, exploited UN resolutions to the full, much to the irritation of would-be partitionists.

Whatever the pros and cons of US power-projection that the world has witnessed recently, it has certainly attracted the same kind of virulent criticism as during the later Vietnam years.

Gore Vidal sums up current policy as follows:

> Bush Junior has a sense of mission about completing his father's work in Iraq, a country with vast oil reserves but small current production. However, the real target is the conquest of Eurasia to which Afghanistan is the traditional gateway, as the English know from the past.[17]

Clearly, then, 'geopolitical' considerations have clear implications for any serious consideration of the Cyprus dispute, particularly because recent events such as the bombing of Yugoslavia and Iraq have weakened UN authority, the latter being particularly important as regards Cyprus.

CYPRUS' US ROLE

In terms of precise US objectives, Cyprus has not, despite Kissinger's machinations, been an unqualified success for US strategy in the region, largely because even the USA, for all its power, has refused to recognise the 'Turkish Republic of Northern Cyprus', despite its close alliance with Turkey. This is probably because to do so would, at least at this stage, seriously bedevil its relations with the European Union, which Cyprus has joined. This in turn explains why, at least presentationally and theoretically, the USA is content with the *modus vivendi* approach, as in 1969 (see Chapter Five), apart from the obvious fear of a new international border, which would render the treaties invalid and probably lead to *enosis* with Greece for unoccupied Cyprus. Behind the scenes, Cyprus is important to the USA in terms of its Middle East policy of supporting Israel and weakening Iraq, Iran and Syria, and because Greece and Turkey are NATO members. Since the USA's objective is to strengthen and enlarge NATO, to officially recognise the division of Cyprus could easily be exploited by a still powerful Russia, as well as attract enormous criticism through the UN, but particularly from the EU. In this sense, the EU has replaced the USSR as the main counterweight to the promoters of formal partition.

The US position is to support Turkish EU membership, as a way of keeping the Turkish government happy, albeit in the full knowledge (see later) that the latter will continue to insist on independence for, or the annexation of, Northern Cyprus. Without tacit Turkish condoning of American policy towards Iraq, the USA would find it very difficult to pursue its current actions with impunity. Turkish sensitivities towards the Kurdish question (see Chapter Nine) are particularly germane here. They explain Turkey's refusal to allow a full-scale American attack on northern Iraq through its territory. Turkey has been doing what it can to weaken Kurdish autonomy both within Turkey and in northern Iraq, a policy that has come into conflict with American aims in Iraq.[18] One is bound to speculate as to the extent that this could influence the USA's tacit support — or at least turning a blind eye — to Turkey's rigid position over Cyprus.

Cyprus is important to the USA, in the context of the latter's support for Israel, as an extra western flank to defend Israel in the event of a large-scale attack.

Hence the latter's support for the Israel–Turkey military agreement. The US government puts it this way:

> US military cooperation with Turkey and Israel is a matter of long-standing policy and practice. As a NATO ally and friend with Turkey and as a special ally with Israel, both democracies and key regional players, the United States shares core values and actual security and political objectives in the Eastern Mediterranean. Israel and Turkey have likewise found that they share common objectives, in part from confronting the same set of neighbors which have pursued weapons of mass destruction programs, have been sponsors or supporters of terrorism, and which have been inimical to democracy, the rule of law and regional stability.[19]

What these shared core values are is a moot point, but the US listening posts in occupied Cyprus form part of an elaborate military structure connected to Turkey's allowing its bases to be used, with Israel and Turkey forming a common front against Syria (which claims Iskenderun) and, if it proves necessary, Iran. Iran is, of course, part of Bush's 'axis of evil'. In the case of Cyprus, the whole question becomes more poignant when one recalls the imprisonment in early 1999 of two Israeli Mossad agents in Cyprus, for spying on sites, where Russian S-300 missiles were due to be installed.[20] In this connection, one needs to recall that President Makarios supported the Arab position (only vocally, of course) following the Six Day War, and that any unwelcome tendencies on the part of a more independent Cyprus as an EU member to adopt a pro-Palestinian attitude (in line with current EU policy) would be resisted by the USA and Israel. Thus again we see the importance of Cyprus as a simple strategic tool.

US Middle East objectives alone are not enough to begin to understand US policy towards Cyprus. Perhaps the two most significant underlying factors, closely intertwined, are the 'special relationship with Britain' and the growing divergence between US and EU strategic perceptions. They are intertwined because, in military strategic matters, the UK is now firmly entrenched behind US policy, to the irritation, in particular, of France, which for example, pulled out of the periodic bombing of the 'no-fly zone' in Iraq, on the grounds that it was illegal. Enough has been written about the Blair government's support of the 'unaccountable hegemon's'[21] objectives in Iraq not to require elaboration. Britain's motives are bound up in the question of its attitude to Europe.

THE USA, BRITAIN AND EUROPE

With Cyprus' membership of the European Union, the questions of European defence, Greek–Turkish relations and EU–Turkish relations, not to mention US–EU relations, have been thrown into sharp relief. With the inception of an EU Common Foreign and Security Policy (CFSP) – as distinct from the European Defence and Security Initiative, seen by some as a British ploy to ensure that NATO remains in charge – some have come to see this as a first step 'towards a separate

European capacity to wield and project power that will diverge from that of the United States',[22] while others simply think that NATO and the EU will 'need to adapt'.[23]

As a way to counterbalance the increasing coordination of EU members in defence matters, the USA is very much in favour of NATO enlargement, particularly from EU applicants, so as to 'increase the Atlanticist voice in the new Europe'.[24] One expert has written:

> The one entity with the capacity to challenge the United States in the near future is the European Union, if it were to become a tight federation with major military capabilities and if relations across the Atlantic were allowed to sour.[25]

Some souring there has undoubtedly been, as we have seen above. To this we can add the banana and steel trade disputes, the Israel–Palestine conflict and tension over the US attack on Iraq, to mention some of the more publicised topics. It is however the NATO–EU question that worries the USA most. The latter's tactic is to push for NATO enlargement willy-nilly, since the USA has always been more than *primus inter pares* in the organisation, with the supreme commander always an American.

Elias Demetracopoulos, a well-informed Greek journalist in Washington, says succinctly that America simply wishes to 'split Europe by NATO expansion'.[26] His thinking is inherently logical, since most of the batch of the new East European members look to the USA more than the EU.

Since the fall of the Berlin Wall, when the 'Communists lost their God, and the Capitalists their devil',[27] NATO, designed to 'keep the Americans in, the Russians out and the Germans down',[28] has been in search of an adversary and a common purpose. A handful of 'rogue states' and conflict in the Balkans was not exactly on a par with the Warsaw Pact. Nevertheless, East European countries, in the 'post-communist stress disorder' have understandably queued up to join the organisation. The 11 September outrage and the spectre of international terrorism came as a welcome – if horrible – boost to NATO's transmogrifying purpose. This is where the EU's CFSP comes into the picture. Britain and America wish to undermine it. Apart from occasional blips, such as under the Heath premiership, Britain has always opted for the USA when forced to choose.[29] At the sentimental level, there is 'an instinctive, almost reflex tendency to look first across the Atlantic rather than the Channel'.[30] Blair is but the most recent in a queue of British prime ministers keen to please US presidents.[31]

This policy naturally serves US military-strategic interests in Europe, justifying to a certain extent President de Gaulle's 'nightmare scenario' of Britain as an American Trojan horse. Certainly, thus far, US–British policy has been preponderant in the embryonic EU CFSP that was planted at Maastricht. The primary US objective is to ensure that NATO remains at the top and to weaken any attempt to create a supra-national European Army that would compete with NATO or even render it otiose.

Hence the British and NATO-sponsored 'European Security and Defence Identity' (ESDI), not to be confused with the CFSP. The ESDI has now become the ESDP (Policy). It is under ESDP auspices that the European Rapid Reaction Force has been agreed on. Although the ESDP has been institutionalised by the establishment of the Political and Security Committee (PSC), it is intergovernmental, rather than supra-national, reporting to the EU Council of Ministers. It therefore circumvents, to US and British relief, the European Commission. To engage in military action, it will require the permission of national governments and parliaments. Crucially, it will operate when NATO as a whole is not engaged,[32] in other words, when the USA decides it can leave matters to the Europeans. It will also use NATO assets, thus detracting further from its independence or rapidity of action. The inter-governmental aspects of ESDP have been promoted, through, *inter alia*, the Trilateral Commission and the Rockefeller Foundation (the latter supports the former financially)[33] by the likes of Lord Owen, the former British foreign secretary.

The ESDP also provides for NATO-EU members to be consulted. This is where the Cyprus question comes into its own, explaining at one and the same time both US and British support for rapid EU and NATO expansion. The latter ensures an Atlantic flavour to European defence. Behind the expansion policy comes the promotion of Turkey's bid to join the EU, but, more important, giving to Turkey a role in European defence even while still outside the EU. This will render Cypriot military cooperation with the EU difficult.

Rapid EU enlargement weakens EU supra-nationalism, so inimical to US and British interests. At the same time, it further weakens it by bringing in the USA's most crucial allies in the Middle East, Turkey and Israel. US policy is unequivocal:

> Turkey's goal has been to broaden and deepen the European and trans-Atlantic ties, which the US strongly supports and which, ultimately, is in Greece's self-interest [no reason is given]. A Turkey integrated in Western and European institutions and adhering to Western values should, we believe, be encouraged.[34]

Thus we come to the crunch. Turkey's nightmare would be a Cyprus as a member of a future European defence force, already coordinated with Greece in defence matters, weakening Turkey's position not only in relation to Cyprus, but also in the Eastern Aegean, where Turkey claims several islets.

The USA and Britain are striving as hard as they can to strengthen Turkey's hand, with the dual objective of keeping their finger in the Cyprus pie and, concomitantly (as a natural corollary) to weaken the independence of action of an EU force.

This explains why in December 2001, the USA, Britain and Turkey signed the above-mentioned document in Ankara without EU authorisation, guaranteeing Turkey a say in any European operations around Cyprus and the Eastern Aegean, in return for which Turkey would agree to drop its veto on the release of NATO assets for putative European military operations. Greece at first rejected the idea and threatened to veto both the agreement and EU enlargement, if the worst came to the worst.

At the EU Seville Summit at the end of June 2002, Greece secured additions to the British–US–Turkish paper, guaranteeing that no NATO member (for which read Turkey) would threaten the use of, or use, force, against an EU member (Greece).

Matters were not however clear: the Danish prime minister denied that the EU had reached a common position, saying 'We have not negotiated a common position. We have noted that a common position has been reached with Greece. But there will still be talks with Turkey.'[35]

Even with such an unclear situation, Turkey continued to prevaricate until the EU Summit in December. Despite the recent clear mandate given to the Islamic party, Turkey is still claiming islets, although (see Chapter Sixteen), the EU has now agreed to keep Cyprus out of ESDP operations.

'CONSTANT ONGOING PROCESS'

In a double tautology, the US ambassador to Greece recently described Greek–Turkish negotiations over Cyprus as 'a constant, ongoing process'.[36] The recent ambassador's penchant for verbal bulimia and tautology betrays the American policy of keeping the '*modus vivendi*' going, to keep control while planning, with Britain, to ensure that its interest in keeping Cyprus within its strategic ambit is not threatened. It also seeks to ensure that Turkey's hand in Cyprus and the Aegean is not compromised by the European Union.

Behind this policy lies the possibility that a solution to avoid conflict between Greece and Turkey over Cyprus will involve the USA and/or NATO guaranteeing Cyprus' integrity, rather than only Britain, Greece and Turkey, who have so obviously failed.[37] The only question is whether the USA would take over from Britain, Greece and Turkey, or simply join them. Given Britain's territory on Cyprus, the likelihood is that first and foremost, the USA and Britain will guarantee Cyprus' defence, along with Turkey, while Greece will – obviously – also have a role. Only the EU can prevent this.

The possibilities for crisis are manifest, since Greece will stress the EU role, while Turkey will continue to pursue its interests, which could lead to a confrontation, for example over oil exploration rights around Cyprus.

The secret negotiations – as opposed to the intercommunal talks – are intense. The complications for the USA and Britain (because of its bases) are obvious since, even if the Cyprus government were persuaded that the USA would be the best guarantor of future peace, this has enormous implications for European Union law. This whole question will be further analysed in Part III.

In the meantime, we have the 'constant ongoing process' of the intercommunal process. We now turn to the Turkish point of view.

9 The Ottoman Legacy and Turkey's View of Cyprus

In the 1920s the Turkish government had actually encouraged the Turkish Cypriots to emigrate to the mainland in pursuance of Ataturk's policy of national homogeneity.[1]

INTRODUCTION

It may appear strange and inconsistent that some fifty years after Turkey renounced any future rights to former Ottoman-occupied territories and ceded Cyprus to Britain, its army invaded and reoccupied part of the island. Such are the vagaries of relations between states, which should serve as a lesson to those theory-prone pundits of international relations who try to formulate slick and convenient models.

It is only in history that we can find some rationale to explain how, in contrast to Ataturk's 'peace at home, peace in the world' policy[2] encouraging Turkish-speaking Cypriots to return to the homeland, around 100,000 Turks have actually settled in occupied Cyprus since 1974.

Turkey was born out of the final collapse, in 1923, of the Ottoman Empire,[3] which had stretched well into modern-day Austria,[4] itself today a remnant of the Austro–Hungarian Empire that collapsed almost at the same time as the Ottoman Empire. Both had maintained an 'unholy arrangement' through much of the nineteenth century, to maintain as best they could their respective shares of the Balkans.

Although the Selçuk Turks had moved west into Byzantine-controlled Anatolia in the eleventh century, and the Ottoman (Osmanli) Turks later consolidated their grip on Anatolia and the Balkans, it was not until the Ottoman conquest of Constantinople in 1453 that the Turkish tribes began to identify themselves with Anatolia, although ethnically they were still a minority, there being, *inter alia*, large Greek, Kurdish and Armenian populations. The final collapse of the Byzantine Empire gave an enormous impetus to the Ottoman ability to conquer other peoples, particularly in the Balkans and along the Danube, as Byzantium no longer existed as a buffer zone for Western Europe. Under Selim the Grim (an admirer of Alexander the Great)[5] and Suleyman the Magnificent, massive expansion occurred, helped by an alliance with France, directed principally against the Hapsburg Empire. The fratricidal Thirty Years' War in Europe further helped the Ottomans to push west. It also marked a turning point for the Hapsburgs, who gave up their dream of uniting Europe under a Roman Catholic banner and turned their attention increasingly to the Balkans, where, as noted above, they eventually came to an accommodation with the Ottomans, thanks largely to Metternich. The First World War alliance between Vienna and Constantinople was very much a matter of convenience. By the end of the war, both empires had lost most of their territories and, in the case of the Ottomans, there was even the possibility that much of Anatolia would be broken up. The Treaty of Sèvres envisaged the ceding of Thrace to Greece and the placing under Greek administration of Smyrna (Izmir), with a referendum to be held after five years. Events, however, overtook the treaty and the Greek armies that had landed in Anatolia in 1919 found themselves deserted by their allies: after a number of successes, they were pushed back, resulting in the infamous catastrophe of 1922, when almost all the Greeks of Anatolia 'left' for Greece proper. By attempting to take Ankara, the Greeks had gone 'a bridge too far'.

ATATURK'S LEGACY

The hero of the moment was Ataturk who, quite rightly, was hailed both as the saviour of Turkey and as the founder of a new Turkish state. The Treaty of Lausanne of 1923 recognised the new situation: Turkey kept Eastern Thrace and Izmir and there was a (forced) exchange of populations: the Orthodox Christians had already been forced to leave, while the Muslims of Greece – many from Crete – 'left' for Turkey.

Importantly, and significantly for today, the Muslim and Greek Christian Orthodox populations of Western Thrace (Greece) and Constantinople were exempted from the population exchanges, as was Cyprus, which now formally became a British colony. Today, only about 2,000 Greek Christian Orthodox remain in Istanbul, an irony, seeing that the Greek-speaking Patriarch of the Orthodox Church is based there. In contrast, the Muslim population of Western Thrace has thrived.

The Ottoman Empire was avowedly (Sunni) Muslim, and ruled its subjects by religion more than simple race. At the negotiations for the Treaty of Lausanne, the Turks refused to recognise ethnic minorities. Thus, the treaty bound Turkey to protect its citizens 'regardless of creed, nationality or language'. Although the Greek-speaking Christian population of Constantinople was therefore protected (theoretically), the Kurds – Muslims like the Turks – were unable to obtain any special protection clauses.

Ataturk's vision may not have been overly well achieved, but he is revered today in Turkey as a quasi-religious figure. He established a secular state, changed the visually pleasing Arabic script to the functional Roman one and stressed that Turkey should be a 'western' country. His portrait is to be found everywhere in Turkey, far more than that of the Queen or Winston Churchill is found in England.

Not everybody has shared a positive view of Ataturk. Writing in the 1930s, the American journalist John Gunther described Ataturk as a 'blond, blue eyed combination of patriot and psychopath', who had changed his name seven times, from 'Mustafa' and 'Mustafa Kemal' respectively, to 'Mustafa Kemal Pasha', 'Ghazi Mustafa Kemal Pasha', and 'Ghazi Mustafa Kemal', 'Ataturk', 'Kemal Ataturk' and finally 'Kamal Ataturk'. Despite his 'Turkishness', he was actually half-Albanian and, according to Arnold Toynbee, may have had Jewish blood.[6] He was born in Thesaloniki, which had a very big Jewish community. The Jews had fled from the Iberian peninsula during the Inquisition and been welcomed by the Ottomans, possibly to serve as a counterweight to the Greek population.

Although he was loved by most Turks and is still respected today, it is worth quoting some of Gunther's acerbic observations (with apologies to any Kemalists who might be reading this book):

> Kamal Atatürk, a somewhat Bacchic character, the full record of whose personal life makes you blink, is the dictator-type carried to its ultimate extreme, the embodiment of totalitarian rule by character. This man, in personality and accomplishments, resembles no one so much as Peter the Great, who also westernised his country at frightful cost. Kamal Atatürk is the roughneck of dictators. Beside him, Hitler is a milksop, Mussolini a perfumed Dandy [...][7]

ATATURK'S ATAVISTIC LEGACY

It no exaggeration to state that today Turkish national consciousness is based on the originally benign nationalism, secularism and modernisation ('westernisation')[8] of Ataturk, although there are of course intellectually-minded detractors. Deeper down lies the Ottoman heritage. Just as the British, and, to a lesser extent, the French national psyche is afflicted by a tacit consciousness of past supremacy, this can occasionally lead to bouts of 'post-imperial *rigor mortis*', of which the Suez campaign can be seen as an example.

In the case of Turkey, there is also a contradictory conundrum surrounding national identity, which is not shared to anything like the same extent by the British, French or Greeks. One of the main ingredients of this conundrum is the Kurdish question. Estimates of the number of Kurds (in Turkey alone) range from 7.1 per cent of the population of Turkey (Turkish government estimates) to 24 per cent (Kurdish estimates). There must be at least between 17 and 18 per cent (ten to eleven million people).[9] Before the latest trouble, the Kurds had revolted in 1925, 1930 and 1936–1938.[10] In 1999, following Turkish threats, Syria asked a prominent Kurdish guerrilla leader, Oçalan, to leave, whereupon he turned up, with unofficial Greek help, at the Greek embassy in Nairobi, only to be snatched by

Turkish agents – probably with Israeli help – and whisked back to Turkey, where he is now languishing in prison. The affair was particularly embarrassing for the Greek government, which denied any official involvement in the affair and even took official proceedings against those who had helped him while he was briefly in Greece.

The Kurdish problem continues to be a major thorn in the side of the Turkish authorities, who are loath to treat the Kurds as an official minority with special rights, although they are slowly yielding to European pressure. However, the issue is big enough to stir up neo-Kemalist nationalism, which can be somewhat exaggerated, since Ataturk has an almost pharaoh-like status in some quarters. This nationalism has in the past reached near farcical proportions. Ataturk himself, for example, personally sponsored the so-called 'Sun Theory', a theory of language postulating that the earliest Turks were sun-worshippers who derived their conceptions of life from the idea of the sun, and that this 'sun language' was the parent of all other tongues. In 1936, the British ambassador to Ankara wrote:

> The theory, which I am privately informed on the best expert authority, is entirely devoid of a scientific basis, is personally sponsored by Kamal Ataturk, whose interest in it is sufficient to explain the enthusiasm by which it was expounded by Turkish delegates to [the Third Turkish Language] Congress, and the tactful silence of the foreign scholars.[11]

Ataturk's legacy is a somewhat difficult ingredient of today's Turkish identity, particularly given the Kurdish quest for autonomy, and it is compounded by political and religious factors.

ISLAM, POLITICS AND THE ARMED FORCES

Another spanner in the works of the Kemalist utopia – or perhaps spicy ingredient would be a more accurate term – is Islam. Among the various somewhat exaggerated 'westernisation' measures taken by Ataturk, such as abolishing Arabic script and introducing an entirely phonetic language based on the Roman alphabet,[12] was the total separation of Church and State, to the point of forbidding religious dress in public places and even the wearing of the fez (this latter more because of its Ottoman imperial connotations than its religious ones). Despite various constitutional modifications since Ataturk's era, the armed forces are still the legal guarantors of the Turkish constitution. This has led to confrontations between Islamic parties that 'overstep the Kemalist mark', and secular (Kemalist) parties. The most recent example of this was when the leader of the (now banned) Welfare Party, Necmettin Erbakan, came to power as prime minister in December 1995, but was forced to resign eighteen months later, following pressure from the National Security Council.[13] The Islamist political parties – under whatever name they operate – are feared by the traditional secular Kemalist-minded establishment, not only because they are the largest political force in terms of votes, but because they have supporters in the armed forces, hence occasional purges of the latter. Thus, questions about whether women can wear headscarves at state universities tend to polarise public opinion and party politics into extreme factions.

Until recently, right-left extremism was also particularly rampant, accounting for many killings in the 1960s and 1970s. Today, the extreme right wing is still strong. The National Action Party, with its youth organisation, the Grey Wolves, for example, was involved in the killing of two Greek Cypriots on the Green Line in 1996.

The multifariousness of the Turkish polity, combined with the difficult tri-chotomy of purist anachronistic Kemalists, 'modern westernisers' and Islamists has not been a happy mix. The socio-political instability that has resulted has contributed to a particularly shaky economy, which has to support the Turkish armed forces. Turkey has NATO's second largest army. Just as the dying Ottoman empire was granted huge loans, particularly by Britain, so today the International Monetary Fund periodically does its best to bail the Turkish government out of one crisis after another.

The power of the military is crucial. Turkey has had three recent official military interventions, in 1960, 1971 and 1980. Today, the military is still ready to step in and prevent what it sees as any Islamist excesses.

A Turkish author sums up the situation succinctly:

> The significant role that the military plays in the political process, the high degree of political violence and a polarised political system have contributed to the disorder and instability prevalent in Turkish democracy [...] Despite such a high degree of instability (what [sic] can sometimes be described as chaos) in Turkish domestic politics, however, there has been a remarkable degree of stability in the conduct of foreign policy.[14]

CONSISTENCY ON CYPRUS

Turkey had no strong policy over Cyprus until the British government successfully bedevilled relations between the two main communities on Cyprus and brought in Turkey as a major player in 1955 (see Chapter Two). The deterioration in relations between Greece and Britain over Cyprus meant that British–Turkish cooperation over Cyprus would increase by default. Governmental instability in Turkey and Greece also contributed to radicalism. Thus the tails began to wag – as they still do to a certain extent – the Greek and Turkish dogs.

The Turkish government had little option but to support the increasingly radicalised Turkish-speaking minority and, as we have seen, the British helped with the necessary propaganda. By the time of the 1960 agreements, the socio-nationalistic structures on both sides of the divide were so psychologically entrenched, that it was only a matter of time before a crisis occurred.

The crisis, when it came, was exacerbated by unstable governments in both 'mother countries'. Thus, the Greek Cypriot EOKA and Turkish 'TMT' ('Turkish

Resistance Organisation') were able to run rampant, aided by unchecked elements in politically unstable Greece and Turkey.

By 1963, when Makarios tried to introduce his 'Thirteen Points', with the full knowledge and cooperation of the British high commissioner (see Chapter Three), Cyprus was ready to crack. The crack resulted in thousands of Turkish Cypriots fleeing their homes, and in near war between Greece and Turkey several times between November 1963 and well into the summer of 1964. Turkish warplanes even bombed Cyprus briefly. With the USA afraid of a war between Greece and Turkey and the USSR threatening the latter, the Turkish government was able to do no more than overfly Nicosia and mobilise troops to invade Cyprus. It was particularly frustrated by UN Resolution 186 of 4 March 1964, because the resolution called on the (legitimate) government of Cyprus to restore law and order. From the Turkish point of view, this was tantamount to UN support for Greek Cypriot excesses – and there were plenty – since the Turkish Cypriots were by now already out of the Cypriot government and running their own affairs. Soviet insistence upon a strong UN role proved crucial.

From the Turkish point of view, partly justified, the troubles were the result of an ill-conceived and clumsy attempt by the Greek side illegally to amend the constitution, by means of the secret 'Akritas Plan',[15] with the aim of crushing Turkish Cypriot opposition to *enosis* which, although not allowed under the Treaty of Guarantee, was still on the political agenda.

The diplomatic defeat suffered by Turkey and its Cypriot protégés was, however, to prove an Achilles heel for the Greek side, which clumsily consolidated its position,[16] thereby further antagonising Turkey. The 1967 crisis was thus hardly a surprise, particularly since Greece had by then sent 12,000 troops to Cyprus. This encouraged the Turkish government to reciprocate in kind (with the TMT) and prepare for military action, incensed by what it saw as an injustice. Most of the Turkish Cypriots were by then ensconced in their 'ghettos'.

In the event, the new Greek Junta was humiliated, and had to withdraw the troops (as well as Grivas), thus weakening the military position of Cyprus in terms of a Turkish attack. The cracks were only papered over, and intercommunal talks began in 1968, almost as a necessary diversion from the need to come to a hard-and-fast solution. By now, the Turkish government was already moving towards a policy of partition and future statehood, helped by the extremism not only on their own side, but among certain Junta leaders, particularly Brigadier Ioannidis. The clumsy 'Sampson' coup in July 1974 gave Turkey not merely an excuse to land on Cyprus, but a reason to do so, invoking Article IV of the Treaty of Guarantee, in particular the sentence that had been inserted therein (ominously) on Turkish insistence fifteen years previously:

> In so far as common or concerted action may not prove possible, each of the three guaranteeing powers resume the right to take action with the sole aim of re-establishing the state of affairs created by the present treaty.

Although Turkey did not exactly fulfil the second part of the clause – re-establishing the previous state of affairs – she was certainly able to justify her initial landing, given the frustrating years of what she saw as UN bias against Turkish Cypriots.

Through almost four decades of intercommunal negotiations, and despite expectations of a breakthrough on various occasions, the Turkish position has remained remarkably consistent, perhaps because of its sheer simplicity: complete autonomy, at the very least, for the Turkish Cypriots. While the Turkish Cypriots regarded the 1960 independence arrangement as an end in itself, the Greek Cypriots regarded it as a means to an end: eventual *enosis*. This, in Turkey's eyes, meant colonisation by the Greeks.[17] Thus, ever since the invasion, the Turkish position, semantics apart, has slowly but inexorably hardened. Hence the proclamation of the 'Turkish Republic of Northern Cyprus' in 1983, and recent threats to annex Northern Cyprus (and perhaps to do more) if Cyprus joined the European Union. The Turkish view is that only two independent and sovereign states can facilitate cooperation.[18] This is however, somewhat disingenuous, since this would render the 1960 treaties meaningless.

In contrast to the Greek position, which is finely tuned to international law and UN resolutions, the Turkish side stresses 'political realities'. This explains its irritation at the above-mentioned Resolution 186, among others, and its view that the resolution established an 'erroneous international mandate' vis-à-vis Cyprus.[19] Turkey is in powerful company when it comes to its view towards the role of the United Nations. The USA has recently questioned UN authority in Iraq, while Israel has for years ignored various UN resolutions relating to the occupied territories.

GEOPOLITICAL PAWN

The vigour of the Turkish position on Cyprus can be explained not only by an apparent wish to protect the minority Turkish-speaking population, but also by a desire to use Cyprus as a tool, weapon even, in its broader objective of maintaining its claims on some Greek islets and the continental shelf, as well as on territorial sea and airspace limits (see Chapter Eleven), and of its desire to join the EU. Paradoxically, it is unlikely that it would happily countenance Greek – and Cypriot – recognition of occupied Cyprus, since this would create a new international border. In such a scenario, an entirely new international legal framework would have to be created, while EU membership for Southern Cyprus could eventually lead to *enosis*, thus strengthening Greece's and Southern Cyprus' position against Turkey.[20] Hence the Turkish government's continuing recognition of the 1960 Treaty of Establishment, at least as regards the sanctity of the British sovereign territories. Here, the Turkish position converges with the British one, since two entirely separate and independent states, or one independent one plus an annexed Northern Cyprus, would destroy the 1960 arrangement, thus calling into question the validity of British sovereignty over the bases.[21]

In short, the Turkish position is to ensure separation of the communities, while making sure that, whatever arrangement ensues, the Greek Cypriots will not be independent as regards their own defence.

THE TURKISH HUB

Turkey's vigorous position on Cyprus and its solitary recognition of the occupied part has been facilitated by its strategic importance to the USA and NATO, an importance which arguably goes back to Metternich's support for the Ottoman Empire, to maintain a tacit agreement to control the Balkans. Britain's Disraeli also supported the Ottomans as a buffer against Russian power. More recently, Turkey has been crucial to the West as a cold war buffer against the USSR, as the Cuban Missile Crisis so poignantly demonstrated, when the USSR cited the stationing in Turkey of US nuclear missiles as justification for doing the same in Cuba. Since then, with the development of the Arab–Israel–Palestinian problem to include Iraq and Iran, US support for a strong Turkish state has grown exponentially. Thus, the USA strongly supports Turkish–Israeli military cooperation, both to protect Israel from Syria and Iraq, and to strengthen its and Israel's position in the Middle East following the break-up of the Soviet Union.[22]

The most obvious recent example of Turkey's importance to the USA was the 1991 Gulf War,[23] when Turkey offered the Inçirlik airbase to the US-led coalition. It was then used to bomb the 'no-fly zones' in Iraq. In return, Turkish armed forces were able to operate with impunity against Kurdish fighters in Iraq. Turkey again briefly offered Inçirlik as a base from which to bomb Iraq, in return for financial sweeteners and military support,[24] although the question caused considerable divisions within the country, divisions which led Turkey to deny its territory to American troops to invade northern Iraq. Turkey is in effect trading its support for US policy on Iraq and the Kurdish problem for support for its EU and Cyprus policy. Britain follows.

The Turkish government is fully aware of its central role in US objectives in the Middle East, and is adept at skilfully exploiting this fact. At a time when NATO's role is under scrutiny,[25] there is a recognition that the USA's 'going it alone', or almost alone, could undermine the very raison d'être of the organisation. Here Turkey, with NATO's second-largest army, plays a pivotal strategic and institutional role. In March 2002, a senior member of the Turkish military warned that Turkey might seek closer relations with Russia and Iran, in preference to the European Union.[26] This would obviously have implications for NATO. Six months later, the head of the Turkish Armed Forces warned the EU that if it accepted Cyprus as a member of the EU without taking Turkish needs into account, there would be a 'period of protracted crisis in the Eastern Mediterranean with all sides involved, including the European Union'.[27]

CONCLUSIONS

The Turkish position can be summed up as the recognition that the USA would ideally like the whole of Cyprus, and later Turkey, to become EU members,[28] and that if it cooperates with American wishes it will obtain US recognition for a two-state Cyprus, with an amended 1960 Treaty of Guarantee. This would ensure that the Greek Cypriot state could not join a future European Defence Force on its own, nor push for *enosis*. As one academic has written:

> It may be that Cyprus has lapsed into a form of diplomatic and political stasis from which two states will emerge with full international recognition. There are, after all, sixteen member states in the United Nations with populations smaller than the TRNC [...][29]

Behind the whole question of Cyprus, and Turkey's relations with Greece, which are closely intertwined, lies an atavistic mutual distrust. Greece, after all, had to defeat the Turks to gain independence, while Turkey had to repel a near-successful Greek invasion to establish its modern state. The Cyprus question has seriously bedevilled Greek–Turkish relations on territorial issues which, while theoretically distinct from Cyprus, are part and parcel of the same 'macro-problem'. It is indeed arguable that without Cyprus, the Treaty of Lausanne would have been respected, and that Greek–Turkish relations would be on an even keel. Now, however, with the tension mounting because of Cyprus' EU membership, we turn to the Greek point of view.

10   Greece's Cyprus View: The Foreign Yoke

We cannot leave her [Cyprus] a prisoner in the hands of the unjust interests of England.[1]

INTRODUCTION

It is no exaggeration to say that Greece has, by recent tradition, been pulled in different directions by competing allegiances to outside powers, and that it has been subject to a high – and often unwarranted – degree of foreign interference. Although other small countries, for example the Netherlands, with its post-war foreign policy polemics between French-influenced European federalists and British-influenced Atlanticists, has also been subjected to outside pressures, few can equal the case of Greece.

In its early years, Greece was run by competing 'English', French' and 'Russian' parties, with a Bavarian king in charge. The most blatant case of foreign interference was the 'Don Pacifico' affair of 1850. Don Pacifico was a Gibraltarian Jew whose Athens house had been plundered during rumbustious anti-Jewish demonstrations at Easter. To enforce compensation, the British blockaded Piraeus, even refusing a French offer to mediate; King Otto finally yielded, but only a small sum was paid in compensation.[2] Nevertheless, the case aroused nationalist feeling in a still irredentist state. Despite traditional pro-English 'Byronesque' emotions, Greece understandably favoured Russia against the Turks during the Crimean War, thus provoking an Anglo–French occupation of Piraeus. In 1916, British and French troops even attempted to enter Athens to 'persuade' the neutral Greek government to enter the Great War on their side. They were beaten back, but got their 'revenge' by recognising the pro-British and anti-monarchist government of Venizelos, whereupon Greece joined the fray.

It was not until 1923 that Greece was formally freed from the 1832 guarantee of the 'protecting powers' of Britain, France and Russia. Between the wars, German economic influence in Greece increased exponentially, but by the end of the war,

Britain's position as the most important foreign influence in Greece had been re-established. Greece had stood alone with Britain for several months and Churchill's rating was high, although, as we have seen, British involvement in the civil war (see Chapter One) was to alienate the left and contribute to considerable political tensions within Greece. Britain's 'handover' of Greece to the USA, and the 'Truman Doctrine' and Marshall Plan marked an important re-adjustment of Greek foreign policy, particularly as regards the Cyprus issue, which had lain reasonably dormant since the 1931 riots.

GREEK PERPLEXITY

Since relations between the Greek establishment and the British government were cordial, particularly following the Second World War, the Greek government was entitled to expect *enosis*, particularly in 1947, when the Dodecanese islands were handed to Greece. On the Cyprus issue, however, the British government was, as we have seen, not even prepared to discuss the question, and Sir Oliver Harvey's prediction (see Chapter One) of the Greeks 'turning to the methods of the Irish, Jews, Hindus and Egyptians' was to prove correct. One of the best-known British authorities on Greece describes Britain's refusal to even discuss yielding sovereignty as 'perverse'.[3] Another (Greek) authority demonstrates how the British were by 1953 asking the Turkish government to pressure the Greeks into not putting the Cyprus question onto the UN agenda, albeit with mixed results.[4] Yet another (British) expert writes that the British seemed to argue the Turkish case 'before the Turks had even thought of it', adding that Britain's real motive was to retain a base in the Eastern Mediterranean because of the impending Suez crisis of 1956.[5]

Greek governments, having to respond both to the genuine desire of the vast majority of Cypriots and to Greek nationalist sentiment, had little choice but to be drawn into 'diplomatic loggerheads' with an intransigent Britain, hence a feeling of genuine embarrassment and perplexity.[6] It is not beyond the bounds of possibility that what Britain feared most was a Greek–Turkish understanding on *enosis* in return for a Turkish military base and special safeguards for the Turkish-speaking community,[7] since this could have led to pressure on the British to get out of Cyprus.

Although *enosis* had been on the Greek agenda since at least the beginning of the war of independence, it was not until the early 1950s that Cyprus was to become a serious bone of contention between Greece, Britain and Turkey, to a large extent because of British intransigence in the face of US pressure. Atavism reared its ugly head. The Greeks recalled the conquest of Constantinople, which continues to be the seat of Christian Orthodoxy, of hundreds of years of Turkish occupation, its war of independence and subsequent reclaiming of more Greek-speaking territories in 1881, 1913 and 1947. All this, coupled with Turkey's alliance with Germany in the First World War and her neutrality in the Second generated a nationalist fervour over Cyprus that was to prove difficult to temper. This suited British policy, since

Britain believed that political confrontation, particularly between Greece and Turkey, was the best way of retaining Cyprus. The Treaty of Friendship and Mutual Assistance between Yugoslavia, Greece and Turkey in 1953 therefore presented a danger to the British, particularly when it led to the Balkan Pact and military co-operation shortly thereafter. The dénouement of British Cyprus policy came in 1955 with the start of the EOKA campaign and Britain's cynically contrived tripartite conference (see Chapter Two), which resulted in the atrocities against the ethnic Greeks of Istanbul and led Turkey to 'intensify its pressure upon Greece by expanding the conflict in a wide range of other fronts'.[8] From 1955 onward, the Cyprus problem became inextricably intertwined with a string of other problems: Turkish claims on some Greek islands; Turkish insistence that Greece demilitarise the Dodecanese; her questioning of Greece's airspace and sea limits and continental shelf; and accusations that Greece was mistreating Turkish-speakers in Western Thrace (see Chapter Eleven for a brief analysis of other problems). The (British-planned) failure of the 1955 conference had as another side-effect the disintegration of the Balkan Pact, although it is also true that an improvement in relations between Yugoslavia and Russia may have contributed to this. By now the Greek government was openly hostile to Britain, and Turkey had aligned itself with Britain over Cyprus. The Balkan Pact was a dead letter. For all the criticism that one can level at Greece and Turkey for occasional bouts of atavistic jingoism, it is fair to remind ourselves of the historical rhetoric used by both President Bush and Prime Minister Blair at the height of the Iraq campaign.

THE BRITISH AND US FACTORS

Greece, already under American military, political and economic influence, now turned increasingly to the USA for help over Cyprus, exploiting the crisis in US–British relations over the Suez affair. The attitude of the Greek intelligentsia in 1956 is best summed up in an article by Vassilis Spanopoulos, the editor-in-chief of the conservative *Kathimerini*, remarkable for its perceptiveness, despite some (understandable) skilful journalistic rhetoric that must appear old-fashioned to the modern reader:

> The English are not interested in Cyprus as such [...] it is their machine against the Americans [...] The English are not so naïve as to think that by hanging heroic youngsters [in Cyprus] they will not enrage national sentiments and make Greece an enemy [...] They have worked in such a way that our hostilities will be expressed by our leaving NATO. If we leave NATO, America will lose military bases of great importance in the Mediterranean [thus Britain would remain 'supreme' in Cyprus] [...] Thanks to the Cypriot matter, England managed, to the detriment of America of course, but also of Continental Europe, to dissolve the Balkan Pact. [...] The English always loved to divide and rule [...] the English wish to use us to bait the Russian bear. During the [German] occupation they delivered us to the EAM and ELAS. Then they helped us with arms during the Civil War [...] the English did what they could

to keep us out of NATO [...] before the Americans came to Greece, when the English were the organisers of the Greek army, they had told us very cynically to get organised for the Desert War [...] the English are using Cyprus to wreck the Arab world [...] we should run to it at least until the day of the UN comes [...] In the meantime we must help the holy struggle of Cyprus openly or secretly and enlighten international public opinion; we cannot leave her a prisoner in the hands of the 'unjust interests of England'.[9]

Spanopoulos was obviously disillusioned by Britain's stance, particularly since he had helped British intelligence consistently during the German occupation. For all the rhetoric, this was the feeling in many quarters at the time.

By 1956, Britain was using Cyprus as a diplomatic and military tool to safeguard its dying Middle East interests. Eden put matters brutally (see Chapter One) when he said: 'No Cyprus, no certain facilities to protect our supply of oil [...] It's as simple as that.'[10] Thus, the Greek government did its utmost to convince the USA to put pressure on Britain to free Cyprus.

THE US DISAPPOINTMENT AND THE COLD WAR

By now, however, although the USA disapproved of British intransigence and methods in Cyprus, it was fast coming to the conclusion that Cyprus would have to remain firmly in the western camp. As early as 1950, the State Department was favouring the continuation of British rule for 'strategic considerations'.[11] Although there were powerful dissenting voices in the USA, strongly critical of the way in which America was 'aiding and abetting' British colonialism,[12] the intensification of the cold war and McCarthyism, combined with Britain's heavy diplomatic pressure on the USA (see Chapter Two), meant that America had decided by 1955 to pressure Britain into moderating its actions rather than into giving up Cyprus willy-nilly. There, the Greek government's hopes were dashed. Its policy, particularly from 1956, under the premiership of Karamanlis, was less confrontational, and concentrated on pressuring Makarios to accept the London and Zurich agreements. *Enosis* was shelved, and the Greek government even rejected Makarios' Thirteen Points in 1963.[13] Karamanlis' successor, George Papandreou, took a different line: while chiding Makarios for going it alone, he put more emphasis on a UN solution rather than on a NATO one, and the *enosis* idea remained, albeit on the back-burner.

CONFUSION AND INVASION

By now, active *'enosism'* was largely an underground phenomenon, but a dangerous one. The confusion in Greek political life, exacerbated by the constitutional crisis between Papandreou and the king, grew steadily worse. When the military coup occurred, the colonels had been left a very hot potato by Papandreou: the presence of Grivas and thousands of Greek troops in Cyprus. If one adds to that the independent attitude of Makarios, bordering on disdain, vis-à-vis the Junta, and extremist elements inside the Junta, only a spark was needed to set off a crisis. In short, Greek policy became inconsistent during the Junta. Makarios noted that, diplomatically, the Greeks were stressing independence for Cyprus, while the military were at the same time shouting for *enosis*.[14]

The US-friendly Junta's relations with Makarios were, then, extremely delicate at that time, to put it mildly. The death in 1970 of Pipinelis, the experienced (civilian) foreign minister, sounded the death knell for whatever modicum of consistency and moderation that remained. By this time, the Cyprus tail was wagging the Greek dog, at least in foreign policy.[15] Following the Ioannidis takeover in November 1973, the Junta was more deeply split than ever about what action to take to remove Makarios and achieve some form of *enosis*, almost certainly with a strong dose of secret American connivance. The essential US objective was at the same time still to achieve lasting partition, since this would entail a NATO solution. Up to the invasion, there was confusion in Greek foreign policy formulation, 'aided and abetted' by the crisis in the US administration, which gave Kissinger, the CIA and even darker forces a freer hand than usual. The result was a twisted and bastardised version of the Ball-Acheson Plan of 1964, but without, for the time being, the *enosis* elements. The colonels' legacy was a certain level of subtle apprehension between the Greek and Cypriot governments. This apprehension was disguised by the international outcry at the excesses of the Turkish invasion and by enormous Greek humanitarian assistance to Cyprus. The colonels' legacy was the division of Cyprus.

CONSOLIDATION AND RECOURSE TO THE LAW

Since 1974, the Greek government has ensured that the Cyprus question remains an international problem and has supported the UN-sponsored intercommunal talks as the only appropriate avenue towards a solution. It may appear paradoxical that the 1960 agreements were reached over the heads of the Cypriots (apart from Makarios being invited in at the end of the negotiations), while now great lip service is paid to the on-and-off series of negotiations – so far abortive – between the Greek and Turkish Cypriots. It is also clear that the legal part of Cyprus is more independent of Greece than is the occupied part of Cyprus of Turkey.

Both the Greek and Cypriot governments constantly stress the letter of the law, while the Turkish government stresses the need for a political solution (i.e. not one based on the niceties of current international treaties and UN resolutions). Despite the intercommunal talks, the basic positions have remained unchanged: Turkey demands international recognition of the occupied zone before it will begin substantive negotiations, while Greece, using the latest UN formula of a 'bi-zonal, bi-communal federation', insists on a solution that will preserve the integrity of Cyprus. Behind this charade lie important NATO interests (mainly

American and British), which appear to have been bedevilled by Cyprus' joining the European Union.

TURKISH INTRANSIGENCE

From the Greek government's viewpoint, Turkey appears to have grown increasingly frustrated and bellicose, particularly since the acceptance of Cyprus' EU application. Greece has been able to 'play the Cyprus card' to a certain extent, by vetoing the distribution of various EU funds to Turkey, but then withdrawing its veto to Turkey's application to join the EU. Although Turkey is now formally a candidate, this has not altered her insistence that Northern Cyprus be recognised, and has led the Turkish government to table a whole host of other claims, often in a rather bellicose fashion. The Turkish parliament has declared, for example, that a Greek extension of its maritime limits to twelve nautical miles – as permitted under the UN Law of the Sea Convention – would be a *casus belli*.

Following the declaration in November 1993 of the Greece–Cyprus 'Joint Defence Doctrine', the Turkish government began to 'up the ante'. First, two Cypriot demonstrators were brutally killed on the Green Line in Cyprus, provoking US and EU condemnation,[16] and then the 'Imia' incident occurred: a Turkish ship ran aground on the Greek islet of Imia (claimed by Turkey) in December 1995. In January, 1996, Turkish 'journalists' replaced the Greek flag on Imia with the Turkish one and Turkish commandos landed. Greek forces then entered the area and a clash (that could have resulted in war) was narrowly averted, with intense American involvement, 'while Europe slept' (see Chapter Eleven).[17]

The atmosphere of tension continued, with Turkish warplanes periodically overflying Greek airspace (some of which Turkey does not recognise), and Turkish sabre-rattling. Greece responded by supporting Cyprus' purchase of a sophisticated Russian ground-to-air missile system, the S-300. Following US and EU pressure, a compromise was reached in 1998, whereby the system was delivered to Crete.

Following the resumption of intercommunal talks and, concomitantly, a series of major earthquakes in Turkey and Greece respectively, the superficial atmosphere between the two countries temporarily improved, largely due to Greek and Turkish rescue teams helping each other, and the conclusion of a series of bilateral commercial, tourism and cultural agreements. These developments are, however, cosmetic, in that they have not altered the Turkish standpoint on Cyprus or its other bilateral claims. Turkey has also refused to submit its claims to the International Court of Justice, as Greece has suggested.

Although a minority view holds that Greece should 'trade' a Cyprus solution (and peace in the Aegean) by encouraging Turkey's EU application, many think that Turkey is simply interested in what she can get and that if Greece gives an inch, Turkey will take a mile. This can be justified by the fact that despite Greece having dropped its veto on Turkey's application to the EU, it has seen no reciprocal measures; hence the 'Joint Defence Doctrine', whereby an attack on unoccupied Cyprus would be considered as an attack on Greece.

CONCLUSIONS

The official Greek position on Cyprus was to support the UN formula, the inter-communal talks and Cyprus' accession to the EU, to the point of vetoing enlargement had any EU member opposed Cyprus' accession. With Cyprus' membership the stakes are getting higher.

A purist Greek attitude to the Cyprus problem, written by a Greek ambassador, Themistocles Chrysanthopoulos, who was also Greek consul-general during the expulsion of most of the ethnic Greek population of Istanbul in 1964, reads:

> The Cypriot constitution of 1959 was applied more or less satisfactorily until the July 1974 Greek coup to overthrow President Makarios, the President of Cyprus.
>
> Turkey then intervened militarily 'to restore constitutional order.' Constitutional order was restored almost immediately with the return of Archbishop Makarios. The Turkish occupation troops are still there, supposedly to protect the Turkish Cypriots, who were in no way involved in the coup, despite a whole series of UN resolutions calling upon Turkey to withdraw them. The Turkish government also sent 80,000 [now 100,000] settlers and set up a quisling Government in northern occupied Cyprus. Were these measures taken to restore constitutional order? The Turkish troops of occupation are still there [...] Any solution in the presence of troops of occupation would be politically and legally wrong. It would legalise military invasion and occupation, creating a disastrous precedent. It would disappoint the peoples of Cyprus and Greece, and have unpredictable political repercussions.
>
> If there is to be a viable solution to the Cyprus question, the Turkish troops, the Turkish settlers and the quisling Turkish Cypriot government must evacuate Cyprus, before any negotiations between the parties concerned. And once they are gone, there might well no longer be a Cyprus question to solve.[18]

Although it is unlikely that the current Greek government would dare to enunciate such a solution, for fear of upsetting Washington and Ankara, it nevertheless represents the 'ideal' Greek view. Greece is essentially juggling its own national interests by maintaining the Joint Defence Doctrine, to deter Turkey from attacking free Cyprus, and at the same time sticking firmly to the UN line on Cyprus. The tradition where Greece is pulled in different directions by foreign powers is, however, also still a factor of Greek foreign policy, visible in the massive arms purchases it is obliged to make, although there has been some recent cost-cutting. The USA exerted immense pressure on Greece to buy the 'Patriot' anti-missile system rather than the Russian 'S-300'. Similarly, after Greece had announced its participation in the Eurofighter consortium, it curiously postponed this, amid some journalistic accusations of yielding to US pressure. It is worth bearing in mind here the 'Lockheed bribery scandal' of the 1970s, in which Prince

Bernhard of the Netherlands (titular head of the Dutch air force) was censured, and a highly placed Italian committed suicide.

Apart from the arms lobby, foreign influence, particularly US and British, is also strong in education. Thousands of Greek students unable to gain a place at a Greek state university attend sometimes mediocre private and purely profit-motivated American colleges (not recognised by the Greek Ministry of Education), where they are sometimes fed a diet of US foreign policy objectives, through ambassadors' visits and the like. 'Alternative' views by staff are suppressed by staff being fired with no reason given. Those who remain are either cowed or 'sweetened'. The US ambassador himself (whose wife has taught at a college) has been pressing the Greek government to recognise even the mediocre colleges. Some journalists and others have wondered whether some of these 'establishments' are front organisations, at best, or merely spearheading 'cultural imperialism' at worst, particularly since one refuses to reveal its accounts. At one college, Kissinger's book *Diplomacy* is the recommended course book on a course entitled 'Diplomacy'. Far from teaching the ins and outs of diplomacy, the book is essentially a personal view of power politics. Thousands of Greek students go to the EU and US to study, with Britain the most popular destination. Thousands more attend UK-franchised establishments in Greece, some good and some bad. French, once Greece's de facto second language, has completely lost out to English – of total worldwide entrants to the Cambridge Certificate of English, half are from tiny Greece.

Even terrorism, in the form of the notorious 17 November group, has not escaped speculation about foreign interference in Greece. The organisation, which named itself after the date of the 1973 demonstrations that led to the Ioannides takeover (see Chapter Six), began its serial killing in 1975, with the shooting of the head of the CIA station in Athens, Richard Welsh, following up with more Americans and a Turkish diplomat, then returning to Greek targets. Its final killing was of the British military attaché, Stephen Saunders, on 8 June 2000, as he was driving to discuss an arms deal with the Greek government. Unfortunately, his driver happened to be ill that day, and Saunders drove himself. The killing resulted in Scotland Yard officers being allowed into Greece to help with investigations. In late summer 2002, a member of the group was injured when a bomb he was carrying went off, leading to a spectacular series of confessions and arrests. For some of the press, it all seemed too simple. How could such an efficient organisation that had killed twenty-four people in almost thirty years without any convictions resulting, suddenly collapse like a pack of cards?

A British embassy guard allegedly tried to commit suicide on 23 June 2000, claiming in a letter that he felt guilty about not having informed Saunders about two men on a motorbike who had been watching the embassy. A television station, Antenna, actually went round to the guard's house and filmed the guard's wife holding his letter, which was transmitted on the afternoon news. It ended with a PS saying 'May God forgive my country for killing its children.' The story then appears to have been suppressed, the suppression campaign being run by the head of station at the British embassy in Athens, who, after working night and day, was sent to do a sabbatical. Many of the embassy staff were posted on, some not even knowing about the 'Dunford PS'. When the guard recovered three days later, he was whisked straight from hospital to the embassy. It appears that nobody – at least publicly – has asked the guard what he meant by his PS, and whether he simply staged the attempted suicide to protect himself through publicity. According to the embassy, the guard (who had been working there for sixteen years, locally engaged) was still working at the embassy in July 2003, as an internal messenger. This is most curious, since any embassy employee who attempted suicide, particularly in a way likely to attract publicity, would almost certainly be considered a security risk, or be pensioned off, or given extended leave. On the other hand, he is in safe hands at the embassy. His wife has since died. When this author contacted the embassy guard to clear up the above, he immediately said: 'I'm sorry, I can't talk…it's my job…contact the Embassy Press section.'[19] The embassy told this author that they could not discuss staff matters.[20] While this is understandable, the tale is a curious one.

Saunders' wife, Heather, was and is particularly angry, since shortly before her husband's murder, his security protection rating was not increased by the deputy head of mission, despite the fact that Dunford and M16 knew of a security risk; in fact, the head of stations' advice to increase Saunders' level of protection was studiously (or stupidly) ignored. This author discussed the whole story with the head of the Greek Intelligence Service. At the end of the discussion, Mr Apostolides (who had been, uncharacteristically, appointed to the position from an ambassadorial rank in the Greek diplomatic service) said that he would try to find Dunford's suicide letter. He was unable to find it.[21] There has even been speculation that Saunders was killed for leaking information about bombing targets in Serbia (he was known to be a humane man).

Greece provides a rich environment for all manner of conspiracy theories, some serious and some less so. The 17 November story is still unfolding, with some suspecting that the organisation had been infiltrated by powerful foreign business interests and was used as a cover/front organisation to 'dispense with' perceived risks. Whatever the truth about 17 November, the saga illustrates the speculation about foreign interference that occasionally runs rife in Greece. Greece is now becoming increasingly integrated with the European Union. The country's postwar tradition of being pulled between the USA and Britain has been overtaken by a new tug-of-war, between the EU and the US–UK partnership. The Cyprus problem adds poignancy, as the island's EU membership develops. The Greek government probably hopes that the sheer force of the EU will eventually, somehow, bring a lasting agreement. The government is however keen to please the USA in defence matters, and is currently being strongly pressed to take a US/UK line over Cyprus, helped by some of the US- and UK-supported academics who advise the Greek government.[22]

PART III

Keeping the Fingers in the Pie

INTRODUCTION

The third and last part of this book is devoted to considering and evaluating current topics, themes and developments germane to Cyprus' position in the world. It will offer some prognoses, by considering various 'possibilities and probabilities'. As such, the history of the secret diplomatic contortions in Part I, and the policies of the poker players set out in Part II provide sufficient ingredients to undertake this part. The inadequacy of the responses of some governments to the author's questions (Chapter Fourteen) should be seen in conjunction with these final chapters. Reasons for the inadequacy of those responses are one or a combination of the following: the Cyprus question is still in the melting pot; current policy-making is still rather confused; some governments do not wish to be seen to be taking sides, and are adopting the 'wait and see' approach while they keep whatever cards they have close to their chest; and transatlantic tensions on the future of European defence. Those who did respond with some degree of clarity may be so sure of the outcome that they do not mind answering questions.

The geopolitics[1] surrounding the Cyprus question has, given the 'European question', become more intense. Before embarking on our critique, it is important to consider Greek–Turkish relations.

11 Graeco–Turkish Relations: The Cypriot Thorn

Like Greece, Turkey did not view the Cyprus problem in isolation, but as an important bargaining counter.[1]

INTRODUCTION

Ever since Britain's cynically contrived conference, in September 1955, on 'political and defence questions in the Eastern Mediterranean, including Cyprus', various Graeco–Turkish disputes have reared their ugly heads.

The anti-Greek rioting in Istanbul on the night of 6 September 1955 was the most obvious example of how the British colony had become a tawdry tool to destroy the painstaking work by Venizelos and Ataturk to maintain stable relations. Another blatant example was the expulsion of almost the whole of the 80,000-strong ethnic Greek community of Istanbul at the time of the intercommunal troubles in the mid-1960s. It is hardly coincidental that the Turkish invasion of Cyprus was preceded by infringements of Greek airspace by Turkish military aircraft, by the dispatch of a Turkish survey ship and thirty warships to Greek waters and by the granting of oil exploration rights. Then, only three days before the invasion, Turkey claimed sovereignty of the whole continental shelf east of the median line between the Greek and Turkish mainlands 'regardless of the location of Greek islands'.[2] Since then, whenever there has been a crisis in Cyprus, or Turkey's efforts to hamper Cyprus' accession to the EU have been frustrated, there has been a concomitant crisis in Graeco–Turkish relations, papered over occasionally by meetings between the Greek and Turkish foreign ministers or by actions such as the recent bout of 'earthquake diplomacy'[3] resulting in the signing of a series of agreements in the fields of culture, tourism, commerce and illegal immigration. Greece has made no claims on Turkish territory since the signing of the Treaty of Lausanne in 1923, while Turkey has increasingly made claims in the following areas: territorial waters, airspace, the continental shelf, islands, and the Muslim population of

Western Thrace, which Turkey considers 'Turkish' (although it does not officially claim the territory).

This chapter is not an attempt exhaustively to set out and argue the legal, legalistic and moral rights and wrongs of the Turkish claims, but rather to set them out succinctly, since they are inextricably linked to the Cyprus question, insofar as the latter has led to the claims being made with increasing stridency.[4]

THE AEGEAN-IMIA

Although the Treaty of Lausanne was meant to resolve the question of ownership of the Aegean islands, Turkish probing and questioning of borders grew as the Cyprus problem intensified. The most poignant example was the Imia crisis, which almost led to war. Although even the US National Imagery and Mapping Agency indicates that the Imia (Kardak in Turkish) islets belong to Greece,[5] the captain of a Turkish bulk carrier that ran aground on Imia on Christmas Day 1995 refused Greek assistance, on the grounds that Imia was Turkish. This was despite the fact that the Italo–Turkish Agreements of 1932, which traced the sea frontier between Turkey and the Dodecanese, placed Imia on the (Italian) Dodecanese side. The Turkish government addressed to the Greek government a note claiming the islets, which was rejected. The mayor of nearby Kalymnos then planted the Greek flag, which was torn down and replaced with the Turkish flag by a group of Turkish journalists. On 31 January 1996, Turkish commandos landed on the smaller of the two islets. There was a military stand-off. Thanks to American intervention, the two sides agreed not to fly their respective flags on Imia. The EU approach to the affair was dithering and incompetent, to the chagrin and irritation of the Greek government. The then Turkish prime minister, Tansu Ciller, threatened war, while the Turkish Foreign Ministry stated: 'There are hundreds of little islands, islets and rocks in the Aegean, and their status remains unclear.'[6]

Ciller estimated the number of these islands to be around a thousand, while the Turkish government even laid claim to a non-Aegean island, Gavdos, off the southern coast of Crete, in the Libyan Sea.

As regards Imia, Turkey claims that the Italo–Turkish Convention of 4 January 1932 and a *Procès Verbale* of 28 December the same year, which stipulated clearly that Imia was Italian, are invalid because of the 'particular political situation of the pre-Second World War era'.[7] In addition to this rather nebulous and curious statement, the Turkish government then points out that the legal procedures were not completed, since the *Procès Verbale* was not registered at the League of Nations; and that the Greek government had subsequently proposed talks with Turkey to 'ascertain the validity of the agreements'.[8] There was also no mention of examples of Greek sovereignty, such as a lighthouse or other installations. The Turkish government's position suggests that islands not mentioned in the Treaty of Lausanne and the Paris Peace Treaty of 1947 are 'fair game', thus further enriching the legal landscape.

THE DODECANESE AND OTHER EASTERN AEGEAN ISLANDS

Since the Imia crisis, which can be viewed as the tip of the iceberg of Turkey's unilateral statements about 'grey zones', Turkey has repeatedly put forward other reasons to justify its claims. One is that neither the 1914 'Athens decision of the Six Powers', which ceded most of the Aegean islands to Greece, nor the Treaty of Lausanne, mentioned islets or rocks by name and that the latter treaty only uses the term 'adjacent islets'. More significantly, the Turkish government points to the Paris Treaty of 1947, which stipulates that the Dodecanese 'shall be and shall remain demilitarized', which they are not.

More generally, the Turkish view is that the Aegean should not be a 'Greek lake', and that Turkey is entitled to an equitable share of the Sea's resources. On the question of Greece's right to extend its territorial waters to twelve miles (under the UN Law of the Sea Convention, which Greece has signed and Turkey has not), Turkey has threatened war with Greece, should the latter attempt to enforce her twelve-mile limit. Turkey nevertheless enforces its own twelve-mile limit in the Black Sea. Were Greece and Turkey to extend their limits to twelve miles, then their respective shares of the Aegean Sea would increase from 35 per cent and 7.6 per cent to 64 per cent and 8.8 per cent respectively, thus eroding Turkish claims to its continental shelf, which Turkey considers to include that of some Greek islands.

The purist Greek riposte to Turkey's Aegean claims is summed up comprehensively in the following interpretation, written by a former Greek ambassador, Themistocles Chrysanthopoulos:

> All the islands in the north Aegean Sea, Lemnos, Samothrace, Mytilene, Chios, Samos, Icaria, Imbros, Tenedos and the Lagousae Islands, were occupied by the Greek navy during the first Balkan War in 1912. The 1913 Peace Treaty [...] of London was the final decision regarding the status of these islands, reached by the then Great Powers, namely Great Britain, Austro–Hungary, France, Germany, Italy and Russia (Article 5). Although this treaty was never ratified, the relevant Article 5 was restated in Article 15 of the then 1913 Peace Treaty. Ultimately, the six Great Powers, by a decision taken in London on 13 February 1914, gave Greece the above first six islands in the north Aegean Sea, on the condition that all Greek troops evacuated northern Epirus. Greece complied immediately, and the decision of the Great Powers was finally confirmed by Article 12 of the Lausanne Peace Treaty. The three remaining islands, Imbros, Tenedos and Lagousae, were returned to Turkey under the same Article 12. Although Article 14 established a régime of self-government for the Greek-speaking population of these islands, this was ignored by the Turkish government. Under Article 13 four Greek islands, Mytilene, Chios, Samos and Icaria, were placed under partial demilitarisation. Flights over these islands, and the opposite coast of Asia Minor, were also mutually prohibited.

LAUSANNE CONVENTION ON THE STATUS OF THE STRAITS
24 JULY 1923

Under Article 4 of this convention, together with the demilitarisation of the Straits, the remaining two Greek islands, Lemnos and Samothrace, were also demilitarised, together with the aforementioned three Turkish islands.

MONTREUX CONVENTION ON THE STRAITS, 20 APRIL 1936

During the deterioration of world affairs in the 1930s, Turkey succeeded in convening an international conference, aimed at ending the demilitarisation of the Straits. The conference took place in Montreux and the Convention was signed on 20 April 1936:

1. The foreword [preamble] of the Convention states that it 'substitutes' for the Lausanne Convention of 1923. This means that the Lausanne Convention was abolished and no longer exists. This is confirmed by the indices of international agreements of both the United Kingdom and France. In the British Index 1101–1968 Volume 3, page 69, it is stated that the 1923 Lausanne Convention on the Straits was abolished by the Montreux Convention. The Lausanne Convention is not even mentioned in the French Index. As for the Lausanne Peace Treaty, it is stated that it is valid insofar as it has not been modified by the Montreux Convention.

2. There is no mention in the Montreux Convention of the abolition of the demilitarisation of the Straits, although this was the purpose of the conference. But since the Lausanne Convention had been terminated and replaced by the Montreux Convention, there was no need to deal with the abolition of the demilitarisation of the Straits. With the abolition of the 1923 Convention, full sovereignty over the Straits, and the Turkish and Greek islands that had been demilitarised under the Lausanne Convention, was restored. Only in the Protocol attached to the Convention is it stated that Turkey could remilitarise the Straits and the Turkish islands, upon the signature of the Convention. As for the other dispositions of the Convention, they were to start to be applied by Turkey, as of 15th August 1936.

There is no mention in the Protocol of the two demilitarised Greek islands (Lemnos and Samothrace). Therefore the abolition of their demilitarisation took effect only with the ratification of the Convention according to Article 26.

3. As for the partial demilitarisation of the remaining four Greek islands (Mytilene, Chios, Samos and Icaria) which had been imposed under Article 13 of the Lausanne Peace Treaty, it could be said that it continues to be effective, since these islands were not mentioned in the 1923 Convention of the Straits. However, it could also be claimed that, since the partial demilitarisation of the four islands was due entirely to the demilitarisation of the Straits, there was no longer any reason for the four Greek islands to continue to be partially demilitarised. This is also the interpretation of France. The French Index states that all dispositions of the Lausanne Peace Treaty, which are contrary to the Montreux Convention, have been tacitly abolished. The writer agrees with this interpretation.

CONCLUSIONS:

1. Remilitarisation of the Straits and the Turkish islands, after the signature of the Montreux Convention.
2. Remilitarisation of the two Greek islands demilitarised under the Lausanne Convention, after its ratification. Similarly, remilitarisation of the remaining four Greek islands, their original demilitarisation being incompatible with the 1936 Montreux Convention.
3. In spite of the two Conventions relating to the Straits of 1923 and 1936, the Straits remained closed to the allies during WWII, because of the neutrality of Turkey.

DODECANESE ISLANDS

During the war of Italy against Turkey in 1911, aimed at colonising Libya, Rome decided to occupy the Dodecanese Islands, in order to open up a second front. In the ensuing Peace Treaty between the two countries, in which Libya was ceded to Italy, it was also agreed that the Dodecanese Islands would remain under Italian rule, until the Libyan resistance movement ended. Eventually the Dodecanese Islands were definitely acquired by Italy under Article 15 of the 1923 Lausanne Peace treaty.

Subsequently, the sea frontier between the Dodecanese Islands and the Turkish mainland was established in detail by two Italo–Turkish agreements, both signed in Ankara, dated 4 January and 28 December 1932. The first was registered with the League of Nations on May 23rd 1933 (Vol. CXXXVIII Page 244). The second agreement was not registered, being considered a supplement of the first.

During WWII, the Dodecanese Islands were occupied, first by German troops, and eventually by British forces. Finally the Dodecanese Islands were ceded to Greece under Article 15 of the Paris Peace Treaty with Italy, in 1947.

During the discussion on the subject, the Greek delegation requested that the two Italo–Turkish agreements of 1932 be mentioned in the Treaty, but this was considered unnecessary. In any case, these two agreements are binding, for Turkey as a signatory, and for Greece, which succeeded Italy, the original signatory.

Under the same Article 15, the islands were demilitarised, at the request of the former USSR. Moscow had originally endeavoured to acquire one of the islands to serve as a Soviet naval base in the Mediterranean. Once this proved unattainable because of the resistance of the other allies, the USSR delegation finally agreed that the Dodecanese Islands should be ceded to Greece, but on the condition that they be demilitarised, so that they could not be used as naval bases by the United Kingdom.

Turkey is completely opposed to the remilitarisation of the Dodecanese Islands, but its claims are groundless for the following reasons:
1. The demilitarisation was decided upon at the insistence of the USSR, for its own reasons
2. According to Article 16 of the Lausanne Peace Treaty, 'Turkey renounces all titles or rights of all nature, to territories that lie beyond its frontiers, as

established by the present Treaty, as well as to islands, except those, the sovereignty of which remains with it (Turkey),' the ultimate sovereignty over these territories and islands having been established, or to be established, by the interested parties.

3. Turkey is not among the signatories of the 1947 Peace Treaty with Italy, not having participated in the war against Italy. According to article 89 of the Treaty, the dispositions of the Treaty cannot be invoked by states that have not signed, or acceded to, it. Therefore Turkey has no right to invoke the demilitarisation of the Dodecanese Islands.

DEMILITARISATION

According to Article 51 of the UN Charter, the right of self-defence is established for all territories of all the member states. This right naturally covers all demilitarised territories as well. The Greek islands offer free passage to both naval and commercial vessels to and from Turkish ports.

The Greek islands cannot be used strategically for an eventual military landing on the coast of Asia Minor, nor is there any such Greek intention, now, or in the future. Strategically speaking, any such landing would necessarily embark from the Greek mainland. On the other hand, the IV Turkish Army, stationed along the coast of Asia Minor, and supplied with a large number of landing craft, constitutes a permanent threat to Greece.

ABOLITION OF DEMILITARISATION IN GENERAL

After the creation of the two post-war major alliances (NATO and the Warsaw Pact), the demilitarisation of the Italian islands Pantelaria, Lampedousa, Lampione and Linosa was unilaterally abolished. West Germany too was remilitarised. On the Eastern side, Bulgaria, Romania, East Germany, Hungary and Poland were also remilitarised. Therefore the concept of demilitarisation has been mutually abolished, de facto. It is therefore not acceptable that Turkey should demand the demilitarisation of the Dodecanese Islands for the supplementary reason that they belong to Greece, a state which, together with Turkey, belongs to the same alliance, namely NATO.

TERRITORIAL WATERS AND THE
CONTINENTAL SHELF

All islands have their own territorial waters and continental shelf, according to Article 121 of the Code of the Law of the Sea, singed in Montego Bay, Jamaica on 10 January 1982.

Beyond territorial waters, the sea is open to all. Therefore there cannot be 'grey zones' which are claimed by states beyond their own territorial waters, nor can there be claims on 'unnamed islands' within the territorial waters of another state. 'Continental Shelf' is a recent concept. It refers exclusively to the bottom of the sea and has no connection with the surface.

CONCLUSIONS

A. The Greek islands in the Aegean Sea belong to Greece, with definite sea frontiers with Turkey, for the following reasons:
1.Greeks have inhabited them since time immemorial.
2.They have been ceded to Greece by international treaties.
B. The islands do not constitute impediments, either economic or military, to access to and from the Turkish mainland. In any case, both Greece and Turkey belong to the same alliance, NATO. This requires peaceful relations between the two countries.
C. The original demilitarisation restrictions on the islands through international treaties and conventions have since been lifted by the 1936 Montreux Convention regarding the Straits, and by the *de facto* international abolition of all demilitarised zones. The Greek islands are now, therefore, all under the full sovereignty of Greece.
D. According to the Code of the Law of the Sea of 1982, the Greek islands all have their own territorial water and continental shelf.
E. Beyond the territorial waters of the Greek mainland and the Greek islands, lies the open Aegean Sea. There can be no gray zones' or 'unnamed islands, islets or rocks,' as claimed by Turkey. All unnamed islands, islet or rocks within the territorial waters of Greece belong to Greece. If there are any such islands, islets or rocks, beyond the territorial waters of Greece, they belong to no one.
F. According to Article 16 of the 1923 Lausanne Peace Treaty, Turkey has renounced all titles and rights to all territories or islands ceded to other states. Therefore Turkey cannot have any claims on Greek islands.
G. Turkey, as a candidate for entry to the European Union cannot have territorial claims against Greece, a full member of the same European Union. In any event, when Turkey eventually enters the European Union, these claims would lose all significance.[9] [ends]

AIRSPACE

Since the invasion of Cyprus, Turkey has questioned Greece's ten-mile airspace limit, on the grounds that it extends beyond that country's six-mile (Turkish recognised) sea limits. Athens responds by saying that no state has ever questioned its adoption, in 1931, of a ten-mile airspace limit, and that the International Law of the Sea Convention defines national airspace as an element of the territorial sea. To complicate the issue further, Turkey contests the Athens Flight Information Region (FIR). In August 1974, as it was invading Cyprus, it issued a unilateral 'Notice to Airmen (NOTAM), moving the limits of the Istanbul FIR westwards, up to the middle of the Aegean. This led to dangerous confusion, since pilots did not know whether to report to Athens or to Istanbul and whose instructions to follow. Greece responded with its own NOTAM, stating that it could not accept responsibility for traffic information or safety measures on the international air routes of the Aegean. The International Civil Aviation Organisation declared the

Aegean a danger area. Although Turkey withdrew its NOTAM in 1980, it continues to 'violate the rules of international airspace within the Athens FIR'.[10]

THE MINORITIES IRRITANT

Although the ethnic Greek (officially 'non-Muslim') populations of Istanbul and the islands of Gökçeada (Imvros) and Bozcada (Tenedos) are now on their way to extinction, the ethnic Turkish (officially 'Muslim') population of Western Thrace continues to thrive. The Treaty of Lausanne exempted these two groups from the population exchange and guaranteed their rights. As we have seen, the extinction of the 'non-Muslims' is a direct result of the Cyprus problem. Although the treatment of the non-Muslims in Turkey is clearly indefensible, the Muslims of Western Thrace – particularly those of ethnic Turkish origin, rather than gypsies and Pomaks – have not exactly been encouraged to stay put and there has been some emigration. The Greek government has also expropriated land in Western Thrace (as elsewhere), an act which has naturally been exploited for political purposes by the Turkish government, particularly during times of crisis. In 1923, 'the Turkish community' represented two thirds of the population of Western Thrace, owning eighty-four per cent of the land. By 1990, the 'Turkish community' represented thirty-four per cent of the population, owning twenty per cent of the land.[11] Many of the Muslims have, however, left because of the strength of the drachma (now the euro) against the Turkish lira, and set up businesses elsewhere.

Greek governmental intervention in local affairs has also caused irritation in the past. For example, until the military Junta, the muftis (local Muslim religious leaders) were elected; but in 1973, the minister of religious affairs appointed a gypsy Muslim as mufti, infuriating the ethnic Turks.[12]

Whatever the debate about who has been 'nastier' to whom, the figures speak for themselves: there are few 'Christians of Greek stock' left in Turkey, while there are plenty of Muslims in Greece, including those of Turkish stock. Nowadays, perhaps because of past excesses, the Greek government is particularly scrupulous in ensuring the equal rights of Muslim Greeks. As for the ethnic Greeks of Istanbul, their dwindling number makes them an increasingly weak stick with which to beat Greece when times are tense in Cyprus.

Were the Greek government to adopt an aggressive position vis-à-vis the Turkish claims, it could of course make counter-threats. For example, it could lay claim to Imvros and Tenedos on the grounds that Turkey has ignored the rights of the island's now minute ethnic Greek population, in contravention of Article 14 of the Treaty of Lausanne, part of which reads:

> The islands of Imbros and Tenedos remaining under Turkish sovereignty will benefit from a special administrative organisation comprising local elements and affording a complete guarantee to the indigenous non-Moslem population, as regards local administration as well as the protection of people and goods.

The maintenance of order will be assured by police who will be recruited among the local population and placed under the authority of the above-mentioned administration.

CONCLUSIONS

Turkey's position regarding its claims is essentially political and somewhat legalistic, while Greece has scrupulously defended its position by constant reference to international law. Turkish overtures to Greece to discuss all the problems bilaterally as a package have been interpreted by the Greek government as an attempt to make it recognise that Turkey's claims have some basis in law. Thus, Greece has repeatedly invited Turkey to submit its claims to arbitration at the International Court of Justice. The Turkish government has in turn repeatedly refused to take its claims to arbitration, which has weakened its position. The only issue on which the Greek government is flexible is that of the continental shelf, but there has been no progress, since Turkey continues to insist on a bilateral 'package deal'.

Turkey's claims on territory that Greece considers Greek make some other claims look like a friendly game of tiddlywinks. For example, Britain and the Republic of Ireland both claim the islet of Rockall (south of Iceland), while Denmark claims Rockall's continental shelf. Despite years of fruitless negotiations, there has never been even the hint of military aggression. Similarly, the Netherlands wishes to 'polderise' part of the Eems-Dollart estuary. Germany resists the suggestion. A joint commission meets periodically, agrees to disagree and goes home. German jets do not 'buzz' the Eems-Dollart. Humour apart, neither Rockall nor the Eems-Dollart is a matter of vital national interest to the parties involved, while the opposite can be considered true in the case of Greece and Turkey, at least from their perspective. It is the Cyprus problem that, almost by default, influences the agenda of Greek–Turkish relations. This connection was made abundantly clear in the (EU) Helsinki Council of Ministers' stipulation in 1996 that 'candidate states' should settle any outstanding border disputes or bring them to the International Court of Justice. Britain, perhaps because of its interests in Cyprus, has done its best to avoid agreeing with Greece's position on questions such as the remilitarisation of the island of Limnos, tending to give non-committal replies for fear of 'upsetting the Turkish apple cart'. It is however significant that in 1972, a senior FCO official referred to 'what looks *prima facie* like a strong Greek case in law'.[13]

We now turn to a necessarily brief – there are few diplomatic files available – overview and exegesis of the Cyprus problem since 1974. Hopefully, the foregoing eleven chapters should facilitate the task.

12 The Current Occupation Period

One safe conclusion is that negotiations alone cannot bridge the wide gap between the two communities.[1]

INTRODUCTION

The bulk of the pertinent 'backstage' diplomatic documentary evidence for the years between 1975 and today has not yet been released, although the 1975 papers were released as this book was being sent to the publishers. We shall have to wait until 2035 for a reasonably clear picture of current diplomatic dealings – and double-dealings – over the Cyprus poker chips. Most of the written material enabling us to plot the course of post-1973 diplomatic developments comprises press reports, books, academic analyses and government statements to the press, but there is a dearth of primary source material. Some of the books and press columns are speculative, partisan, or opinionated.

We are, however, entitled to attempt to make reasoned assumptions, by combining what we do know today with the earlier diplomatic documents, since the latter serve very much as pointers to the future. There has been only marginal movement, public relations apart, on the Cyprus impasse since the invasion. Positions have coagulated, despite numerous apparent 'near breakthroughs', superficial bonhomie, crises and US commitments to 'solve the problem'. Foreign policy formulation and implementation tend to be slow processes and, *force majeure* apart, tend to remain on the same 'selfish' national railtrack. The only new potential power-broker is the European Union. Russia's influence is arguably considerably less than in the days of the USSR, while America's has increased. Yet we are still in a position of stalemate, which may almost by default lead to one of the scenarios that we shall discuss in the final chapter.

In attempting to highlight some of the major elements, we need to bear in mind that the public positions adopted by the poker players do not necessarily reflect their secret objectives. In 1955, for example, one of Britain's objectives in calling for the fateful tripartite conference was to stir up trouble between Greece and Turkey, in order to hang on to Cyprus. Had the Greek government, or the American public, been aware of this secret objective, the Greek government would never have attended the conference in the first place. Today, Britain's objective, given its recent updating of its electronic spying facilities, is to keep its finger in the pie. At the same time, it is adopting as low a profile as it can on the question of the bases, particularly in view of the problem of its 'Dependent Territory', Gibraltar, which it is currently discussing with Spain. Although Britain and Greece publicly support UN resolutions on Cyprus, it is worth bearing in mind the quotation: 'All that glisters is not gold {...} gilded tombs do worms infold.'[2]

The main elements to consider are Graeco–Turkish relations, outside powers, and international efforts, which are of course connected to the intercommunal talks.

GRAECO–TURKISH RELATIONS

As we have seen in the previous chapter, the Cyprus problem has been central to Graeco–Turkish relations since 1955. It exercises a considerable influence on Greek and Turkish internal politics. The most obvious example of this is that the Cyprus problem led to the collapse of the Greek Junta and to a more aggressive Turkish stance towards Greece. Similarly, when Greece joined the European Community in 1981, there was a mutual hardening of relations, leading to the declaration of the 'Turkish Republic of Northern Cyprus' two years later. Crises over Cyprus and in Graeco–Turkish relations have often become intertwined, to the extent that they merge into a morass of competing problems. It is no coincidence that the following events took place in the seventeen months between March 1995 and August 1996: the announcement by the EU Council of Ministers that Cyprus' accession negotiations would begin six months after the conclusion of the 1996 (EU) Intergovernmental Conference; the EU Summit in Madrid in December 1995, when Germany poured cold water on Turkey's EU aspirations;[3] the Imia crisis immediately thereafter; and the killings by Turkish extremists of two Greek Cypriots on the Green Line in August 1996. This was followed by the 'S-300 crisis'. It is not unlike a Corneille play, where events occur at an increasing pace.

While it is obvious that Cyprus' accession negotiations with the EU led to increased Turkish intransigence and aggressive diplomacy, it is equally true that the Greek and Cypriot governments have themselves felt sufficiently emboldened not to budge substantively; and even to 'cock a snook' at Turkey and the Turkish administration in Cyprus. The S-300 crisis can be seen in this context. On the other hand, it can also be suggested that Turkey timed the Imia incident to coincide with the early weeks of the new Greek government of Costas Simitis, when the foreign minister, Pangalos, proved somewhat ineffective, for all his clever rhetoric and intellect.

Neither Greece nor Turkey has offered substantive changes in its policies vis-à-vis Cyprus. Matters inevitably boil down to the Greek side insisting on compliance with UN resolutions, while the Turkish side insists on recognition for Northern Cyprus before substantive talks can begin between the two communities. Obviously, the Greek and Turkish governments support 'their' respective Cypriot communities.

The Greece–Cyprus Joint Defence Doctrine, announced in 1993, has also further demonstrated how Cyprus affects Greek defence, as well as foreign, policy. It has come to a point where, if Greece were to 'give up on' Cyprus and abandon the 'Joint Defence Doctrine' of joint military exercises, withdrawing its air support for Cyprus, the Greek government would then still feel vulnerable about some of its own islands, since the Turkish military would interpret the demise of the Greece–Cyprus axis as weakness. Moreover, given the troubled relations between previous successive unstable Greek governments and the more stable – but less sovereign – post-1964 Cyprus government, there is a subtle yet almost palpable lack of confidence between the two governments at the diplomatic level.

Although, at least presentationally, the recent Simitis government pursued a conciliatory line towards Turkey, this was not reciprocated. For example, following a European Court of Human Rights judgment in May 2001 that Turkey was guilty of 'massive and continued violations of human rights arising from its 1974 invasion of Northern Cyprus', the Turkish foreign minister said: 'There is no limit to what we can do to avert Cyprus' accession to the EU.'[4] This is another example of how, as in the case of Greece, the Cyprus problem is key to Turkish foreign policy. As for Greece's seemingly bland and non-confrontational prime minister, who served until March 2004, even he has pointed out that 'Graeco–Turkish relations cannot improve much further as long as the present stalemate on Cyprus continues.'[5]

Each country is using Cyprus as a stick with which to beat the other. Notwithstanding the Greek government's less bellicose stance, it can still be criticised for unnecessarily needling the Turkish establishment, particularly via the official information sheets that some of its embassies distribute. Such headings as 'The Arduous Task of Helping Turkey Become European', 'Ankara Isolated, Defiant, Aggressive',[6] 'Old Turkish Habits Die Hard'[7] and 'Cyprus Within Reach of the EU: Turkey Fulminates'[8] are hardly designed to foster good relations. Normally, one would expect such government rhetoric (whether justified or not) to be disseminated in a subtle fashion, such as the British government's way of distributing 'unattributable' texts (in brown envelopes) via the successor to the 'disbanded' Information Research Department of the Foreign and Commonwealth Office.

Graeco–Turkish relations have been particularly volatile since the British-inspired conference in 1955, and are unlikely to undergo any genuine *détente* until a proper and mutually agreed solution to the Cyprus problem has been worked out. If the wallpaper is merely pasted over the cracks again, that will be a recipe for future conflict.

OUTSIDE POWERS AND INTERNATIONAL AFFAIRS

Here, we are talking about the main poker players, the USA and Britain, together with the United Nations. As we have seen, the USA has assumed ever-increasing responsibility for areas under former British and, to a lesser extent, French influence. Until Makarios' unnecessary death in 1977, America's fear of him dictated that country's policy to the extent that the USA decided that its listening posts and the British bases would be better protected in a divided Cyprus, hence the Acheson/Ball plan of 1964 and the Turkish invasion of 1974. Now, as then, NATO's interests have proved more important to US foreign and defence policy than pressuring the Turkish government to withdraw and allow the island to reunite. Thus, although America has presentationally supported various UN resolutions calling for the withdrawal of occupying troops and for the reunification of the island, her main concerns are her Middle East strategy, the Turkey–Israel military pact and NATO's interests. Therefore, until 1980, the USA tended to take 'a relaxed attitude towards peacemaking in Cyprus'.[9] Being relaxed did not, however, mean that American policy was lackadaisical. In 1978, together with Britain and Canada, the USA proposed a British-inspired plan calling for a bi-communal federal state with two constituent regions. Since the plan would have severely curtailed the extent of the central government's power, restricted freedom of movement, left the Turkish side with an area greater than their population merited and curtailed property rights, it was rejected by the Cypriot government. A political parallel can be drawn with the so-called 'Annan Plan' of November 2002 (see Chapter Fifteen).

From 1980, concerned at the continuing impasse and wishing to ensure that the Cyprus stalemate did not further bedevil Graeco–Turkish relations, the USA began to become increasingly active in seeking a settlement. The generally populist – and at times presentationally anti-American – stance of the Andreas Papandreou government, together with political instability in Turkey, led to a warming of relations between the USA and Turkey, particularly after the military coup of September 1980. Although the State Department generally favoured the Greek position,[10] the Pentagon, more concerned with keeping Turkey's huge army firmly NATO-friendly, tended to support the Turkish government's position on Cyprus. So, it appears, did the CIA. When the 1980 coup in Turkey occurred, the duty officer in the 'Situation Room' of the National Security Council said to the official in charge of the Middle East, (a career CIA member, whose last foreign posting had been head of the CIA station in Ankara), 'Paul [Henze], you boys have finally pulled a coup!'[11] When Carter lost the election and Reagan became president, US policy began to place even more emphasis than before on keeping Turkey stable. The amount of US aid to Turkey increased dramatically.[12] When the Reagan administration managed, despite opposition from Congress, to obtain $855 million for Turkey, Denktash announced the establishment of the 'Turkish Republic of Northern Cyprus'. This would have been difficult to 'establish' while Carter was still in power. It is perhaps unfortunate that during the presidential campaign, Carter did not have the time to resolve the problem.

Despite howls of protest from Congress and the State Department, or perhaps because of them, the Reagan administration intensified its efforts to bring about a Cyprus solution, while continuing to attach considerable importance to Turkey. Hence it supported any initiative likely to suggest a solution to the Cyprus impasse. Although the proximity talks in New York in 1984 were conducted by the UN, and were to lead to a summit between Denktash, and the Cypriot president, Kyprianou, in January 1985, US 'cooperation' was intense. The reason for unofficial but intense US involvement was to play down the role of the UN, since the latter's prominence strengthened the Soviet Union's policy, which was to push for a more centralised and independent Cyprus, rather than a (loose) federation. 'In reality,' writes one seasoned observer, 'UN diplomats played second fiddle to the Americans.'[13]

By the time of the summit, the UN – with obvious US and subtle British participation – had prepared a 'draft framework agreement', which would form the basis of an 'historic' agreement to be signed by the leaders of the two Cypriot communities. The US government media relations machine then got to work and prepared the media for this historic agreement. According to one writer, the US knew that President Kyprianou would have to reject the agreement, thereby strengthening Turkey's position by default.[14] The actual agreement was, according to the Cypriots, presented as a *fait accompli*, entailing, *inter alia*, the following: a 70:30 Greek–Turkish ratio in the Cabinet, an 80:20 ratio in the Lower House of Parliament, and a 50:50 one in the Upper House; 25 per cent of territory for the Turkish Cypriots; passports to be issued by the central government; political equality not to imply numerical equality of the two communities; and Turkish troops to be withdrawn after signature of the agreement.[15] Kyprianou rejected the paper, while Denktash accepted it. A disappointed world press depicted the former as responsible for the failure. The reality was that Denktash refused to negotiate over a document that, he claimed, the UN had agreed should be cast in stone, while Kyprianou considered it only as a basis for discussion. Thus he had to shoulder most of the blame, although it is significant that Denktash then rejected Kyprianou's suggestion of a second summit, citing impending Turkish Cypriot elections.[16] Shades of the present.

All negotiations up to the time of writing have come to little, despite the fall of the Berlin Wall, the much vaunted 'new world order', and express commitments by US presidents to bring about a settlement in Cyprus. The obvious sticking point is the Turkish side's insistence on prior recognition as a state, clearly unacceptable to the Greek side. The UN Security Council recently noted that progress remained disappointingly slow and that a target date of June 2002 for an agreement had not been met, also observing that the Turkish Cypriot side has been less constructive in its approach so far.[17] Certainly, the USA, especially now with its even greater reliance on Turkey in the matter of Iraq, is continuing to champion the massive influx of International Monetary Fund financial aid to Turkey. It is therefore unwilling to exert too much pressure on Turkey over Cyprus, knowing that the former can simply use its position vis-à-vis Iraq as a lever. If we also take into account America's current unilateral tendencies and its lack of regard for the UN, it is not easy for the beleaguered original Turkish Cypriot community – that which is left – to pressure Denktash to follow the official UN line. Basically, whatever the rhetoric, Turkey is currently so important to the strategy of the USA that the latter will not seriously irritate her, particularly because of the US–Turkey–Israel arrangement.[18]

The United Nations has theoretically been in charge of fostering a settlement ever since its involvement more than forty years ago, but the Security Council has failed to comply with General Assembly resolutions calling for the removal of the occupation troops, thus illustrating that it is really the poker players who determine matters. Both Greece and Turkey use Cyprus as a foreign policy tool against each other, while the USA and Britain insist, perhaps somewhat disingenuously, that the problem is merely 'intercommunal'. The impasse is essentially the result of 'years of shortsighted policy and manipulation by outside powers – Great Britain, Greece, Turkey and the United States'.[19] What then, of the former colonial controller, and current owner of parts of Cyprus, Britain?

BRITISH POLICY

As emphasised at the beginning of this chapter, we have no access to the most crucial British diplomatic documents for the last thirty years and must base our evaluation of British policy on reasoned assumption. While Britain has had its ups and downs with the USA, particularly during the Wilson and Heath eras, and to a lesser extent during Callaghan's tenure, she has never seriously impeded America's attainment of her strategic objectives. Although the Callaghan government was clearly upset by the Turkish invasion, it eventually went along with US policy on Cyprus. This cooperation was strengthened during the Thatcher era, when Mrs Thatcher even visited Turkey. Britain on its own would never have had the power to force the Turkish armed forces to leave Cyprus. She was more concerned with keeping her sovereign territories than with the niceties of international law. Thus, as we have already seen, Britain's policy was to obfuscate the legal issues and nurture the knowledge that the US Sixth Fleet would not intervene to stop a Turkish invasion. In 1974, Britain depended on the USA to convince the Turkish Army not to push even further south than it did (although there was a dangerous confrontation at Nicosia airport). Even then, she lost twelve of her thirty-one military and intelligence sites and installations in Cyprus, whereas US sites continued to operate in occupied Cyprus.[20] The main thing was the retention of the sovereign territories, which continue to operate today, in close cooperation with the USA. In 1987, the Thatcher government even blocked an attempt by MPs to examine how British policy could be changed to find a solution.[21]

It is paradoxical that the USA, rather than Britain, is the most involved outside power in the Cyprus game. Paradoxical, because while the USA has little historical and no legal *locus standi* in Cyprus, Britain's legal responsibility, as a co-signatory of the Treaties of Establishment and Guarantee, is clear to see. As the former colonial power, it also bears more historical responsibility than most for Cyprus' condition. Were Britain to take a more legal stand, rather than beat about the bush – as we have seen in its contorted (internal) attitude to the Treaties – this would of course clash with US policy, which is not currently overly concerned with abiding by the niceties of international law. There are considerations which transcend the rights of the people of a mere Mediterranean island like Cyprus, namely British and American policy towards EU enlargement, Britain's sovereignty and, concomitantly, British and American support for Turkey's application to join the EU. Behind it all lie Britain's bases, and other 'retained sites', which, according to the Director of Graeco–Turkish relations at the Greek Foreign Ministry,[22] make Cyprus (at least through its territory) fully accessible to NATO as if it is a de facto member. Blair now stands shoulder to shoulder with Bush on the latter's unilateral strategy, whatever the semantics. Neither Blair nor Bush could stomach a repeat of Edward's Heath's action in denying use of the sovereign base areas to help Israel in the Yom Kippur war. The question of the bases is likely to be a continuing sore between Britain and Cyprus, as well as one that is easy to exploit. Giant antennae have recently been erected at the British bases, leading thousands of Greek Cypriots to demonstrate against the very existence of the bases. According to a Cypriot MP, Britain asserted that Iraq had targeted these bases.[23] Many Cypriots argued that Britain was involving Cyprus in war.

Whatever the polemics, it is clear that Cyprus – and the British bases – are now part and parcel of American Middle East strategy, which is further to strengthen Israel and exercise control over the Middle East. Geostrategic and political factors therefore appear to be crucial to Britain and the USA as regards Cyprus. Yet for those who still prefer to follow law and morals more than geostrategic interest, there are other factors, to which we now turn.

13 Legality, Reality and Morality: The Difficult Triangle

Justice will only be achieved when those who are not wronged are as indignant as those who are.[1]

INTRODUCTION

Our weary world is well aware of the periodic bouts of hypocrisy in the conduct of international relations during which, all too often, selectivity and expediency are the order of the day. Looking for morality in international relations is like looking for a needle in a haystack. The national interests of the powerful tend to take precedence. The phenomenon is not new, although increasing unilateralist tendencies and globalisation in the 'new world disorder' are throwing into relief cases of inconsistency and double standards. It is useful to refresh our memories with a few events unrelated to the specific case of Cyprus, yet pertinent, in that they are all connected to the controversial area of double standards in the conduct of international relations. Recent history shows us how American President Wilson lectured the Europeans on the rights of self-determination (the Fourteen Point Plan et al.), while the blacks and indigenous Americans continued to be treated as second-class citizens. When Germany and the Soviet Union invaded Poland, Britain and France declared war only on Germany. The USA has consistently turned a blind eye to Israel's weapons of mass destruction, while making Iraq's apparent ability to develop such weapons a *casus belli*. Britain, keen to lease Diego Garcia to the USA, forced its own subjects to leave their homeland on US insistence, yet sailed across the world to defend its subjects in the Malvinas (Falkland Islands). Although NATO circumvented the United Nations and bombed Yugoslavia for seventy-eight days to 'save' the ethnic Albanians of part of Yugoslavia, Kosovo, it has done nothing to help the ethnic Chechens of Russia. Nor has it prevented Israel from mistreating the hundreds of thousands of Palestinians whom she expelled from their land, and their descendants. The USA and Britain protect the Kurds of Iraq (no such luck for the 'displaced' Cypriots in 1974), yet have hardly lifted a finger to help the mistreated Kurds of Turkey. The French Secret Service blew up Greenpeace's 'Rainbow Warrior' in New Zealand, and France's Defence Minister, Charles Hernu, had to resign when caught lying. The Soviet Union continued until its break-up to insist that Nazi Germany was responsible for the Katyn massacre of Polish officers. The Iran Contra scandal, with the USA secretly funding terrorists in Nicaragua, is another example of the lack of scruples of states when they believe that their interests are threatened. The list goes on, showing that self-interest is not always a good bedfellow of international law. International politics, like politics, can bring out the worst in human nature. Let us now consider some of the legal aspects of Cyprus' situation, since these have a bearing on whatever kind of arrangement is to be made.

THE TREATY OF LAUSANNE

There is a legal case for denying Turkey any rights whatsoever in Cyprus, and Britain, Greece and Turkey can be held to account for ignoring Article 16 of the Treaty (see Chapter Two), by which Turkey renounced all rights beyond its borders. By Article 20, Turkey also recognised Britain's annexation of Cyprus. Although the Greek government did point out in 1958 that Turkey had surrendered all her rights, the British prime minister countered by saying that Greece had also accepted the British annexation.[2] Implicitly, Greece had done so, by signing the Treaty. On the other hand, this cannot detract from the fact that Britain, as well as Greece and Turkey, ignored Article 16. Greece accepted British, not Turkish, control over Cyprus. Since Greece did, however, agree to attend the ill-fated 1955 conference and subsequently became a guarantor power, it is highly unlikely that she would have any *locus standi* today, if she tried to invoke Article 16. It is no use crying over spilt milk, and the water has long gone under the bridge.

Turkey's efforts to hamper Cyprus' accession to the EU are also relevant to the Treaty of Lausanne, with Turkey claiming that the balance between Greece and Turkey established by the Treaty would be upset by Cypriot membership and would even amount to *enosis* between Greece and the Greek-controlled part of Cyprus. The Turkish argument appears somewhat specious, legally, since the treaty nowhere refers to the establishment of a balance between Greece and Turkey.[3] The only thing that was undeniably established was peace. In the words of a group of international legal experts, 'the Treaty of Lausanne of 1923 neither provides any rights in favour of Turkey relating to the maintenance of "balance" in the region of the eastern Mediterranean, nor does it purport to establish such a balance.'[4]

Turkey's concerns, although legally shaky, are nevertheless well founded in terms of its own political perceptions. Depending on what arrangement is eventually reached over Cyprus' accession to the EU, it is indeed possible that Greece and the free part of Cyprus could agree to unite, on security grounds alone, particularly if progress on the CFSP is slow and continues to be bedevilled by 'NATO complications'. Even if Greece and Cyprus do not wish to unite, the fact that they would be members of a developing European security structure which excluded Turkey would alter the 'balance of power' in Greece's favour. From this we can, however, conclude that whatever arrangement is worked out, the USA and Britain will do their utmost to prevent independence of action by the Greek and Cypriot governments vis-à-vis Turkey, perhaps by an enhanced US military presence. The USA already has electronic spying posts in the occupied north. This is where Turkey's other arguments against Cyprus' accession to the EU come into play.

THE EU FACTOR

As we have seen, the EU factor is the new cat among the pigeons of the previous – and still current – arrangement under which the Republic of Cyprus was established in 1960, notwithstanding the abuse to which this arrangement has been subjected by Britain, Greece and Turkey. Apart from Turkey's reference to the Treaty of Lausanne, she has invoked Article 1, Paragraph 2 of the Treaty of Guarantee, which states:

> The Republic of Cyprus undertakes not to participate, in whole or in part, in any political or economic union with any state whatsoever. It accordingly declares prohibited any activity likely to promote, directly or indirectly, either union with any other state or partition of the island.

Were the EU a single state, then the Turkish argument that Cyprus cannot join would be correct. Turkey has therefore preferred to stress that Cyprus' accession to the EU would constitute de facto *enosis* with a single state, Greece, and that this would be in breach of the Treaty of Guarantee. This is however legally untenable, since the EU is still a supra-national organisation, separate from the state authority of the member states.[5] Therefore, even if the EU has power over and above that of its constituent parts, this is only in certain areas. To strengthen the argument, Austria joined the EU in the face of Article 4 (1) of the Austrian State Treaty of 1955, which forbade union with Germany. Again, the EU was considered a supra-national organisation, rather than a sovereign state.

The British government strongly supported Austria's and Cyprus' application, but her reasons for so doing were hardly altruistic. Given Britain's historic attempts (Edward Heath's government apart) to bedevil the creation of an integrated and sovereign European state, to reject the applications of Cyprus and Austria would have implied British recognition that the EU was – at least potentially – a sovereign state. Britain's objectives are, however, to give up as little sovereignty as possible, and stress the idea of an intergovernmental organisation. The more new members join, the more distant, in British eyes, is the 'federast'[6] ideal of one Europe, since the greater the number of members, the more difficult it is to manage integration – hence strong British and American support for Turkey's application. Greece's current support for Turkish membership is more of a diplomatic ploy to appear friendly and reasonable, in contrast to Britain's motives. Britain's insistence at the Dublin Summit in June 2004, on watering down the EU constitution, reveals her marked resistance to sharing sovereignty in defence, foreign policy and financial policy. A Cyprus able to fully merge its foreign and defence policy with the EU would be strongly resisted by Britain, essentially because it would call into question the compatibility of the British bases on Cyprus with a future EU defence policy.

The paradox is that when, or if, the EU does end up with its own completely independent armed forces and foreign policy, and becomes concomitantly a single sovereign state, then Cyprus' membership of the EU could be considered to have been – *a fortiori*, therefore – in breach of Article 1 of the Treaty of Guarantee. By then, however, EU law will presumably have superseded the Treaty of Guarantee. If not, then there could be difficulties to be exploited by Turkey, assuming that she is not yet a member, and of course by Britain, if she is not a core member. Here, the USA would support Britain and Turkey, if they were to object to a European army with Greeks and Greek Cypriots (or by that time Cypriot Greeks) facing their Middle Eastern ally, Turkey. Such considerations reveal the delicacy of the problem from the British and American viewpoints and why they are so keen for Turkey to gain EU membership. In the obvious absence of that for the foreseeable future, they will do their best to champion NATO, ensure that the European Rapid Reaction Force remains subservient, and impede serious moves toward European integration. Whatever conditions are imposed on Cyprus' EU membership regarding defence and *enosis*, a united sovereign Europe would not willingly inherit such restrictions as the 1960 treaties on part of its territory, since this would detract from its own sovereignty. These are the problems currently exercising the minds of the poker players, and this explains why (see next chapter) some of them were so reluctant to provide specific answers to the author's questions. They are themselves either confused, or desperate not to reveal their true intentions.

It can be seen that Turkey's arguments against Cyprus' accession have not been successful, perhaps partly because of Turkey's attitude towards the Council of Europe, of which it is still a member. Although the Council of Europe, once intended to be the first step towards a federal Europe, was then reduced to an intergovernmental talking shop, it nevertheless serves as a political pointer. This leads us to the 'Loizidou case'.

LOIZIDOU

The Loizidou case has become a *cause célèbre* for critics of Turkey's attitude towards the Cyprus problem and is used as a diplomatic weapon by those seeking to portray Turkey as insufficiently prepared, politically, organisationally and economically, to join the EU. Titina Loizidou is a Greek Cypriot who was refused access, as are all Greek Cypriots, to her property in Kyrenia. Following her temporary detention on the 'Green Line' in 1989, by Turkish Cypriot police, she sued the Turkish government in the European Court of Human Rights. Initially, she encountered legal problems: Turkey had not signed the protocol granting individuals the right to turn to the Court, until 1987, and Loizidou was unable to demonstrate that she had been physically mistreated. Such legal niceties were soon swept away as the affair gathered momentum and, to cut a long and legally tortuous story short, the Court finally decided that Turkey, with its occupation army, was responsible for paying compensation, rather than the (unrecognised) part of Cyprus. The Court ordered Turkey to compensate Loizidou for 'material losses', expenses and 'moral tort', to the tune of £468,000.[7] The Turkish government at first refused to pay, insisting that the case was the responsibility of 'the Turkish Republic of Northern Cyprus'. More poignantly, if all those deprived of their property in the north were compensated, this would cost some sixteen billion dollars,[8] coincidentally the same amount that the IMF is currently lending Turkey. Even if the court were to recognise the occupied north, it is unlikely that any compensation would be paid, since the flood of claims currently in the pipeline would become a deluge. A small minority of members of the Ministerial Committee of the Council of Europe, led by Britain and keen not to embarrass Turkey further, has thus far protected her from being threatened with suspension or expulsion for her non-compliance. Hence there is a whiff of double standards: Greece was pressured into withdrawing from the Council of Europe in 1970, on human rights grounds, while Russia was suspended for its 'activities' in Chechnya. For the record, by June 2001, 193 judgments made by the European Court of Human Rights against Turkey, had not been implemented, even partially.[9]

Perhaps understanding some of the flaws in its attitude, the Turkish government offered in June 2003 to compensate Loizidou, but only on condition that the plethora of other pending cases would be adjudicated by Denktash's administration. This was an obvious attempt at getting the legal government to recognise the 'TRNC', and the offer was therefore rejected. Since then, submitting to international pressure, the Turkish government has agreed to compensate Loizidou, but not yet to grant her access to her property.

The Loizidou case highlights the plight of ordinary people, the pawns in the game of Cyprus, as well as the highly complex legalistic pirouetting of international lawyers, politicians and officials.[10] The attitudes of the Cyprus government and the administration in occupied Cyprus towards abandoned properties are very different. The former has allowed Turkish Cypriots living outside Cyprus to sell their properties, which are protected by law, while many abandoned properties are simply left empty. Those Greek Cypriot refugees from the north who reside in abandoned Turkish Cypriot properties in legal Cyprus are allowed to do so only on a provisional basis. Conversely, Turkish Cypriot refugees from free Cyprus can declare their abandoned properties to the Turkish Cypriot administration and be compensated with an abandoned Greek Cypriot property.[11] In this way, the Turkish Cypriot administration is cementing a 'final solution' and pre-empting the issue, while the Cypriot government is trying to manage a situation which it apparently hopes will be temporary, so as not to prejudice any future negotiations. All told, there are about 200,000 Greek Cypriot and 50,000 Turkish Cypriot refugees.[12] In the case of the latter, the Cyprus government argues that most of those Turkish Cypriots who left did so of their own free will in the year after the invasion.

THE BRITISH BASES

One of the reasons that Britain still recognises the Treaties of Establishment and Guarantee is that not to do so could expose it to pressure on its moral right to hang on to the Areas (see Chapter Seven). It has admitted as much in private.[13] This helps to explain the shroud of secrecy currently enveloping the Cyprus question. Then there is an unavoidable link with Gibraltar, which enables Britain and, by extension, the USA to control the entrance to the Mediterranean. Although the circumstances surrounding England's acquisition of Gibraltar and the sovereign base areas are different, both are indisputably British-controlled territories in other countries. One is led to wonder what the attitude of the British government would be if France owned sovereign territory in Cornwall. Now that Britain has already conceded its readiness to discuss the question of sovereignty with Spain, a fellow EU member, then it follows that Cyprus as an EU member might well feel it had the right to do the same. While Britain can point to the Treaty of Establishment in support of its retention of Cypriot territory, its legal reason for keeping Gibraltar is the rather archaic Treaty of Utrecht. Britain could well be held to be in breach of the treaty if Jews or Moors live in Gibraltar, since Article 109 states:

> His Britannic Majesty, on the demand of the Catholic King, consents and agrees to not allowing for any motives, Jews or Moors to live in and have their domicile in the said town of Gibraltar.

Although there may well be international conventions on human rights that could call into question this racist (by today's standards) clause, such as the UN Charter itself, that in itself could be construed by some Spanish lawyers as undermining the validity of the whole treaty, or at least those articles relating to Gibraltar. There has certainly been at least one Gibraltarian Jew, Don Pacifico (see Chapter Ten).

At any rate, given the intricacies of international law and the different interpretations of treaties, Cyprus' membership of the EU could well lead to pressure on Britain to give up its bases.[14] In this connexion, Article 27 of the Vienna Convention on the Law of Treaties states: 'A party may not invoke the provisions of its internal law as justification for its failure to perform a treaty.'

PEACE, PROFITS, PRINCIPLES AND EXPEDIENCY

When the Berlin Wall was torn down in 1989, there was some temporary euphoria in naive circles that the end of the cold war would have a knock-on effect on Cyprus, since it was assumed that it would no longer be of strategic value in the

'New World Order' so strenuously fanfared by George Bush Senior and a gaggle of politicians, journalists and think-tankers. This has, of course, proved to be illusory. If anything, divisions have hardened over Cyprus.

As the armchair strategists are still trying to re-order the world, new wars which would have been unthinkable during the cold war have resulted in the very raison d'être of international law being either put under the microscope or ignored. Selectivity appears to be on the increase, at the same time as NATO is challenging the UN's authority. The eleven-week bombing of Yugoslavia (see Chapter Eight) is a case in point. NATO simply circumvented the UN Security Council and went ahead with its self-proclaimed 'humanitarian intervention'. The Kosovo Liberation Army, previously described as terrorists by the American envoy to the Balkans, Robert Gelbard[15] (to the delight of anti-Albanian Serb fanatics), were transmogrified by the next envoy, Richard Holbrooke, into heroes well before the bombing began. One particularly knowledgeable expert writes that one of NATO's main objectives was to promote its fiftieth anniversary.[16] The North Atlantic Treaty was designed to last for fifty years and, therefore, to expire in April 1999. Far from that, it welcomed three new members, having started bombing at the end of March 1999. Although the media messages put out claimed that the bombing was designed to protect values rather than interests, the expert points out:

> This was a classic example of image taking precedence over substance, which is not uncommon in today's political world. It is often associated with a rhetorical style that is more concerned with effect than with accuracy.[17]

He also says that the available evidence supports the widespread impression that the negotiations at Rambouillet were designed to fail, ensuring a free run for NATO. Thus, for the first time since the Second World War, a European country was bombed, and for seventy-eight days into the bargain. Thanks to 'smart' bombs (although one can wonder about the cluster bombs), 1,500 Serb civilians were killed,[18] as well as the Albanian Yugoslavs who died at the hands of enraged extremist Serb militiamen.

Juxtaposing the somewhat heavy-handed NATO reaction to Milosevic's excesses and NATO's reaction to the 'ethnic cleansing' in Cyprus, the latter is actually non-existent, obviously because Turkey is a NATO member and considered vital to US interests, whereas Yugoslavia was proving a thorn in the side of American plans. Clearly, the US put the interests of Kosovo Yugoslavs above those of Cypriots, Turkish Kurds and millions of dead Rwandans.

If Kosovo does become a sovereign state (which, without Serb and UN agreement would be in breach of the UN Charter), this would have a knock-on effect for Cyprus, since it would set a precedent for occupied Cyprus. The same would apply if Kosovo were partitioned.

An intense academic, governmental and journalistic debate is raging about the effects of the end of the cold war, globalisation, the free market and unilateralism, which impinges on the very concept of state sovereignty. It has yet to develop into anything coherent. The legal adviser to the Kosovo delegation at the ill-fated Rambouillet talks has written:

> The connection of the legal humanitarian action with the aim of achieving FRY/Serb acceptance of the Rambouillet package in its entirety, if it is maintained, would represent an innovative but justifiable extension of international law.[19]

Such a semantically flexible and utilitarian approach could be interpreted as the thin end of an anarchistic wedge in international law. The whole relationship between the interpretation of international law and the current unilateralist trend of US (foreign) policy is confused and confusing. The maelstrom of 'new ideas', unilateralism, and emotional, moralistic sloganising, such as 'axis of evil', 'crusade' and 'with us or against us' does not lend itself to rational policy formulation. As such, this maelstrom is open to dangerous exploitation. The US–UK 'special relationship' is asserting itself in an almost 'D-Day' spirit. Washington is attempting to make NATO a worldwide policeman,[20] while continuing to question the already battered authority of the UN. The atrocities of 11 September 2001, the bombing of Afghanistan and attack on and occupation of Iraq have given an enormous public emotional – and, therefore, political – impetus to the extremists' crusade to stamp out the new-found enemy, terrorism, even if behind the scenes, its true diplomatic antagonists are France and Russia.

The stand-off in the UN Security Council, where the USA and Britain insisted on attacking Iraq, while France, Russia and China urged a diplomatic solution, suggests that despite the disintegration of certain states since 1989, Eurasia, but more pointedly, the continental EU, is nevertheless subtly challenging current American geopolitical objectives. As regards Cyprus, its importance to US Middle Eastern policy and, by extension, to Israel, means that the island is likely to continue to be a strategic tool.

CONCLUSIONS

The current jockeying for power between a partially united would-be European state and a united American state, the former stressing the UN's authority, is likely to characterise any Cyprus arrangement. Cyprus' position as a US staging post for the Middle East, and therefore as part of the US–Israel–Turkey strategic axis, must also be considered in any arrangement, particularly because of the 'unholy alliance' between the Christian fundamentalist-influenced Bush administration and the Zionist lobby. The question is whether, in the coming 'arrangement', Cyprus' sovereignty will be as adulterated as it was in 1960.

We now turn to 'living history', where we record the responses of a number of governments to a similar set of questions posed in July 2002. The results reflect the current confusion among some of the poker players in formulating clear policies for the Cyprus conundrum.

14 How the Players Responded

INTRODUCTION

This chapter is necessarily written in the first person, not to make it appear more relevant or exciting, but because it is literally 'finger on the pulse' writing. By using the third person, I could run the risk of detaching the reader from current reality. It is an analysis of how a number of 'key' governments handled a similar set of questions that I asked about Cyprus. Although the questions and answers are now history, they will be fundamental to the Cyprus issue for some time to come.

One of the most important tasks of an embassy is to promote good relations between the country it represents and that to which it is accredited. To this end, a typical embassy will invariably be keen to explain and justify its country's policies: large sums of money are devoted to this activity, whether it be conducted through publications, helping friendly journalists in one way or another or supporting various 'educational' establishments. When people ask embassies reasonable questions, they respond, even if the questions are tricky. Stephen Milligan,[1] a former *Economist* editor, once visited me at the embassy in The Hague, in my capacity as Information Officer, at very short notice to ask sensitive questions about Dutch defence policy. The military attaché and I obliged.

With Cyprus, however, the situation changes. Some of the embassies were reasonably efficient in their responses, some dilatory, some downright inefficient and a small number essentially unhelpful. At the time of writing, I am still awaiting the French, Russian and Dutch responses. I shall now list the questions and the responses, to be followed by an analysis. The questions were all submitted in early July 2002, with a covering letter to the ambassador or an official. (Some had to be faxed a second time, because they had been 'mislaid'.) The respondents were the Israeli ambassador, the Turkish minister counsellor, the deputy chairman of the (Turkish) Motherland Party, Bulent Akarcali, the head of the Department of Greek–Turkish Relations of the Greek Foreign Ministry, the Cypriot counsellor, the US State Department and the Political Section of the British embassy.

THE QUESTIONS AND RESPONSES

Question One: Does your government recognise the 1960 Treaties of
    a. Establishment,
    b. Guarantee and
    c. Alliance?

Israel:	'Israel fully recognizes the Cypriot Government.'
Turkey:	'Yes to all three treaties. What is invalid is the state of affairs created following the 1960 treaties, which can be blamed on the Greek side.'
Bulent Akarcali (Deputy Chairman, Motherland Party):	'Turkey recognizes that the Treaties of Guarantee and Alliance are still in force. As regards the Treaty of Establishment, since the "Republic of Cyprus" was destroyed by the Greek Cypriot acts of violence in 1963, which resulted in the forceful expulsion of the Turkish Cypriot partner from all the state organs, Turkey is of the view that the Treaty of Establishment is no longer in force except its provisions relating to the sovereign British bases areas.'
Greece:	'Yes, we recognize them, but they have ceased to function effectively.'
Britain:	'The UK is a Party to the 1960 Treaties of Establishment and Guarantee but not the Treaty of Alliance. In strict legal terms, states are either parties and, therefore, bound by the terms of a treaty or not. Notwithstanding any political support for the subject matter provided for in a treaty, neither States nor Governments "recognize" treaties in any formal sense.'
Cyprus:	'We support the Treaty of Establishment, but Turkey has made matters difficult. The Treaty of Guarantee should have been respected, but events have not shown that it is. We have the "joint defence doctrine" with Greece.'
USA:	'The United States is not a party to these treaties.'

Question Two: Does your government recognise Greece's border with Turkey?

Israel:	'Israel recognizes Greece and Turkey in full terms and the existing borders of each country.'
Turkey:	I did not ask.
Greece:	I did not ask.
Britain:	'Yes, the UK recognizes Greece's border with Turkey in that the land border is delineated by the 1923 Treaty of Lausanne, to which the UK is a party.'
Cyprus:	'Yes.'
USA:	'Yes, but not all of the territorial waters implications which Greece

asserts. We have not taken a position on sovereignty over Imia/Kardak, in part because of the lack of an agreed maritime boundary.'

Question Three: Does your government recognise Greece's twelve nautical mile limit and ten nautical mile airspace limit?

Israel: 'The Ambassador did not wish to answer this question.'
Turkey: I did not ask.
Greece: I did not ask.
Britain: 'The UK recognizes Greece's right to establish its territorial sea (with the consequent air space above) in accordance with Section 2 of the UN Convention on the Law of the Sea 1982.'
Cyprus: 'Yes.'
USA: 'Greece claims a six-mile territorial sea and a ten-mile territorial airspace. We recognize the six-mile territorial sea claim and a claim to the superjacent air space. We do not recognize Greece's claim to territorial air space seaward of the outer limit of its territorial sea. See Roach and Smith, U.S. Responses to Excessive Maritime Claims 367–369 (Nijhoff 1996).'

Question Four: Does your government recognise the Treaty of Lausanne?

Israel: 'Israel respects all bilateral and multilateral agreements signed between countries in the area.'
Turkey: 'Yes.'
Bulent Akarcali: 'The Treaty of Lausanne is one of the basic documents underlying the establishment of the Turkish Republic. Therefore, as a party to that Treaty, Turkey recognizes that it is valid and still in force.'
Greece: 'Yes.'
Britain: 'The UK is a party to the 1923 Treaty of Lausanne.'
Cyprus: 'Yes.'
USA: 'The United States is not a party to the Treaty of Lausanne.'

Question Five: Does your government recognise the Italo–Turkish Agreements of 1932?
Israel: 'Same as for question four.'
Turkey: 'Turkey never ratified the agreement. Turkey refused several Greek requests to ratify. The Paris Peace Treaty [formally ending the Second World War] does not mention them.'
Bulent Akarcali: 'The 4 January 1932 Agreement between Turkey and Italy is in effect. The 28 December document between Turkey and Italy, on the other hand, is not valid. Neither domestic nor international legal procedures with regard to the latter were completed. The

	document was not approved by the Turkish Grand National Assembly. It was not registered with the League of Nations. Therefore, it has never entered into force.'
Greece:	'Greece inherited the agreements. Greece therefore recognizes what Italy recognized.'
Britain:	'The UK is not a party to the Italo–Turkish agreements of 1932.'
Cyprus:	'Yes, and this is covered by the Joint Defence Doctrine with Greece.'
USA:	'The United States is not a party to these agreements.'

Question Six: Does your government recognise all UN resolutions on Cyprus?

Israel:	'Yes.'
Turkey:	'Not all of them. The UN was given an erroneous mandate in Cyprus.'
Bulent Akarcali:	'The Greek Cypriot side does not represent the whole island nor does it possess the right or authority to act or speak on behalf of Cyprus as a whole. However, the UN Resolutions are based on the false assumption that "the 1960 Republic of Cyprus", which in fact was destroyed in 1963 by the Greek Cypriot party's forceful expulsion of its Turkish Cypriot counterpart from the state organs, and thus became a Greek Cypriot Republic, still continues. They also do not refer to the equal status and political equality of the Turkish Cypriot side. Therefore, Turkey does not consider the UN resolutions as a basis for reaching a comprehensive settlement since they do not reflect the realities of the island.'
Greece:	'Yes.'
Britain:	'The UK has voted in favour of UN resolutions on Cyprus since its independence.'
Cyprus:	'Yes.'
USA:	'The US Government supports UN efforts to bring about a resolution to the division of Cyprus and strongly supports the UN Secretary General's Good Offices Mission. As a member of the Security Council, we have voted for and supported UN Resolutions on Cyprus over the years.'

Question Seven: Does your government now support the idea of two states within a state i.e. a confederation, for Cyprus, or does it support a 'bi-zonal, bi-communal federation'?

Israel:	'Israel supports all UN resolutions concerning Cyprus.'
Turkey:	'There should be no preconditions.'
Bulent Akarcali:	'Turkey wants a freely negotiated, mutually acceptable, compre- hensive and viable settlement in Cyprus. Cyprus is the home for

two nations and there exist two states in the island. The relationship is not one of majority and minority. These two peoples in Cyprus should be able to co-exist and cooperate under a new partnership structure on the equality and sovereign status of the two Partner States. The new partnership structure will have a single international personality with the competence assigned to it by the two parties.'

Greece: 'Greece supports the UN formula of a "bi-zonal, bi-communal federation." One should not go beyond that framework.'

Britain: 'The Government believes that it is for the two sides in Cyprus to agree the terms of a settlement, and for Greek and Turkish Cypriots to endorse the outcome. The UK has always said that it supports a settlement, which would establish a bi-communal, bi-zonal federation in Cyprus. It still does. The preferred outcome of the British Government is for the two leaders in Cyprus to reach a just, lasting and comprehensive settlement which allows for a reunited island to accede to the EU. In our view, for a settlement to be viable, the new Cyprus would be able to speak with one voice internationally, to meet its full range of international obligations (advancing implementation of the EU acquis), and to have a single international legal personality.'

Cyprus: 'A qualified yes.'

USA: 'Our effort is to encourage all parties involved to engage in constructive efforts to reach a peaceful resolution of their differences so as to achieve a just, lasting peace on the island. The United States believes that a Cyprus solution should be based on a bi-zonal, bi-communal federation, and that it is possible to reach a settlement that addresses the legitimate concerns of both sides and promotes regional stability.'

Question Eight: Would your government support Cyprus' possible membership of NATO?

Israel: 'Given that Israel is not a member of NATO, there is no official position regarding Cyprus' membership in the organization.'

Turkey: 'We have no specific position on NATO. Turkey supports the original "Ankara Text" [signed between the US, UK and Turkey]. One should build on WEU.'

Bulent Akarcali: No response.

Greece: 'Why not? On the other hand, the British Sovereign Base Areas are in any case *de facto* NATO bases.'

Britain: 'Cyprus has not made any application to join NATO, nor suggested
                that it will. If Cyprus were to apply, the UK would decide its
                response in the light of the circumstances at the time.'

Cyprus: 'Cyprus has been trying to get into the "Partnership for Peace
                Program." But Turkey is against this. If Cyprus were a member of
                NATO, then the British Sovereign Base Areas would become less
                important.'

USA: 'Cyprus has not applied to join NATO. It is not a candidate for
                NATO membership.'

THE SCALLYWAGS

Three governments were unable or unwilling to answer the questions I posed.
They were those of Russia, France and the Netherlands. I wished to ascertain the
answers of the latter, because of the Dutch parliament's known opposition
to admitting Cyprus to the EU before a solution. It is worth recording these
governments' reactions, or rather those of their officials.

RUSSIA

Having faxed my letter and questions to the Russian ambassador, his assistant
faxed me back almost immediately, asking me to contact the Russian Ministry of
Foreign Affairs Press and Information Department. This I did immediately, by
fax, following up with a telephone call. I heard nothing, so got in touch again
with the assistant. To cut a long story short, the assistant faxed me three months
from the date of my original request, writing: 'I am awfully sorry to inform you
about that [sic] but H. E. Mr. M. Botcharnikov is not competent to give you such
an interview. Contact Dep't for Information in MFA in Moscow.' My response
was to fax her back (4 October 2002) asking whether she could ask the
ambassador to ask the Russian Foreign Ministry to reply. I have heard nothing.

FRANCE

The French method of avoiding my questions was more tortuous than the Russian
one. The head of press at the French embassy asked me to telephone both the
'Service de Presse' at the Foreign Ministry in Paris and their embassy in Cyprus,
simply to confirm my *bona fides*. This, he explained, would enable him to obtain
the information for me. Despite several subsequent telephone calls and a further
letter to the French embassy, I heard nothing. The head of press then gave me
the name of an official in Paris, whom I contacted, and who promised me that
there would be no problems. In December 2002, the Ministry of Foreign Affairs

telephoned me to say they would send me the information soon. They did not. France, of course, has its own sensitivities and interests in Cyprus in the shape of a broadcasting station *cum* listening post for the Middle East, set up against British wishes at Cape Greco in the early 1970s.[2] There is a strong element of stonewalling.

THE USA (THE NEAR SCALLYWAG)

Following my letter to the American ambassador, I telephoned the press officer at the embassy. He asked me to fax the State Department Press Relations Bureau, which I did, following up with a telephone call. Hearing nothing, I contacted the press officer again. He agreed to 'push them'. Two months after submitting my questions, he then told me that 'there were problems with some of the questions.' I suggested he answer those which he could. He then asked me to send my questions to the US embassy in Cyprus, which I did, following up with telephone calls. Nothing happened until I suggested to the Athens embassy press officer that matters were slightly absurd, whereupon he gave me another telephone number in the State Department. To cut a tedious and long story short, the 'Office of Southern European Affairs' then telephoned me to say that they 'were trying to answer my questions, but needed clearance from different departments'. On 18 November 2002, I was informed that the answers were awaiting clearance 'at the Cyprus desk'. This was five months after I had put my questions. On 27 December 2002, the Office of Southern European Affairs telephoned me to say that my questions were awaiting final clearance. I remained sceptical. On 9 January 2003, I rang the State Department yet again, and surprisingly received a facsimile the following day, the answers which you have just read. I have included the USA in this 'miscreant' section, because I cannot escape the nagging feeling that it was only my pressure that finally occasioned a reply.

THE NETHERLANDS

Before this account begins to lose *gravitas*, suffice it to say that the Dutch, for all their help, have proved unable to answer the questions, or even some of them. The ambassador's assistant sent the questions to her Ministry of Foreign Affairs, assuring me on several occasions that they were to reply. Each time I told her that they had not yet replied, she appeared to be genuinely surprised. Finally, she even gave me the telephone number of the official in the ministry, who asked me whether, in the light of recent developments, answers were still relevant. *I replied that they were even more relevant.* At 3.16 p.m. (Greek time) on 22 November 2002, I found the following message on my answerphone:

> Hello. This is [name omitted] from the Dutch Ministry of Foreign Affairs. I'm terribly sorry, but I'm afraid I have to disappoint you regarding our – well, my

– promise to come back to you today with an answer to your questions. It's just that we've been overwhelmed these days with all that is happening on the Cyprus issue – er – we have visits of Simitis,[3] Erdogan[4] and de Soto.[5] It's been incredibly busy and – er – I'm afraid I cannot yet answer your questions. Maybe you can call me back on this, so that we can discuss it. Thank you very much. Bye, bye.

I telephoned once more, to be told that they could not answer before the presentation of the Annan Plan (see next Chapter), nor even after.

One is inclined to wonder whether the Dutch government's policy formulation on the Cyprus question is clear-cut. I am suspicious about their future motives.

COMMENTS

In the case of the 'scallywags' one can conclude that the current period of uncertainty suggests that the French, Russian and Dutch governments do not have a clear policy on Cyprus, whereas those of Britain, Israel, Turkey, Greece and Cyprus are at least prepared to show that they have a position. The miscreants may, however, have formulated or reformulated policies, which they do not wish to reveal, for fear of irritating certain governments upon publication of this book. The other possibility is that they are confused by the plethora of related issues – NATO enlargement, ESDP, the latest UN plan (see following chapter) – and are still trying to fine-tune their policies.

The legal ramifications are indeed particularly complex, largely because of the 1960 'solution', the invasion and, now, the question of Cyprus in the European Union. It is nevertheless surprising that those countries are not prepared to provide even anodyne answers such as 'we support the UN approach' (as indeed the Israelis did, even if, in their own case, they often ignore the UN). Something is therefore afoot. Perhaps some countries, such as France, are afraid of unduly upsetting Turkey, particularly because of their business dealings. We are forced to speculate.

The case of Russia is curious, because even now, their support for the United Nations is unwavering, while they have traditionally supported the idea of a unified and independent Cyprus. On the other hand, Russia worked hard to ensure that Turkey did not offer too much help to the USA in attacking Iraq, and may have been indulging in some secret backstage horse-trading over Cyprus, to keep Turkey reasonably sweet.

The American response is odd, particularly since they have a regiment of 'public affairs' people in Athens and an army of them in Washington. Their initial dilatory and confused approach to my questions contrasts with their response to some questions I asked in 1998. Then, I asked, *inter alia*, the following:

Now that the USA has signed the UN Law of the Sea Convention, does it recognise Greece's 12-mile sea limit?
and

Why does the USA *not* recognise Greece's 10-mile air limit (established in 1931, with no objection from Turkey)?

The response then was:

As a Law of the Sea (Los) signatory, the US recognises Greece's right to extend its territorial seas to 12 nautical miles (NM) of territorial seas and 10 NM of air space is unique. Under international law and customary practice, territorial seas and air space are coincident. Under international law, adherence to international agreements supersedes national legislation. Let me underscore that differences of interpretation on this matter in no way affect the strong and close relationship between the United States and Greece; for our part, we prefer to concentrate on issues where we agree and where we can further build on our cooperation.[6]

This reply is itself open to interpretation. It could mean that the USA recognises Greece's right to a twelve-mile sea limit and a twelve- (not even ten-) mile airspace limit. It could mean that Greece should reduce its sea limit to ten miles, or increase its airspace limit to twelve miles to be coincident. On the other hand, the answer does not deny that the USA does not recognise Greece's ten-mile airspace limit.

This studied American fuzziness about the precise delimitation of Greece's Aegean borders with Turkey is not new, and can be traced back to at least 1977, when the aspiring ambassador to Greece, William Schaufele, had to appear – as aspiring ambassadors do – before the Senate Foreign Relations Committee. He referred to the 'unusual arrangements' governing Greek sovereignty over its islands near the Turkish coast. His words led to an outcry from the 'Greek lobby' and the State Department issued a correction, stating: 'This ownership is based on longstanding international agreements *which the United States fully supports.*'

The State Department, however, then slyly ordered the last six words of the correction (in italics) to be deleted, obviously not to annoy the Turkish lobby. This was immediately spotted by the Greek journalist Elias Demetracopoulos, who informed the Greek government, which in turn refused to accept Schaufele as ambassador.[7] Schaufele was posted to Poland. The whole tawdry tale suggests that the USA tends to support Turkey's positions if it thinks it can get away with doing so.

At the time of the 1998 American response to my questions, the British response to my precise questions was vague in the extreme. I was sent mainly irrelevant material and directed to a website. Thus the brisk British response this time is, in contrast, refreshing. The speed of the Israeli response also contrasts starkly with the American shilly-shallying. This is surprising, since the USA and Israel are each other's closest allies. Let us now comment on the questions and answers.

THE QUESTIONS AND ANSWERS

Does your government recognise the 1960 Treaties of
a. Establishment
b. Guarantee and
c. Alliance?

The Israeli answer is oblique. It is presumably implying that, since it recognises the Cypriot government, it therefore recognises the 1960 treaties. This contrasts with Bulent Akarcali's response, which states clearly that from Turkey's point of view the treaty is no longer in force, except its provisions relating to the British sovereign base areas. The Greek response that Greece recognises them, while realistically pointing out that they have ceased to function effectively, suggests regard for international law. Following Makarios' attempt to alter the constitution and his known aversion to the terms of the treaties, and the Turkish invasion, the Cypriot government's response shows that it needs to keep its options open, while paying lip service to the treaties, even though it believes that the Treaty of Guarantee has not been respected. Britain says, in a surprisingly precise vein, that it supports the treaties, and is bound by the terms of the two treaties to which it is a party. Yet it then lapses into mildly convoluted – or at least legally ambiguous – language in saying that 'Notwithstanding any *political support* for the subject matter provided for in a treaty, neither States nor Governments "recognize" treaties in any formal sense.' One is left wondering about the definition of 'political support'. In Chapter Four we saw how, in 1967, the law officers had noted the force of the argument that the Treaty of Guarantee was contrary to Article 2.4 of the United Nations Charter, and completely overridden by Article 103. In Chapter Seven, we saw how the Foreign and Commonwealth Office legal advisers had agonised over the treaties, admitting that any questioning of the Treaty of Guarantee would affect the Treaty of Establishment and thus expose Britain to 'moral pressure on the right to hang onto the Areas'. The answer to my question, however, does not betray any backstage misgivings or concerns. It is clear that Britain regards the 1960 agreements as a package deal, and does not wish to rock the boat, since its prime purpose is to hang on to its sovereign territory in Cyprus.

The American response is difficult to analyse, since the US government is using the fact that it is not a party to these treaties to avoid giving a view.

Does your government recognise Greece's border with Turkey?
and
Does your government recognise Greece's twelve nautical mile limit and ten nautical mile airspace limit?

Israel's response that it recognises the existing borders of each country is perhaps ominous, given the otiose use of the word 'existing' and the implication that this could mean 'current' or even 'temporary'. But perhaps I am reading too much into the reason for the use of the world 'existing'. The answer at any rate contrasts worryingly with the Israeli ambassador's refusal to answer the question about air and sea borders. Israel's military agreement with Turkey clearly plays a role here.

The American response to the two questions is imprecise: the US government recognises Greece's border with Turkey, but not 'all the territorial waters implications which Greece asserts'. It does not say which. Over Imia/Kardak, they have not taken a position, because of the 'lack of an agreed maritime boundary'. This is close to the Turkish position and directly contradicts the Greek one. As regards the air and sea limits, it is obvious that the USA recognises only six miles of Greece's sea and airspace limits, and not the rest. Again, this is close to the Turkish view, despite the UN Law of the Sea Convention, which Turkey has not signed. One cannot help but wonder how far the USA will go in 'obtaining' Turkish acquiescence in its occupation of Iraq.

US policy has altered radically: not long ago, the US ambassador told an audience of students that Imia was marked as lying in Greek waters on a US naval map. That was before George Bush Junior came to power.

Does your government recognise the Treaty of Lausanne?

Israel respects it; Turkey, Greece and Cyprus recognise it, the USA is not a party to it, while Britain is a party to it. Here, thankfully, there is apparently little conflict of opinion, although it is obvious that Turkey has not abided by the clauses protecting the Christian (mainly ethnic Greek) minority in Turkey.

Does your government recognise the Italo–Turkish Agreements of 1932?

The Israeli response that it respects the agreements is bizarre in light of the fact that the ambassador refused to answer the question about Greece's air and sea borders. Once this book is published, the Israeli government will doubtless wish to clarify its position. Britain's statement that it is not a party to the agreements obviously enables it to keep its options open, while the Greek, Cypriot and Turkish responses are predictable.

Does your government recognise all UN resolutions on Cyprus?

The Turkish government clearly does not recognise any resolution that it dislikes, hence its ignoring of UN resolutions concerning Cyprus calling for the removal of occupation troops. Since the involvement of the UN following the 1963 troubles, Turkey has been put on the defensive regarding its policy towards Cyprus, being of the view that the UN should give more recognition to the Turkish Cypriot component.

The Israeli response ('yes') is intriguing, given the close military cooperation between Israel and Turkey, and even more intriguing given the vast number of UN resolutions on Palestine that Israel has simply ignored. Both Turkey and Israel have ignored UN resolutions with apparent impunity (and tacit US consent), while other countries such as Iraq, do not enjoy this luxury.

Britain's reply ('has voted in favour et cetera') presumably means 'yes', but could also detract from Britain being firmly committed to upholding these resolutions. This roundabout reply suggests that it is 'greying' precision, given the latest UN plan (see following chapter), which the Foreign and Commonwealth

Office clearly helped to draft. This plan is rather vague about previous UN resolutions. The straightforward affirmative replies of Greece and Cyprus underline their attachment to international law as an integral element of their Cyprus policies.

The American reply presumably means 'yes', but does not use the word 'recognise'.

Does your government now support the idea of two states within a state i.e. a confederation, for Cyprus, or does it support a 'bi-zonal, bi-communal federation'?

Israel's slightly oblique answer presumably means that it supports the UN sponsored 'bi-zonal, bi-communal federation', while the Turkish government stresses that there should be no preconditions. This again reflects Turkey's suspicion of the UN role, and suggests that she is keen to play down the UN's authority in any potential deal. Similarly, Bulent Akarcali's reply does not mention the UN, but clearly favours a confederation, in other words two sovereign states in partnership.

The Greek and Cypriot responses support the idea of a federation, in other words one sovereign state, with local autonomy for the two main communities. This again underlines their preference for a 'UN-weighted' solution, which would in their book favour the return of refugees and the withdrawal of the occupation troops (negotiation under occupation is almost a contradiction in terms).

The US statement that America supports a 'bi-zonal, bi-communal federation' is slightly odd, since the 'Annan Plan' (see following chapter) tends more towards a confederation, even mentioning the 'Swiss' model.

Britain's response, while supporting the UN solution, is perhaps a little disingenuous in emphasising that responsibility lies with the two sides ('sides' which she herself helped to create) and the two leaders, given its covert record of favouring the Turkish Cypriots and the obvious fact that its main concerns are her sovereign territory and ensuring that European integration is diluted by a strengthened NATO role in European defence. Nevertheless, its attachment to the UN idea and mention of Cyprus being able to speak with one voice internationally are broadly in line with the UN and Greek and Cypriot positions. The big question is whether the UK would really support Cyprus as an EU member with the same sovereign rights as, say, France or Germany.

Would your government support Cyprus' possible membership of NATO?

Israel has taken the easy way out by intimating that because it has no *locus standi* as a non-member, it has no official position. This is somewhat contrived, given its close military cooperation with Turkey, NATO's second largest member. One can assume that its government will go along with the Turkish position, which implies support for the intergovernmental, NATO sponsored ESDP, into which the WEU (where Turkey had consultative status) has now been subsumed. This, however, is contingent upon Turkey's requests for full consultation and involvement in ESDP's ERRF operations.

Greece sees NATO membership for Cyprus as a way of enhancing Cyprus' sovereignty, which would not be to Turkey's liking. Cyprus has clearly implied the same as Greece. Turkey, again fearing Cyprus' attempts to be part of the NATO 'Partnership for Peace' programme, has been against Cypriot participation, since this would detract from Turkish political control over Cyprus' status.

The American response studiously avoids answering the question.

CONCLUSIONS

Out of this quagmire of wriggling, it is clear that the responses are predicated on certain major backstage factors. These are: Britain's dependence on, and attachment to, the 1960 treaties; the UN's ability – or otherwise – to solve the problem; the EU factor; the ESDP and NATO factors; and the US–Israel–Turkish military triangle. Former Greek prime minister Constantinos Mitsotakis says that Cyprus is considered important to Israel's defence.[8] Kissinger's 1957 idea of Cyprus as a staging post for the Middle East again springs to mind. Cyprus thus becomes, from the US and British standpoint, part of the overall geopolitical strategy for controlling the security of what we call 'the West'. This is being exercised through American–British use of NATO to control European sovereignty. Constantinos Mitsotakis agreed on the latter with this author.[9]

In this sense, Cyprus can be seen as the thin end of an American–British wedge to promote and expand NATO power by trying to link Turkey's entry to the EU to a 'solution' to the Cyprus problem. This is evident in the latest UN plan for a settlement (see next chapter). The plan's very preparation, combined with the related questions of EU membership, NATO and the ESDP, perhaps explains why the responses to my questions have been so difficult to prepare.

We now turn to the UN plan. It is akin to writing and scrutinising history as it happens.

15 The United Kingdom Nations Plan

The plan we offer is not negotiable!

INTRODUCTION

On 11 November 2002, Kofi Annan presented a 'basis for agreement on a comprehensive settlement' to President Clerides and Mr Denktash. This was just nine days before the NATO summit in Prague, at which seven new countries were invited to join the organisation and where Turkey continued to refuse to agree to the release of NATO assets for the European Rapid Reaction Force. It was one month before the EU Summit in Copenhagen, where Cyprus and nine other countries were to be officially invited to join the EU. In the days before the presentation of the plan, there were inspired leaks to the media to the effect that the plan would follow the Swiss (confederal) model, rather than the previous model of a 'bi-zonal, bi-communal federation'. Behind-the-scenes diplomatic activity – and pressure – was intense: on the morning of 15 November, Britain's special envoy for Cyprus, Mr David Hannay, visited President Clerides. The gist of the conversation, as revealed by a journalist, went:

> Hannay: The plan we offer is not negotiable!
> Clerides: If you mean that, I'll tell you, no. We want to negotiate.
> Hannay: Listen!
> Clerides: Don't you speak to me that way! I'll tell you once more. We are not going to take the plan on a take it or leave it basis. If you do not want to take my 'no' now, don't repeat that I must take it or leave it.[1]

Hannay left, possibly frustrated.

IMPOSITION

Before we look at the plan itself, we have to make a number of important observations. First, Clerides and Denktash were asked to signal their initial agreement to the plan by 18 November, and to sign a document by early December agreeing to the main articles in the 'Foundation Agreement'. By 28 February, they were to agree to the annexes to the agreement. Each 'side' would then hold a referendum on 30 March 2003. The reason for this indecent haste was the EU Summit on 12 and 13 December and the date scheduled for the EU accession signing ceremony, 16 April, 2003, with the invitees actually joining on 1 May 2004.

Although both Clerides and the Greek government accepted the plan 'as the basis for negotiations on a comprehensive solution', Denktash and the Turkish government prevaricated. At first, the reason given was that Denktash was recovering from a heart operation in New York, but despite the fact that he was reported as working a few hours each day, he continued to obfuscate.

Quite apart from the inadequacy (see below) of the plan itself, to insist that 137 pages be accepted so quickly is tantamount to imposition. Quite apart from the strong-arm tactics employed, it is reasonable to assume that the plan was drafted mainly by Hannay's staff, in close consultation with the USA, and then imposed on the flexible Mr Annan, who, in effect, passed on the 'imposition'. Although Turkey did not respond within the timescales, this was because the whole plan was devised to facilitate Turkey's entry into the EU, while ensuring that Cyprus would not, even as a putative member, be able to veto its application. Second, Turkey had used its refusal to allow the release of NATO assets for ERRF operations to pressure the EU into allowing its EU membership. Again, Cyprus is the tool. Concomitantly, it is clear from the plan that Cyprus could not be an effective ERRF member. What, then of the plan itself?

BUILT ON FAILURE

We have seen how the Foreign and Commonwealth Office itself doubted the compatibility with UN law of the package of treaties establishing the nominal sovereignty of the Republic of Cyprus in 1960. We have seen how those treaties established a system of government and security that was doomed from the start to promote divisions[2] which led – with British high commissioner Clark's help – to Makarios' attempt to amend the constitution, and then to bloodshed. We have also seen how those treaties were essentially handed to Makarios on a take it or leave it basis, with the archbishop being given very little time to engage in substantive negotiations.

The parallel today is stunning. The failed treaties again assume a central, indeed *the* central role, in the new document:

> The Treaty of Establishment, the Treaty of Guarantee and the Treaty of Alliance remain in force and should apply *mutatis mutandis*[3] to the new state

of affairs. Upon entry into force of this agreement, Cyprus shall sign a treaty with Greece, Turkey and the United Kingdom on matters related to the new state of affairs in Cyprus, along with additional protocols to the Treaties of Guarantee and Alliance.

This shows that, whatever was to be agreed, Britain's main concern was its territory on Cyprus. If the whole package disintegrated, Britain could still hang on to its treaties, although there could be legal problems about compatibility with EU law as Cyprus' EU membership solidified, since the legitimate government could well take the matter to the European Court of Justice.

To detractors from the plan, it must appear to have been devised both ingeniously and ingenuously, given that it appears to have been designed to ensure that the sides will never be able to agree on matters of substance, particularly on anything which impinges on Britain's land. First, the minority will be able to apply the veto, since the 'common state' parliament's senate will be composed of twenty-four Greek and Turkish Cypriots respectively, meaning potential deadlock if disagreement arises. Second, the office of Head of State will be vested in a presidential council of six, including two Turkish Cypriots. Although a simple majority (four to two) will suffice to agree on a decision, at least one member from each of the two component states will have to be in the majority. If this is not the case, the deadlock will have to be passed to the Supreme Court, composed – again, disproportionately – of three Greek and three Turkish Cypriots respectively and three non-Cypriots (not from Britain, Greece or Turkey). Assuming that agreement is reached on the appointment of the three non-Cypriots (presumably by the UN), it is they who will decide the issue, whether it concerns the British territories, or an attempt to alter the constitution – which will of course be based, just like the fatal 1960 constitution, on the failed 1960 treaties, *mutatis mutandis*.

HEADLESS CHICKEN

The 'single international personality' that the 'new' state is intended to have will, in effect, be invested in the three non-Cypriot judges and the guarantor powers of Britain, Greece and Turkey, making Cyprus, in fact if not in name, a weak protectorate. Although the draft plan does not deal with the division of powers between the Supreme Court (in effect, the three non-Cypriot judges) and the guarantor powers, it is the latter that will presumably prevail if they disagree with any Supreme Court decision, in which they will point to the Treaty of Guarantee. If one of the guarantor powers disagrees with the other two, as happened in 1974, then there is the possibility of conflict. Here, matters are further complicated by the EU factor.

THE ACHILLES HEEL, THE EU AND NATO

The 'UN' plan not only seriously undermines what remains of Cyprus' sovereignty, but also infringes EU independence. First, the draft states that 'Cyprus shall sign and ratify the Treaty of Accession to the European Union.' Apart from this major infraction of sovereignty, which, in effect, takes away Cyprus' choice in the matter, it also means that the EU as a whole takes in the 'failed' treaties of 1960, which could create conflict between an EU member (Greece) and an aspirant member (Turkey), should disagreement occur. A larger infringement of EU independence is to be found in the paragraph in the 'Foundation Agreement' that says *'Looking forward to joining the European Union and to the day when Turkey does likewise.'*

This destroys in one fell swoop the painstakingly constructed Greek and Cypriot policy of separating the issues of a solution on Cyprus and that of Cypriot membership. It also applies pressure on the EU to accept Turkey. Third, the Cyprus problem is the tail wagging not only the Greek and Turkish foreign policy dogs, but also the EU mastiff. The potential for a major disagreement among EU members is strong, since, under EU law, issues such as defence, foreign policy and enlargement must be *unanimously* approved in the Council of Ministers. Even more restrictively, the document includes this clause:

> Cyprus shall maintain special ties of friendship with Greece and Turkey, respecting the alliance established by the Treaty of Guarantee and the Treaty of Alliance and this agreement, *and as a European Union member shall support the accession of Turkey to the Union.*

This last phrase detracts even more from the idea of an independent state, and also prejudges any future vote by an EU member regarding the accession of new states. As such, it conflicts with EU sovereign rights. Indeed, it literally forbids the right of a (potential) EU member to vote on an issue with the others. The UK obviously introduced this clause (as she did the other mention of Turkish EU membership) at the behest of Turkey, with American support.

To drive the nail home, there is a stipulation that the heads of the Department (Ministries) of Foreign Affairs and European Union Affairs shall not come from the same component states. This creates more potential deadlock. As far as this author is aware, there is no separate Ministry of European Union Affairs anywhere in the world.

Apart from stipulating that Cyprus 'shall be a member of the European Union', the document goes on to say that the governments of the 'component states' shall participate in the formulation of policy in the European Union, without even specifying which areas of policy, thus confusing the question of the rights of the 'common state', which is meant to represent Cyprus internationally. In another stab at EU authority, one clause states:

> The European Union shall authorise Cyprus to accord equal treatment regarding entry and residency rights with respect to Greek and Turkish nationals without prejudice to policies and arrangements applying to entry and residency rights of Turkish nationals in other member states of the European Union.

This could complicate Cyprus' putative membership of the Schengen agreement, and unrestricted intra-EU travel. It also appears to contradict, or at least befuddle, the interpretation of another clause, which restricts the number of Greek (and Turkish) nationals in Cyprus. This goes against EU law on the right of residence in another member state. The plan is also clearly intended to bedevil the European Court of Human Rights' judgment in favour of the Greek Cypriot Tina Loizidou, and stem the tide of petitions to the court (see Chapter Thirteen). In short, it is going to keep a large number of lawyers bogged down for quite a time.

From just a cursory consideration of some of the plan's apparent objectives, it seems clear that it is an ill-disguised attempt by Britain and the USA, both of which strongly support Turkish membership of the EU, to ensure that the British territories (which are not even mentioned in the plan) remain sacrosanct, while promoting an entirely impotent non-sovereign state to membership of the European Union, at the same time undermining EU authority. This certainly corresponds with the line of thinking of the journalist, Elias Demetracopoulos, who thinks that Washington, by expanding NATO, is trying to split Europe and weaken independent European defence.[4] An expert on US foreign policy objectives, Professor Couloumbis of Athens University, also Director General of the Hellenic Foundation for European and Foreign Policy, says that the USA does not want a competitor and may wish ultimately to control European defence. He makes the unreasonable (for many Europeans) sound reasonable by stressing the importance of shared decision-making.[5] Demetracopoulos gives us a more perceptive insight into the US strategy of strongly promoting the 'Annan Plan': its basis is Iraq, because the USA needs to please Turkey in order to ensure its support in its occupation. Hence, for example, the references in the plan to Turkey's joining the EU. The USA's essential motive for attacking Iraq is not human rights. According to Demetracopoulos, it is because Iraq represents a military threat to Israel.

Before turning to some of the other criticisms that have been expressed about the plan, let us briefly consider its defence and security arrangements.

INDEFENSIBLE DEFENCE

First, the plan stipulates that Cyprus shall have no armed forces of its own, although the police (an equal number from both communities) may carry arms. Second, under a new treaty to be signed by Britain, Greece, Turkey and Cyprus, Greece and Turkey will be allowed to station an equal number of troops on Cyprus, thus creating even more disproportionality than before in the population ratio. Curiously, the plan states:

> The participation of Cyprus in the European Security and Defence Policy shall fully respect the provisions of the Foundation Agreement and [again!] the provisions of the Treaties of Guarantee and Alliance and the Additional Protocols thereto, and in no sense undermine these provisions.

How such a state can effectively participate in the ESDP is anyone's guess, but, again, the instruction to Cyprus that it will participate, further undermines the concept of Cypriot and EU independence.

Annan Plan or no Annan Plan, Cyprus continues to be a 'place d'armes', with the significant difference engendered by Cyprus' EU membership, namely that Britain now controls territories in two EU states, Spain and Cyprus. Although former prime minister John Major's aim of putting Britain 'at the heart of Europe' has proved illusory, Britain is certainly stuck on the EU's long bottom, from Gibraltar to Cyprus.

GENERAL CRITIQUE

The above are merely observations about the British-inspired UN plan. The latter is itself a 'revamp' of the failed 1960 agreements. Other criticisms need to be made. First, it is a vehicle for Turkey to push for EU membership, by using both the references in the plan, but also by offering to give way on the question of releasing NATO assets. Second, it does not refer to *specific* UN resolutions calling for foreign troops (Turkey's occupying force) to leave, thereby virtually sanctioning the Turkish invasion and occupation. Third, as three former Greek ministers have pointed out, the majority of the illegal settlers will be allowed to remain, as only those who have resided there for fewer than seven years must leave.[6] Thus, the plan legitimises illegality. Fourth, the stipulation that, following the 'transitional period', the offices of president and vice-president shall rotate every ten months makes a mockery of consistent government. It means in effect, as one expert has pointed out, that ministers would have to reside permanently in Brussels, rather than Cyprus, simply to vote at the various EU Councils of Ministers' meetings.[7] Fifth, although it is claimed that the plan is modelled on the Swiss system, the component states will also have their own citizenship (obviously of a secondary nature), whereas there is only one Swiss citizenship. Moreover, there are four, not two, recognised groups in Switzerland, and certainly no Romansch, Italian, French or German secondary citizens. Sixth, Cyprus would have fewer ministerial portfolios than Switzerland, insufficient to conduct the affairs of a real state efficiently.

The most obvious difference is that Switzerland is perhaps one of the most independent states in the world, while Cyprus would be a de facto protectorate, without true sovereignty. Switzerland's Supreme Court has no foreign members.

Another expert says that the make-up of the Supreme Court is closer to the Bosnia-Herzegovina model than the Swiss one.[8] In Switzerland, freedom of movement and settlement between cantons is guaranteed, while in Bosnia it is severely restricted, as it would be in Cyprus.

In Bosnia, politicians were unable to agree even on such apparently mundane matters as passport design, or vehicle licence plates. A solution had to be imposed by a high representative.[9] To think that the plethora of such down-to-earth yet crucial issues can be resolved in a few weeks, or even months, is naive. According to Elias Demetracopoulos (see above), the 'highly complicated' plan was doomed.[10]

The two simultaneous referenda stipulated in the 'Annan Plan' look like a travesty of the term referendum. Although the document refers to one question, it then goes on to list four, which must be answered as a single package. The question is, or rather the questions are:

Do you:

i. Approve the Foundation Agreement and all its Annexes, including the Constitution of Cyprus;

ii. Approve the Constitution of the 'Component State' and the provision as to the laws to be enforced for the 'Component State';

iii. Approve the terms of the draft Treaty between Cyprus, Greece, Turkey and the United Kingdom on matters related to the new state of affairs in Cyprus and require [sic] the signature by the Co-Presidents of the Treaty;

iv. Approve the accession of Cyprus to the European Union in accordance with the conditions laid down in the draft Treaty concerning accession of Cyprus to the European Union, and require [sic] the signature and ratification by the Co-Presidents of the Treaty?

Yes [ ]
No [ ]

The documents to be approved or being referred to in the referendum question shall be made available free of charge to any voter so requesting in Greek, Turkish or English and shall be placed on a common web site in the same languages.

To be able to understand properly what they were to vote for, voters needed to read through almost 138 pages. Theoretically, this meant that around fifty million pages would have to be delivered to voters, if they all asked to receive the document free of charge. Whether or not the typical voter would understand all the implications of the document was a moot point, but it was asking a lot of the voter to give a simple 'yes' or 'no' to a series of questions masquerading as one question. Finally, since there are currently about 250,000 Greek Cypriot and around 30,000 'legal' Turkish Cypriot voters respectively, this means that 16,000 Turkish Cypriot voters could have vetoed the vote of 264,000 voters,[11] since both 'component states' must agree to the plan.

CONCLUSIONS

The imposition of Mr Hannay's UN plan in the guise of a 'Swiss model' was not a serious attempt to solve the Cyprus dispute. Italian Swiss, German Swiss, or French Swiss do not look to their country of ethnic origin for their state identity in the way that has happened in Cyprus. Any attempt to claim that the UN plan emulates the Swiss model is not serious, since the failed 1960 treaties and the conservation of the British bases are the main 'hidden' elements of the whole exercise, together with the attempt to make Cyprus' entry into the EU contingent on Turkish entry, thereby weakening the EU.

It is no coincidence that former French President Valéry Giscard d'Estaing, former chairman of the convention preparing a future constitution for the EU, has stated quite bluntly that Turkey is 'not a European country', that it has a 'different culture' and that its admission would quite simply 'mean the end of the EU'.[12] His statement directly contradicts British and US policy of controlling EU defence through NATO and of reducing the EU to what British governments – apart from the Edward Heath 'blip' – always wanted, namely a large inter-governmental group of free-market economies, with none of this 'airy-fairy "federastism"'.

In the hurried effort to push a weakened Cypriot protectorate and Turkey into the EU, the British government has shown considerable inconsistency; on 25 September 2002, the official British government's view was to support a bi-communal, bi-zonal *federation* in Cyprus,[13] while two months later Mr Hannay was supporting what was quite clearly a confederation, with an emasculated central government. To drive this home, the British ambassador to Greece made his government's support for the plan quite plain. He added for good measure that the EU was a 'collection' of nation states and that EU defence policy should not be separated from NATO. When he was asked precisely whether his government would support Cyprus' entry into the EU even if the two sides failed to agree on the plan, he answered carefully that if no blame could be attached to President Clerides, then he assumed that the *EU* would say 'yes'.[14] Yet he did not say whether his own government would say the same.

The Turkish position, however, was to stall, so that the EU Summit on 12 December 2002 (see next chapter) had to consider the ERRF, Turkey's accession to the EU (a fixed date for negotiations to begin) and Cyprus' accession simultaneously. The Anglo–American 'logic' would run like this. Turkey gets a date in return for 'being nice' and agreeing to release NATO assets for the ERRF, and at the same time instructs Denktash to sign the UN plan, thus putting the onus on Clerides to do the same, even though negotiations would not yet have taken place. Therefore, the plan, despite its obvious shortcomings, would – theoretically at least – be cast in stone. Turkey would probably offer Varosha as a sweetener to show 'moderation', but this would not prevent disagreements and stonewalling. Each side would then try to attach blame to the other, while Britain, possibly using the Netherlands, would persuade the EU not to admit Cyprus until the two sides have agreed. Greece would then be faced with having to veto enlargement, or with giving in over Cyprus. This was one of the reasonable scenarios – based on historical observation. However, it did not go as planned, as we shall see.

Another worry was that the negotiations would go so badly that extremist elements would rear their heads, persuading the EU to ignore Cyprus, which may well be what Britain also wanted, to keep its bases sacrosanct, and free from any potential EU interference. On the other hand, that would have meant the death of the attempt to bring outdated 'post-colonial' treaties into the EU. Both Britain and the USA could nevertheless live with both options.

Finally, even if the EU conjured up a complex deal on Cyprus' accession that saved Turkey's face while keeping a specific date for negotiations at bay, this would not have prevented a continuation of Turkish pressure on Greece's borders. In this sense, the poker players would simply call for a break, and continue the *modus vivendi*. This is in fact what occurred (see final chapter).

In the concluding chapter, we shall look at what happened at the Copenhagen summit and after, and at the likely scenarios in the international context (Iraq, Israel, NATO et al). Cyprus has been placed firmly in a tug-of-love (or war?) between NATO and the EU. What seems certain is that the USA and the UK do not want the legitimate government of Cyprus to 'renounce' its occupied territory and create new international borders, since this could cast doubt on the compatibility with EU law of the 1960 treaties. In short, the UK and the USA wish to gain UN sanction for the 1960 treaties, because they are overridden by, or contrary to, the UN Charter; and because they are not properly compatible with EU law.

16 NATO vs EU

War is the continuation of politics by other means.[1]

INTRODUCTION

The period between the presentation of the 'Annan Plan' and the EU Summit's decision on enlargement on Friday 13 December 2002 was subsumed into a manic maelstrom of meetings, telephone calls and telegrams. To the onlooker, the frenetic activity was similar to a Racine play where, although the essential outcome is known, nobody can guess exactly how, in the psychologically charged atmosphere, matters will proceed to the *dénouement*. The maelstrom included the following sample of related events: the visit of the bellicose American deputy defense secretary, Paul Wolfowitz, to Ankara, to persuade Turkey to accommodate the American plan to attack Iraq; former French President Giscard d'Estaing's strong statement against Turkey's EU aspirations (see previous chapter); visits of the leader of the Turkish Justice and Development Party, Erdogan, to the USA and various European capitals, including Athens; Denktash's periodic – and possibly synchronised – bouts of illness and obfuscation on the question of signing the Foundation Agreement of the 'Annan Plan'; alterations to parts of the plan concerning territory, settlers, troop numbers and various transitional arrangements; a joint declaration by the French and German governments underlining not only their future cooperation on EU issues, but also stipulating that they favoured a review in December 2004 of Turkey's progress towards fulfilling the EU's political criteria which, if deemed successful, would entail opening accession negotiations the following year; a flurry of telephone calls by President Bush to EU leaders, attempting to pressurise them into opening entry negotiations with Turkey; and Erdogan's depiction of the EU as a Christian Club.[2] This latter statement contradicted the official Turkish policy of separating politics and religion. The Turkish delegation's behaviour at the summit prompted even a British diplomat to comment that Turkey's public statements 'did not always make things easier for its friends'.[3]

During the summit, the Greek Cypriot and Turkish Cypriot teams worked frenetically with the UN negotiator, de Soto, while Denktash went into hospital in Ankara. His envoy, Ertuguroglu, had no authority to sign anything, despite American and British pressure, and Annan himself called off his hoped-for triumphal trip to Brussels. American pressure on the EU to open accession talks with Turkey in 2003 was intense and led to considerable annoyance among European leaders. The French industry minister accused the USA of interfering in EU business, while the EU's trade commissioner said:

> It's certainly not up to the President of the United States to interfere in something so important and which mainly concerns Europeans [...] It's a classic case of US diplomacy to want to put Turkey in Europe. The further the boundaries of Europe extend, the better US interests are secured. Can you imagine the reaction if we told them that they had to enlarge into Mexico?[4]

Once it had become obvious that Anglo–Turko–American pressure was not going to prevail, Denktash somehow found the strength to leave his hospital bed and appear on Turkish television to rule out signing any agreement on Cyprus. Ertuguroglu walked out. Later that afternoon, the Danish EU Presidency issued a statement, of which the parts relevant to Cyprus read:

> Cyprus will be admitted as a new member state to the European Union. Nevertheless, the European Council confirms its strong preference for accession to the European Union by a united Cyprus [a sop to the UK and the Netherlands]. In this context it welcomes the commitment of the Greek Cypriots and the Turkish Cypriots to continue to negotiate with the objective of concluding a comprehensive settlement of the Cyprus problem by 28 February 2003 on the basis of the UN Secretary General's proposals [...] In case of a settlement, the Council, acting by unanimity on the basis of proposals by the Commission, shall decide upon adaptation of the terms concerning the accession of Cyprus to the EU with regard to the Turkish Cypriot community. The European Council has decided that, in the absence of a settlement, the application of the *acquis* to the northern part of the island shall be suspended, until the Council decides unanimously otherwise.[5]

The use of the word 'unanimously' is particularly significant, since it means that any EU member can veto the application of the *acquis* to Northern Cyprus, even if the two sides do manage to agree.

As regards Turkey, the summit statement was clear enough:

> If the European Council in December 2004, on the basis of a report and a recommendation of the Commission, decides that Turkey fulfills the Copenhagen political criteria, the European Union will open accession negotiations with Turkey without delay.

Thus far, it is clear that the European Union, to a large extent in the shape of a renewed 'Franco–German axis', is increasingly gaining in influence when faced with the 'Anglo–American axis', at least to the extent that the EU did not give in to pressure and reward what many have interpreted as Turkey's and the USA's pushiness. 'Old Europe' (the US Secretary of State, Rumsfeld's, infamous and indelicate phrase) particularly in the form of France, Germany, Belgium and Luxembourg, announced at the European summit in Athens in April 2003 the joint defence project that, unlike the NATO-linked ESDP, would, if built on and activated, be entirely independent of NATO institutionally. It would be jumping the gun to think that the move was simply Franco–German posturing following the clash at the UN over the US and British insistence on bombing Iraq. Such measures are not taken frivolously. It also represents a suggestion to the new East European EU aspirants that it would be better to toe the line. Although we have seen that Cyprus is now precluded from active participation in the ESDP, if Greece were to join in the Franco–German initiative, this would put a different complexion on matters, since the legal government of Cyprus could still claim that it had the right to join a body that does not use NATO assets to operate. Britain, the USA and Turkey would resist such a development, since Cyprus as a fully fledged member of a defence body independent of NATO would represent a threat to their Eastern Mediterranean and Middle East interests.

Let us now examine the various factors that need to be considered in any attempted prognostication of the likeliest scenarios for the Cyprus question. These are Turkish and Greek defence, the US–Turkish–Israeli triangle, American foreign policy per se, the 'US–UK axis', Iraq and last, but not necessarily least, Cyprus itself.

THE TURKISH QUESTION

Although the Turkish minister, Gul, said at the end of the summit that Turkey had taken a very definite step 'on the road to the EU',[6] events since then have underlined the instability inherent in the Turkish polity on the one hand and the all-embracing, albeit often hidden, power of the military on the other. The confusion is almost palpable. In contrast to Erdogan's and Gul's conciliatory attitude vis-à-vis the EU, only five days after the summit, the Foreign Ministry issued a statement saying: 'Turkey does not accept the EU Copenhagen decision on Cyprus either legally or politically.'[7] The same day the UN Security Council called for intensive talks, expressing regret that the Turkish Cypriot leadership 'has not responded in a timely way'.[8] Denktash had emphasised the separateness of his territory, insisting that the EU sign a separate agreement with Northern Cyprus, but suspend it until Turkey also joins.[9] It is hardly surprising then, that there have been large pro-EU demonstrations against Denktash in occupied Cyprus, nor that, according to an opinion poll, Denktash's approval rating is higher in Istanbul (50.7 per cent) than in his 'own' territory (28.6 per cent).[10] Even though Denktash has demanded a ban on the return of refugees to the North, as well as permanent joint presidential powers,[11] the Turkish government, which means the military and the Foreign Ministry, openly supports him. Despite Erdogan's massive electoral victory, Turkish policy is still that of the former prime minister Ecevit, who said before losing the election that only

Greece, Turkey and Britain could contribute to a solution, and that the EU should 'stop showing an interest'.[12]

The Greek Foreign Ministry thinks that the situation in Turkey remains equivocal and ambiguous for as long as the new political equilibrium between the post-Kemalist establishment and the AKP party of Erdogan remains in the air.[13] Apart from obvious policy divergences between the ruling party on the one hand and the strictly secular military and senior Foreign Ministry officials on the other, Erdogan's own position was confused until recently. On the one hand, he is the clear leader of his party, yet could not become prime minister because of the ban imposed on him for being convicted of reciting a poem considered to be too religious. Even though parliament voted to lift the ban, President Sezer then rescinded that decision; parliament in turn lifted the ban again, enabling Erdogan to stand in a by-election in February 2003. The president decided not to appeal to the Constitutional Court. The Constitutional Court banned Erdogan on 22 February 2003 as leader of his own party, whereupon he was immediately re-instituted as leader by his party. Although the legalistic toing and froing then came to an end, and Erdogan is now prime minister, tension remains under the surface.

The tension was enhanced by US efforts to 'buy' Turkey's cooperation in its war against Iraq, by offering a special aid package. Although parliament passed a motion to the effect that the UN weapons inspectors' initial report must be considered before Turkey supported a war, the USA, in the shape of senior Department of Treasury officials, visited Ankara at the end of 2002 to offer money. In the end, Turkey refused US requests for its army to attack Iraq from Turkey.

The implication for Cyprus is that the USA will support Turkish policy on Cyprus even more strongly than before, because Turkey is now an integral part of its Middle East strategy. There is, of course, the ever-lurking danger of an about-turn in Turkey, despite huge amounts of dollars, as occurred in Iran in 1979. Certainly, the ingredients are there: an increasingly rigid but nevertheless powerful military as the real ruler of Turkey; an increasingly restive alliance between the 'Muslim' tendency and intellectually minded democrats; and, crucially, the spectre of increasing autonomy for the Kurds of Turkey, particularly if Turkish and Iraqi Kurds try to unite. Turkey already suspects that the USA wishes to establish an autonomous Kurdistan in northern Iraq. Although *prima facie*, US money and political support for the military is likely to prevail in the immediate term, this may not necessarily work in the longer term. It may also be that the military is forced to indulge in an overt, or at very least a covert, takeover, which would be the fourth since 1960. Israel, for its part, would try to ensure that the USA would continue to underpin the Israeli military alliance with Turkey. If the complexities of Turkey's relations with the EU, its policy on Cyprus and its relations with Israel are a curious cocktail, one can assume that Greece is also being affected.

YESTERDAY'S GREECE

The Greek government, although inherently more stable than that of its eastern neighbour, is also in a difficult position over Cyprus, as it has been in the past. On the one hand, it has sensibly and cautiously welcomed the 'Annan Plan' as a constructive idea, and supported Turkey's European aspirations. On the other, Turkish violations of Greek airspace have increased recently. There were fifty violations on 18 December 2002 alone. In 2002, Turkish violations increased by 296 per cent compared to the previous year.[14] This sort of pressure (for example, the Imia incident) tends to whip up atavistic anti-Turkish fervour in Greece, not confined to fringe politicians, but extending to sections of the two leading parties, PASOK and New Democracy. There is scope for division in either party between the more Atlantic way of thinking nurtured, perhaps, by Couloumbis and others (see previous chapter) and more European-minded politicians such as the former prime minister, Constantinos Mitsotakis. Although any Turkish-style instability, let alone a military coup, is simply a non-starter, political confusion, and therefore a weakness in foreign policy formulation, is possible. Nevertheless, thus far (barring 'democratic disagreements' about the viability and acceptability of the 'Annan Plan'), the government has maintained a mature stance almost by default, letting Turkey's and Denktash's beating about the bush do its work for it. Thus, following the Turkish government's initial refusal to recognise Cyprus' EU accession, the Greek prime minister, Simitis, was able to question, by implication, the 1960 treaties, which must have caused British palms to sweat. He said:

> I would prefer it, if it were possible, that neither Greece nor Turkey should act as guarantors of Cyprus' security. I believe that Cyprus itself, with its EU accession, will guarantee the security of all its inhabitants and that these agreements are not necessary.

Diplomatically, he continued:

> But if this has to continue, because the interested parties and the UN believe in it, then, of course, we will agree to such a guarantee.[15]

In one fell swoop, Simitis revealed the true objective of Greek foreign policy on the Cyprus issue: to replace the Treaty of Guarantee with an EU security guarantee. This, of course, went hand in hand with Greece's attempt to press for a common EU border police force. This would imply EU recognition of Greece's borders vis-à-vis Turkey, as well as Cyprus' borders, which would entail EU engagement with Turkey in Cyprus and the Aegean. Thus, although Greece is paying lip service to the 'Annan Plan', it does not agree with some of its most basic aspects, the 1960 treaties (or parts of them), since they give Turkey a role in Cyprus, and, therefore, in the EU, when Cyprus joins. Of course, matters are not quite that simple, as interviews with the international secretary of the leading opposition party (New Democracy) – now in power – and with the foreign minister's spokesman suggested. The former acknowledged that Britain has a different view of Europe and European security to that of the French and Greek governments in particular, since she views the EU as a free-trade area. Unlike Britain, New Democracy supports the idea of future independent European armed forces. On the difficult question of the 1960 treaties, New Democracy says that they are technically valid but dormant, and that new realities have appeared since 1974. A full member of the European Union should not need such anachronistic treaties. The spokesman says that it is in the first instance up to the Cypriots to decide. As regards the 'Annan Plan', New Democracy considers some of the plan to be 'incompatible with EU logic', while it considers Simitis' statement (see above) that the (1960) agreements are not necessary, to be a 'theoretical wish'. When asked whether Cyprus forms part of US and Israeli defence planning, the spokesman diplomatically said that there was an element of truth in this.[16]

Comparing these answers with those of the Greek foreign minister's spokesman revealed a more tentative, but not dissimilar approach; tentative in comparison, because it is usually easier for the opposition to be more robust and precise in its stated views, especially since New Democracy in opposition was not subject to the intense backstage diplomatic pressure from the USA and Britain as was the government. Thus, rather than openly supporting the idea of genuinely independent EU armed forces in the future, the foreign minister's spokesman said that the EU should develop its own policies on security and defence, and that, at the end of the day, there should be independent EU armed forces; that it was first and foremost for the Cypriots to formulate their views on the 1960 treaties; that the government supported the 'Annan Plan' provided that it ended up as a functional solution following negotiations; and that, on the question of Cyprus' role in Israeli/US defence, 'Cyprus was of strategic importance in the region.'[17]

The latter's position also came across as more coy than that of the then New Democracy opposition because the government party, PASOK, is in some disarray over the plan, with some members of parliament and former ministers openly against it. Indeed, when this author tried to obtain an official PASOK view, he was directed to the foreign minister's spokesman who, as a career diplomat, is also the Foreign Ministry spokesman.

Disagreement in Greek political circles over the plan, especially under the surface, is inevitable, given the capacity for divisiveness of the Cyprus problem. As we have seen, this is replicated in Turkey, with Denktash and parts of the military establishment still adopting a 'tough' approach, while the prime minister and the leader of the majority party (whose position and authority are still open to question) are more flexible. In the background is the obvious concern among those in power that overt Turkish support of US policy on Iraq will irritate most EU countries, just as Turkey is aspiring to join.

What, however, of defence?

GEOSTRATEGIC DEFENCE PAWN

Whether or not readers agree with the contention that Cyprus is a geopolitical pawn in the hands of competing power-brokers, it is difficult not to see the significance of the whole question of defence, bound up as it is with British, American, Turkish and, increasingly EU and Israeli security considerations. Despite the fact that the 'Annan Plan' would take defence out of Cypriot hands and would therefore render the Joint Defence Doctrine with Greece anomalous, this doctrine still exists, as confirmed by the Greek Ministry of Foreign Affairs.[18] Cyprus in the EU without the 'Annan Plan' allows the continuation of the Joint Defence Doctrine, since EU law permits military cooperation between states.

On the other hand, to complicate matters, the USA and Britain achieved their main – but not well-publicised – objective at Copenhagen: the dropping of the Turkish objection to the release of NATO assets for the ESDP's ERRF in return for a guarantee that Cyprus would not take part in any EU military operation using NATO assets. Thus, even if the 'Annan Plan' becomes a dead letter, Cyprus and, by extension, the EU, will have lost some sovereignty on defence. This is in line with the Anglo–American strategy to ensure NATO control, and to keep a genuine (CFSP) EU army at bay. This is where the American–Israeli–Turkish military triangle comes into play.

THE TRIANGLE

The Turkish–Israeli military axis *per se* has been dealt with previously. In the current scenario around Cyprus, Turkey's consultative status in the ESDP and possible participation in ERRF operations, at least by invitation, gives Israel itself a tactical connection with Cyprus and the EU by default, because of its military cooperation with Turkey. If Turkey were ever to join the EU, then she would 'bring in' Israel militarily, by default, unless she abrogated the military agreement. The USA, however, would strongly resist a weakening of the Israel–Turkey alliance, in which it plays its own part, because of Turkey's importance to its Middle East strategy. Moreover, if Cyprus were to play a part in the defence of Europe, this would be anathema to Turkey and, by extension, to Israel, since EU policy (Britain apart) is far more supportive of the Palestinian cause than the USA's. The USA, by promoting Turkish involvement in putative EU military operations and at the same time promoting the Turkish–Israeli military axis, can bedevil and dilute a strong EU position on Palestine. The regular 'triangular' military exercises in the Eastern Mediterranean, the latest one in January 2003, underline the American, Israeli and Turkish pressure in the face of, for example, Israel's enemy Syria. It should not be forgotten that Syria claims Iskenderun (the Hatay) from Turkey. As one expert puts it 'this alliance, which the US has encouraged, guided and participated with in full, seems to be a serious stumbling block for the EU's distinctive strategy in the Middle East.'[19] As long as Cyprus, or at least part of it, can be kept within the Turkish military ambit, this suits Israel and the USA. Recently, there has been a body of new thinking on Palestine and NATO, to the extent that there have been calls for NATO to take over from Israel in Palestine, to 'oversee the building of a democratic Palestinian state while uprooting the terrorist infrastructure'.[20] Such a solution, if ever attempted, would serve the dual purpose of extending NATO control over the Middle East and of involving Israel in close cooperation with NATO. It is worth bearing in mind here the Israeli ambassador's refusal to answer the question about recognition of Greece's airspace and sea limits (Chapter Fourteen).

Turkish–Israeli military cooperation is a *sine qua non* of the so-called American Greater Middle East initiative. Some Arab regimes, particularly that of Syria, and Islamic extremism, are common enemies of both states. Whatever official displeasure the Turkish government periodically expresses about Israeli army excesses against Palestinian civilians, the security and industrial-military partnership is strong.

Apart from complicating a common EU defence policy, the 'triangle' assures Turkey of the support of the strong Israeli lobby in the US administration and business world, thus counteracting the influence of the Greek lobby. Hence, Cyprus' future is – at least partially – contingent on the Israel–Turkey–US military triangle. Kissinger's strategy of using Cyprus as a springboard for the Middle East comes to mind yet again.

THE BEHEMOTH

Although we have already looked at the development of American policy on Cyprus, there have been sufficient recent developments while I have been writing this book to justify a final look at current American policy. Rather than having altered in any dramatic way, American policy has simply become more unilateralist and, it has to be said, intrusive and strident in tone.

First is the USA's use of NATO to promote its policies. Hence its plan – agreed at the November 2002 NATO summit in Prague – to establish a rapid reaction force to operate anywhere, even without a request from the government of a country in which a NATO target might be located.[21] Apart from further spreading American military control over ever wider areas, such a force obviously detracts from the cohesion of the ERRF, and can divide EU members, since some of the new EU members are still looking far more to the USA than to the EU. The foreign policy spokesman of the German Christian Democrats sums up the mood in certain circles: 'The influence of the United States will be fostered by the Central and East European countries which look more to the US than to Europe.'[22]

The current Iraq crisis illustrates the American (and British) obsession with using NATO enlargement as a tool to weaken the EU. When France and Germany expressed their joint opposition to the war against Iraq, American Defense Secretary Rumsfeld said:

> You're thinking of Europe as Germany and France. I don't – that's the old Europe. If you look at the entire NATO Europe today, the center of gravity is shifting to the East. And there are a lot of new members.[23]

In short, the new EU members are far more pro-USA and NATO than most of the old members. This obviously detracts considerably from the classic idea of the EU as a serious global force in competition with the USA. Enlargement will, for the time being at least, slow down European integration.

A perfect example is the case of Poland, whose president recently denied being an American Trojan horse in the EU.[24] Yet, only three weeks after this denial, the Polish government rejected offers to buy French Mirage 2000–5 or Swedish Gripen fighter aircraft, opting instead to purchase forty-eight Lockheed Martin F-16s, to the tune of $3.5 billion. The deal, accompanied by US government 'sweetener loans' of $3.8 billion, was attacked by the Chairman of Dassault as political. Tellingly, the European Defence Industries Group accused the Americans of using 'any method they can to try to kill the European aircraft industry'.[25] Poland also delayed agreement on a European constitution.

For the USA, European security has a strong business dimension. Despite such 'European disappointments' as the Polish purchase, the EU's defence industry is coming together, often in the face of American opposition. In March 2002, the EU decided to proceed with its own E3.6 billion 'Galileo' satellite navigation system,[26] to the anger of the US government. There has been a number of national and intra-European mergers, such as France's Aerospatiale with Matra in June 1999. Only four months later, the new aerospace and defence electronics combine merged with Germany's Dasa to form the European Aeronautic Defence and Space Company, which then swallowed Spain's CASA.[27]

EU–US competition in the defence industries is as intense as in economic, ideological and juridical spheres, all of which have witnessed a rampant expansion in the parameters of US foreign policy projection since the collapse of the USSR.[28] A strong element of the Cyprus conundrum hinges on the currently confused, and confusing, EU–NATO relationship. According to one group of experts:

> The effort to resolve the NATO–EU security relationship satisfactorily is already seriously undermined by the problem posed by the non-EU members of NATO, and in particular, Turkey, which have serious concerns about the implications of the development of the EU's Common Security and Defence Policy. The addition to NATO of more members that are not also members of the EU could exacerbate the current dilemmas unless these are resolved before the new members take their seats at the alliance's decision-making tables.[29]

Turkey's concern referred to above is of course centred on Greece and Cyprus, hence the US and British success at the Copenhagen summit in keeping Cyprus out of ESDP operations using NATO assets, and, by extension, questioning the Greece–Cyprus Joint Defence Doctrine.

Current American behaviour sits uneasily with the EU's cautious, diplomatic and non-confrontational approach to world problems. President Bush has even been described as thinking that foreign policy is military policy.[30] Many will remember how, on taking power, Bush was considering a contained foreign policy bordering even on isolationism, but that this somehow transmogrified into the thrusting and domineering policy of today, aided, obviously, by the 11

September outrage. Hawkish Deputy Defense Secretary Wolfowitz was able to resuscitate a paper that he had 'spearheaded' under a group of 'intellectuals' in the dying days of the Bush (Senior) administration.[31] The paper includes the rumbustious statement:

> Our forces will be strong enough to dissuade potential adversaries from pursuing a potential military build up in hopes of surpassing or equaling the power of the United States.

Since September 11 we have witnessed an almost surrealistic series of statements and events, which by their very nature, begin to render the very notion of reasoned and moderate intellectual argument redundant. Phrases such as 'with us or against us' and 'axis of evil' betray an essentially (dualistic) Manichaean way of thinking,[32] which simply leads to fanaticism and extremism. American avoidance of international norms, such as the extra-judicial questioning of Al-Qaeda suspects (many are simply ageing shopkeepers and the like, snatched from the streets) in Guantanamo, and the appointment of the controversial Kissinger to head the Commission of Enquiry into 'September 11' are actions which appear to be taken without regard for, at the least, European sensitivities. Even if Kissinger subsequently resigned, apparently because of 'conflicts of interest', the damage has been done. Usually moderate journalists like Richard Norton-Taylor of *The Guardian* end up writing articles entitled 'The US will be legislator, judge and executioner',[33] while an American professor writes:

> The campaign against Iraq is part of a global strategy, imposed on Washington by a small clique of Cold War nostalgics and founded on their vision of the strategic military, ideological and economic interests of the United States.[34]

Certainly, a whole host of American objectives is being subsumed into the fight against terrorism, for presentational purposes. Thus, attacking Iraq has somehow been connected to 'September 11', as is making NATO a military organisation with worldwide reach. Under the anti-terrorism label, the USA has managed to justify – at least to itself – and implement the creation of new, and the strengthening of existing, bases, all over the Middle East and along Russia's 'soft underbelly'. These bases are likely to remain, as a 'hedge against terrorism' and to strengthen the Wolfowitz idea of a new world order. Should there be a crisis over Cyprus, as there could be if Turkey decides that its perceived interests are threatened by an independent but potentially hostile 'southern' Cyprus in the EU, the US reaction could well be one of inaction, since a Turkish advance could be interpreted as both 'testing' and weakening Greek and EU notions of joint defence. Although the British, more subtle than their American counterparts, might well baulk privately at Turko–American excesses, they would do little if anything to protect Cyprus, apart from ensuring, by arrangement, the security of their bases. It is indeed the US–British NATO partnership, along with its antithesis, the traditional Franco–German EU partnership, which will determine what happens.

ROBIN AND BATMAN

Britain's position – trying to be 'at the heart of Europe', while supporting American policies that are unpopular with most European governments – is designed to promote 'intergovernmentalism' and now (on America's back) NATO power, to prevent any European sovereignty in defence matters. This is not only manifested in prime ministerial rhetorical statements such as 'we must accept that there is a significant part of the world that is deeply inimical to all we stand for.'[35] It can be seen in British industrial defence cooperation with American companies, in preference to European ones. As one expert writes: 'The British are trusted with technology, and are allowed to buy into the US market, in a way that the French and Germans are not.'[36]

British thinking was not always so Atlantic. In 1975, Prime Minister Harold Wilson said:

> There is no future for Europe, or for Britain, if we allow American business and American industry to dominate the strategic growth of our individual countries that [sic] they, and not we, are able to determine the pace and direction of Europe's industrial advance [...].[37]

Plus ça change. Britain is now so openly supportive of US strategies that its defence secretary, Geoffrey Hoon, said in November 2002: 'NATO is and will be the only organization for collective defence in Europe.'[38]

Britain's apparent readiness to provide land and facilities for the basing of missile defence interceptor rockets, as part of Bush's 'son of star wars' programme, is another example of Britain's intense relationship with America. This can be most graphically understood from maps computed by *Petroleum Economist* and Arthur Anderson, the Comité Professionnel du Pétrole, the CIA, the US Energy Information Administration, NATO, and the US Defense Department. In November 2002, there were thirty-six permanent or 'temporary' Anglo–American military and naval bases in the Middle East, stretching from Bichkek in Kirghizstan in the East to Cairo and, of course, Cyprus in the West.[39] The proximity of these bases to existing and projected oil pipelines is remarkable.

Whatever the occasional 'spats' between Britain and America, usually due to Britain's legal commitments to EU legislation, the emotion which characterises the special relationship is currently in the ascendant, emotion which is complemented by the close business and defence relationships between the two countries.

Thus Cyprus, with its British and American listening posts and British sovereign territories, and its usefulness as a lever with which to weaken European integration in any 'solution' can be seen, at least from the Anglo–American view, as a chess-piece. Perhaps it is no longer a pawn, owing to the EU factor; it might even be a knight, but nevertheless still a chess-piece. One expert sums up the nature of Anglo–American strategy in Cyprus thus:

> The US with support from Britain has managed to turn the issue of [Cyprus] accession into one more instrument of pressure in order to advance another burdensome political settlement that eventually legitimises the conditions

created by Turkey's invasion and occupation. If this gambit is allowed to succeed, an agreement between the government of Cyprus and the Turkish Cypriot community prior to the Cypriot accession will pre-empt the applicability of European norms and will provide major derogations from these norms in the case of Cyprus.[40]

These precocious and perspicacious words, written before the presentation of the 'Annan Plan', provide a pointer and underline the argument that any Cyprus 'solution' will detract from EU cohesion, at least from Batman's and Robin's point of view.

On the face of things, Cyprus can be seen as a violated Aphrodite in a tug of 'love' between the US–UK Atlantic NATO axis and the Franco–German European one. Certainly, this image has its inner tensions, which detract from the simple picture. For example, minor countries like the Netherlands sometimes tend towards the Atlantic NATO view. On the other hand, as Bismarck said: 'Holland will annex itself.' In other words, the Netherlands is so bound up with the German economy that she cannot afford to go against the Franco–Germans when they are in full swing.

As regards Cyprus, the USA and the UK share the same strategy, namely to ensure that the island does not become a fully fledged and independent EU member, whether divided or not. Here, however, they have to contend with the EU. With the weak state of coordinated EU defence, the US–UK attitude is likely to prevail, at least in the short term. We now need to consider the impact on a Cyprus solution of the Anglo–American attack on Iraq.

BABYLON BASHING

The whole Iraq affair has come in for a good deal of international criticism, particularly since many consider Israel's programme of weapons of mass destruction to be for more dangerous than Iraq's, if indeed, Iraq had one. Many saw the attack on Iraq as an attempt to maintain Israel's regional control (over the Arab world); second, to ensure the secure supply of oil, particularly to the USA; and third, to establish US control over the Middle East, before 'dealing with' Iran and, later, Korea, the latter as a 'way into China'.

Any Cyprus 'solution', then, will be influenced by considerations of Israeli security and, crucially, will tend towards what Turkey wants, given the latter's continuing strategic importance and its part in the above-mentioned military triangle. The war against Iraq has distracted attention from Cyprus and provided Turkey – and the USA – with the perfect excuse to stall on a clear-cut Cyprus solution, which has continued in the aftermath of the attack, as the USA confronts Russia over Iran. Before we consider the likely outcome for Cyprus, and the possibility of conflict, let us turn to a less-discussed factor, namely the leverage of Cyprus itself.

CYPRUS

One of the main themes of this book is that the Cypriot people themselves and, by extension, their leaders, have little room for manoeuvre in deciding their destiny. Clearly, the lack of agreement between the Greek- and Turkish-speaking communities has stymied any notion of united action. Both the dividing of the communities and the British-influenced radicalisation of the two sides, as well as the 1960 treaties, left a state that is handicapped. Despite this, we have seen how Makarios was able skilfully to be a strong 'piggy in the middle', until political immaturity in Greece and confused American policy formulation led to the 1974 invasion. By that time, however, American fear of a conflict between two NATO partners allowed Makarios and his successors some degree of international clout, but never enough to alter radically the so-called *modus vivendi*. Certainly, the outcome of the S-300 saga (see Chapter Ten) can be seen as determining the limits of the official Cyprus government's independence, along with America's turning a blind eye to the illegal occupation.

It is the EU factor which has radically altered matters, to the extent of causing friction between the EU on the one hand, and the USA and Turkey on the other, with Britain playing its by now traditional role of trying to be all things to all men, while supporting US and Turkish policies, particularly by allowing Turkey to use Cyprus as a hostage to gain membership of the EU.

Economically, Cyprus is a positive step for the EU, as well as for itself. Its accession will boost the EU's shipping fleet by twenty-five per cent, increasing the EU's share of world shipping from sixteen to twenty per cent.[41] Moreover, Cyprus and Syria have been building an undersea gas pipeline[42] which, when completed, would mean that Cyprus would export gas to the rest of the EU. Naturally, there have been problems, because of delays in the construction of a related pipeline from Egypt to Syria and the fact that Syria is the strategic enemy of both Israel and Turkey. A strong Cyprus is clearly in EU interests, since it would enhance the EU's economic and political influence in the Middle East. This, however, is precisely what Israel, the USA and Britain wish to avoid, since the EU is too pro-Palestinian for their liking.

At the moment, the Cypriot government knows that its own room for manoeuvre is limited, to the extent that it has been coy about giving specific answers to specific questions. Following an interview with the counsellor of the Cypriot Embassy in Athens (see Chapter Fourteen), the Embassy then suggested that I put a series of questions to President Clerides. They were as follows:

1. What is your attitude towards the Treaties of Establishment, Guarantee and Alliance?
2. What is your attitude towards the Treaty of Lausanne?
3. Do you support Cyprus' possible membership of NATO?
4. Are you aware that Britain was against Cyprus joining NATO in 1960?
5. Do you think that the USA and Britain are only interested in a resolution that is good for NATO, rather than for the EU?

6. Do you think that Cyprus should be part of a future European Army?
7. If a solution is found based on a bi-zonal, bi-communal federation, who is going to be responsible for defence and foreign policy?
8. Do you believe that the British Sovereign Territories should remain?
9. How can negotiations take place under an illegal occupation?

Although the questions were sent on 16 September 2002, the answers (from the new president) did not arrive until 8 July 2003, to the genuine embarrassment of the embassy. My reading is that the current diplomatic activity is like quicksilver and that the Cyprus government literally could not afford to say certain things in public, for fear of upsetting major poker players or simply because they were keeping their options as open as they could. This underlines that Cyprus itself is the least influential of the forces making up its destiny. The fact that answers did eventually arrive suggests that the Cyprus government has now adopted a reasonably cohesive policy. Some analysis is however necessary now. To the first question, President Papadopoulos concluded that 'the United Kingdom and Turkey have not honoured their obligations under either of the Treaties and/or they have abused and violated the rights or alleged rights they have under the Treaties.'

To question 2, the president said that ever since the 1950s (see Chapter Two), Turkey has violated the Treaty of Lausanne with British support, since the Treaty explicitly stated that Turkey had no rights regarding Cyprus. The president drove this home by citing, as evidence of the violation, the London–Zurich agreements of 1959, the drafting of the 1960 constitution and the granting to Turkey of rights as a guarantor power. This is highly significant, since it suggests that behind the scenes, the Cyprus government wishes to ditch the whole anachronistic 1960 package, and those parts of the Annan Plan that attempt to revitalise the 1960 treaties (see previous chapter), and to seek genuine independence through the EU.

The answers to questions 3 and 4 show that the Cyprus government believes that Turkey has violated the Treaty of Lausanne and stymied Cyprus' attempts to improve relations with NATO, while the answer to question 5 is an indirect way of stressing the UN resolutions calling on Turkey to cease the occupation.

The answer to question 6 shows that Cyprus must go along with what was agreed at the Copenhagen Summit, but begs the question as to what its attitude would be *regarding a future European Army independent of NATO*.

The answer to question 7 is understandably and necessarily curt. Since the representatives of the two putative 'constituent states' could well disagree, then one is back to the Annan Plan, with three foreign judges and the Guarantor Powers having to decide (see previous chapter). This whole question is obviously the subject of intense secret talks.

The answer to question 8, that the government of Cyprus has no intention of asking the British government to open or re-examine the Treaty of Establishment, suggests that the question of the British territories is far too sensitive for Cyprus to rock the boat without EU support.

The answer to question 9, where President Papadopoulos agrees that no negotiations should take place while the occupation continues, but that 'our desire for a resolution of the Cyprus problem is so ardent, that we have abandoned this stand or principle' is startlingly frank, betraying an ethical dilemma: on the one hand, he accepts negotiations with an illegal regime supported by an occupation force, but on the other criticises the maxim 'might is right'.

RECENT DEVELOPMENTS

When researching for and writing a book that attempts to bring the reader up to date by connecting the past to the present, it is difficult to decide when to stop and apply the guillotine. Now is the moment, as we move towards the end of 2004.

After the Copenhagen summit, the poker-playing became even more frenetic, more 'high-low' than 'seven card stud'.[43] The British and Americans continued to push for acceptance of the Annan Plan (or at least signature of the Foundation Agreement), despite several postponed deadlines. The British government, in its keenness to obtain the signatures, even offered Cyprus forty-five square miles of its territory in Cyprus, provided that 'there was agreement by both sides to the UN's proposals'. The election of a new President of Cyprus, Tassos Papadopoulos, appears to have had little substantive effect on the policy of the Cyprus government, particularly since the astute Papadopoulos kept his canny predecessor, Cleridis, as his adviser for the negotiations.

A key date was 16 April 2003: Cyprus signed the Treaty of Accession to the EU, and has since ratified it. A protocol attached to the Treaty effectively ensures that while the whole island is acceding to the treaty, the *acquis communautaire* would be suspended in those areas of Cyprus where the legitimate government did not exercise effective control, in other words the part of the European Union under Turkish occupation when Cyprus became a member of the EU on 1 May 2004.

These developments have placed the Turkish government and Denktash under increasing pressure. Opposition from Denktash and the Turkish government to a UN settlement based on the Annan Plan continued, despite conflicting signals from different parts of the Turkish establishment. It rested largely on Denktash's apparent desire for his state to be recognised as legitimate by the Cyprus government before any substantive talks took place. Thus, on 23 April 2003, Denktash eased travel restrictions to the South, and opened occupied Cyprus to visits from the South. By 11 May, 238,000 Greek Cypriots and 88,000 Turkish Cypriots had crossed the buffer zone.[44]

Although the UN secretary general stated that Denktash bore prime responsibility for the failure to agree,[45] the latter tried to keep a dialogue open, but mainly as a way to achieve recognition, rather than pursue a UN solution. In this connection, he has so far rejected an EU aid package to allow the export of Turkish Cypriot products through ports in unoccupied Cyprus, on the grounds that this 'would put his administration' under the signature and stamp of the Greek Cypriot government.[46] Consultation with the Turkish government is close, as the Turkish government's offer to reimburse Loizidou (see Chapter Thirteen) provided that the other claims were settled directly with Denktash's administration, showed. The tension is only just under the surface: while an increasing number of Turkish Cypriots are now applying for (legitimate) Cypriot passports,[47] Turkish jet fighters have increased their violations of Greek airspace and Denktash has even threatened to settle the 'ghost town', Varosha, unless the Greek Cypriots agree to reopen Nicosia airport.[48] On 17 July 2003, Denktash stated that the Annan Plan was unacceptable.

Denktash's intransigence was skilfully tempered by the formation in January 2004 of a new administration in occupied Cyprus, the head of which, Mehmet Ali Talat, is a supporter of negotiations and reunification. His Turkish Republican Party is balanced in the coalition by Denktash's son's Democratic Party, which is less flexible. In this opaque situation, the commander of the Turkish Fourth Army warned the Turkish government not to make concessions:

> Some people in Turkey believe we should make concessions to get rid of problems. This country has always given birth to wonderful people, but lately it has begun to breed traitors.[49]

At the same time, the Greek and Cypriot governments rejected a request by the UN secretary general to hold referenda in Cyprus irrespective of negotiations. The Greek prime minister stated: 'Our aim is always for a solution to be just, viable and functional, to follow UN resolutions and the [EU's] *acquis communautaire.*'[50] He had a point, since holding referenda on issues that are still subject to negotiation is hardly logical.

Perhaps most significant, however, is that when the Greek prime minister announced the holding of general elections for 7 March 2004, two months earlier than required, he cited Cyprus developments as the reason.[51] Whether this was because he thought that his party would lose and wished to hand the problem (and the administration of the Olympic Games) to the opposition party is of course a moot point. But it does bring back the spectre of 1974, when the Cypriot tail wagged the Greek dog, as well as the Turkish wolf.

Following intense US pressure, Denktash performed a diplomatic U-turn by agreeing to continue negotiations. Significantly, this followed a statement by the Turkish National Security Council in favour of negotiations.[52] On 10 February 2004, the two sides agreed in New York to resume negotiations in Cyprus. Negotiations would continue until 22 March, when Greek and Turkish negotiators would join in. If issues still remained unresolved, Annan would himself 'fill in the gaps', and the plan would be put to referenda on 24 April. A poll of 800 Greek Cypriots at the end of February resulted in sixty-one per cent expressing opposition to the plan as it currently stood, twenty-seven per cent in favour and twelve per cent not replying.[53] This is despite the fact that Britain would give up almost half its territory on Cyprus, if an agreement were reached.

On 27 February, Mr Denktash rejected as 'physically impossible' a request by President Papadopoulos to endorse all the 114 EU laws that Nicosia had so far adopted.[54] He was reported to want all mainland Turkish settlers to remain in

Northern Cyprus, and to delay by several years the return to the North of Greek Cypriot refugees.[55] Such demands were unacceptable to President Papadopoulos, who was also reported to be irritated by US envoy Thomas Weston's comment that a 'no' vote would come at a heavy price.[56] According to the Turkish ambassador in Athens, Yigit Alpogan, it was possible that Annan would be left to try and sort matters out.[57] He was proven correct: at the end of March, the 'Cyprus roadshow' arrived in Switzerland, where intensive negotiations were conducted between representatives of the two sides in Cyprus, and of Turkey and Greece. Mr Denktash, to show his disapproval, did not attend. It transpired that at these negotiations, President Papadopoulos had submitted amendments, most of which were rejected, while eleven amendments put forward by the Turkish Cypriots were accepted.[58] It was indeed Annan who filled in the gaps of what was by now the fifth plan. The date for a referendum on the plan was set for 24 April.

On 7 April, President Papadopoulos gave a televised statement, coming out firmly against the plan. Some of the most significant points he made were that while the Republic of Cyprus would be scrapped, there was no firm guarantee that Turkey and the Turkish Cypriots would implement the plan. Yet, if both sides voted in favour of the plan, the invasion and occupation would be 'written off'[59] and Turkish Cypriot citizens would benefit fully, while Greek Cypriot demands would be postponed for years, and be contingent on Ankara's and the Turkish Cypriots' goodwill. He stressed the danger and perverseness of doing away with an internationally recognised state at the very moment that its political weight was being strengthened through membership of the European Union. He pointed out that the plan was weighted in favour of the Turkish Cypriots, and that the best solution was to pursue a more equitable solution through the European Union. This galvanised the US and British governments into introducing a Security Council resolution providing guarantees for the plan, which did not go far enough for the Cypriot government. In a sign of its increasing resistance to Anglo–American plans for the 'Greater Middle East', Russia vetoed the resolution.[60] In the run-up to the referenda, the pressure intensified, with both US and EU politicians making unspecific threats that this was the last chance. The EU enlargement commissioner, Günter Verheugen, even said that he felt cheated by the Cyprus government, and that President Papadopoulos had distorted the provisions of the Annan Plan. This was rebutted by the Cypriot government.[61] Both the US State Department spokesman and the EU's high commissioner for common foreign and security policy stated that if the Greek Cypriots voted against, and the Turkish Cypriots in favour of, the plan, the latter could not be left out in the cold.[62]

In unoccupied Cyprus, only Nikos Anastasiadis' right-wing Democratic Rally party came out firmly in favour of the plan, while the left-wing AKEL demanded more guarantees before it could accept it. In Turkey, the government came out in support (in the almost certain knowledge that the Greek Cypriots would reject the plan). Denktash continued to oppose it, while in Greece the opposition PASOK leader, Yiorgos Papandreou, supported it. The prime minister, Kostas Karamanlis, ingeniously managed to cautiously support the plan, while stressing that he would respect the Cypriots' decision.[63]

The referenda took place, with seventy-six per cent of the Greek Cypriots rejecting the plan, but only thirty-five per cent of the Turkish Cypriots. Perhaps rather perversely, the Turkish settlers also voted. The difference between the (minority) original Turkish Cypriots and the (majority) Turkish settlers is well epitomised by Shener Levent, publisher of *Avrupa* (now called *Africa*), a newspaper calling for the departure of all foreign troops and a united, independent Cyprus free of foreign interference. Levent was actually put on trial as a 'Greek spy' (he has Greek Cypriot friends), but was freed for lack of evidence. Interestingly, he is still publishing his newspaper at the time of writing, perhaps because of the influence of the *acquis communautaire*.[64]

At any rate, perhaps predictably, there was a somewhat intemperate and 'withering barrage of criticism' from the European Union, directed towards the Greek Cypriots. The enlargement commissioner claimed that the 'political damage was large', and the Council of Ministers initiated talks to provide an aid package to occupied Cyprus.[65] The Cypriot government welcomed this package, the main problem being whether occupied Cyprus would accept this aid via the legal government or whether the EU would try and allocate the aid package directly to occupied Cyprus.

There was also some criticism of the 'no' vote in Greece, expressed mainly through more fervent PASOK parts of the media. For example, the *Athens News* published an article, riddled with historical inaccuracies and errors, that actually called for AKEL to support a new plan, 'have Papadopoulos resign' and for Athens to assist in 'implementing this decision',[66] thus evoking the policy pursued by extremist elements in the Greek Junta towards President Makarios. There have even been unsubstantiated rumours that the Bilderberg group has 'appointed' someone to overthrow President Papadopoulos.

What, however, were the Cypriots asked to vote for? The actual question was:

> Do you approve the Foundation Agreement will all its Annexes, as well as the constitution of the Greek Cypriot/Turkish Cypriot State and the provisions as to the laws to be in force, to bring into being a new state of affairs in which Cyprus joins the European Union united?

How much time were the Cypriots given to digest the plan before voting? Most voters probably understood the basics, namely that the 'bi-zonal state' would have a 'single international presence' and that Greece, Turkey and Britain would remain guarantor powers; that a 'reunified Cyprus' was obliged to support Turkey's EU accession; and that Greek and Turkish troops would be limited to 6,000 each until 2011 and 3,000 by 2018 or until Turkey joined the EU. The Turkish Cypriot area would cover 28.5 per cent of the island. For nineteen years, or until Turkey joined the EU, each group would constitute up to eighteen per cent of the other sector; and, finally, for fifteen years, or until per capita income of Turkish Cypriots reached eighty-five per cent of that of Greek Cypriots, up to eighteen per cent of each group could purchase land in each other's area.

While a certain number of voters had the time and the inclination to peruse the 182 pages of the (fifth) plan, published on 31 March 2004, the 9,000 pages of annexes were not issued until the day before the referendum. In fact, *the United Nations did not place the full plan on its website until 23:59 GMT on 23 April*. This may help explain the large 'no' vote. Some other considerations may also help one to understand the opposition.[67] First, thousands of displaced Greek Cypriots would have been denied the right of return; second, the plan, by establishing a new 'state of affairs', would have deprived Cypriots of the right to bring certain cases before the European Court of Human Rights, and frozen applications to the Court in respect of actions taken by Turkey; third, the plan would have undermined democratic principles by giving eighteen per cent of the (legal) population fifty per cent of the seats in the senate; and fourth, it would have legalised the presence in Cyprus of most of the illegal settlers.

Given the above, it is not unreasonable to conclude that many voters, apart from not being given time to properly digest the plan, must have thought that the United Nations was seeking to legitimise the illegitimate and turn a blind-eye to military aggression and illegal occupation. Certainly, the contrast between what the United Nations did in Kuwait in 1991 and what they have not done in Cyprus is remarkable.

The dust of the 'no' vote has yet to settle. Mr Annan's report on the plan's failure contained some only barely disguised criticism of the Greek Cypriots (and those Turkish Cypriots who voted 'no'): 'The decision of the Greek Cypriots must be respected. However, it is a major setback [...]. If they remain willing to resolve the Cyprus problem through a bizonal, bicommunal federation, this needs to be demonstrated.'[68] Stung by this indirect criticism, President Papadopoulos riposted on 7 June, pointing out that Annan had exceeded his mandate by presenting a fifth version of the plan, and denouncing the fact that the illegal settlers were allowed to vote, and that they would be allowed to remain, with the possibility of further settlement. Cuttingly, President Papadopoulos wrote:

> The fulsome praise [of the Turkish side] in the report is also designed to secure an unlawful objective, namely to give Turkey's subordinate local administration in occupied Cyprus the economic attributes of an independent state without formally recognising it [...]. It is an attempt to by-pass a rule of international law that forbids recognition of the fruits of aggression. That rule is the reason why Security Council Resolutions 541 (1983) and 550 (1984) [forbidding recognition of the breakaway state in the occupied north] were passed. Yet not a single word in the report indicates that the Republic of Turkey is in unlawful military occupation of 36.4% of Cyprus.[69]

Since then, the debate has focused on the question of de facto recognition of occupied Cyprus. Mainly at British instigation, the European Union is considering how to open occupied Cyprus to international trade, while the USA is considering ways of aiding occupied Cyprus. On 15 June, the Organisation of the Islamic Conference (OIC), meeting in Istanbul, referred to the 'Turkish Cypriot state'.[70] At the same meeting, the Turkish foreign minister called on the OIC to monitor the condition of Greece's Muslim minority in Thrace, claiming that it was not able to fully enjoy its basic human rights. This attitude contrasted with that of the Turkish prime minister when he visited Thrace in early May, during an official visit to Greece, resulting in a friendly but vague joint communiqué. Significantly, however, Mr Karamanlis stated that the talks on the continental shelf would continue beyond December, when the EU would decide whether to set a date to begin accession talks. This is inconsistent, given that the 1999 Helsinki Council of Ministers summit stated that failing agreement on the issue by December 2004, the issue should be taken to the International Court of Justice. Mr Erdogan, for his part, stated that the Christian Orthodox seminary in Halki 'would soon reopen'.[71] Yet, three weeks later, at the end of May, nine formations of Turkish military aircraft entered the Athens Flight Information Region without first submitting flight plans. In one encounter, jet fighters flew close to a Cyprus Airways passenger jet.[72] This last incident, one of many, serves to remind one of the intractability of Turkey's claims to Greek islets and airspace, and how, despite the much-avowed 'de-coupling' of the Cyprus question from other problems of Greek–Turkish relations, the military establishment in Turkey still exploits the linkage to the full. Paradoxically, and as if to underline the volatility and inconsistencies in Greek–Turkish relations, the Greek and Turkish governments recently announced to each other large cuts in their arms procurement programmes. Whether this is simply window-dressing, a result of economic necessity, a genuine desire to achieve full rapprochement, or a combination of these factors, is currently a moot point; but it must have set alarm bells ringing in defence companies, particularly the American ones, which have the lion's share of the Greek–Turkish market. Peace can be expensive for some.

As this final chapter is being sent to the publishers, two developments pertinent to Cyprus' future have taken place. First is agreement on the watered-down EU constitution, with Britain, predictably, coming under heavy criticism, for insisting on its future veto on social security, taxation and foreign policy and defence matters. President Chirac summed up the criticism by referring to 'the *non possumus* clearly and strongly put forward by the United Kingdom', and to the delay in the creation of a Europe that would avoid being blocked by a single country. The German delegation was similarly critical. Britain, however, was forced to give way on the creation of an EU foreign minister, closer military procurement cooperation, a plan for willing countries to take part in special combat units and, crucially, the idea of a two-speed Europe, allowing groups of countries to cooperate more closely, particularly on defence issues.[73] The Cyprus government is likely to use whatever legal methods it can to cooperate militarily with the EU. Its chief spokesman says that membership in a common foreign and security policy is a final objective for Cyprus, but that it is 'dangerous to push it now'.[74] The second – connected – development is that Turkey is coming under pressure to recognise the legal government of Cyprus. To comply with its customs agreement with the EU, Turkey must deal with every new member, including Cyprus. This was made clear in the Dublin Summit's final conclusions. The Turkish prime minister has merely said – to CNN – that he expects Cyprus to be fully incorporated into the customs union, without giving a date.[75]

The situation is likely to remain legally expedient, confusing and, therefore, tense. An EU solution would be preferable in the long term, but if the Turkish government is still trying to use Cyprus as a foreign policy tool – with US and UK backing – to force its way into the European Union, this is unlikely to please the hardcore EU members, whatever Britain and the USA want.

TENTATIVE PROGNOSTICATIONS

The diplomatic history surrounding Cyprus for at least the last fifty years, combined with the current strategic objectives of the USA, Israel, Turkey and Britain on the one hand, and of Greece, Cyprus and the EU on the other, point towards a tense time and ever more acrasial behaviour from some of the poker players.

Every EU member state was ratifying the enlargement agreement at the same time as the two sides in Cyprus were being pressured by Britain to sign an agreement recognising the 1960 treaties, and thus Britain's territories. It was not beyond the bounds of possibility that the Netherlands would try to complicate Cyprus' accession before an agreement between the two communities led to a united Cyprus. Britain, however, would probably have resisted such a move, in the full knowledge that this could have endangered the accession of all ten new members, thereby leading to a more solid and entrenched EU, and not the large and organisationally complicated group of twenty-five states that Britain and the USA were so keen to see. Their eagerness to see this derived from the belief that, with an expanded NATO including the new EU members, the EU would be divided, and therefore paralysed, on serious defence matters, leaving the USA and Britain to take the lead in a NATO context.

The big 'if' in this scenario, unwelcome to the British, is that, unless the Cypriot government's arm is twisted to sign an agreement underpinning the 1960 treaties, the government could try to divest itself of the post-colonial shackles of the 1960 agreements, and achieve full independence, albeit in truncated form, within the EU.

A big sticking point will be the joint defence doctrine with Greece. Although the EU has agreed, owing to British, Turkish and American pressure, to keep Cyprus out of ESDP operations involving NATO assets, this does not preclude a new and independent truncated Cyprus from its legitimate defence, especially if the 1960 agreements bite the dust.

Turkey, with its 40,000 troops, will keep up the pressure on Cyprus and Greece. At the same time, it is possible that many of the remaining Turkish Cypriots (one half have already left) will be granted official Cypriot nationality, and leave for the South, leaving only the illegal settlers and the Turkish army.

This in turn could lead to the 'semi-integration' of Northern Cyprus by Turkey,[76] and de facto annexation, or an independent state recognised initially only by Turkey. In the long term, this could lead to international recognition, which would thereby create a new international border, either with Turkey or with the new state. This is precisely what four former Greek ambassadors argued in 1995, on the grounds that it is far more difficult to violate a (de jure) international border than a de facto illegal one.[77] This solution would not negate the eventual application of the *acquis communautaire*, if and when occupied Cyprus were to reunite (à la Germany). On the other hand, if occupied Cyprus were to continue to fill up with settlers, this would cause problems. It could also put Turkey on the spot vis-à-vis the Loizidou case (see Chapter Thirteen) since Turkey argues that the 'TRNC' government is responsible, rather than its own.

Such a 'solution', however, would be resisted by those who believe in the letter of international law, since it would contradict UN resolutions calling for a united Cyprus. Britain, in particular, would baulk at a new international border, since this would render the 1960 agreements even more meaningless than they already are, particularly if the legal government of Cyprus and Greece refuse to sign another British-inspired document underlining the sanctity of the 1960 agreements. Apart from this, a new internationally recognised 'state of Northern Cyprus' would hardly be ready to join the European Union, for many years.

Ideally, if Erdogan and the moderate part of the American establishment prevail, then legal Cyprus' EU membership could lead to reunification at a later date, without linkage to Turkey's accession hopes, but, rather, stronger trade links between the EU and Turkey. Such moderate solutions are unfortunately not the current order of the day, when one considers the statements flying around.

Turkey is, therefore, likely to continue to use Cyprus as a lever to pressure the EU to open its door, and, to pursue its claims on Greek islets and airspace, which will lead to increasing indignation in Brussels. One plan, which Greece and unoccupied Cyprus may have already considered, is *enosis* following Cyprus' accession to the EU. This would be one answer to Turkish pressure over the Aegean and around Cyprus. In such a scenario, Britain may already have contingency plans to give up its base at Akrotiri, while strengthening its Dhekelia base, since the latter borders with the occupied zone of its Turkish partner. The Cypriot government (or, perhaps rather fantastically, the then Greek government) would simply stop its border at the Dhekelia base. This is some of the meta-thinking required, when one attempts to prognosticate.

Of particular significance was a statement by President Papadopoulos about the Annan Plan, which indicates that he prefers an EU to a NATO solution:

> We have indications that many circles in the European Commission are not very happy with the principles of the plan that they believe constitute great diversions from the *acquis communautaire*. Our hope is that this will strengthen our bargaining power and these diversions will change during the negotiations.[78]

This suggests that, behind the scenes, Cyprus is still very much a 'hostage to history'. This time it is, however, not a hostage of the old East–West political conflicts, but of the emerging jockeying for position between the EU and the Anglo-Saxon world. It is perhaps slightly troubling that Cyprus' accession to the EU in May 2004 happened to coincide with Greece's last-minute frenetic preparations for the Olympic Games and a new government, a time when certain politicians were more susceptible than usual to the covert influence of foreign powers.

Following the collapse in December 2003 of the talks on an EU constitution, caused to a large extent by Polish intransigence, and the emergence of an EU operational military planning unit, there is speculation that the core EU members will eventually integrate alone, perhaps with their own constitution, even if the current constitution is ratified by all current members, while the more Atlantic-minded ones, Britain included, will form their own loose 'intergovernmental' outer ring.[79] The question for Cyprus is whether it will be able, if it wishes, to join such a putative inner core, although it may be less difficult for Greece to do so. Turkey, Britain and the USA, to name but some main players, will strive to ensure, as they already have, that Cyprus will lack the kind of sovereignty that enables it to act sufficiently independently in its international relations so as to choose its friends. The background tension around Cyprus and in the Aegean will not dissipate, and could, depending on the degree of regional instability, increase.

On current form, whatever is signed, it is likely that the situation will remain sensitive for some time. The real 'macro-issue' is the nature of the relationship between NATO's, the USA's and Britain's Eastern Mediterranean and Middle Eastern military, political and economic interests on the one hand, and those of a putative strengthened European defence entity (and perhaps of Russia) on the other. This central issue encompasses various objectives from the Anglo–American standpoint. These are: the continual strengthening of NATO and its transmogrification into a worldwide policeman; the concomitant weakening of any putative European armed forces entirely independent of NATO; the promotion of intergovernmentalism in the EU in order to weaken the process of European integration; the effort to bring Turkey into a weakened EU, thereby further weakening European integration; the defence of Israel; and the perceived need to control the Middle East.

The US and British essential objective is to resuscitate and strengthen the 1960 treaties, even if the latter have already been shown to have failed (and virtually admitted by the FCO, at least in the case of the Treaty of Guarantee, to be contrary to the UN Charter). Not to revive those treaties would give the EU a greater measure of power as regards Cyprus' own sovereignty. Much will depend on how far the EU is prepared to turn a blind eye to the Treaty of Rome, and how many derogations it is prepared to accept in accepting Northern Cyprus. Whatever is agreed, it seems that the arrangement will be highly expedient, with the bemused Cypriots themselves having only a minimal say in the matter, whatever the frontstage handshakes. In 1960, it took very little time for the 1960 treaties to show their unworkability. The situation now is likely to be yet more complex, and once the dust has settled, if it does, some hard positions are likely to be taken, particularly if an allegedly reunited Cyprus realises that it is the least sovereign member of the EU. Whatever happens, Britain, the USA and Turkey will continue to use the Cyprus question (and, quite possibly, the Aegean problem) to push for Turkey's admission to the EU.

The current 'solution' may look convenient in international relations terms, but historically, Cyprus may well remain a hostage to externally owned strategies. A senior research fellow at the Athens Academy hopefully concludes:

> [...] no doubt should remain that these deviations from community [EU] rules do not constitute a major setback from a European Union point of view. Further, the realities of the post-accession situation and particularly the realities of market forces could well lead to the amelioration of otherwise inflexible provisions of the Annan Plan. In the last analysis, it is not at all certain that these protective clauses will prohibit the smooth coexistence of the two communities on the island.[80]

Such a statement, coldly realistic, reflects the fact that ever since Britain cynically pulled Turkey into the Cyprus equation in 1955 (despite Article 16 of the Treaty of Lausanne), division is indeed an effective control-mechanism. As long as Britain can claim that the 1960 treaties are still valid and/or as long as the government of Cyprus – whether a united Cyprus or not – is not a wholly independent member of Europe, responsible for its own defence, then Britain can withstand pressure on the validity of its bases. If, however, Cyprus were ever to be allowed to join NATO or an independent European army, then the bases would undoubtedly become less relevant. To date, the Cyprus government has not officially questioned their existence, although legally, it can be argued that they are an anomaly, or at least, in the words of one expert, unique.[81] A British expert on Cyprus recently described the bases as an anachronism.[82] It is not impossible that the government of Cyprus could begin to exercise pressure on the bases, for example by holding a referendum on the question of negotiating with Russia over a naval base, or granting the Russians overflying rights – as Britain enjoys. Britain, the USA, Turkey and Israel could, however, react unpredictably to such moves, given the current use of the bases as part of their Middle East strategy. A leading expert on the bases recently pointed out their massively increased use during the build-up to, and during, the war against Iraq. Any pressure to remove the bases would undermine the Israeli–Turkish military agreement, which has not been affected by the public rhetoric of Mr Erdogan against Mr. Sharon's behaviour. In this connection, a former Greek ambassador to Cyprus thinks that the military agreement is detrimental to Greece's and Cyprus' interests.[83] Clearly, this is so, given that American and British Middle East 'initiatives' are supported by Israel, but not by the mainstream EU, which includes Greece and, by extension, Cyprus. It is in British and US interests to 'Taiwanise' Cyprus, thus maintaining their version of a *modus vivendi*, while ensuring that there cannot be full recognition of occupied Cyprus. Beyond that, Russian influence is slowly increasing. As Moscow continues to reconstitute a forward security zone in Central Asia,[84] this clearly has a knock-on effect, as witnessed in the above-mentioned veto of the Security Council Resolution on the Annan Plan. In the UN connection, it is perhaps paradoxical that Turkey is now praising and courting the UN, when it was blatantly ignoring and criticising it from 1964 onwards.

At the end of the day, in terms of international relations theory, Cyprus is caught between the utilitarian 'realists', namely British and American foreign policy, and the 'functionalists', those who wish to abide by the rule of international law and promote multi-polarity. In the not too distant future, one could end up with a hardcore 'old Europe', with its own defence and foreign policy, surrounded by a US-friendly group of East European countries led by Britain. This prospect is bringing, and will bring, Moscow closer to Paris and Bonn in security terms. Cyprus is likely to be held hostage to these developments, unless it can skillfully become part of 'hardcore' Europe. Greece's position will be important in this respect. Much will depend on whether Greece's politicians have the courage to intensify ties with Paris, Bonn and Moscow, or whether they will choose a halfway house.

CONCLUSIONS

Lin Yutang wrote that he distrusted all dead and mechanical formulas for expressing anything connected with human affairs or human personalities. Putting human affairs in exact formulas, he said, showed in itself a lack of sense of humour and therefore a lack of wisdom.[85] In short, you cannot trap the human mind. If we apply this to international relations, with its ever-increasing plethora of 'conflict-resolution' techniques and theories, it becomes obvious that these serve as a distraction as much as an attempt to analyse, evaluate and prognosticate. If you cannot trap the human mind, it follows that you cannot trap society. Thus, whether you are a proponent of critical theory, postmodernism, constructivism, Marxism, liberalism, realism, neo-realism or rationalism, to name but some of the main international relations notions put out by earnest social scientists, it is unlikely that one will be much the wiser in gaining a deep understanding of the likelihood of future events.

If one looks at the history of the biped as a social beast, anthropologically, biologically and, as in the case of this book, through the prism of diplomatic history, one comes up with certain constant factors. In the case of Cyprus, it is the desire for states to control other states, hence the ugly yet unavoidable term 'geopolitics'. The British, unable to control the whole of Cyprus, adopted the tactics of division and brought in extra geopolitical actors or, as I have written, poker players, in order to keep what she could of the island. It is not fair to accuse only Britain of 'post-colonial *rigor mortis*': Spain, with its Moroccan territories of Ceuta and Melilla, is in a similar boat, and Britain can therefore cock a snook over its possession of Gibraltar. Britain is in fact the only EU member that owns territory in another EU state. (The Irish government might also claim that Britain is occupying part of Ireland, but that is another ball game!)

Much of the current secret diplomatic scurrying around Cyprus is more likely to involve Cyprus' future relationship with the ESDP. As long as the USA and

Britain can keep NATO in control of Europe, and Britain can keep at least Dhekelia, then it will live with Cyprus in the EU, even without the 1960 Treaties of Guarantee and Alliance. However, as the ten, albeit slowly but inexorably, become integrated into the EU, and adopt a more *communautaire* and less Atlantic approach, Cyprus' security will be further enhanced as the Franco–German machine gains a new lease of life. An outer ring of EU members could well include Turkey, eventually leading to the reunification of the island.

The path of common sense and reason, however, is confronted by an immoderate climate. In America, the Christian evangelical fundamentalists are posing as mainstream policy-makers, in alliance with Jewish fundamentalists and an extreme right-wing Israeli government, while in several Muslim nations, the likes of al-Qaeda and other extreme Islamic fundamentalist groups are growing in strength. Moderate, reasoned international relations have given way to the opinions and soundbites of extreme leaders, who are irresponsibly using religion as a political weapon, a sure path to further bloodshed. One cannot fail to see a connection between current American unilateralism (to put it diplomatically) and insatiableness (to put it more strongly).

This unilateralism has been fuelled by the collapse of the USSR. Since the fall of the Berlin Wall, the imbalance in the United Nations has become more obvious. The world's second and third strongest countries in terms of the size and power of their economies, Japan and Germany, are not even permanent members of the UN Security Council, as if they are still being punished for losing the Second World War. A more logical reflection of world power should entail Britain and France giving up their seats on the Security Council to the EU, and Japan joining.

If there is to be further conflict in Cyprus, or between Greece and Turkey, it is likely to destabilise the EU as much as NATO. Turkey, or rather its neo-Ottoman 'Kemalist' establishment, may well continue to provoke and probe, in the belief that it can exploit occupied Cyprus and its claims on Greek territory, because the USA is obliged to support it for strategic reasons. Whether there is a conflict or not will depend on the leeway given to Turkey to push its Aegean claims and support Denktash or whoever succeeds him. In 1974, Kissinger gave Turkey that leeway and, given an inch, Turkey took a mile. These are the imponderables of (human) international relations. One can only hope that the likes of Kissinger, Wolfowitz and Condoleezza Rice learn the art of diplomacy and practise it, rather than mistake it for power politics. They could take a leaf out of Churchill's book, and apply more jaw, and less war and killing. The Atlantic community needs more stable, deeply and broadly educated leaders than it currently has.

For the time being, the dividing line in Cyprus has nothing to do with a 'clash of civilisations' in the simplistic Huntingdonian sense of Muslim versus Christian. It has rather to do with the moderate forces of Europe against the forces of extreme Christian, Jewish and Muslim geopolitical brinkmanship and 'pre-emptive action', which make up the current vociferous fashion in Atlantic politics, and which are the real 'axis of evil'. To avoid, or stave off, extreme actions, Cyprus may well have to give up its northern bit and plump for the EU, in the hope that a continuing policy of neo-Ostpolitik will eventually lead to reunification. In the meantime, the Cypriots can console themselves with the fact that there are other divided islands, such as Timor, Ireland, Borneo, New Guinea and Hispaniola (Haiti and the Dominican Republic). These divisions are all, to a greater or lesser extent, the stings in the tail of colonialism. If war is the continuation of politics by other means, then it is also the failure of diplomacy and the triumph of greed.

EPILOGUE

As this book goes to print, the main factor relevant to Cyprus' future has been Turkey's persistence, supported strongly by Britain and America, in persuading the European Commission to set a date for opening EU accession talks. Before the European Commission's heavily qualified 'yes' (see below), there were moments of farce when, for example, in the space of only a few days, the Turkish government magically decriminalised adultery, by holding an extraordinary session of parliament on 26 September 2004, at which an amended set of 'EU-compatible' laws were agreed on.[1] The fact that the offending law on adultery was even originally considered is surprising, given the Turkish government's apparent keenness to take Turkey into the EU.

Of considerable significance, too, was the French government's decision to hold a referendum to amend the French constitution, so as to introduce referenda on any future EU enlargement, in the knowledge that a majority of French citizens are opposed to Turkey's accession.

The period up to 6 October, when the European Commission made its recommendation, was punctuated by considerable international media interest, some of it clearly partisan. For example, *The Economist* indulged in some rhetorical scare-mongering and linguistic bulimia, when it wrote: '…a "no" to Turkey would have catastrophic consequences.' The magazine, however, did not choose to elaborate on, and demonstrate, what these 'catastrophic consequences' would be; it merely wrote that a 'no' would be 'a blow against all Islam' and that 'it would threaten Turkey's own reforms.'[2] The latter could easily be interpreted as an inadvertent insult to Turkey, since it implies that Turkey depends on external factors to run its own affairs.

At any event, as expected, the European Commission expressed itself in favour of opening membership talks with Turkey. Although some may choose to interpret this as a 'future *fait accompli*' for Turkish membership, the reality is very different, given the number of – unprecedented – conditions attached to the 'yes.' The report includes the following:

> a. an open process whose results cannot be guaranteed in advance;
> b. in the event of serious and persistent violation of the principles of freedom, democracy, respect for human rights and fundamental liberties, the Commission recommends the suspension of negotiations, and the [European] Council will decide by majority voting;
> c. permanent safeguard clauses could be envisaged for the free circulation of workers and
> d. despite important efforts [in political reforms], implementation must be further consolidated.

Apart from these conditions and restrictions, the report makes clear that regional and agricultural aid will be subject to specific rules. Turkey would not, therefore, be able to swallow up EU funds nor drastically affect the EU budget. Indeed, it would be treated as a special case.

Particularly disappointing to the Turkish government is the likelihood that negotiations may not begin until 2006. According to *Le Monde*, the referenda on the European Constitution will slow down the whole process, and that each year there will be a general examination of the political reforms in Turkey. This will allow a new report before the European Council's meeting in December 2005, which in turn could be used as 'a final security net' before the opening of formal talks in 2006.[3] As if all this is not enough, the European Commission has stipulated that Turkey could not join before the EU has agreed its budget from 2014.

What, however, of Cyprus? The report avoids mentioning the obvious fact that Turkey would have to recognise Cyprus before any meaningful negotiations could take place, restricting itself to the statement that negotiations 'take place within the framework of an intergovernmental conference comprising all the member states of the Union', thus implying recognition by Turkey.

For the time being, both Cyprus and Greece have 'welcomed' the European Commission's report, perhaps hoping to trade an agreement over Cyprus and Turkey's claims on Greek territory and airspace with progress on Turkey's membership aspirations. President Papadopoulos has stressed international law by stating: 'The number of Turkish soldiers in northern Cyprus and the settlement policy of Turkey are against international rules. Before negotiations start, this has to be changed.'[4] As for its attitude towards the British government which, as this book has attempted to demonstrate, has been clearly biased towards Turkey in the latter's policy vis-à-vis Cyprus, the Cypriot government has made it plain that if there is to be a future reduction in UN troops on the island, then British UN troops should leave first. The essential reason is that Britain has favoured the Turkish Cypriot side.[5]

It is clear that there will be a continuation of tension and hard bargaining in the question of not only Cyprus and Turkish hopes to join the EU, but in Turkish claims in the Aegean. As regards the latter, although, as we have seen previously, Turkey was meant to take its claims to the International Court of Justice, the Greek government has yielded to pressure and agreed to negotiate separately, thereby theoretically unlinking the problem from Turkey's putative membership talks. The Greek Foreign Ministry has however stressed to this author that unless Turkey recognises Cyprus, it will not be able to join the EU and that it will need to behave in the Aegean.

An optimistic scenario from the Greek and Cypriot viewpoint would be that Cyprus is reunited under one strong independent government, with Turkey dropping its claims on Greek territory, as it moves closer to European norms. Britain and the US would however resist this, since Britain's bases would look even more anachronistic than they already are. Britain, the US and Israel are more interested in their perceived Middle Eastern interests than in a truly independent Cyprus.

A pessimistic scenario for Greek and Cypriot security, which would suit Britain's and America's interests, would be to maintain as much control as possible over the Eastern Mediterranean and Middle East by ensuring a controlled measure of tension, and by keeping EU defence away from the area. This brings the danger of 're-Balkanisation'[6] in Greece, with Greek governments feeling a moral obligation towards Cyprus, and being subject to orchestrated provocations such as the Imia incident of 1996 and the almost daily incursions of Turkish jet fighters, that are continuing as this is being written. In such a scenario, with the US, as we have seen, not recognising areas such as Imia as Greek, and Turkey's military ally Israel avoiding questions about Greece's air and sea borders with Turkey, the danger is that Greece and Cyprus will be left out of mainstream Europe, and belong to a second-tier EU led by Britain, and including Turkey, the recent East European members and, later, Israel, all avid supporters of NATO.

The potential 'joker in the pack' is Russia, which is not only increasing its economic grip – particularly in the form of gas exports – over parts of eastern Europe, but still keeping an eye on developments around Cyprus, while at the same time improving its links with Berlin and Paris. Thus, in a future two-tier Europe, Greek and Cypriot diplomacy will need to be of an extremely high quality to circumvent the many obstacles to stability caused, among other things, by Cyprus' unfortunate proximity to the Middle East. The best and the most realistic solution is for a strong EU, with Moscow's support, to bring Turkey into its own future security ambit, with, of course, many of the provisos set out in the European Commission's report (see above). The current backstage bargaining, in advance of the European Council meeting on 17 December, is intense, with Britain, the US and Turkey trying to water down the conditions attached to the European Commission's report, and to speed up the whole process with indecent haste. It is easier to confuse in order to control, than to control in order to confuse: power without responsibility is easier than responsibility without power.

THE END

NOTES

FOREWORD

1   Pluto Press, London, 2003.

PREFACE

1   Nicolson, Harold, *Peacemaking 1919*, Universal Library Edition, USA, 1965, p. 207.
2   Cable to Overton, 28 February 1972, *Memorandum*, PRO FCO 82/179, file AMU 2/3.
3   *Economicos Tachidromos*, 14 August 1997. The article took Kissinger's words from the *Turkish Daily News* of 17 February 1997. The former editor of *Economicos Tachidromos*, Yiannis Marinos, now a Member of the European Parliament, confirmed the story's veracity to the author on 17 July 2002.
4   Sked, Alan (ed.), *Europe's Balance of Power, 1815–1848*, Macmillan, London, 1979, p. 7. Sked quotes de Bertier de Sauvigny in *Metternich and his Times*, Darton, Longman and Todd, 1962, p. 251.
5   Op. cit., Nicolson, p. 35.
6   Ibid., p. 242.
7   Kissinger, Henry, *Nuclear Weapons and Foreign Policy*, Harper & Brothers, New York, 1957, p. 165.
8   Leigh Fermor, Patrick, *Roumeli*, Penguin, London, 1983 (first published by John Murray, 1966), p. 171.
9   *Athens News*, 24 August 2001, article by George Lardner, syndicated from the *Washington Post*. According to Lardner, the publication 'would have given the CIA heartburn'.
10   In this connection, readers would do well to compare two books of the same title, *Diplomacy*, one by Harold Nicolson (Oxford University Press, 1939, revised 1969), the other by Henry Kissinger. Their only similarity lies in the title, and one finds oneself comparing chalk with cheese. Nicolson's book is clearly a studied and judicious attempt to describe and promote the art of diplomacy, while Kissinger's would be better entitled 'How Abuse of Power is the key to Killing Diplomacy'.
11   Richard, Oliver P., *Mediating in Cyprus*, Frank Cass, London, Portland, OR, 1998, p. xii.

INTRODUCTION

1   Winston S. Churchill, British Embassy, Beirut, to FO, 21 December 1956, letter enclosing *Greek Government Booklet*, which quotes Churchill, PRO FO 953/1708, PG11928/230.
2   Clogg, Richard, *A Concise History of Greece*, Cambridge University Press, 1992, p. 159.
3   Mallinson, William, *Portrait of an Ambassador*, Athens, 1998, p. 105.
4   Following Turkish threats and pressure from the USA and some EU countries, notably Britain, the S-300 system was moved to Crete. This represents the first major commercial inroad into Europe for a sophisticated Russian armament.
5   West, Nigel, *The Friends: Britain's Post-War Secret Intelligence Operations*, Weidenfeld and Nicholson, London, 1988, p. 75. The claim is also repeated by O'Malley,

Brendan and Craig, Ian in *The Cyprus Conspiracy*, I.B.Tauris, London, 1999, p. 74, who refer to *The Friends* and a biography of Richard White, then Head of M16, *The Perfect English Spy*, by Bower. Curiously, Peter Wright does not mention it in his notorious *Spycatcher*.

6   Costar to Secretary of State, 28 April 1969, PRO FCO 9/785, WSC 1/9, *Valedictory Dispatch*.

7   Sir David Hunt, former British High Commissioner in Cyprus (1965–1967) gave a very incisive comparison between Crete and Cyprus at the Montague Burton Lecture on international relations at the University of Edinburgh, on 28 October 1980.

8   Throughout this book, the terms – although inaccurate – Greek and Turkish Cypriots will be used, for simplicity's sake. British pressure led to the introduction of these divisive terms.

9   There is some disagreement about the precise number of refugees from Anatolia and Thrace. Pentzopoulos, Dimitris, in *The Balkan Exchange of Minorities and its Impact Upon Greece*, Mouton & Co., Ecole Pratique des Hautes Etudes, Paris, 1962, p. 99, provides a table from the Statistical Annual of Greece, from which one can extrapolate the figure of between 1,300,000 and 1,400,000. A good number, however, died or emigrated onwards. Michael Llewelyn Smith, on the other hand, in *Ionian Vision*, Hurst & Co., London, 1998 (first published in 1973), p. 319, writes that in all, 1,500,000 refugees came to Greece in the aftermath of the disaster. To this one can add over 100,000 who came before the disaster (Pentzopulos). Eddy, Charles B., in *Greece and the Greek Refugees*, Allen and Unwin Ltd, London, 1931, p. 57, suggests that 1,300,000 is 'not far from the truth.'

10   In return, Greece had accepted a new king.

11   Op. cit., Hunt. Churchill's quote in 1907 is a far cry from what he wrote in a letter to Lord Quickswood on 2 February 1955: 'I must say, when I think of the risks I ran and the efforts I made on behalf of the Greeks, I feel they qualify for the first prize for ingratitude.' Plus ça change! PRO PREM11/831.

12   Hitchens, Christopher, *Hostage to History*, Verso, London and New York, 1997 (first published 1984).

13   Zambouras, Sergios, 'Current Greek Attitudes and Policy', in Dodd, Clement H. (ed.), *Cyprus: The Need for New Perspectives*, Eothen Press, Huntingdon, 1999.

14   Vital, because disagreement between the USA and the EU over several economic and political issues is growing. See, for example, Nye, Joseph, 'The US and Europe: Continental Drift', *International Affairs*, vol. 76, no. 1, Chatham House, London, January 2000, pp. 51–59, Bergsten, C. Fred, 'America's Two-Front Economic Conflict', *Foreign Affairs*, vol. 80, no. 2, New York, March–April 2001, pp. 16–27, and Broder, David S. 'Europe's Anger Reaches Boiling Point', *International Herald Tribune* (syndicated from the *Washington Post*, 28 March, 2002).

15   Op. cit., O'Malley and Craig, p. vii.

16   *Milliyet*, 16 April 2002 (reported in *Kathimerini*, 17 April 2002).

17   Tebbit to Wiggin, 30 December 1971, *letter*, PRO FCO 82/62, AMU 3/548/10.

18   These authors are particularly scathing about the role of Henry Kissinger in the Cyprus debacle. Hitchens writes: 'A good liar must have a good memory: Kissinger is a stupendous liar with a remarkable memory.' See *The Guardian*, 26 February 2001.

19   *The Guardian*, 9 February 2002.

CHAPTER 1

1   Clogg, Richard, *A Concise History of Greece*, Cambridge University Press, 1992, p. 57. He quotes the British Minister to Greece, Sir Edmund Lyons, in 1841.

2   Woodhouse, C. M., *Modern Greece*, Faber and Faber, London, 1991, p. 167

3   Taylor, A. J. P., *The Struggle for the Mastery of Europe, 1848–1918*, Oxford University Press, 1971, p. 60.

4   Ibid., p. 249.
5   Ibid., p. 249. Taylor, writing in the mid-fifties, could just as well have written the same today, were he alive, given the constant granting of IMF loans to Turkey, essentially to prevent economic – and, therefore social – meltdown; not to mention US attempts to 'buy' Turkey's support in the war against Iraq.
6   Pantelis, Stavros, *The Making of Modern Cyprus*, London, 1990, pp. 59–60.
7   Holland, Robert. *Britain and the Revolt in Cyprus, 1954–1959*, Oxford University Press, 1998, p. 5. Holland does however state that this 'much quoted episode' has been somewhat elaborated in the telling.
8   Ibid., p. 5.
9   Llewellyn Smith, Michael, *Ionian Vision*, Hurst & Co., London, 1998, p. 14.
10   Heurtley, W. A., Darby, H. C., Crawley C. W. and Woodhouse, C. M., *A Short History of Greece*, Cambridge University Press, 1965, p. 123 and op. cit., Woodhouse, p. 196.
11   Op. cit., Heurtley, W. A. et al., p. 130.
12   Op. cit., Pantelis, p. 102.
13   Ibid., p. 104.
14   Leventis, Yiorghos, 'The Politics of the Cypriot Left in the Inter-War Period: 1918–1940', *Synthesis – Review of Modern Greek Studies*, vol. 2, no. 1, 1997, London School of Economics and Political Science, p. 13.
15   Op. cit., Holland, p. 10.
16   Ibid., p. 13.
17   Stefanidis, Ioannis D., *Isle of Discord*, Hurst & Co., London, 1999, p. 3. See also Leventis, Yiorghos, *Cyprus: The Struggle for Self-Determination in the 1940s*, Peter Lang, Frankfurt am Main, 2002, for an incisive account of Cyprus' internal politics in the 1940s.
18   Ibid., p. 3.
19   PRO CO 67/323/3, Woolley to Secretary of State for Colonies, 11 August 1944, *telegram no. 448*.
20   Mallinson, William, 'A Partitioned Cyprus 40 Years After Qualified Sovereignty – Reality vs Morality', *Defensor Pacis*, issue 7, January 2001, p. 30; PRO FO 371/48281, PG 11926/203.
21   Mallinson, William, 'The Dutch, the British and Anti-Communism in the Immediate Post-War Years', *Dutch Crossing*, no. 41, Summer 1990, Centre for Low Countries Studies, University College, London. In this paper, Mallinson argues that anti-communist propaganda was not strictly necessary, and was somewhat overdone.
22   Mallinson, William, 'Turkish Invasions, Cyprus and the Treaty of Guarantee', *Synthesis – Review of Modern Greek Studies*, vol. 3, no. 1, 1999, London School of Economics and Political Science, p. 41– PRO FO 371/67084, R 13462/G.
23   Op. cit., Mallinson, *Defensor Pacis*, p. 31; PRO FCO 371/67084, R 13462/G.
24   Ibid., p. 31.
25   Ibid., p. 32.
26   Ibid., p. 32.
27   Balfour, 17 October 1947, *Memorandum*, PRO FO 371/67084, R 12449.
28   Mazower, Mark, 'British Historians of Greece Since the Second World War', *Synthesis – Review of Modern Greek Studies*, vol. 1, no. 2, London School of Economics and Political Science, 1996, pp. 16–17.
29   Op. cit., Clogg, p. 131.
30   British Ambassador to Greece to Foreign Secretary, 22 December 1943, *letter*, PRO FO 371/43674, R 226/4.
31   Op. cit., Clogg, p. 131.
32   Eden, 7 June 1944, *Memorandum to War Cabinet*, PRO FCO 371/43646, R 9092.
33   Davies, Norman, *Europe*, Pimlico, London, 1997, p. 1037.
34   *Greek Press Comments*, PRO FO 371/48207, R 1335/1335/67.

35   Op. cit., Clogg, p. 139.
36   Ibid., p. 137.
37   12 June 1945, *FO Memorandum*, FO 371/48323, R 10376/48/19.
38   PRO FO 371/4832, R 14448/98/19.
39   Leeper to Foreign Secretary, 18 March 1946, Annual Review, PRO FO 371/58680.
40   *Joint Planning Staff*, 3 December 1945, Report, PRO FO 371/48288, R 21028/G.
41   Op. cit., Clogg, p. 140.
42   Mazower, Mark, (ed.). *After the War Was Over*, Princeton University Press, Princeton and Oxford, 2000, p. 38.
43   Op. cit., Mallinson, W. D. E., 'Turkish Invasions etc.', *Synthesis*, p. 41.
44   Op. cit., Holland, p. 16.
45   Athanasios Ioannis Spanopoulos, son of the former editor-in-chief of *Kathimerini*, told the author that his father's view was that the 'disorganisation' in Greece, even while the Germans were still there, suited the British government in its efforts to distract attention from Cyprus and at the same time use it as an excuse to hang on to the island to counter the Communist threat.
46   Op. cit., Holland, p. 15.
47   Ibid., p. 19.
48   Ibid., p. 22.
49   Ibid., p. 22.
50   Op. cit., Stefanidis, Chapter One.
51   Ibid., p. 25.
52   Ibid., p. 29.
53   British Ambassador, Athens to Secretary of State, 15 February 1954, *Annual Review for 1953*, PRO 371/117612, RG1011.
54   Secretary of State for the Colonies, July 1954, PRO CAB 129/69.
55   O'Malley, Brendan and Craig, Ian, *The Cyprus Conspiracy*, I.B.Tauris, London and New York, 1999, p. 7.

CHAPTER 2

1   Mallinson, William, 'Turkish Invasions, Cyprus and the Treaty of Guarantee,' *Synthesis – Review of Modern Greek Studies*, vol. 3, no. 1, 1999, London School of Economics and Political Science, p. 47, PRO FO 371/17640, file RG 1081/535, Kirkpatrick to Nutting, Foreign Office Permanent Under Secretary of State, 26 June 1955, *memorandum*.
2   Cool, because, for example, during the Second World War, the (neutral) Turkish government introduced unacceptably heavy property taxes on minority citizens, affecting primarily the Greek population, but also the Jewish. Those unable to pay were taken to labour camps far inside Anatolia. Under international pressure, the Turks then withdrew the measures.
3   Stefanidis, Ioannis D., *Isle of Discord*, C. Hurst, London, 1999, p.176.
4   Alan S. Milward (*The Reconstruction of Western Europe, 1945–1951*), Methuen & Co., London, 1987) offers the cogent argument that the USA's politico-moral objectives were underpinned by essentially commercial considerations.
5   O'Malley, Brendan and Craig, Ian, *The Cyprus Conspiracy*, I.B.Tauris, London and New York, 1999, p. 18.
6   Op. cit., Stefanidis, pp. 87–91.
7   Mallinson, William, 'A Partitioned Cyprus 40 Years After Qualified Sovereignty – Reality versus Morality,' *Defensor Pacis*, issue 7, January 2001, pp. 32–33, Bowker to Young, 15 February 1955, *letter*, PRO FO 371/117625, file RG 1081/120.
8   Ward, 27 April 1955, *memorandum*, PRO FO 371/117629, file RG1001/243/9.
9   Hitchens, Christopher, *Hostage to History*, Verso, London and New York, 1997, p. 45.

10 Ward to Nutting, 25 June 1955, *memorandum,* PRO F 371/117642, file RG 1081/622.

11 Ward to Bowker, 21 June 1955, *telegram,* PRO FO 371/11739, file RG 1081/502.

12 Op. cit., Mallinson, William, 'Turkish Invasions etc.', Kirkpatrick to Nutting, 26 June 1955, memorandum.

13 *Editorial Note, FRUS,* 1955–1957, vol. XXIV, pp. 272–273.

14 *Memorandum,* PRO FO 371/117640, file RG 1081/535.

15 Ibid., file RG 1081/536, 28 June 1955, Ministry of Defence, *memorandum.*

16 Mallinson, William, *Portrait of an Ambassador: The Life, Times and Writings of Themistocles Chrysanthopoulos,* Athens, 1998, p. 27.

17 Op. cit., FRUS, Department of State to US Embassy, Athens, 1 July 1955, *telegram,* p. 274, *editorial footnote.*

18 Ibid., FRUS, *telegram,* p. 274.

19 Prime Minister's Private Secretary to Rumbold, 17 July 1955, *letter,* PRO FO 371/117644, file RG 1081/692.

20 Op. cit., O'Malley and Craig, p. 21.

21 Op. cit., FRUS, Butterworth to State Department, 10 August 1955, p. 277, *telegram.*

22 Secretary of State for Foreign Affairs, 3 September 1955, *memorandum* c.p. (55) 117, PRO CAB 129/77.

23 Op. cit., Mallinson, William, *Portrait of an Ambassador,* pp. 26–27.

24 British Consulate General, Istanbul, to Foreign Office, 7 September 1955, *telegram,* PRO FO 371/117721, file RG 10110/1.

25 Op. cit., Hitchens, Christopher, p. 45.

26 Op. cit., FRUS, Hoover to US Embassy, Ankara, 9 September 1955, pp. 281–282, *telegram.*

27 Holland, Robert, *Britain and the Revolt in Cyprus, 1954–1959,* Oxford University Press, 1998, p. 69.

28 Ibid.

29 Ibid., p. 76.

30 Ibid.

31 Wright, Peter, *Spycatcher,* Viking Penguin Inc., New York, 1987, p. 113.

32 Mitsotakis, Constantinos, Athens, 4 November 2002, *interview with author.*

33 Op. cit., FRUS, Macmillan to Dulles, 19 September 1955, p. 297, *letter.*

34 Op. cit., Mallinson, William, *Portrait of an Ambassador,* p. 28.

35 Governor of Cyprus to Secretary of State for Colonies, 12 August 1955, *letter,* PRO FO 371/117652, file RG 1081/900.

36 Pantelis, Stavros, *The Making of Modern Cyprus,* Interworld Publications, London, 1990, p. 173, Pantelis says that by February 1957, the mobile reserve of the Cyprus police consisted of 32 officers and 551 men, of whom none were Greek, but 560 Turkish Cypriots.

37 Op. cit., Wright, Peter, *Spycatcher,* p. 154.

38 Op. cit., Mallinson, William, 'Turkish Invasions etc.', *Defensor Pacis,* p. 36, PRO FO 953/1694, file G11926/23, Cox to Fisher, 13 July 1956, *letter.*

39 Peck to Stewart, 28 May 1956, *letter,* PRO FO 953/1693, file PG 11926/8.

40 Op. cit., Pantelis, Stavros, p. 174.

41 Glass to Fletcher-Cooke, 9 August 1956, *letter,* PRO FO 953/1695, file PG 11926/50.

42 Fletcher-Cooke to Hebblethwaite, 26 July 1956, *letter,* PRO FO 953/1696, file PG 11926/50.

43 Op. cit., FRUS, Rountree to Secretary of State, 13 August 1956, pp. 384–392, *Paper.*

44 Evriviades, Marios, 'The US and Cyprus: The Politics of Manipulation in the 1985 UN Cyprus High Level Meeting', Institute of International Relations, Panteion University, *Occasional Research Paper* no. 3, Athens, October 1992, p. 4.

45 Op. cit., FRUS, p.466, *editorial note* reproducing extract from President Eisenhower's *diary,* at the Eisenhower Library, Whitman File, DDE Diaries.

46 Demetracopoulos, Elias, Athens, 30 November 2002, *interview by author.* Demetracopoulos was chosen following intense negotiations between Prime

Minister Karamanlis and the leaders of the opposition, George Papandreou and Sofoklis Venizelos.

CHAPTER 3

1   Holland, Robert, *Britain and the Revolt in Cyprus 1954–1959*, Oxford University Press, 1998, p. 253.
2   Ibid., p. 237.
3   Ibid., p. 257.
4   Ibid., p. 253.
5   Ibid., p. 255.
6   Ibid., p. 268.
7   Ibid., p. 306.
8   British Ambassador, Athens, to Secretary of State, 16 January 1959, *Annual Review for 1958*, PRO FO 371/144516/RG1011/1.
9   Demetracopoulos, Elias, Athens, 30 November 2002, *interview with author*. Demetracopoulos says that both the Greek prime minister and Queen Frederika pressurised Makarios.
10   Bahcheli, Tozun, *Greek–Turkish Relations since 1955*, Westview Press, Boulder, San Francisco and London, 1990, p. 45.
11   Sonyel, Salahi R., 'New Light on the Genesis of the Conflict', in Dodd, Clement H. (ed.), *Cyprus: The Need for New Perspectives*, Eothen Press, Huntingdon, 1999, p. 25.
12   Ibid., p. 26.
13   Ibid., p. 28. Mirbagheri, Farid, in *Cyprus and International Peacekeeping*, Hurst, London, 1998, p. 19, does not mention Britain's curious role in 'Makarios' 13 Points'. However, the British government's role is indisputable. In a letter of 11 March 1971 from Secondé (Southern European Department, FCO) to Ramsbotham (High Commissioner in Cyprus), the former writes: 'We have been through the 1963 papers, which tend to confirm that the Thirteen Points were indeed framed with British help and encouragement; that the then High Commissioner [Clark] considered them to be reasonable prospects; and that our intention was to promote their acceptance by the Turks.' Ramsbotham wrote later to Secondé: 'Makarios, ever the gentleman, took sole responsibility for the Thirteen Points.' PRO FCO 9/1353–WSC 1/1.
14   Dodd, Clement H., *The Cyprus Issue*, Eothen Press, Huntingdon, 1995, p. 4.
15   O'Malley, Brendan and Craig, Ian, *The Cyprus Conspiracy*, I.B.Tauris, London and New York, 1999, p. 112. Packard had clandestinely arranged for Turkish Cypriots to return to their villages. Only one day before this was due to happen, he was whisked back to London. He had done his job too well, for the likes of Ball and his British sympathisers, who wanted partition. His original report was mislaid. Athens, 6 November 2002, *interview by author*.
16   Ibid., p. xi.
17   Hitchens, Christopher, *Hostage to History*, Verso, London and New York, 1997, p. 59, and op. cit., Mirbagheri, *Cyprus and International Peacekeeping*. The US State Department tried to strengthen NATO's hand by liaising with Grivas.
18   Parsons, 16 June 1964, PRO FO 371/174762/C1193/10G, *memorandum*.
19   An interesting 'inside story' is that at 3.00 a.m. one January morning, the US consul-general in Istanbul telephoned his Greek counterpart, Themistocles Chrysanthopoulos, asking to see him. The courteous Chrysanthopoulos duly obliged, and was told that the US State Department wanted Makarios to accept the 'Ball Plan'. The US consul-general asked Chrysanthopoulos if he would contact the ecumenical patriarch to ask him to convince Makarios to accept the plan. Chrysanthopoulos – quite rightly – said that he had no instructions, and that it

was in any case curious for the patriarch to try and persuade the head of an autocephalous church to take political action. Chrysanthopoulos was also concerned that such action might provide the Turkish government with the excuse to attack the patriarch (a Turkish citizen) for involving himself in politics. Chrysanthopoulos therefore refused, but telephoned the patriarch's assistant, to say that the US consul-general wished to see him. The patriarch then agreed to contact Makarios, but only if the Turkish prime minister was willing that he do so. Inonu gave his permission, whereupon the Patriarchate tried to telephone Makarios, but was lambasted by the Turkish telephone operator. The Valli ('governor') of Istanbul was then asked to put the call through on behalf of the patriarch, but Makarios could not be found. When the patriarch finally found him some hours later, Makarios told him that he had already turned down the 'Ball Plan'. Such are the frenetic behind-the-scenes realities of international crises. For the record, the rumbustious Ball hated Makarios, personally and politically (see op. cit., Hitchens, p. 58) and, according to the British consul-general the US consul did not like Chrysanthopoulos. The British consul-general, (Warr), however, wrote: 'Chrysanthopoulos acts as sort of Foreign Minister to the Patriarch [...] done his best for his people and personally I think highly of him. He is intelligent, agreeable and very hard-working.' (PRO FO 371/147813, CE 103144/28).

20 Mallinson, W. D. E., 'Turkish Invasions, Cyprus and the Treaty of Guarantee', in *Synthesis – Review of Modern Greek Studies*, vol. 3, no. 1, London School of Economics and Political Science, 1999, p. 46, PRO CAB 129/116, Prime Minister, 2 January 1964, *Memorandum*.

21 Ibid., British Embassy, Washington to Foreign Office, 7 July, 1964, *telegram 8541*, PRO FO 371/174766, C1205/2/G.

22 Allen to FCO (enclosing Ambassador's report), 16 September 1964, PRO DEFE 13/626-MO 5/1/4, *telegram*.

23 Op. cit., Dodd, *The Cyprus Issue*, p. 33 and Çelik, Yasemin, *Contemporary Turkish Foreign Policy*, Preager, Westpoint, 1999, p. 49.

24 Joseph, Joseph S., *Cyprus: Ethnic Conflict and International Politics*, St Martin's Press, London and New York, 1997, p. 66.

25 Washington to Foreign Office, 5 June 1964, *telegram No. 2075*, PRO FO 371/29840.

26 Ibid., Mottershead to P.U.S., *letter* of 27 April 1964, enclosing *brief of Defence and Overseas Policy (Official) Committee D.O. (0) (64) 26*, with appendix. It is perhaps ironic that, since the invasion, over half the original Muslim Cypriots have, in any case, left the occupied zone of Cyprus, many for London, but not so many to Turkey, as Ataturk would have preferred.

27 Record of conversation between Prime Minister and NATO Secretary General, 25 June 1964, MOD *telegram*, PRO DEFE 13/625 – MO 5/1/4 pt.5..

28 Ibid., Major General Sir Alec Bishop (Nicosia) to Athens, 25 August 1964, *telegram 2152*.

29 Chrysanthopoulos, Themistocles, 6 February 1995, Athens, *interview with author*.

30 Ibid.

31 Man, British Embassy, Ankara, to Foreign Office, 13 April 1964, PRO FO371/174813, file CE 103144/6, *Letter*.

32 An acquaintance of Turkish nationality, living in Greece, who wishes to remain anonymous.

33 Warr to Murray, 15 June 1964, *letter*, PRO FO 371/147813/CE103144/28.

34 Barnes, British Embassy, Athens, to Dobson, Foreign Office, 13 April 1964, Letter, PRO FO 371/174813, 103144/5.

35 Ibid., The official was Pilavakis.

36 My view is supported by an FCO telegram, reporting a meeting in Washington among the British, Canadians and Americans, to assess Greek and Turkish forces in Cyprus: British Embassy, Washington to Foreign Office, 8 July 1964, *telegram*

2474, PRO FO 371/174766, file C 1205/11/G. One is left with a slightly worrying suspicion that the USA, at least, was not against the infiltration of Greek and Turkish forces, provided it led to a more solid partition and an Acheson plan-style 'double-*enosis*'.

37 Op., cit., Mallinson, William, 'Turkish Invasions', op. cit., p. 48, Hunt to Foreign Secretary, 17 December 1966, *Valedictory Despatch*, PRO FO 371/185620, CC 1015/16.
38 Op. cit., Dodd, *Cyprus: The Need for New Perspectives*, p. 37.
39 Mirbagheri, Farid, *Cyprus and International Peacekeeping*, Hurst & Co., London, 1998, pp. 42–43.
40 Pantelis, Stavros, *The Making of Modern Cyprus*, Interworld Publications, London, 1990, p. 215.

CHAPTER 4

1   Allen to Secretary of State, *Diplomatic Despatch on Turkish Foreign Policy*, 3 February 1965, PRO FO 371/180153/CT 1022/1.
2   Mirbagheri, Farid, *Cyprus and International Peacekeeping*, Hurst & Co., London, 1998, p. 53.
3   *New York Times*, 1 April 1965.
4   Hunt to Foreign Secretary, *Valedictory Dispatch*, 17 December 1966, PRO FO 371/185620/1015/16.
5   *The Providence Journal*, 21 September 1965.
6   Joseph, Joseph S., *Ethnic Conflict and International Politics*, St Martins Press, London and New York, 1997, p. 72.
7   Allen to Foreign Secretary, *Annual Review for 1965*, 5 January 1966, PRO FO 371/185824/CT 1011/1.
8   Sykes to Walker, *Annual Report for Greece for 1964*, 6 January 1965, PRO FO 371/180004/CE 1011/1.
9   *Press Release of Greek Orthodox Archdiocese of North and South America*, 29 September 1965.
10 Parsons to Edes, *letter*, 19 November 1965: PRO FO 871/180167/CT 1781/2.
11 Greek Embassy, *letter*, 2 December 1965; PRO FO 371/180013/CE 103144/29.
12 Bahcheli, Tozun, *Greek–Turkish Relations since 1955*, Westview Press, Boulder, San Francisco and London, 1990, p. 65.
13 Op. cit., Mirbagheri, p. 77.
14 Woodhouse, C. M., *Modern Greece*, Faber and Faber, London and Boston, 1968, revised 1991, p. 287.
15 Allen to Dodson, *letter*, 13 December 1965, PRO FO 371/180153/ CT 1022/1.
16 Op. cit., Bahcheli, p. 68.
17 Ibid., p. 68.
18 Ibid., p. 68.
19 Ibid., p. 68.
20 *The Boston Globe*, 4 March 1965.
21 Foreign Secretary, 22 July 1965, PRO/ CAB 128/39/ pt. 2.
22 Op. cit., Woodhouse, p. 288.
23 Op. cit., Mirbagheri, p. 78.
24 Ibid., p. 75.
25 Wood to Central Department, FCO, 21 April 1966, *letter* enclosing *Pravda* article, PRO FO 371/ 185661/CE 103138/2.
26 Agee, Philip, *On the Run*, Bloomsbury, London, 1987, pp. 130–131.
27 O'Malley, Brendan and Craig, Ian, *The Cyprus Conspiracy*, I.B.Tauris, London and New York, 1999, p. 126.

28   *The Boston Globe*, 28 April 1967.
29   *Avgi*, 6 August 1965 and *New York Times*, 9 August 1965.
30   Edwards to Gorham, *memorandum* enclosing *Record of Meeting*, 18 June 1969, PRO FCO 9/836/WSG 541/11. See also Murray to Foreign Secretary, 17 January 1966, *Annual Review for Greece for 1965*, where the British Ambassador alluded to the Greek Secret Service being used as an instrument of a small party clique within the Papandreou government to tap the telephone lines of ministers and to plant listening devices in their homes – a case of wheels within wheels!
31   Murray to FCO, *telegram*, 11 May 1967, PRO FCO 9/163/CE2/7.
32   Hunt to Foreign Secretary, *Valedictory Despatch*, 17 December 1966, PRO FO 371/185620/ CE 1015/16.
33   *Ministry of Defence Paper*, JP (59) 163, 1 January 1960, PRO DEFE 13/99/MO/5/1/5.
34   Ibid.
35   Ibid. Brief for Cyprus Ministerial Committee on Membership of International Organisations CY (M) (60) 1.
36   Diggines to Moreton, *memorandum*, 5 May 1967, PRO FCO RAIL 359/9/MN 3/1.
37   Op. cit., Bahcheli, p. 72 and Mirbagheri, p. 69.
38   *Tass statement* of 4 July 1967, PRO FCO 9/71/CC 3/5. One is inclined to wonder at the fortuitous timing of the statement – the Day of American Independence!
39   Ibid.
40   Evriviades, Marios, 'Alliances and Alignments in the Middle East: The Turkish-Israeli Axis', Arvanitopoulos, Constantine (ed.), *Security Dilemmas in Eurasia*, Panteion University of Social and Political Sciences, Athens, 1997.
41   Daunt to Tyler, *letter*, 31 August 1967, PRO FCO 27/105/MF 2/20, pt. B.
42   Mallinson, William, 'Turkish Invasions, Cyprus and the Treaty of Guarantee,' in *Synthesis – Review of Modern Greek Studies*, vol. 3, no. 1, London School of Economics and Political Sciences, 1999, p. 42 – *United Nations Security Council Document* S/8248 of 16 November 1967, PRO FCO 9/164/ CE 3/8. See also op. cit., Mirbagheri, p. 54.
43   Op. cit., O'Malley and Craig, p. 129.
44   *FCO Brief for visit of Soviet Ambassador* to Foreign Secretary, 5 July 1967, PRO FCO 9/70/CC3/4.
45   Harold Wilson to George Brown, *letter*, 28 April 1967, PRO FCO 9/164/CE3/8.
46   *Christian Science Monitor*, 27 April 1967.
47   Op. cit., Foreign Office file CE3/8 (PRO FCO9/164).
48   Ibid., Murray to Hood, *letter*, 15 May 1967.
49   Allen to Hohler, *letter*, 9 September 1967, PRO FCO 9/71.
50   Foreign Secretary to Cabinet, 23 January 1967, *Record of Discussion*, PRO CAB128CC (67).
51   Op. cit., Mallinson, *Turkish Invasions etc, memorandum- Position of United Kingdom Government in International Law in Relation to the Threatened Turkish Action Against Cyprus*, 24 November 1967, PRO FCO 27/166/MF/10/41.
52   Ibid., para. 2.
53   Ibid., para. 4.
54   Ibid., para. 5.
55   Ibid., para. 6.
56   Ibid., Moreton to McPetrie, *memorandum*, 14 December 1967.
57   Ibid., McPetrie to Moreton, *memorandum*, 1 March 1968.
58   Ibid., Background Note.
59   British Embassy, Athens, *internal memorandum* from (name and date deleted) to Ambassador and Messrs James and Hinton, PRO FO RAIL 359/9/CE3/220. Some credibility is lent to the thesis that the Turkish government was bluffing, since its army (at least according to the British Military Attaché at Ankara) was not overly efficient. The Attaché's assessment for the state of the Turkish Army in 1968 (it would not have been intrinsically different for November 1967), has the following illuminating extracts: 'But they [conscripts] only serve for two years, of which a large

number spend their first four months learning to read, write and in many cases even to speak Turkish (...) Personal bravery they do not lack, but (...) an awe of their superiors that amounts almost to an abject servility, a lack of readiness to take a decision, or conversely to delegate responsibility (...) a marked lack of initiative (...) laziness and/or just plain lack of ability. Thus in CENTO and NATO we see most of the detailed staff work done by the foreign officers though often signed by a Turk, the foreign officers not wishing to be part and parcel of the muddle that would otherwise ensue (...) They would certainly fight as individuals and units, but not for long as a cohesive modern army.' – PRO FCO 9/1109/WST10/11.

60   Ibid., *Internal British Embassy Memorandum.*
61   Clogg, Richard, *A Concise History of Greece*, Cambridge University Press, 1992, p. 212.
62   Maury, Jolen, *Memorandum of Conversation*, Athens, 28 January 1967, FRUS vol. XVI, document no. 251.
63   Talbot to Department of State, 9 April 1967, *telegram*, ibid., document no. 269.
64   Talbot to Department of State, 21 April 1967, *telegram*, ibid., document no. 273.
65   Ibid., 28 April 1967, *telegram*, document no. 282.
66   *Memorandum of Meeting between President Johnson and King Constantine*, 11 September 1967, ibid., document no. 301.
67   Pattakos, Stylianos, *Tête-à-tête*, Athens, Alter TV Channel, 11 December 2002.
68   Talbot to Brewster, *letter*, undated, ibid., document no. 343.
69   Talbot to Department of State, 13 December 1967, *telegram*, document no. 345.
70   Packard, Martin, Athens, 6 November 2002, *interview by author.*
71   Stewart to Foreign Secretary, *Annual Review for Greece 1968*, 14 January 1969, PRO FCO/9/785/1/WSC1/9.
72   Dodson to Snodgrass, *letter*, 18 April 1969, PRO FCO 9/864/WSG3/304/1.
73   Talbot to State Department, op. cit., *telegrams* of 3 and 14 April 1967, document nos. 269 and 271.
74   Ibid., *telegram*, document no. 271.
75   Ibid., *telegram*, document no. 272.
76   Ibid., *telegram*, 9 January 1968, document no. 353.
77   See Woodhouse, C. M., *Modern Greece*, Faber and Faber, London and Boston, 1991, p. 318-320.
78   Daskalothanassis, Harilaos H., 'As Greek Junta Declined US Debated Its Stance', *National Herald*, 16–17 February, 2002. At the meeting, the US ambassador to Athens referred to the differences between Greece and countries 'like Chile and Brazil' [dictatorships]. For example, the latter did not have a 'Demetracopoulos' to effectively oppose US policy in Greece. Kissinger replied: 'We're just letting Demetracopoulos' particular group make policy.' In fact, Demetracopoulos was a one-man lobby.
79   Ibid.
80   Papandreou, George to Heath, Edward, *letter,* 16 January 1972, PRO PREM 15/945.
81   Costar to Permanent Under Secretary, *letter*, 11 October 1968, PRO FCO9/830/1/WSG1/5.
82   Stewart to Foreign Office, *telegram* no. 66 of 22 January 1968, PRO FCO RAIL 359/9, CE3/22.
83   FCO *Working Paper*, 14 June 1968, PRO FCO 9/166/CE3/8.
84   Ibid., *Report of Meeting*, 20 June 1968.

CHAPTER 5

1   Stewart to Secondé, *letter*, 17 April 1970, quoting the French radical politician, Jean Jacques Servan Schreiber, in interview, PRO FCO 9/1188/WSG1/3; see also *The Guardian,* 15 April 1970.

2   Stewart to Secretary of State, 20 January 1970, *Greece: Annual Review for 1969*, PRO FCO 9/1192/WSG1/10.

3   Beattie (BHC) to Fearn, 16 December 1970, *letter*, PRO FCO9/1150/WSC1/3. Mirbagheri, Farid, in *Cyprus and International Peacekeeping*, Hurst & Co, London, 1998, p. 58, writes that it was confusing for the Turkish Cypriots to hear one thing from the Greek Cypriot interlocutor assuring them of an independent Cyprus with guarantees for the Turkish Cypriots, and then see Makarios making public statements to the contrary about *enosis*.

4   British Ambassador Ankara to Secretary of State, *Turkey: Annual Review for 1968*, PRO FCO9/1091/WST1/6.

5   Folsom (US State Department) to Smart (British Embassy, Washington), *letter*, 6 February 1969, *enclosing State Department Policy Statement on Cyprus*. PRO FCO 9/971, WSC3/3 18/2. This shows that, in the USA at least, US–British policy on Cyprus was coordinated in 1969.

6   This oxymoron certainly looks like a contradiction in terms, since, as a rule, the idea of a *modus vivendi* tends to detract from that of a long term and, therefore, hard-and-fast settlement.

7   Op. cit., FO9/971, WSC 3/3 18/2, *Informal State Department Memorandum*, entitled 'Semantic Problems', accompanying *Country Policy Document*.

8   My emphasis.

9   Kissinger, Henry A., *Nuclear Weapons and Foreign Policy*, Harper & Brothers, New York, 1957, p. 165.

10 Jackling (British Embassy, Bonn) to Wiggin, *letter*, 8 December 1971, PRO FCO 82/63/AMU 3/548/10.

11 Ibid., Tebbit (British Embassy, Washington) to Wiggin, *letter*, 30 December 1971.

12 See Hitchens, Christopher, *The Trial of Henry Kissinger*, Verso, London and New York, 2002.

13 Agee, Philip, *On the Run*, Bloomsbury, London, 1987, p. 130.

14 Ibid., p. 131.

15 Stylianos Pattakos, 13 June 2002, *interview by author*.

16 Edmonds to Gorham, 19 June 1969, *memorandum*, enclosing record of conversation, PRO FCO 9/836/WSG1/11.

17 *Boston Globe*, 28 April 1967.

18 Papahelas, Alexis, *The Rape of Greek Democracy: The American Factor, 1947–1967*, Estia, Athens, 2001 (tenth edition), p. 23.

19 Hemans (British Embassy, Moscow) to O'Brien, 24 September 1968, *letter*, enclosing translation of *Pravda*'s journalist Mr Bragin interview with Makarios, PRO FCO 27/82/MF2/1.

20 Secretary of State to Stewart, 20 June 1968, *despatch*, PRO FCO 9/166/CE3/8.

21 Ibid. The objectives listed were precisely the same as those listed two years later in the secretary of state's despatch to Stewart, an FCO *brief* for the prime minister's visit to Washington, 7 January 1970, PRO FCO 9/1215/WSG3/548/1.

22 Daunt (British High Commissioner, Nicosia) to Tyler, 5 April 1968, *letter*, enclosing extract of minute by Jenkins, reporting on his lunch with Zavazov, counsellor at the Soviet Embassy, PRO FCO 27/82/MF2/1.

23 FCO record of Anglo–Canadian–US talks on Cyprus, 18 November 1969, PRO FCO 790/WSC1/9.

24 Prendergast to Tyler, *letter*, 19 November 1969, PRO FCO 786/1/WSC1/9. The same problems exist today: Asil Nadir, the highly unorthodox businessman wanted by the British police, is reported to be alive and kicking in the north of Cyprus; so is Brian Brendan Wright – aka 'Mr Big'. See *The Guardian*, 15 June 2002.

25 Secondé to Edwards, letter, 20 February 1970, enclosing Tass statement; Stewart to British Embassy, Moscow, *telegram*, 19 February 1970; and Wilson (Moscow) to FCO, 18 February 1970, *telegram*, PRO 9/1158/WSC3/303/2. Baron, John, in KGB, Corgi, London, 1979, p. 225, claims that the KGB were giving out disinformation.

26 PRO9/1366/WSC3/303/1. In November 1947, the Information Research Department (IRD) was set up at the British Foreign Office, the culmination of increasing government concern at Soviet propaganda directed against colonialism, the British Empire and the role of British – and then American – troops in Greece. IRD's essential role was to combat, in Britain and overseas, communist policy and tactics seen as a threat to Britain's interests. Above and beyond the usual information work of any British Embassy, namely the projection of British policies, the work of IRD included the dissemination of – often – unattributable texts to trusted contacts in the media, civil service and parliament, in a brown envelope. The effect of government 'information' work on editors, journalists and reporters is often underestimated; they are often too busy to check their facts, but need to fill up their publications. IRD was wound up in 1977 by the foreign secretary, David Owen, but it would be naive to think that IRD has not transmogrified into something else. See Mallinson, W. D. E, 'The Dutch, the British and Anti-Communism in the Immediate Post-War Years', in *Dutch Crossing*, Center for Low Countries Studies, University College, London, no. 41, and Smith, Lyn, 'Covert British Propaganda: the Information Research Department, 1947-1977', *Millennium*, vol. 9, no. 1, Spring 1980.

27 Wilberforce to Waugh (Ministry of Defence), *letter*, 22 October 1971, PRO FCO9/1366/WSG/303/1.

28 Ibid., *letter*, 17 November 1972 [sic, 1971].

29 Costar to Secretary of State, 28 April 1969, *Valedictory Despatch*, PRO FCO9/785/WSC1/9.

30 See note 26 (above).

31 Empson (BHC, Nicosia) to Seaward (IRD), *letter*, 19 March 1969, PRO FO9/786/WCG1/9.

32 Stewart to Secondé, *letter*, 20 July 1970, PRO FCO9/1213/WSG3/304/1.

33 PRO FCO 9/1190/WSG1/9, parts A and B.

34 Op. cit., Stewart to Secondé, letter, 20 July 1970.

35 Stewart to Secondé, *letter*, 17 April 1970, PRO FCO9/1188/WSG1/3; see also *The Guardian,* 15 April 1970.

36 FCO *brief* for Meeting of Permanent Members of Council of Western European Union, 9 July 1969, PRO FCO9/862.

37 Op. cit., Hitchens, Christopher, p. 109. He presents a compelling case to show that the Junta could rely on 'various agencies of the US government' in, for example, kidnapping and smuggling back to Greece an anti-Junta Greek journalist (Demetracopoulos) living in the USA.

38 FCO *brief* for Anglo-German Talks on 13 and 13 May 1969, PRO FCO 884/WSG/548/24. See also *telegram* from British Embassy, Rome, to Permanent Under Secretary of State (responsible for liaison with M16). See also top secret telegram 919 from British Embassy, Rome, to Permanent Under Secretary: King Constantine told the ambassador that Colonel Rufoghallis (deputy head of the Greek Security Ministry) had said that the Greek government had proof that the assassination attempt on Papadopoulos was engineered from Cyprus. Rufoghallis also thought that the British Secret Service had engineered it to create bad blood between the Greek and Cypriot governments. The king had pointed out the absurdity of this but was not 'at all sure that he had convinced him'. PRO FCO 830/WSG/1/5. Folios 1 (telegram no. 887) and 2 (a Minute of 27 September 1968) have been 'closed' until 2009. All very sensitive.

39 *Telegram* of 19 March 1970 from British Embassy, Washington to FCO; PRO FCO9/1209/WSG2/7.

40 O'Malley, Brendon and Craig, Ian, *The Cyprus Conspiracy*, I.B.Tauris, London and New York, 1999, p. 134.

41 Ibid., p. 133.

42 Edwards (British Embassy, Ankara) to Snodgrass, *letter*, 12 December 1969, PRO FCO 856/WSG 2/2.
43 Stewart to Secretary of State, *Greece: Annual Review for 1968*, 14 January 1969, PRO FCO9/838/WSG1/20.
44 Stewart to Secondé, *letter*, 13 July 1970, PRO FCO9/1194/WSG1/13.
45 Op. cit., Pattakos, *interview*.
46 Miles to Fearn, *letter*, 19 July 1971, PRO FCO9/1368/WSC3/358/1.
47 Beattie (BHC, Nicosia) to Fearn, *letter*, 9 November 1971, PRO FCO 9/1369/WSC3/358/2.
48 Op. cit., Pattakos, *interview*.
49 Powell-Jones (British Embassy, Athens) to Secondé, *letter*, 17 February 1970, PRO FCO9/1217/WSG3/548/4.
50 PRO FCO9/1410/WSG22/1.
51 Hooper (British Ambassador, Athens) to Secondé, *letter*, 7 July 1971, PRO FCO9/1394/WSG2/4.
52 Bahcheli, Tozun, in *Greek–Turkish Relations Since 1955*, Westview Press, Boulder, San Francisco and London, 1990, p. 86, makes it quite clear that Grivas would never have been involved in an assassination attempt on Makarios, but that he was, rather, concerned that Papadopoulos might try to kill him (Grivas), because of his own differences with the Junta!
53 Edwards to FCO, *telegram*, 18 September 1971, PRO FCO9/1368/WSC3/358/1.
54 Ibid.
55 Edwards to Secondé, *letter*, 26 November 1971, enclosing *record of conversation* of 23 November 1971, PRO FCO9/1357/WSC1/1.
56 Op. cit., Edmonds to FCO, *telegram*, 18 September 1971.
57 Edwards to FCO, *telegram*, 18 September 1971, PRO FCO9/1368/WSC3/358/1.
58 Ramsbotham (British High Commissioner, Nicosia) to Secretary of State, *Cyprus: Annual Review for 1970*, 1 January 1971, PRO FCO9/1358/WSC1/2.
59 Ramsbotham to Secondé, *letter*, 5 January 1971, PRO FCO9/1361/WSC1/C.
60 Edmonds to Secretary of State, *Diplomatic Report 'Makarios versus Grivas'*, 6 December 1971, PRO FCO 9/1365/WSC1/19.
61 Edwards to FCO, *telegram* 38, 19 January 1972, PRO FCO 9/1496, file WSC1/5.
62 Ibid., *telegram* 39.
63 Secondé to Ramsbotham, *letter*, 11 March 1971, PRO FCO9/1353/WSC1/1.
64 Edwards to Wiggin, *letter*, 25 October 1971, PRO FCO9/1357/WSC1/1.
65 Savell to FCO, *telegram*, 29 April 1971, PRO FCO9/1400/WSG3/318/1.
66 Ibid., Edwards (Ankara) to Wilberforce, *letter*, 6 August 1971.
67 Edwards (Nicosia) to Secretary of State, *Draft Despatch*, 27 August 1971, PRO FCO 9/1355/WSC1/1.
68 Ibid.
69 Evriviades, Marios, 'Alliances and Alignments in the Middle East: the Turkish-Israeli Axis', in Arvanitopoulos, Constantine (ed.), *Security Dilemmas in Eurasia*, Institute of International Relations, Panteion University, Nereus Editions, 1997, p. 236.
70 Op. cit., Savell to FCO, *telegram*, 29 April 1971.
71 PRO FCO9/1401/WSG3/548/1 – Visit of Commander in Chief of Greek Armed Forces to Britain, at invitation of Chief of Defence Staff, 7–15 October 1971.
72 PRO FCO9/1362/WSC1/10 – Intercommunal talks in Cyprus.
73 Savell to Secretary of State, 'The Turkish Cypriot Administration', *Diplomatic Report No. 503/72*, 25 October 1972, PRO FCO 9/1499, file WSC1/12.
74 Hooper to Secretary of State, 'Political Role of the Greek Armed Forces', *Diplomatic Report No. 507/72*, 22 November, PRO FCO 9/1516, file WSG1/5.
75 Op. cit., Costar to Secretary of State, *Valedictory Despatch*, 28 April 1969. See also note 3 of introductory chapter of this book.

CHAPTER 6

1   Costar to Secretary of State for Foreign and Commonwealth Affairs, 28 April 1969, *Valedictory Despatch*, PRO FCO 9/785/WSC1/9.
2   Stylianos Pattakos, 13 June 2002, *interview*.
3   Papahelas, Alexis, *The Rape of Greek Democracy: The American Factor, 1947–1967*, Estia, Athens, 1997. Papahelas managed to obtain a US intelligence Field Report, which he reproduced in his book. The report, dated 20 December 1966 (with sensitive names blanked out), lists the 'leadership of the rightist military conspiratorial group' that met on 13 December. The source is probably a Greek CIA informant. Papahelas told the author that he had to take the CIA to court to obtain documents, but that just before the date of the hearing, some documents were produced. Thus, the hearing did not take place. This selective 'chicken feeding' of documents to a journalist was undertaken perhaps because of the suppression by the US government of the distribution of its own already printed *Foreign Policy of the United States, 1964–1968*. The volume, including the document Papahelas 'obtained', has since been released.
4   Bahcheli, Tozun, *Greek–Turkish Relations Since 1955*, Westview Press, Boulder, San Francisco and London 1990, p. 84.
5   O'Malley, Brendan and Craig, Ian, *The Cyprus Conspiracy*, I.B.Tauris, London and New York, 1999. Somewhat contradictorily, the authors state on page 139 that Ioannidis 'was not a long-time client of the CIA', while on page 165 they say that the CIA 'had long term contacts with Ioannidis'. Svolopoulos, Konstantinos, in *Greek Foreign Policy, 1945–1981*, vol. II, Estia, Athens, 2002, pp.172–174, writes that Ioannidis can be quite reasonably assumed to be the 'close link' with the US Secret Services.
6   Venizelos, Kostas and Ignatiou, Michalis, *Kissinger's Secret Files: The Decision to Dissect*, A. A. Livani, Athens, 2002, p. 431.
7   Op. cit., O'Malley and Craig, p. 152.
8   Hitchens, Christopher, *The Trial of Henry Kissinger*, Verso, London and New York, 2002 (paperback edition), p. 83.
9   Ibid., p. 78.
10   Op. cit., Pattakos, *interview*, 18 June 2002.
11   This information was imparted to me, in a *telephone interview* on 15 July 2002, by a former career officer at the State Department, who served in Greece and Cyprus. He does not wish his name to be revealed.
12   Op. cit., O'Malley and Craig, p. 154.
13   Agee, Philip, *On the Run*, Bloomsbury, London, 1987, p. 13.
14   Op. cit., Svolopoulos, pp. 172–174.
15   Ibid.
16   Op. cit., O'Malley and Craig, p. 147.
17   Kissinger, Henry A., *Nuclear Weapons and Foreign Policy*, Harper & Brothers, New York, 1957, p. 165.
18   Constantinos Mitsotakis, Athens, 4 November 2002, *interview by author*.
19   Elias Demetracopoulos, Athens, 30 November 2002, *interview by author*.
20   Goodison to Davies, 1 March 1973, *memorandum*, PRO FCO 9/1677–WSC3/304/1.
21   Prendergast to Hitch, 6 March 1973, *memorandum*, PRO FCO 9/1738–WS9 10/9.
22   Denson to Head of Chancery, 10 September 1973, *memorandum*, PRO 9/1725-WSG3/304/1 and Hooper to Goodison, 15 November 1973, *letter*, PRO FCO 9/1712-WSG1/5.
23   Hooper to Goodison, 18 October 1973, *letter*, PRO FCO 9/1725-WSG3/304/1.
24   Hooper to FCO, 20 November 1973, *telegram* 398, PRO PREM 15/1611.
25   Hooper to Goodison, 29 November 1973, *letter*, PRO FCO 9/1712-WSG1/5. Karamanlis also told the ex-king that the student riots were not particularly

spontaneous, but were Communist inspired – see Acland to Goodison, 23 November 1973, *memorandum*, PRO PREM 15/1611.

26 Hooper to FCO, 26 November 1973, *letter*, PRO FCO 9/1712-WSG1/5.

27 Ibid.

28 Hooper to FCO, 6 December 1973, *telegram* 435, PRO FCO 9/1721-WSG 2/2.

29 Ibid.

30 Op. cit., O'Malley and Craig, p. 151.

31 Op. cit., Svolopoulos, pp. 168–69.

32 *National Herald*, 16–17 February 2002.

33 Op. cit., O'Malley and Craig, p. 153. On 14 July, the day before the Sampson coup, Turkey announced the granting of four oil exploration permits. Three days later, Ankara claimed sovereignty of the entire continental shelf of the median line between the Greek and Turkish mainlands, regardless of the location of Greek islands. All rather fortuitous!

34 Op. cit., Bahcheli, p. 86.

35 Hitchens, Christopher, *Hostage to History*, Verso, London and New York, 1997, p. 79.

36 Ibid., pp. 78–81.

37 The epithet 'Castro of the Mediterranean' is wholly inaccurate, since Makarios was not a communist. Such a label betrays the blinkered, bigoted and parochial 'thinking' of McCarthyism.

38 Op. cit., O'Malley and Craig, p. 155.

39 This information was imparted to me by a former senior member of Her Majesty's Diplomatic Service, who was good enough to tell me the truth, but who said he would have to obtain permission from the FCO if he was to be quoted. The author does not wish to put him through the paranoid process of trying to obtain permission for such a nugget.

40 Op. cit., O'Malley and Craig, p. 193.

41 Pattakos, Stylianos, *21st April, 1967, Why? Who? How?*, Viovivl, Athens, 2002 (7th Edition), pp. 213–215.

42 Ibid., *interview*, 13 June 2002.

43 Ibid.

44 Op. cit., Hitchens, *Hostage to History*, pp. 88–89.

45 Op. cit., Demetracopoulos.

46 Hitchens, Christopher, *The Trial of Henry Kissinger*, Verso, London and New York, 2002, p. 78.

47 Cable to Acland, 31 July 1973, *memorandum*, PRO PREM 15 1983.

48 Sykes to Brimelow, 22 August 1973, *letter*, PRO FCO 82/286-AMU 3/507/1.

49 Mirbagheri, Farid, *Cyprus and International Peacekeeping*, Hurst, London, 1998, p. 89.

50 Ibid., pp. 89–90.

51 Op. cit., O'Malley and Craig, p. 211.

52 Op. cit., Venizelos and Ignatiou, pp. 433–34.

53 Op. cit., O'Malley and Craig, p. 221.

54 Joseph, Joseph S., *Cyprus: Ethnic Conflict and International Politics*, St Martin's Press, London and New York, 1997, (2nd edition, reproduced 1999), p. 73.

55 Op. cit., Mirbagheri, p. 113.

56 Marinos, Yiannis, *Telephone interview*, 17 July 2002.

57 Argyrou, Fanoula, *Conspiracy or Blunder?*, Adouloti Kyrenia, Nicosia, 2000, p. 288. Argyrou cites an article in *Ta Nea* of London, of 29 September 1979.

58 Op. cit., Hitchens, *The Trial of Henry Kissinger*, p. 88.

59 Kissinger, Henry, *Years of Upheaval*, Simon and Schuster, New York, 1999, p. 192.

60 Op. cit., O'Malley and Craig, p. 159.

61 Ibid., pp. vii and 198.

62 Jina Page to author, *e-mail* of 14 March 2002. O'Malley and Craig do not give the name of the MP to whom Callaghan spoke; and Callaghan refuses to be interviewed by me (as well as by O'Malley and Craig). All very cloak and dagger.

INTRODUCTION TO PART II

1 Bahcheli, Tozun, *Greek–Turkish Relations Since 1955*, Westview Press, Boulder, San Francisco and London, 1990, p. 71.

CHAPTER 7

1 Hastings, Max, 'How Britain Ignored the Modern World' (Review of Barnett, Corelli, *The Verdict of Peace*, Macmillan, London, 2001), *Evening Standard*, 20 August 2001.
2 See Wallace, William, 'Foreign Policy and National Identity in the United Kingdom', *International Affairs*, vol. 67, no. 1, Chatham House, London, January 1991, for a piercing analysis of British foreign policy.
3 Nutting, Anthony, *Europe Will Not Wait*, London, 1960, p. 5.
4 Garton Ash, Timothy, 'Is Britain European?', *International Affairs*, vol. 77, no. 1, Chatham House, London, January 2001, p. 9.
5 O'Malley, Brendon and Craig, Ian, *The Cyprus Conspiracy*, I.B.Tauris, London and New York, 1999, p. 124.
6 Ward (FO) to Pearle (British Embassy, Athens), 15 April 1955, *letter*, PROFO371/117630/RG107/290.
7 Ministry of Defence *Brief for Ministers* of 1 January 1960, PRO DEFE 13–99/MO5/1/5, pt. 1.
8 Steel (Legal Advisers, FCO) to Fearn, 10 February 1971, *Memorandum*, PRO FCO 9/1374/WSC3/548/5.
9 Ibid.
10 Empson (BHC, Nicosia) to Seaward (IRD), 19 March 1969, *letter*, PRO FO9/786/WCG1/9.
11 Fearn to Steel, 8 February 1971, *letter*, PRO FCO 9/1374/WSC3/548/5.
12 Ibid., Graham (FCO) to Moon (Prime Minister's Office), 17 February 1971, *letter*.
13 See Dilks, David, 'Britain and Europe 1948–1950', in Poidevin, Raymond (ed.), *Histoire des Débuts de la Construction Européenne*, Brussels, Milan, Paris, Baden-Baden, 1988.
14 Coker, Christopher, 'Britain and the New World Order: The Special Relationship in the 1990's', *International Affairs*, vol. 68, no. 3, Chatham House, London, July 1992, p. 407.
15 Ibid., p. 408. Coker quotes Kissinger, in Kissinger, Henry, 'Britain and the United States: Reflections on a Partnership', *International Affairs*, vol. 58, no. 3, Autumn 1983, p. 587.
16 See Dahrendorf, Ralf, 'The Third Way and Liberty – an Authoritarian Streak in Europe's New Center', *Foreign Affairs*, vol. 78, no. 5, New York, September/October 1999 and Mallinson, William, 'The Road with the Snakes', *Nemesis*, Athens, August 2000.

CHAPTER 8

1 Albright, Madelaine K., 'The Testing of American Foreign Policy', in *Foreign Affairs*, vol. 77, no. 6, New York, November–December 1998, p. 63.
2 Rountree to Secretary of State, 13 August 1956, *memorandum* enclosing paper on Cyprus, FRUS, 1955–1957, vol. XXIV, pp. 385–388.
3 Nye, Joseph S, 'American Strategy after Bipolarity', *International Affairs*, vol. 66, no. 3, Chatham House, London, July 1990, p. 521.
4 Bush, George, 'The Hard Work of Freedom', in O'Tuathail, Gearóid, Dalby, Simon and Routledge, Paul (eds.), *The Geopolitics Reader*, Routledge, London and New York, 1998.

5   Parenti, Michael, *Inventing Reality*, St Martin's Press, New York, 1993, p. 164.
6   Pettifer, James, 'We Have Been Here Before', *World Today*, vol. 54, no. 4, Chatham House, London, April 1998; Lutovac, Zoran, 'European and American Diplomacy in Kosovo', *Eurobalkans*, no. 32, Aegina, Greece, Autumn 1998; and Mallinson, William, 'Using Kosovo to Promote the European Defence and Security Initiative', *Eurobalkans*, nos. 36–37, Aegina, Greece, Autumn–Winter 1999–2000 (Translated in *Ethnikes Epalxeis*, vol. 9, no. 45, April 2001).
7   McCgwire, Michael, 'Why Did We Bomb Belgrade?', *International Affairs*, vol. 76, no. 1, Chatham House, London, January 2000, p. 14.
8   Ibid., p. 16,
9   Lord Wallace, 'Repairing European and Transatlantic Institutions', *World Today*, vol. 59, no. 5, Chatham House, May 2003, p. 16.
10   Cox, Michael, 'American Power Before and After 11 September: Dizzy with Success?', *International Affairs*, vol. 78, no. 2, Chatham House, London, April 2002, p. 268.
11   Ibid., p. 16.
12   Bennis, Phyllis, 'The United States is Undermining International Law', *Le Monde Diplomatique*, Paris, December 1999.
13   Op. cit., Cox, Michael, p. 274. See also Conesa, Pierre and Lepick, Olivier, 'Washington is Dismantling the International Security Architecture', *Le Monde Diplomatique*, Paris, July 2002.
14   Pilger, John, 'The Rogue State', *Daily Mirror*, London, 4 July 2002.
15   Boutros-Ghali, Boutros, *Unvanquished*, I.B.Tauris, London and New York, 1999, p. 198.
16   Op. cit., McCgwire, Michael.
17   'Gore Vidal – This Evil War for Oil', *Sunday Express*, 2 February 2003.
18   See Oliphant, Thomas, 'Turkey's Dubious Pressure in Northern Iraq', *International Herald Tribune*, 10 July 2003.
19   Karagiannis, Alexander (Counsellor for Political Affairs, US Embassy, Athens), to Mallinson, William, 12 August 1998, *letter*. See also, Mallinson, William, 'The Death of Veracity: Diplomacy, Greece and Cyprus', *Atlantis*, Athens, November 1998.
20   Safire, William, 'Turkey, Israel, US: A Phantom Alliance Haunting the Middle East', *Athens News*, 6 February 1999 (syndicated from the *New York Times News Service*).
21   Op. cit., Cox, Michael. The author refers to Fred Halliday's use of the term 'unaccountable hegemon' in *The World at 2000: Perils and Promises*, Palgrave, Basingstoke, 2001, pp. 90–109.
22   Nye, Joseph S., 'The US and Europe: Continental Drift?', *International Affairs*, vol. 76, no. 1, Chatham House, London, January 2000, p. 51.
23   Wallace, William, 'From the Atlantic to the Bug, From the Arctic to the Tigris', *International Affairs*, vol. 76, no. 3, Chatham House, London, July 2000, p. 491.
24   Walker, Martin, 'Variable Geography', ibid., p. 472.
25   Nye, Joseph S., 'The American National Interest and Global Public Goods', *International Affairs*, vol. 78, no. 2, Chatham House, London, April 2002, p. 243.
26   Demetracopoulos, Elias, Athens, 30 November 2002, interview by author.
27   Chrysanthopoulos, Themistocles, in Mallinson, William, *Portrait of an Ambassador*, Attica Tradition Educational Foundation, Athens, 1998, p. 50.
28   Yost, David S., 'Transatlantic Relations and Peace in Europe', *International Affairs*, vol. 78, no. 2, Chatham House, London, April 2002, p. 293.
29   Warner, Geoffrey, 'The United States and the Western Alliance', *International Affairs*, vol. 71, no. 4, Chatham House, London, October 1995, p. 818.
30   Mangold, Peter, 'Pivotal Power,' *World Today*, vol. 58, no. 3 Chatham House, London, March 2002, p. 26.
31   Ibid.
32   Terriff, Terry, Webber, Mark, Croft, Stuart and Howorth, Jolyon, 'European Security and Defence Policy After Nice,' *Briefing Paper*, new series no. 20, Chatham

House, London, April 2001. For those wishing to grasp the fundamentals of a complex question, this paper is cogent and, therefore, helpful.

33   Owen, David, *telephone interview*, with author, Athens, 23 October 1999.
34   Op. cit., Karagiannis, Alexander.
35   Athens News, 28 June 2002.
36   Economist Conference: 'Round Table with the Government of Greece,' Athens, 17-18 April 2002. Another example of Ambassador Miller's penchant for tautology was his exhortation to graduating students at the University of Indianapolis' Athens branch, on 29 May 2002, that 'Your future is your future.'
37   Dimitrios Pavlidis, *interview with author*, Athens, 22 July 2002.

CHAPTER 9

1   Woodhouse, C.M., *Modern Greece*, Faber and Faber, London, 1991, p. 222.
2   Fouscas, Vassilis K., 'Reflections on the Cyprus Issue and the Turkish Invasions of 1974', *Mediterranean Quarterly*, vol. 12, no. 3, Summer 2001, p. 126.
3   The Caliphate was not, however, formally abolished until 1924.
4   In 1683, the Ottoman armies reached Vienna (for the second time) and were decisively defeated by the King of Poland, John Sobieski.
5   Dunan, Marcel (ed.), *Larousse Encyclopaedia of Modern History*, Crescent Books, New York, 1987, p. 30.
6   Gunther, John, *Inside Europe*, Hamish Hamilton, London, 1936, p. 403.
7   Ibid., p. 400.
8   Ibid. The westernisation programme was not Ataturk's brainchild. He appropriated it from the Young Turks.
9   Çelik, Yasemin, *Contemporary Turkish Foreign Policy*, Praeger, Westport, 1999, p. 2.
10   Ibid., p. 3.
11   Morgan to Eden, *despatch*, 18 September 1936, PRO FO 371/20094,E5890.
12   For example, the Arabic word for school, 'mektep' was used by the Turks. Ataturk changed the word to 'okul', from the French 'école', which in turn derives from the Greek 'scholion'. See also op. cit., Gunther, pp. 399–340, for an amusing list (e.g. Table d' Hôte became 'tabldot'). Today, some Turks still use Arabic words.
13   The National Security Council was created following the military coup in 1960, thus establishing the Armed Forces as the main (behind-the-scenes) force in the Turkish polity.
14   Op. cit., Çelik, p. 22.
15   Dodd, Clement H., *The Cyprus Issue*, Eothen Press, Huntingdon, 1995, p. 4.
16   Ertekün, Necati Münir, 'The Turkish Cypriot Outlook', in Dodd, Clement H. (ed.), *Cyprus: The Need for New Perspectives*, Eothen Press, Huntingdon, 1999, p. 100.
17   Ibid., p. 98.
18   Ibid., Mustafa Ergün Olgun, 'Turkey's Tough Neighbourhood', p. 254.
19   Günay, Atila (Counsellor, Turkish Embassy, Athens), 19 July 2002, *interview with author*.
20   Theodhoropoulos, V., Lagkakos, E., Papoulias, G. and Tzounis, I., *Reflections and Considerations About Our Foreign Policy*, Athens, 1995, p. 13.
21   Gazioglu, Ahmet C., *Two Equal and Sovereign Peoples*, CYREP, Cyprus, 1999, p. 97.
22   Lindley, Dan, 'The Military Factor in the Eastern Mediterranean', in op. cit., Dodd, *Cyprus: The Need for New Perspectives*, p. 205.
23   Hale, William, 'Turkey, the Middle East and the Gulf Crisis', *International Affairs*, vol. 68, no. 4, Chatham House, London, October 1992.
24   Bekdil, Burak, 'Turkey Nods to US Plans for Iraq', *Kathimerini* (English Language edition), Athens, 23 July 2002.

25   Diehl, Jackson, 'NATO's Future is at Stake', *International Herald Tribune*, 17 September 2002.
26   Brewin, Christopher, 'Endgame', *World Today*, vol. 58, no. 5, Chatham House, London, May 2002, p. 23.
27   *Kathimerini* (English Language Edition), 29 August 2002.
28   Moran, Michael, *Sovereignty Divided*, CYREP, Cyprus, 1999, p. 177.
29   Coughlan, R, 'From Corporate Autonomy to the Search for Territorial Federalism'; Guy, Y. (ed.) *Autonomy and Ethnicity: Negotiating Competing Claims in Multi-Ethnic States*, Cambridge University Press, 1999, p. 236. See also op. cit., Moran, 'Proposal for a Lasting Solution in Cyprus', by Rauf Denktash, p. 242.

CHAPTER 10

1   Spanopoulos, Vassilis, 'What England Wants', *Kathimerini*, 17 May 1956, *Leader Article*.
2   Woodhouse, C. M., *Modern Greece*, Faber and Faber, London, 1991, pp. 164–165.
3   Clogg, Richard, *A Concise History of Greece*, Cambridge University Press, 1992, p. 150.
4   Stefanidis, Ioannis D., *Isle of Discord*, Hurst, London, 1999, pp. 54–55.
5   Op. cit., Woodhouse, p. 271.
6   Ibid., p. 271; Woodhouse writes: 'Successive Greek governments were increasingly embarrassed by the campaign for *enosis*.'
7   Bahcheli, Tozun, *Greek–Turkish Relations Since 1955*, Westview Press, Boulder, San Francisco and London, 1990, p. 38.
8   Zambouras, Sergios, 'Current Greek Attitudes and Policy', in Dodd, Clement H. (ed.), *Cyprus: The Need for New Perspectives*, Eothen Press, Huntingdon, 1999, p. 114, and Mallinson, William, *Portrait of an Ambassador*, Athens, 1998, p. 83. During the 1964 Cyprus troubles, the Turkish government abrogated the Establishment Treaty of 1930, expelling Greek nationals (even some dead people were ordered to leave!) and also forcing most ethnic Greeks with Turkish nationality to leave.
9   Op. cit., Spanopoulos, Vassilis.
10   O'Malley, Brendan and Craig, Ian, *The Cyprus Conspiracy*, I.B.Tauris, London and New York, 1999, p. 7.
11   Op. cit., Stefanidis, p. 181.
12   Ibid., p. 191.
13   Mirbagheri, Farid, *Cyprus and International Peacekeeping*, Hurst, London, 1998, p. 28.
14   Ibid., p. 70.
15   Ibid., p. 69. Mirbagheri quotes *The Guardian* of 7 September 1967, as writing that one of the main reasons for the military takeover in Greece was to solve the Cyprus problem one way or another. This author thinks that another reason was to keep Andreas Papandreou out of Greek politics.
16   Afendoulis, Ino, 'Turks Kill Civilians in Cyprus', *Hermes*, no. 3, Athens, September 1996, pp. 18–19.
17   Brewin, Christopher, 'Turkey, Greece and the European Union', in op. cit., Dodd, p. 158.
18   Op. cit., Mallinson, William, pp. 106–107.
19   Dunford, Athony, *brief telephone conversation with author*, 24 February 2003.
20   Flessati, Francesca, *brief telephone conversation with author*, 27 February 2003.
21   Apostolides, Pavlos, *face-to-face discussion with author*, 12 December 2003. His secretary then informed me on 9 February 2004 that Mr Apostolides had been unable to locate the letter.
22   It would not be politic of me to name these people, notwithstanding their protestations that they are working for the cause of freedom and stability.

INTRODUCTION TO PART III

1   According to the *Penguin Dictionary of International Relations* (Evans, Graham and Newnham, Jeffrey, London, 1998, p. 199) the term 'geopolitics' has now acquired some academic respectability.

CHAPTER 11

1   Mirbagheri, Farid, *Cyprus and International Peacemaking*, Hurst & Co., London 1998, p. 141.
2   O' Malley, Brendan and Craig, Ian, *The Cyprus Conspiracy*, I.B.Tauris, London and New York, 1999, p. 153.
3   A series of earthquakes in Greece and Turkey in August and September 1999 led to each country sending in teams of rescue experts to help the other, leading to an – unfortunately temporary – convivial climate, and a (well-promoted) friendship between the then Turkish foreign minister, Cem, and his Greek homologue, Papandreou. The latter even ended up performing a Greek dance in front of Cem, who did not however reciprocate with a Turkish fling. Cem has since resigned.
4   Bahcheli, Tozun, *Greek–Turkish Relations since 1955*, Westview Press, Boulder, San Francisco and London, 1990, p. 128.
5   Arvanitopoulos, Constantine and Syrigos, Angelos, *The International Legal Status of the Aegean,* Ministry of Press and Mass Media, Athens, 1998, p. 49.
6   Ibid., p. 55.
7   Ibid., p. 51.
8   Ibid., p. 51.
9   Chrysanthopoulos, Themistocles, 'The Sea Frontier Between Greece and Turkey', *Diplomatic Life*, Athens, March 2001, pp. 22–23.
10   Op. cit., Arvanitopoulos and Syrigos, p. 42.
11   Op. cit., Bahcheli, p. 178.
12   Ibid., pp. 181–182.
13   Hitch to McLaren, *memorandum*, 7 September 1972, PRO FCO 9/1525, file WSG 3/318/1.

CHAPTER 12

1   Mirbagheri, Farid, *Cyprus and International Peacekeeping*, Hurst & Co., London, 1998, p. 160.
2   Shakespeare, William, *The Merchant of Venice*, Act II, Scene vii, lines 65–69.
3   Brewin, Christopher, 'Turkey, Greece and the European Union', in Dodd, Clement H. (ed.), *Cyprus: The Need for New Perspectives*, Eothen Press, Huntingdon, 1999, p. 150. In December 1999, the German Chancellor said that it would be hypocritical to pretend that the EU could 'digest' 63 million Turks at the same time as reuniting Eastern with Western Europe.
4   Embassy of Greece (London), *Greece-Background-News-Information*, no. 46, June 2001.
5   Ibid.
6   Ibid., no. 40, December 2000.
7   Ibid., no. 45, May 2001.
8   Op. cit., no. 46, June 2001.
9   Op. cit., Mirbagheri, p. 111.
10   Ibid., p. 143.
11   Evriviades, Marios, 'The US and Cyprus: The Politics of Manipulation in the 1985 UN Cyprus High Level Meeting', Panteion University, Athens, Institute of International Relations, *Occasional Research Paper,* no. 3, Athens, October 1992,

p. 6. Evriviades quotes from the *New York Times* of 27 January 1983 and from Birand, Mehmet Ali, 'The Generals' Coup in Turkey: An Inside Story', *Brassey's Defence Publications*, London, 1987, p. 185.

12   Op. cit., Mirbagheri, p. 144.
13   Op. cit., Evriviades, p. 10.
14   Evriviades, Marios, Athens, 12 December 2002, *telephone interview by author*.
15   Op. cit., Mirbagheri, pp. 133 and 148. He quotes the Greek Cypriot daily *Avgi* of 16 December 1984.
16   Ibid., p. 135.
17   Vassiliou, Dr. George, 'A Deal to Be Done', *World Today*, vol. 58, no. 10, Chatham House, London, October 2002, p. 13.
18   See Parks, Bill, 'Bridgehead or Bridge?' in op. cit., *World Today*, pp. 7–9, for a cogent and succinct analysis of Turkey's geostrategic position and its importance to the USA.
19   Op. cit., Mirbagheri, p. 144. He quotes Bruce, Leigh H., 'Cyprus. A Last Chance,' *Foreign Policy* (58, Spring 1985, pp. 115–133).
20   O'Malley, Brendan, and Craig, Ian, *The Cyprus Conspiracy*, I.B.Tauris, London and New York, 1999, p. 223.
21   Ibid., p. 229.
22   Clis, Elias, Athens, 23 July 2002, *Interview with author*. Clis was then head of the Department for Graeco–Turkish Relations at the Greek Foreign Ministry.
23   Smith, Helena, *The Guardian*, 30 September 2002.

CHAPTER 13

1   Mallinson, William. *Portrait of an Ambassador*, Athens, 1998, p. 12.
2   Gazioglu, Ahmet C., *Two Equal and Sovereign Peoples*, Nicosia (Mersin, Turkey), 1997, p. 23.
3   Crawford, James, Hafner, Gerhard and Pellet, Alain, 'Does the Treaty of Lausanne 1923 Confer on Turkey Any Specific Rights with Respect to Cyprus?', in Markides, Alecos (ed.), *Cyprus and European Union Membership*, Nicosia, 2002, p. 53.
4   Ibid., p. 55.
5   Ibid., p. 19.
6   The word was used by the former Dutch Foreign Minister, Dirk U. Stikker, in his memoirs *Men of Responsibility*, London, 1966.
7   Bertrand, Gilles and Rigoni, Isabelle, 'Turcs, Kurdes et Chypriotes devant la Cour Européenne des droits de l'homme: une contestation judiciaire de questions politiques', *Etudes Internationales*, vol. XXXI, no. 3, September 2000, p. 432.
8   Ibid., p. 434.
9   Konstas, Dimitris, *Diplomacy and Politics*, Livani, Athens, 2002, p. 318.
10   Op. cit., Bertrand etc.
11   Ibid., p. 434.
12   Greek Cypriot and Greek Cypriot influenced sources usually cite the figure of 200,000 Greek Cypriot refugees, while Turkish Cypriot and Turkish Cypriot influenced sources cite a lower number. Dodd, Clement H., in *The Cyprus Issue: A Current Perspective*, Eothen Press, Huntingdon, 1995, p. 1, cites the figure of 140–160,00, while Bahcheli, Tozun, in *Greek–Turkish Relations Since 1955*, Westview Press, Boulder, San Francisco and London, 1990, cites nearly 180,000.
13   Steel (Legal Advisers, FCO) to Fearn, 10 February 1971, *memorandum*, PRO FCO 9/1374/WSC3/548/5.
14   Pantelis, Stavros, in *The Making of Modern Cyprus*, Interworld Publications, London, 1990, p. 232, writes that when Turkey invaded, Britain was willing to withdraw from Cyprus and abandon its military bases, but that Kissinger vetoed the idea. According to Pantelis, Britain's suggestion was later explained as 'a

temporary aberration, and that the Cyprus bases were as much a part of Britain as Devon and Cornwall'. The British government's behaviour may well have been an act of brinkmanship to ensure that it could hide behind the USA, and rely on it, to protect the British bases. The diplomatic files are not yet available.

15 Pettifer, James, 'We Have Been Here Before', *World Today*, vol. 54, no. 4, Chatham House, London, April 1998 and Lutovac, Zoran, 'European and American Diplomacy in Kosovo, *Eurobalkans*, no. 32, Autumn 1998.

16 McCgwire, Michael, 'Why Did We Bomb Belgrade?' *International Affairs*, vol. 76, no. 1, Chatham House, London, January 2000, p. 22.

17 Ibid.

18 The Serbs claim that 3,000 civilians were killed.

19 Weller, Marc, 'The Rambouillet Conference on Kosovo', *International Affairs*, vol. 75, no. 2, Chatham House, London, April 1999, p. 251. The article was of course written before the bombing of Yugoslavia began, but perhaps in anticipation.

20 'Washington Presses for Worldwide NATO Strikeforce', *Reuters Report* in *Athens News*, 27 September 2002.

CHAPTER 14

1 This former editor of *The Economist* turned Conservative MP developed a close interest in defence questions. He was found asphyxiated on his kitchen table in Black Lion Lane, West London, with an orange in his mouth, and a cord around his neck. Most of the press assumed that he died accidentally in an attempt at self-gratification, but there were also dark rumours – never substantiated – that he had become involved in something dangerous. At around the same time, a former member of the British Intelligence Services, Alan Rusbridger, was found hanging in oilskins from the ceiling of his west country cottage. He had apparently been preparing a book on the intelligence services.

2 Minutes of meeting held at Ministry of Defence, 14 September 1970. PRO FCO9/1160, file WSC3/312/1, document no. D/DSTI/31/2/1(CN). See also Fouscas, Vassilis, *Zones of Conflict*, Pluto Press, London and Sterling, Virginia, 2003, p 113.

3 Greek prime minister.

4 Leader of the recently elected (Islamic) Justice and Development Party. He was not actually yet allowed to be prime minister, despite his landslide victory, since he had been convicted for reciting a poem (with, apparently, anti-secular tendencies) in public! He did eventually become prime minister.

5 UN mediator for Cyprus.

6 Karagiannis, Alexander (Political Counsellor, US Embassy, Athens) to author, 12 August 1998, *letter*. See also Mallinson, William, 'The Death of Veracity: Diplomacy, Greece and Cyprus', *Atlantis*, Athens, November 1998.

7 Novak, Robert and Evans, Rowland, 'Greek Concern Over Six Missing Words', *Washington Post*, 6 February 1978.

8 Mitsotakis, Constantinos, 4 November 2002, *interview by author*.

9 Ibid.

CHAPTER 15

1 Lukas Fourlas, journalist with Cyprus Broadcasting Corporation, 22 November 2002, *interview by author*.

2 O'Malley, Brendan and Craig, Ian, *The Cyprus Conspiracy*, I.B.Tauris, London and New York, 1999, p. 78.

3 *Mutatis mutandis* is a weasel phrase legally, meaning 'making the necessary alterations'. It is difficult to agree on what alterations would apply, how necessary they are, and if those alterations are compatible with EU law.
4 Elias Demetracopoulos, Athens, 30 November 2002, *interview by author*. See also *Apogevmatini* of 14 December 2002, where, in an extensive interview, Demetracopoulos says that the 'Annan Plan' is five times worse than the Zurich–London agreements.
5 Theodoros Couloumbis, Athens, 19 July 2002, *interview by author*. ELIAMEP tends to support the Papandreou-connected parts of the PASOK ('Socialist') Greek government.
6 Gilson, George, 'UN Matchmaker Courts Cyprus', *Athens News*, 15 November 2002.
7 Ibid, 'Cyprus Going Swiss via Bosnia?', *Athens News*, 22 November 2002. The expert is a 'well-known Swiss constitutional scholar', who spoke on condition of anonymity.
8 Ibid.
9 Gray, Andrew, (Reuters), 'Bosnia Displays Pitfalls of UN Blueprint for Cyprus', *Kathimerini*, 14 November 2002.
10 Op. cit., Elias Demetracopoulos.
11 Precise figures for the number of current original Turkish Cypriot inhabitants are difficult to obtain, because of differing figures given by the Cypriot government and the Turkish Cypriot administration, respectively. The figure of 30,000 voters is the author's own. Presumably, many Turkish Cypriot émigrés would be allowed to vote.
12 *The Guardian*, 27 November 2002.
13 Burns, Lynda (Political Section, British Embassy, Athens) to author, 25 September 2002, *letter*.
14 Mr David Madden to seminar, New York College, Athens, 22 November 2002.

CHAPTER 16

1 Fouscas, Vassilis K., *Zones of Conflict*, Pluto Press, London and Sterling (USA), 2003, p. 116. Fouscas quotes van Clausewitz.
2 Taylor, Paul, *Kathimerini*, Athens, 13 December 2002 (Reuters Report).
3 Ibid.
4 Vinocur, Paul, 'French accuse US of meddling', *International Herald Tribune*, 13 December 2002.
5 *Athens News*, 'EU Conclusions on Cyprus, Turkey', 20 December 2002 (report).
6 Hacaoglu, Selcan, 'Joy, regret over Cyprus', *Kathimerini*, Athens, 16 December 2002 (Associated Press report).
7 *Kathimerini*, 'Turkey rejects Cyprus' accession', *Kathimerini*, Athens, 19 December 2002 (report).
8 Gilson, George, 'Turkey against itself over Cyprus', *Athens News*, 20 December 2002.
9 'Denktash sees gain without pain', *Kathimerini*, Athens, 23 December 2002 (report).
10 *Athens News*, 20 December 2002, editorial.
11 Op. cit., *Kathimerini*, 23 December 2002 (report).
12 *Athens News*, 8 October 2002 (report).
13 Tritaris, Constandinos (Head of Cyprus Department, Greek Ministry of Foreign Affairs), 20 December 2002, *interview with author*.
14 *Kathimerini*, Athens, 18 December 2002 (report).
15 Ibid., 19 December 2002 (report). Simitis was talking to the Foreign Press Association.

16   Yiannis Valinakis, International Secretary of New Democracy, 21 January 2003, *interview with author*.

17   Panagiotis Beglitis, Greek Foreign Ministry spokesman, 21 January 2003, *interview with author*.

18   Clis, Elias (Head of Department of Greek–Turkish Relations, Greek Foreign Ministry), 19 December 2002, *interview with author*.

19   Op. cit., Fouscas, p. 114. See also: Bekdil, Burak, 'It's Business as Usual Between Ankara and Tel Aviv Despite Turkish Tough Talk', in *Kathimerini*, 1 June 2004; and Evriviades, Marios, 'Alliances and Alignments in the Middle East: The Turkish–Israeli Axis', Arvanitopoulos, Constantine (ed.), *Security Dilemmas in Eurasia*, Panteion University, Athens, 1997.

20   Friedman, Thomas L., 'Israel, Palestine and NATO', *International Herald Tribune*, 12 December 2002.

21   Norton-Taylor, Richard, 'NATO force to bypass states in hunt for terrorists', *The Guardian*, London, 16 November 2002.

22   Vinocur, John, 'The Big Winner in the EU Expansion: Washington', *International Herald Tribune*, 9 December 2002.

23   Hooper, John and Black, Ian, 'Anger at Rumsfeld Attack on old Europe', *The Guardian*, 24 January 2003.

24   Ibid.

25   'Jilting Europe, Poland opts to buy American', *International Herald Tribune*, 28–29 December 2002 (report).

26   Guay, Terence and Callum, Robert, 'The Transformation and Future Prospects of Europe's Defence Industry', *International Affairs*, vol. 78, no. 4, London, October 2002, p. 771.

27   Ibid., p. 759.

28   Op. cit., Fouscas, p. 117.

29   Terriff, Terry, Croft, Stuart, Krahmann, Elke, Webber, Mark and Howorth, Jolyon, 'One in, all in? NATO's next enlargement', in op. cit., *International Affairs*, p. 719.

30   Reeves, Richard, 'General Bush marches as to war', *International Herald Tribune*, 8 October 2002.

31   Sick, Gary, 'Imperial Moment', *World Today*, vol. 58, no. 12, Chatham House, p. 5.

32   Pfaff, William, 'Thinking with a Manichean bent', *International Herald Tribune*, 28 November 2002.

33   Norton-Taylor, Richard, *The Guardian*, 18 November 2002.

34   Klare, Michael, 'The True Designs of Mr. George Bush', *Le Monde Diplomatique*, November 2002. See also Richard Falk's article 'The United Nations taken Hostage' in *Le Monde Diplomatique* of December 2002 for an interesting analysis of US–UN relations.

35   *The Guardian*, 12 November 2002 (report).

36   Guay, Terrence and Callum, Robert, op. cit., *International Affairs*, p. 761.

37   Ibid., p. 775.

38   Norton-Taylor, Richard, op. cit., *The Guardian*, 18 November 2002.

39   Klare, Michael, op. cit., *Le Monde Diplomatique*.

40   Coufoudakis, Van, quoted in Fouscas, op. cit., p. 108.

41   Fouscas, op. cit., p. 103.

42   Ibid., p. 103.

43   'High-low' is a form of poker where one takes big risks to win, whereas 'seven card stud' is a more moderate form, enabling players not to take major risks.

44   *Kathimerini*, Athens, 12 May 2003.

45   *Kathimerini*, 7 April 2003.

46   *Kathimerini*, 5 June 2003.

47   *Kathimerini*, 23 June 2003.

48   *Kathimerini*, 17 July 2003.

49   *Kathimerini*, 20 January 2004.
50   Ibid.
51   Gilson, George, *Athens News*, 9 January 2004.
52   *Athens News*, 9 January 2004.
53   *Kathimerini*, 21–22 February 2004.
54   *Kathimerini*, 28–29 February 2004.
55   *Kathimerini*, 2 March 2004.
56   Ibid.
57   *Interview with author*, Athens, 27 February 2004.
58   Gilson, George, *Athens News*, 16 April 2004.
59   *Athens News*, 16 April 2004.
60   For a trenchant analysis of Russia's reassertion, see Allison, Roy, 'Strategic Reassertion in Russia's Central Asia Policy', *International Affairs*, vol. 80, no. 2, Chatham House, London, March 2004.
61   *Kathimerini*, 22 April 2004.
62   *Turkish Daily News*, 9 May 2004.
63   *Kathimerini*, 23 April 2004.
64   Levent, Shener, *Occupation*, Nicosia 2004.
65   *International Herald Tribune*, 26 April 2004.
66   Mark Dragoumis, *Athens News*, 7 May 2004.
67   Coufoudakis, Van and Kyriakides, Klearchos, *The Case Against the Annan Plan*, London, 2004.
68   Gilson, George, *Athens News*, 4 June 2004.
69   Ibid., 11 June 2004.
70   *Kathimerini*, 17 June 2004.
71   Ibid., 8–9 May 2004.
72   Ibid., 29–30 May 2004.
73   *International Herald Tribune*, 18 and 19 June 2004.
74   Chrysostomides, Kypros, *interview with author*, 7 May 2004.
75   *Kathimerini*, 19–20 June 2004.
76   Savvides, Philippos K., 'Cyprus at the Gate of the European Union', *ELIAMEP* Policy Paper no. 1, Athens, June 2002.
77   Zambouras, Sergios, 'Current Greek Attitudes and Policy', in Dodd, Clement H. (ed.), *Cyprus: The Need for New Perspectives*, Eothen Press, Huntingdon, 1999, p. 117. Zambouras quotes from Theodhoropoulos, Viron, Lagkakos, Efstathios, Papoulias, Georgios and Tzounis, Ioannis, *Reflections and Considerations about Our Foreign Policy*, Athens, 1995, p. 9.
78   Kathimerini, 12 May 2003.
79   See Bonnart, Frederick, 'A Symbolic Step Towards Real EU Defense', *International Herald Tribune*, 23 December 2003 and North, Richard, 'Enlargement Could Spell the End of the EU', *International Herald Tribune*, 15 January 2004.
80   Rizas, Sotiris, 'Fate of Cyprus in the Balance', *Kathimerini*, 20 February 2004.
81   Chrysostomides, Kypros, *The Republic of Cyprus: A Study in International Law*, Martinus Nijhof, The Hague, Boston and London, 2000, pp. 88–89.
82   Brewin, Christopher, 'Towards a European Concept for the Middle East', *Vane Ivanovic Conference on Conflict Prevention; Security Issues and EU Enlargement in the Eastern Mediterranean*, Kingston University, London, 10 and 11 June 2004.
83   Stoforopoulos, Themos, *interview with author*, 7 June 2004.
84   Op. cit., Allison, Roy, 'Strategic Reassertion etc.'
85   Yutang, Lin, *The Importance of Living*, Heinemann, London, 1976, p. 5. First published in May 1938.

EPILOGUE

1   *Kathimerini*, 27 September 2004.
2   *The Economist*, 18–24 September 2004.
3   *Le Monde*, 7 October 2004.
4   *Kathimerini*, 30 September 2004.
5   *Kathimerini*, 4–5 September 2004.
6   At the risk of upsetting some Greek readers, I use this phrase even if it unfortunately (even if wrongly) evokes negative connotations.

BIBLIOGRAPHY

ARCHIVALIA CONSULTED

Foreign Office (from 1970, Foreign and Commonwealth Office) Public Records Office
 Series FO 371 and 956 and FCO Series; PREM (Prime Minister's Office), DEFE
 (Ministry of Defence) and CAB (Cabinet Office)
FRUS (Foreign Relations of the United States) in published form.

WORKS CITED

The following comprises only those sources cited in the book. There are many more
publications that cannot be included. The fact that I have not cited from them as well
(to avoid repetition) should not necessarily be seen as my not considering them
worthy of being read, but merely that I have attempted not to stray too far from
diplomatic history.

Agee, Philip, *On the Run*, Bloomsbury, London, 1987.
Albright, Madeleine, 'The Testing of American Foreign Policy', *Foreign Affairs*, vol. 77,
 no. 6, November/December 1998.
Argyrou, Fanoula, *Conspiracy or Blunder?*, Adouloti Kyrenia, Nicosia, 2000.
Arvanitopoulos, Constantine and Syrigos, Angelos, *The International Legal Status of the
 Aegean*, Ministry of Press and Mass Media, Athens, 1998.
Bahcheli, Tozun, *Greek–Turkish Relations since 1955*, Westview Press, Boulder, San
 Francisco and London, 1990.
Bergsten, C. Fred, 'America's Two-Front Economic Conflict', *Foreign Affairs*, vol. 80,
 no. 2, New York, March–April 2001.
Bertrand, Gilles and Rigoni, Isabelle, 'Turcs, Kurdes et Chypriotes devant la Cour
 Européenne des droits de l'Homme: une contestation judiciaire de questions
 politiques', *Etudes Internationales*, vol. XXXI, no. 3, September 2000.
Boutros-Ghali, Boutros, *Unvanquished*, I.B.Tauris, London and New York, 1999.
Brewin, Christopher, 'Endgame', *World Today*, vol. 58, no. 5, Chatham House,
 London, May 2002.
— 'Turkey, Greece and the European Union,' in Dodd, Clement, H. (ed.), *Cyprus: The
 Need for New Perspectives*, Eothen Press, Huntingdon, 1999.
Brzezwiski, Zbigniew, *The Grand Chessboard: American Primacy and its Geostrategic
 Imperatives*, Basic Books, New York, 1997.
Çelik, Yasemin, *Contemporary Turkish Foreign Policy*, Praeger, Westport, 1999.
Chrysanthopoulos, Themistocles, 'The Sea Frontier Between Greece and Turkey',
 Diplomatic Life, Athens, March 2001.
Clogg, Richard, *A Concise History of Greece*, Cambridge University Press, 1992.
Coker, Christopher, 'Britain and the New World Order: The Special Relationship
 in the 1990s', *International Affairs*, vol. 68, no. 3, Chatham House, London,
 July, 1992.
Coughlan, R., 'From Corporate Autonomy to the Search for Territorial Federalism', in
 Guy, Y. (ed.), *Autonomy and Ethnicity: Negotiating Competing Claims in Multi-Ethnic
 States*, Cambridge University Press, 1999.
Cox, Michael, 'American Power Before and After 11 September: Dizzy with Success?',
 International Affairs, vol. 78, no. 2, Chatham House, London, April 2002.

Crawford, James, Hafner, Gerhard and Pellet, Alain, 'Does the Treaty of Lausanne 1923 Confer on Turkey Any Specific Rights with Respect to Cyprus?', in Markides, Alecos (ed.), *Cyprus and European Union Membership*, Nicosia, 2002.

Croft, Stuart, 'Guaranteeing Europe's Security? Enlarging NATO Again', *International Affairs*, vol. 78, no. 1, January 2002.

Dahrendorf, Ralf, 'The Third Way and Liberty – An Authoritarian Streak in Europe's New Center', *Foreign Affairs*, vol. 78, no. 5, New York, September/October 1999.

Davies, Norman, *Europe*, Pimlico, London, 1997.

Dilks, David, 'Britain and Europe 1948–1950', in Poidevin, Raymond (ed.), *Histoire des Débuts de la Construction Européenne*, Brussels, Milan, Paris, Baden-Baden, 1988.

Dodd, Clement H., *The Cyprus Issue*, Eothen Press, Huntingdon, 1995.

Dunan, Marcel (ed.), *Larousse Encyclopedia of Modern History*, Crescent Books, New York, 1987.

Eddy, Charles B., *Greece and the Greek Refugees*, Allen and Unwin, London, 1931.

Ertekün, Necati Münir, 'The Turkish Cypriot Outlook', in Dodd, Clement H. (ed.), *The Cyprus Issue: The Need for New Perspectives*, Eothen Press, Huntingdon, 1999.

Evriviades, Marios, 'Alliances and Alignments in the Middle East: The Turkish Israeli Axis', in Arvanitopoulos, Constantine (ed.), *Security Dilemmas in Eurasia*, Panteion University, Athens, 1997.

— 'The US and Cyprus: The Politics of Manipulation in the 1985 High Level Meeting,' Panteion University, Occasional Research Paper no. 3, Athens, October, 1992.

Fouscas, Vassilis, 'Reflections on the Cyprus Issue and the Turkish Invasions of 1974', *Mediterranean Quarterly*, vol. 12, no. 3, Summer 2001.

— *Zones of Conflict*, Pluto Press, London and Sterling (USA), 2003.

— 'The Balkans and the Enlargement of NATO: A Sceptical View', *European Security*, vol. 10, no. 3, Frank Cass, London, Autumn 2001.

Garton Ash, Timothy, 'Is Britain European?', *International Affairs*, vol. 77, no. 1, Chatham House, London, January 2001.

Gazioglu, Ahmet C., *Two Equal and Sovereign Peoples*, Nicosia, (Mersin, Turkey), 1997.

Guay, Terence and Callum, Robert, 'The Transformation and Future Prospects of Europe's Defence Industry', *International Affairs*, vol. 78, no. 4, London, October 2002.

Gunther, John, *Inside Europe*, Hamish Hamilton, London, 1936.

Hale, William, 'Turkey, the Middle East and the Gulf Crisis', *International Affairs*, vol. 68, no. 4, Chatham House, London, October 1992.

Heurtley, W. A., Darby, H. C., Crawley, C. W. and Woodhouse, C. M., *A Short History of Greece*, Cambridge University Press, 1965.

Hitchens, Christopher, *Hostage to History*, Verso, London and New York, 1997.

— *The Trial of Henry Kissinger*, Verso, London and New York, 2002.

Holland, Robert, *Britain and the Revolt in Cyprus, 1954–1959*, Oxford University Press, 1998.

Joseph, Joseph S., *Cyprus: Ethnic Conflict and International Politics*, St Martin's Press, London and New York, 1997.

Kissinger, Henry, *Nuclear Weapons and Foreign Policy*, W.W. Norton, Inc., USA, 1969.

— *Years of Upheaval*, Simon and Schuster, New York, 1999.

Konstas, Dimitris, *Diplomacy and Politics*, Livani, Athens, 2002.

Leventis, Yiorghos, 'The Politics of the Cypriot Left in the Inter-War Period: 1918–1940', *Synthesis – Review of Modern Greek Studies*, vol. 2, no. 1, London School of Economics and Political Science, 1997.

— *Cyprus: The Struggle for Self-Determination in the 1940s*, Peter Lang, Frankfurt am Main, 2002

Lindley, Dan, 'The Military Factor in the Eastern Mediterranean', Dodd, Clement H. (ed.), *Cyprus: The Need for New Perspectives*, Eothen Press, Huntingdon, 1999.

Llewellyn Smith, Michael, *Ionian Vision*, Hurst & Co., London, 1998.

Lutovac, Zoran, 'European and American Diplomacy in Kosovo', *Eurobalkans*, no. 32, Aegina, Autumn 1998.

Mallaby, Sebastian, 'The Reluctant Imperialist, Terrorism, Failed States and the Case for American Empire', *Foreign Affairs*, New York, March/April 2002.

Mallinson, William, *Portrait of an Ambassador*, Athens, 1998.

— 'A Partitioned Cyprus 40 Years After Qualified Sovereignty – Reality vs Morality', *Defensor Pacis*, issue 7, Athens, January 2001.

— 'The Dutch, the British and Anti-Communism in the Immediate Post-War Years', *Dutch Crossing*, no. 41, University College, London, Summer 1990.

— 'Turkish Invasions, Cyprus and the Treaty of Guarantee', *Synthesis – Review of Modern Greek Studies*, vol. 3, no. 1, London School of Economics and Political Science, 1999.

— 'Huntingdon's West', *Nemesis*, Athens, November 1999.

— 'Using Kosovo to Promote the European Defence and Security Initiative', *Eurobalkans*, nos. 36–37, Aegina, Autumn/Winter 1999.

— 'The Road with the Snakes', *Nemesis*, Athens, August 2000.

— 'The Death of Veracity: Diplomacy, Greece and Cyprus', *Atlantis*, Athens, November 1998.

Mangold, Peter, 'Pivotal Power', *World Today*, vol. 58, no. 3, Chatham House, London, March 2002.

Maynes, Charles William, 'Squandering Triumph', *Foreign Affairs*, vol. 78, no. 1, New York, January/February 1999.

Mazower, Mark, 'British Historians of Greece since the Second World War', *Synthesis – Review of Modern Greek Studies*, vol. 1, no. 2, London School of Economics and Political Science, 1996.

— *After the War was Over*, Princeton University Press, Princeton and Oxford, 2000.

McCgwire, Michael, 'Why Did We Bomb Belgrade?', *International Affairs*, vol. 76, no. 1, Chatham House, London, January 2000.

Milward, Alan S., *The Reconstruction of Western Europe, 1945–1951*, Methuen & Co., London, 1987.

Mirbagheri, Farid, *Cyprus and International Peacekeeping*, Hurst, London, 1998.

Moran, Michael, *Sovereignty Divided*, CYREP, Cyprus, 1999.

Nicolson, Harold, *Peacemaking 1919*, Universal Library Edition, USA, 1965.

Nye, Joseph, 'The US and Europe: Continental Drift', in *International Affairs*, vol. 76, no. 1, Chatham House, London, January 2000.

— 'American Strategy after Bipolarity', *International Affairs*, vol. 66, no. 3, Chatham House, London, July 1990.

— 'The American National Interest and Global Public Good', *International Affairs*, Vol. 78, No. 2, Chatham House, London, April 2002.

O'Malley, Brendan and Craig, Ian, *The Cyprus Conspiracy*, I.B.Taurus, London, 1999.

Pantelis, Stavros, *The Making of Modern Cyprus*, Interworld Publications, London, 1990.

— *A History of Cyprus*, East–West Publications, London and The Hague, 2000.

Papahelas, Alexis, *The Rape of Greek Democracy: The American Factor, 1947–1967*, Estia, Athens, 1997.

Parenti, Michael, *Inventing Reality*, St Martin's Press, New York, 1993.

Parks, Bill, 'Bridgehead or Bridge?', *World Today*, vol. 58, no. 10, Chatham House, London, October 2000.

Pattakos, Stylianos, *21st April, 1967: Why? Who? How?*, Viovivl, Athens, 2002.

Pentzopoulos, Dimitris, *The Balkan Exchange of Minorities and its Impact Upon Greece*, Mouton & Co., Paris, 1962.

Pettifer, James, 'We Have Been Here Before', *World Today*, vol. 54, no. 4, Chatham House, London, April 1998.

Rice, Condoleezza, 'Promoting the National Interest', *Foreign Affairs*, vol. 79, no. 1, New York, January/February 2000.

Richard, Oliver P., *Mediating in Cyprus*, Frank Cass, London and Portland, OR, 1998.

Savvides, Philippos K., 'Cyprus at the Gate of the European Union', *ELIAMEP Policy Paper* no. 1, Athens, June 2002.

Sick, Gary, 'Imperial Moment', *World Today*, vol. 58, no. 12, Chatham House, London, December 2002.

Sked, Alan (ed.), *Europe's Balance of Power 1815–1848*, Macmillan, London, 1979.

Sonyel, Salahi R., 'New Light on the Genesis of the Conflict', in Dodd, Clement H. (ed.), *Cyprus: The Need for New Perspectives*, Eothen Press, Huntingdon, 1999.

Stefanidis, Ioannis, *Isle of Discord*, Hurst & Co., London, 1999.

Svolopoulos, Konstantinos, *Greek Foreign Policy, 1945–1981*, Estia, Athens, 2002.

Theodhoropoulos, V., Lagkakos, E., Papoulias, G., and Tzounis, T., *Reflections and Considerations About Our Foreign Policy*, Athens, 1995.

Taylor, A. J. P., *The Struggle for the Mastery of Europe, 1848 – 1918*, Oxford University Press, 1991 (first published 1954).

Terriff, Terry, Webber, Mark, Croft, Stuart and Howorth, Jolyon, 'European Security and Defence Policy After Nice', *Briefing Paper*, new series no. 20, Chatham House, London, April 2001.

Tuathail, Gearóid, Dalby, Simon and Routledge Paul, (eds.), *The Geopolitics Reader*, Routledge, London and New York, 1998.

Unsigned, *Economikos Tachidromos* (ed. Marinos, Giannis), Athens, 14 August 1997.

Vassiliou, Dr. George, 'A Deal to be Done', *World Today*, vol. 58, no. 10, Chatham House, London, October 2002.

Venizelos, Kostas and Ignatiou, Michalis, *Kissinger's Secret Files: The Decision to Dissect*, Livani, Athens, 2002.

Wallace, William, 'Foreign Policy and National Identity in the United Kingdom', *International Affairs*, vol. 67, no. 1, Chatham House, London, January 1991.

— 'From the Atlantic to the Bug, From the Arctic to the Tigris', *International Affairs*, vol. 76, no. 3, Chatham House, London, July 2000.

Warner, Geoffrey, 'The United States and the Western Alliance', *International Affairs*, vol. 71, no. 4, Chatham House, London, October 1995.

West, Nigel (aka Rupert Allason), *The Friends: Britain's Post-War Secret Intelligence Operations*, Weidenfeld and Nicholson, London, 1988.

Wright, Peter, *Spycatcher*, Viking Penguin Inc., New York, 1987.

Woodhouse, C. M., *Modern Greece*, Faber and Faber, London, 1991.

Yost, David S., 'Transatlantic Relations and Peace in Europe', *International Affairs*, vol. 78, no. 2, Chatham House, London, April 2002.

Yutang, Lin, *The Importance of Living*, Heinemann, London, 1976 (first published in 1938).

Zambouras, Sergios, 'Current Greek Attitudes and Policy', in Dodd, Clement H. (ed.), *Cyprus: The Need for New Perspectives*, Eothen Press, Huntingdon, 1999.

Zoellick, Robert B., 'A Republican Foreign Policy', *Foreign Affairs*, vol. 79, no. 1, New York, January/February 2000.

NEWSPAPERS

I cannot include the many other newspapers consulted, which have also covered the Cyprus question.

Athens News (Greece)
Le Monde Diplomatique (France)
Daily Telegraph (UK)
The Guardian (UK)
Kathimerini (Greece)
Daily Mirror (UK)
International Herald Tribune (USA)
Boston Globe (USA)
Christian Science Monitor (USA)

National Herald (USA)
Avgi (Greece)
Providence Journal (USA)
Evening Standard (UK)
Washington Post (USA)

INDEX